THE UNITED WAY

THE UNITED WAY

Dilemmas of Organized Charity

Eleanor L. Brilliant

Columbia University Press
NEW YORK

Columbia University Press
New York   Oxford
Copyright © 1990 Columbia University Press

All rights reserved

Library of Congress Cataloging-in-Publication Data
Brilliant, Eleanor L.
The United Way : dilemmas of organized charity /
Eleanor L. Brilliant.
p. cm.
Includes bibliographical references.
ISBN 0–231–05622–2
ISBN 0–231–05623–0 (pbk.)
1. United Way of America. 2. Charities—United States.
3. Corporations—United States—Charitable contributions.
I. Title.
HV97.U553B75 1990
361.8'0973—dc20   90-35436
                                    CIP

Casebound editions of Columbia University Press books are Smyth-sewn
and printed on permanent and durable acid-free paper.

Printed in the United States of America
c 10 9 8 7 6 5 4 3 2 1
p 10 9 8 7 6 5 4 3 2 1

To Richard Brilliant
honoris causa

Contents

List of Tables and Figures	ix
Preface to the Paperback Edition	xi
Preface	xv
Introduction	1

Part I
The Role of History

1. Historical Themes: Origins of American Charity Organization	15
2. From Community Chest to United Way	28

Part II
Planning and Allocations

A Time of Transition	49
3. Community Planning in the United Way	51
4. From Allocations to Alternative Funds	74

Part III
Whose Pie Is It?
Voluntarism and Big Government

5. Donor Option and Controversy in the Combined Federal Campaign	103
6. From Charitable Controversy to Congressional Action (1982–1985)	130

Part IV
The Corporation and the United Way

Introduction to Part IV   151

7. Corporate Responsibility and the United Way   153

8. Changing the Rules of the Game: Corporate Response to Challenge   176

9. Company Choices and United Way Agencies: The Bottom Line   209

Part V
The United Way as a National Organization and as a Charitable Enterprise

10. Structure and Function   229

11. United Way as a National Organization: The Aramony Era   245

Epilogue   260

Appendixes   267

Notes   317

Index   371

Tables and Figures

Tables

4.1	United Way Allocations to Thirteen Selected Agencies, 1973, 1974, 1975	77
4.2	United Way of the Coastal Bend, Allocations—Five Year History	84
5.1	Metro I Donor Option Communities: Comparative Policies	106
7.1	United Way of King County, Boeing Contributions, 1976–1986	172
8.1	Donor Option Designations by AT&T Participating Companies by Campaign Year	192
8.2	United Way of Tri-State Campaign: Ten Top Non-Funded Agencies Selected by AT&T Employees, 1983, 1984, 1985, and 1986	194
8.3	Dollars Raised from Employee Contributions, Ecolab Campaigns, 1984–1986	206
9.1	Percentage of Corporate Contributions Given to Health and Welfare, Education, Culture and the Arts, Civic and Other Activities, 1970–1986	214
10.1	Total Employee Contributions to Alternative Charities, 1985	232
10.2	United Way Allocations to Selected Agencies, 1973–1983–1985	237
10.3	Family and Children's Service of Pittsburgh, United Way Allocations Compared to Other Income (%)	239

Figures

4.1 Timetable of the Corpus Christi Allocations Program, 1982   81

7.1 Letter of October 27, 1982 to Seagram Employees Concerning United Way   167

8.1 AT&T Donor Option Plan Model Card   190

Preface to the Paperback Edition

THIS is a time of great stress for the United Way signalling a new level of concern about its future. Although the United Way has always been subject to criticism in the media, the issues raised in February 1992 are of a different quality. Past criticism has generally been concerned with broad institutional issues—questions about the raising of funds or the way funds were allocated to agencies in the community. In early 1992, however, a new form of criticism emerged in newspaper headlines, with an attack on the personal credibility of the national executive of the United Way of America, Bill Aramony. The *Washington Post* broke a story that subsequently spread across the country. The news story focused attention on the high salary ($360,000) plus benefits (for a total of $463,000), as well as other perquisites Aramony enjoyed, and on questionable staff hirings and actions in connection with several subsidiary organizations of the United Way of America. After twenty-two years as the national executive of the United Way, Bill Aramony was forced to resign and left on March 12, 1992. Kenneth W. Dam, a recent IBM employee, was named interim president of the United Way by the United Way Board of Governors, chaired by Jim Akers, the Chief Executive Officer of IBM. And the United Way Board, faced with a challenge of its own accountability, promised a full investigation of Aramony's activities, hiring an outside law firm to carry it out.

It is not possible to discuss in detail here all the problems indicated in the report issued by the outside law firm, Verner, Lipfert, Bernhard, McPherson and Hand, and the Investigative Group, Inc. Although no criminal charges are being pressed against Bill Aramony, severe shock waves have resulted from the disclosures of the report, and the United Way Board is now instituting tighter financial controls in the national office. In the meantime many local affiliates are withholding their dues from the national organization, which they now refer to as their *trade association*. Local volunteers and donors are upset, and although Aramony has denied the allegations, the charitable community and even the broader public are asking how this could have happened. What has happened to the idea of stewardship in the United Way? And what are the implications of these events for the United Way system as a whole and for charitable fundraising in general?

We cannot of course predict what will happen in future local United Way campaigns or, indeed, to charitable support for other organizations. Despite the efforts at damage control by the national organization, however, is is clear that the United Way will be subject to increased scrutiny at the local as well as the national level. Newspaper attention is being given to salaries and other issues in local United Ways, and it is hard for most community organizations to do business as usual. It is more than likely that upcoming campaigns will be flat in most communities and will decline in others. Some large well-established charities (like the Red Cross) as well as some alternative federated funds (like the Health Funds or social action groups) may even benefit individually as donors reroute their contributions away from the United Way system. But on the whole no one is rejoicing, because the issues raised go far beyond the United Way problems and threaten beliefs and values that are fundamental to the volunteer sector in America.

As this edition is being prepared the American public is reviewing its position in regard to voluntary charitable institutions. Critical questions are being widely discussed, such as (1) What should be the salary of the executive of a major charitable organization? How should it be determined? Should the executive of such an organization earn more (indeed *much* more) than the president of the United States? (2) Is the impaired credibility of the United Way reflective of the weakened ethical postures of many other major institutions in our country? (3) How do these problems differ from concerns in the corporate world or in government, and to what extent is it legitimate for us to expect a higher standard of trust from the leadership of charitable organizations? (4) How widespread are these abuses, and are we likely to find them elsewhere if we look around the country at other national or local charitable organizations? (5) Once these immediate problems appear to be under control, will it be back to business as usual? Or will we continue to be concerned with significant questions about the nature of federated fund-raising in the workplace and how the funds are allocated? (6) What is the proper role of boards in monitoring an executive's performance? How can we ensure accountability as well as fiscal and moral integrity in the voluntary sector?

As stated in the final pages of this book, the United Way is a resilient organization with powerful friends. The corporate leadership of our country is well represented on the national United Way

Board and has a great investment in this institution. Consistent with past commitments, corporate leaders are now taking on the task of correcting organizational problems in an effort to redeem the United Way system. They will not want to fail in this task. But how they go about it and what kind of changes they accomplish have enormous implications for the future of organized charities in our country.

Eleanor L. Brilliant

Preface

PUBLIC philanthropy and private charity exist in many countries, but have taken on a special configuration in America. In no other country has the role of corporate giving become so important, and no other country has created such a vast mechanism for organizing individual giving in the community and in the workplace. The concept of workplace fund raising and corporate support for voluntary social welfare agencies through the United Way can be considered a uniquely American notion, although the idea of workplace giving is spreading to other countries along with the growth of multinational corporations.

This is a study of the development of the United Way concept of organized fund raising from the early days of small federations of community-based agencies to the multilevel structure of a national charitable fund-raising system. Since the organization which embodies this concept celebrated its one-hundredth anniversary just shortly before this book was finished, it covers a large span of American history. The topic is complex. It concerns the relationship of federated organizations to the community and to the corporation, and considers the factors which make federated fund-raising organizations a significant aspect of the myth of American voluntarism in our country. The story basically unfolds on several parallel levels: it analyzes the development of federated fund-raising organizations in America in light of their environmental context, both nationally and locally; and it utilizes community, corporate, and institutional case studies to illustrate particular issues or factors which have propelled federated fund raising and the United Way system into controversy, conflict, and even front page news headlines at particular points of time.

In developing my argument, I have utilized historical materials and data from the United Way of America Information Center and other primary sources. I have benefited from personal observation and interviews with hundreds of people both inside and outside of the United Way in Baltimore, Maryland; Boise, Idaho; Boston, Massachusetts; Corpus Christi, Texas; Denver, Colorado; Des Moines,

Iowa; Hartford, Connecticut; Philadelphia, Pennsylvania; Richmond, Virginia; San Diego, California; Seattle, Washington; Springfield, Missouri; and in a number of communities within the United Way of Tri-State area (a regional organization which includes New York City, Long Island, Westchester County, southeastern Connecticut, and eastern New Jersey). Most of the site visits took place between 1982 and 1985; however, I also built upon my own personal experience as a local United Way staff member from 1975 to 1980, and attendance at many national and regional United Way conferences from 1975 through 1986. I was able to interview many corporate executives connected with the United Way. I also utilized material from my formal survey of 131 local United Ways (Metros I–VII) and 54 local Planning Councils connected with the United Way, based on a representative sample of local United Way Organizations and Planning Councils in the 1981–1982 UWA *International Directory*.

In carrying out this extensive research I have had the cooperation and support of so many individuals, organizations, and agencies that it is impossible to thank them all by name. However, there are some individuals and organizations whose support has been so critical that I wish to acknowledge them specifically. To begin with, quite literally the book would not have been possible without the cooperation of all the staff of the United Way of America. William Aramony encouraged me and Richard O'Brien assisted me in gaining access to United Way data; Henry Smith helped with archival material and the answers to hundreds of questions; William Phillips provided data from the United Way; Thomas Walker and Leo Benade supported my efforts, and Robert Beggan presented a lively challenge to my inquiries. Two other individuals who were at the United Way of America merit a particular thank you: Dennis Murphy, who spoke for my project initially, and Russy Sumariwalla, who offered wise counsel and discussion of the issues.

Former volunteers at the United Way of Westchester gave consultation throughout. I am grateful for the wisdom shared with me by John Riehm and Marjorie Dammann, the advice of Jane Butcher, and the special expertise and understanding of John Pike. Colleagues Robert Gebbia and Ralph Gregory cheerfully answered many queries. I am also deeply indebted to the volunteers and staffs of all the local United Ways, human science agencies, and Community Planning Councils whom I visited or who took time to respond to our survey. Special thanks is owed to Peter Bentley of Toledo, Ohio, and to Planning Council executives Bernard Shiffman and Elmer Tropman. I also want to express my gratitude to the support staff who made me feel welcome at the United Way of America and in the local communities I visited.

Many other individuals and groups assisted me with the gathering of data, including professionals and staff of the Black United Funds, social action groups, and health organizations in local communities. I profited from my attendance at meetings of the alternative funds and from the frequent assistance and intelligent discussion of Robert Bothwell, as well as from the unique insights of Kermit Eady and Nancy Steketee. Elizabeth Essex provided invaluable help with later phases of the research, and in earlier stages I was assisted by graduate students at Columbia University including Jo Ann Yaworski, Catherine Verhulst, Kyung-Hee Nah, Andrea Glick, and Tracy Rosenhand. Natalie Webb provided significant assistance in developing and carrying out the survey of local United Ways and planning organizations, and Bill Gerin and Jim Johnson served as consultants for the survey. Many hands touched the manuscript, but it would not have been completed without the efficient help of Sandy Greene, Carolyn Ambrose, and Selma Almeida. I also want to thank Tanya Strage, Eran Ashany, Edward Croen, Lois Gehrman, Susan Kivelson, Arlene Bernzweig, and Lauren Mosso for their varied efforts.

Alfred J. Kahn encouraged me to undertake the study, and Harold Demone and Paul Glasser supported me in finishing it. Wallace Doud provided a perceptive reading of the whole manuscript, and Franca Brilliant, Livia Thompson, and Stephanie Wald made helpful comments on different sections. I used many libraries, but wish to offer special thanks to the White Plains Public Library, whose reference staff responded to numerous requests.

My research could not have been carried out without the generous financial support of the Aetna Life and Casualty Foundation, the Dammann Fund, Exxon Corporation, the Johnson's Wax Fund, the Morgan Guaranty Trust Company of New York Charitable Trust, the Thomas J. Lipton Foundation, the Metropolitan Life Foundation of the Institute for Research in History, and the Rutgers University Research Council. I acknowledge my debt to the individuals in those organizations who had confidence in the study, and to Virginia Hodgkinson and Robert Payton, who constantly cheered me on.

And finally, I want to thank my family—my husband, Richard,—and Franca, Livia, Myron, Thomas, Stephanie, and Stephen for their considerable patience as I produced the manuscript.

Introduction

Few aspects of American society are more characteristically, more famously American, than the nation's array of voluntary organizations, and the support of time and money that is given to them by its citizens.

The Commission on Private
Philanthropy and Public Needs,
Giving in America

The organizational effects . . . which really operate in social life to regulate organizational survival are matters of political agreement and social definition negotiated between organizations and their environments.

John Meyer, "Strategies for Further
Research: Varieties of Environmental
Variation"

Voluntarism and the United Way

Americans like to organize. Democratic process requires free association, and voluntary organizations are an integral part of our national life. As Alexis de Toqueville observed over 150 years ago, Americans are a nation of joiners. We have a propensity for organizing and characteristically we join together to solve community problems and to realize common purposes. Since de Toqueville's time, voluntarism has become a part of the American self-image, and we have created a variegated, multidimensional voluntary sector to which Americans contribute vast amounts of personal energies, and through which we meet many of our most basic human needs. We organize Little League games for our children, pot-luck suppers for our neighbors, self-help groups to solve personal problems, and civic associations to deal with political concerns.

In order to support this vast array of voluntary organizations, Americans have developed an extraordinary capacity for raising money from their friends and neighbors. Americans are asked to give constantly: in our homes, in our churches, in schools, and at the workplace. We are appealed to on television, and through the mail. And we certainly do give: in 1985 Americans gave about $79 billion in charitable contributions, and donated an estimated 16.1 billion hours of volunteer time, estimated to be worth an additional $110 billion.[1] Altogether Americans supported about 800,000 voluntary organizations in this period, of which over 300,000 were charitable organizations defined as serving the public good under section 501(c)(3) of the United States tax code, and therefore listed as tax exempt organizations by the Internal Revenue Service.[2]

Voluntarism and organized charity on this scale are a uniquely American phenomenon. We characterize the phenomenon variously as the non-profit sector, the voluntary sector, or the independent sector. By any name it embodies fundamental values of community, mutual help, and personal responsibility. It is a third sector, standing firmly between the sectors of business and government in our society. The organizations of which it is composed vary greatly in their focus: some are neighborhood self-help groups, while others are trade associations formed for the purpose of protection of particular business and professional interests.[3] Others are philanthropic or charitable in nature, formed for the purpose of providing valued communal goods outside the mechanism of the private market. As 501(c)(3) organizations, they receive special benefits under our tax laws. Many are also beneficiaries of intensive fund-raising drives, developed to insure financial support for activities presumed to be in the public interest. Among the most well known of all these drives is that of the United Way.

Although voluntarism and organized charity are highly valued as part of American life, their role and function present constant dilemmas for the polity. Thus, in the early 1970s, a group of public officials and private citizens shared a common concern about the changing nature of the voluntary sector and its increasing dependence upon the government in the aftermath of the explosion of social welfare programs in the 1960s. This led to the formation of a prestigious public study group, the Commission on Private Philanthropy and Public Needs, more commonly known as the Filer Commission. With the encouragement of John D. Rockefeller III, the Commission undertook its work in 1973. John H. Filer, chief executive officer of Aetna Life and Casualty Company, became Chairman, and support was provided by the United States Treasury Department.[4] Initially the focus of Commission research was primarily on tax-related issues, but the scope of inquiry was soon broadened to include a range of policy issues about the functioning of the voluntary sector in American life more generally.

One of the major institutions that was subject to critical inquiry in the reports of the Filer Commission was the United Way. In a paper that had widespread implications for charity organization in the next decade, David Horton Smith raised a series of questions about the nature of the United Way system, its accountability to donors, its continued funding of a small group of national agencies, its close relationship to the world of business, and its lack of responsiveness to the demands of a new society.[5] Smith articulated already existing concerns, and his formulation of them provided a central theme around which opposition to the United Way continued to rally through the mid-1980s, serving as fuel for the continuous fires of discontent which were eventually to force change in the United Way system.

This book is about the United Way, organized charity, and voluntarism. Its primary focus is on events that emerged in the 1960s and accelerated after publication of the Filer Commission report in 1974, but it begins with the early history of charity and social welfare development in this country. It is a contextual analysis, because it is my contention that an organization must be understood in the context of the environmental circumstances in which it operates. Much of the argument is presented historically, because the present dilemmas of the United Way have their origins in the initial efforts of the charity organization movement in this country, and the shape of the United Way organization of today reflects responses over time to a constantly changing, frequently hostile environment, with shifting messages about the public interest.[6]

United Way: Description and Definition

Countless numbers of Americans have been exposed to the United Way in some manner. A conservative count would have to include hundreds of thousands who have either given money to the local United Way campaign, or worked in it. Millions more have seen the outstretched arm with the rainbow which is the symbol of the United Way. This visual representation is included often on public service announcements on television, along with the personal vignettes of players in the National Football League (NFL) who explain how "the United Way Works for All of Us." Thus, United Way has become a highly visible symbol of organized charity in our country.

Despite this wide public exposure to the United Way concept, very few Americans appear to have in-depth understanding of the nature of the United Way, how it actually operates in the local community, and what its impact is on public policy at the national level. Factual knowledge about the United Way is not widely disseminated, and the name recognition that it seems to enjoy is not necessarily accompanied by informed opinion. Both my own research and the extensive marketing surveys of the United Way itself suggest that widespread publicity about the United Way has not been matched by the transmission of accurate factual knowledge.

The United Way movement is an offshoot of a charity organization movement which by the early twentieth century had begun to move in two different directions. The first branch was that of direct service, leading to the family service agencies of a later period. The other centered around community coordination of agency services, evolving eventually into councils of social agencies and closely related federated fund-raising organizations.[7] These early functional councils were a kind of association of charities, with autonomous members coming together to coordinate social service activities and to assist in identifying needs and setting standards for agency performance. Thus, the roots of the modern United Way structure and function go back to organizations whose membership was actively involved both in the coordinating-planning role and in the allocation of funds raised for affiliated agencies through a joint, or combined, communitywide appeal. Indeed, membership, and membership agreements, as defined by early community-based federations, were to remain underlying themes of later United Way development, causing internal tensions for the organization.

Local United Ways are still committed to the three major functions of the earlier organizations from which they emerged: coordination and planning for community needs; fund raising; and the distribution, or allocation, of funds raised. However, the way that these core functions are carried out has become considerably more complicated over the years, and it now involves United Ways in another whole set of service activities, including marketing, research, technical assistance to agencies, government relations, and public relations—all related to an increasingly competitive philanthropic environment, and necessitating a more complex organizational structure.

In the mid-1980s the contemporary United Way system was reported to include about 2,200 local United Ways, with approximately

1,200 dues-paying members of the national organization, the United Way of America (UWA).[8] The system included about 20 more diverse state organizations, and at least one notable regional organization, the United Way of Tri-State, consisting of 36 local United Ways from parts of New York, Connecticut, and New Jersey. United Ways are also grouped loosely into regions: in 1986 there were four major regions (northeast, southeast, mid-America, and western) for organizational and administrative purposes, which include data gathering, regional UWA offices, and bi-annual conferences.

In addition, the *1986 International Directory* of the UWA includes 15 affiliated international "United Ways" and their local organizations in countries as far apart and varied as Canada, Japan, and South Africa. Of them all, not surprisingly, the relationship with Canada is the longest and the closest. However, despite the apparent "Americanism" of the contemporary United Way "movement," and its ties to American community life, the UWA continues to encourage the development of these organizations around the world. In some respects this development is analagous to the spread of Americanism around the world generally, and, more specifically, to the spread of American corporate activities in receptive business environments in other countries; and indeed it may be a related phenomenon.

Finally, there are a group of local planning councils which are linked to the United Way system, in varying degrees of closeness, and which in 1981-82 included about 80 local independent, but affiliated, councils officially listed in the United Way *International Directory* and on other United Way lists.[9] The relationship of these planning organizations to the local United Ways in their communities, and to the United Way system as a whole, however, has generally been problematic.[10]

Of all the subsystems or categories in the United Way system, by far the most critical may be the United Way of America's formal classification of local United Ways by the amount of money they raise. Since these categories remained basically the same in the inflationary period of the early 1970s through the mid-1980s, there has been a gradual upward creep of organization numbers, so that the larger-size metro groupings now contain more United Ways than they did in the early 1970s. The Metro Groups in the United States are categorized as follows, with numbers of United Way organizations as listed in the *1986 International Directory* (in parenthesis):

Metro   I $9,000,000 and over   (50)

       II $4,000,000 to $8,999,999   (44)

III	$2,000,000 to $3,999,999	(77)
IV	$1,000,000 to 1,999,999	(116)
V	$750,000 to $999,999	(61)
VI	$500,000 to $749,999	(101)
VII	$200,000 to $499,999	(257)
VIII	$100,000 to $199,999	(172)
IX	50,000 to $99,999	(142)
X	$25,000 to $49,999	(79)
XI	less than $25,000	(58)

On the whole, the argument in this book will focus on United Ways in categories I through VIII, and primarily on the larger United Ways (I–IV). These are the United Ways that in fact set the tone for the whole system, raise by far the largest share of of the monies, and are most accessible for study purposes.

Except for the approximately fifty large United Ways in the Metro I category, most United Ways operate with relatively small staff. In 1987, United Way counted over 4,000 professional staff in its reporting United Ways; most of the non-reporting organizations would in any case be very small (Metro VI or under), and unlikely to have any full-time professional staffing. The education and socialization process of staff members has changed over the years, from the time when it was closely allied with the social work profession and schools (1940s and 1950s) to years (the 1970s) when a business ethos dominated the United Way field, and more recently to a more eclectic mix.

Nationwide the United Way can be considered to be big business. In 1986 United Ways raised a combined total of about $2.4 billion, which by dollar volume of business would rank them high in the list of major American corporations.[11] They funded a reported 37,000 health and welfare agencies and programs, or something over 10 percent of the IRS list of over 300,000 charitable organizations, not all of which would be considered health and welfare related.[12]

In the early 1980s, United Way's share of the total budgets of the agencies it funded was estimated to average about 15 percent;[13] and this share was continually declining. Nevertheless, the funds provided by United Ways have a particular significance for most of the agencies that receive them. United Way support for the traditional members of local federations has tended to be long lasting, remaining fairly constant over time. Indeed, changes in funding have historically been incremental in nature, usually taking the form of increases to a core group of agencies. This group of agencies thus has been able to depend upon the continuity of United Way support while they searched for other more marginal or uncertain sources of funds, or grants, from foundations, individuals, or the government.

The United Way raises a considerable amount of money for health and welfare activities generally, and for some agencies in particular, but it is not just the amount of money raised by the United Way system that makes it so powerful in the voluntary sector. The United Way's special position, in the eyes of its friends and foes alike, seems to be related as much to *how* it raises funds, and *where* it raises these funds, as to *how much* it raises.

From their earliest days federated fund-raising organizations raised money through campaigns aimed at both individuals and businesses in the local community. Over time contributions by business grew as a percentage of all funds raised through the campaign, until the mid-1950s when a change in the focus of the appeal occurred, and funds raised through workplace solicitation became an increasing share of the totals raised. By 1983, nearly 50 percent of United Way contributions came from workers in major corporations and small business, with another 25 percent reported as coming from the gifts of large companies. A smaller but still significant amount was raised through workers in the non-profit and public sector (around 13 percent in all) and from small businesses (around 2 percent.)[14] No other fund-raising organization has yet been able to obtain the same kind of access to the workplace, and the old "community"—or residential—(house-to-house) campaign has almost disappeared.

Issues to Be Addressed: Elements of a Conceptual Framework

One hundred years of history and approximately 2,200 separate locations make the United Way a variegated and complex subject for analysis. Consequently, only certain key issues have been selected to illuminate the dilemmas of organized charity in American life generally. Issues were selected to help provide answers to the basic question about how this community-based charity organization has survived for one hundred years in American history, and how it has adapted and changed to meet new and challenging environmental conditions. The issues addressed should also lead to understanding of how these locally autonomous federated fund-raising organizations developed into an American institution, with national implications, and the constant blessings of presidents of the United States.

Community Values and Community Decision Making

Federated fund-raising organizations and their counterparts in the community planning councils embody a particular model of community decision making—an American consensus model. This model is predicated on the fundamental assumption that there is a sufficient communality of interest around basic values and goals to permit citizens to come together to solve their problems, share valuable resources, gain mutual benefits, and achieve a public good through a rational allocation of resources. This consensus model suggests that conflict will either be minimal or can be dealt with readily through rational argument or negotiation. The alternative is the threat, and indeed the probability, of the loss of community support or the breaking away of parts of the federation, which is held together by contract. The model therefore supports the notion of shared values in American society as a basis for community life, and tends to underplay differences that may exist in power and influence, as well as differences in interests, among groups within a community.

Environmental Challenge and the Capacity for Change

In order to survive, all organizations must have the capacity to adapt to changing conditions and to grow. Federated fund-raising organizations demonstrated this capacity from their formative years. However, in the 1960s American society, and the social welfare system, underwent enormous changes, while it appeared that federated fund-raising organizations remained largely out of the mainstream of these developments. By the mid-1970s, they were no longer allowed that luxury. In this period new and emerging groups that had formerly (in the 1960s) asked only for a share of United Way dollars now began to redirect their energies. Increasingly, competitive groups of agencies and alternative funds began to target their efforts toward gaining equal access to workplaces formerly controlled by the United Way system. Minorities, social action groups, and traditional health agencies, as well as arts and cultural organizations, became more visible as they knocked loudly at the corporate door. Moreover, they were stepping up this pressure at the very time when governmental funds for human services were being reduced, and therefore charitable support for agencies in the non-profit sector assumed greater importance. Thus ideological differences and financial competition served to escalate the controversy around organized charity and United Way hegemony in the workplace.

Ultimately, the issue for the United Way revolved around its capacity to come up with solutions which would allow it to be responsive to new demands from the environment, without giving up the essential power of domain in the workplace.[15] Change, however, is never without a cost, and this cost would involve offering workers more choices. This change would not be made willingly by all parts of the United Way system, but was necessitated by legal challenges arising in the public sector campaign, and as a response to larger environmental factors impinging on the corporate world. Thus, analysis of this issue also helps to focus on an underlying critical question— how has this federated fund-raising system managed to survive all these years, despite constant challenge and criticism?

Public/Private Intersections

The definition of community-based charity organizations seems to place these institutions squarely within the third sector or voluntary sector. However, the boundaries between the three major sectors of our economy—business (or profit-making), public (or governmental), and voluntary (or non-profit)—are far from impermeable, and there is frequent blurring of the lines between them.[16] This is certainly the situation with health and welfare services, and is even evident in a United Way system, considered the eptiome of voluntary movements. Activities of this organization, as with others in the third sector, are conditioned by public policy decisions. These include tax laws and legal decisions made in the federal court about constitutional rights of employees and advocacy or dissenting groups. Challenges to the United Way domain in the work site, and to control of payroll deduction, emerged most dramatically in the Combined Federal Campaign (CFC) in the 1980s, with repercussions in regard to choice in giving which went far beyond the original groups involved (in particular the NAACP and the Black United Fund) and led to a wide-open, almost limitless campaign. But actions taken in regard to a campaign in the public workplace also had ramifications for corporate decision making.

The link between the business sector and the United Way has been discussed frequently.[17] United Ways are considered to be at the crossroads between social welfare interests and the corporate community. Indeed, the issue of the relationships between organized community charities and the business world emerges as a theme almost with the founding of federated fund raising, and seems to revolve around the difficult-to-answer question, Who influences whom? and, In whose best interest?

Congruence of Goals: Corporations, Charities, and Communities

If charity organization in the community is to be based on a consensus mode of decision making, there would have to be some congruence of goals among a number of constituent groups, or stakeholders, involved.[18] In its most obvious sense this occurs when fundraising organizations set campaign goals, or develop campaign strategies, with the concurrence of corporate management and labor leadership. But there are others whose voices may not be equally represented in goal determination, and these include the workers who contribute to goal achievement, the agencies and organizations within the federated fund-raising system, and even more, the groups that have been left out of the process entirely.[19] In relation to goal setting, then, we ask: how are goals determined, and to what extent can there be common interests in goal achievement in a complex organizational environment?

The Role of Myth

For many Americans, the United Way has become a symbol of voluntarism, based on its perceived attachment to basic values of community, workplace, charity, and business. Every since the days of the community chest in the 1930s federated fund-raising organizations appear to have consciously cultivated their connection to fundamental American beliefs, deliberately building on the notion that they represent a "movement" in support of Americanism. Indeed, United Way has consistently helped to promote a myth of organized charity as linked to the very heart of American community life. The myth of the United Way is therefore preserved as a system of beliefs which serve as organizing principles for the representation of United Way organizations to the public and even to its own volunteers and professional staff.[20] Regardless of whether or not the myth corresponds to reality, it is transmitted directly through personal contacts and indirectly through the media and other means, in the workplace, in the community, and in corporate headquarters. Hundreds of thousands of United Way volunteers have helped to transmit the message, and continue to do so.

However, the question remains: what happens when there is cognitive dissonance involved in the belief system—when the perception of reality conflicts directly with parts of the myth which individuals hold to be significant?[21] For example, what happens if volunteers begin to question whether changes actually do take place through a citizen review process, or corporate leaders begin to doubt the efficiency of the United Way system?

National versus Local Leadership

It is traditionally claimed that the United Way is a bottoms-up organization, a loosely organized confederation of community-based federations affiliated with a national organization whose purpose is to provide them with maximum assistance and minimum interference in their own activities. This may once have been true. But in the interactive, high-tech world of the 1980s, it may no longer be so. At some point after the challengers of the 1970s gathered force, the balance between national and local influence seems to have shifted, as national corporate relations and federal government actions (for example in the CFC) became increasingly important to the local United Way organizations.[22] If this is the case, what implications does this change have for the fundamental notion that the United Way is a community-based, community-controlled organization?

Part I

The Role
of History

Chapter 1

Historical Themes: Origins of American Charity Organization

Organizational structures persist over time—and may change to match the context of time and their funding—but the initial context "imprints" the organization and organizational form.

Arthur Stinchcombe, "Social Structure and Organizations"

Financial Federation, which received the support of social work figures like William J. Norton, Street . . . and Edward T. Devine, was not a scheme arbitrarily imposed by businessmen. The chest was the outgrowth of an agency-centered machinery of social welfare which required coordination and a stable income, and also of an industrial, corporate economy with a vast economic surplus to provide the funds it systematically exploited. Federation provided a formal link between the two.

Roy Lubove, The Professional Altruist

ORGANIZED charity and social welfare are two overlapping, related, but not identical spheres of modern life. As the broader term, "social welfare" has come to mean primarily functions of the public sector, including cash assistance for vulnerable populations and insuring the provision of the most basic human needs in education, health, housing, and mental health. Organized charity, on the other hand, generally refers to that part of the voluntary sector covered under the IRS code section 501(c)(3), some of which is also health and welfare—or social welfare—related, but much of which goes beyond that is ordinarily defined as a basic need, such as recreation, the arts, and other goods which are defined as having communal value in a relatively affluent society. Some of these organizations have a particular advocacy stance. Like the NAACP–Legal Defense Fund or the Legal Aid Society, they provide services which are often more controversial. In addition, the term "charity" has a vestigial meaning, related to the giving of financial aid to the needy directly, through religious institutions such as the church and synagogue, or through a variety of other specialized charities, including aid to the poor overseas, through organizations such as C.A.R.E.

In its broadest sense, social welfare can be taken to include the whole range of organizations defined as charitable under the tax code in addition to generally recognized public sector programs and services. The exact lines to be drawn are far from clear, however, and, since they have evolved pragmatically out of changing conditions, they are also constantly subject to change. The boundaries have also become ideological battlegrounds. Both in the public sector and the voluntary sector, organizations which protect individuals or groups against oppressive mainstream forces of society are often unpopular and subject to retaliation by more powerful forces. Much of the history of charity organization in our country revolves around the question of purpose—the degree to which institutions in both the voluntary and public sector can serve the cause of protecting civil liberties as well as that of meeting basic physical needs of individuals for food, clothing, and shelter, and how this can be achieved while protecting what is viewed as the community interest in a productive, well-ordered society. The tension between these various purposes— on the one hand, that of protection of liberty and individual dignity, that of providing for basic care of needy individuals and groups in the community, and, on the other, that of social control (protecting the community from disruption)—pervades the historical development of welfare institutions in our country, and becomes a central concern of charitable organization in a democratic capitalistic society.

Development of Social Welfare Institutions, 1860–1890

From the period of the earliest settlements in the seventeenth century through the mid-nineteenth century, Americans provided charity to the poor through a variety of predominantly local institutions. Urbanization and industrialization had already emerged as aspects of American society in the early 1800s, but until the Civil War aid to the needy and the handicapped (widows, children, the ill) continued to be dominated by colonial traditions and structures. Initially this aid was based largely on neighbor-helping-neighbor, mutual aid, and church responsibility, but increasingly it included town and county public assistance funded by local taxes and delivered through a variety of indoor and outside relief mechanisms—the dole, assigned work, and the almshouse.

The Civil War, however, made a startling change in our nation, in social welfare as in all other aspects of American life. Trends that had started before the war, such as urbanization, industrialization, nationalization, and settlement of the Western frontier, accelerated and began to reshape our national scene. In response to changing environmental conditions and new needs, social welfare institutions expanded rapidly both in the voluntary sector and in the public arena. The Freedman's Bureau (1865–1872), the first major effort at direct social welfare intervention by the federal government, was developed as an effort to help newly freed blacks, and it failed. In the late 1800s, blacks, Orientals, and American Indians—groups that were not part of the majority Western, white heritage—were already separate from the mainstream of American life, and with the demise of the Freedman's Bureau a secondary service system developed for blacks in particular, including educational institutions.[1]

After the Civil War, new public institutions were developed by the states in a move which was paralleled by the growth of private agencies and charities. Concomitantly, coordinating groups began to proliferate as well, in both the public and private sectors.[2] State Boards of Charities were created and national committees and conferences, such as the National Conference of Charities and Corrections (1874). With intensified industrialization and factory development, labor organizations became increasingly significant. The International Labor Union was organized (1878) and foundered (1882), and the Knights of Labor grew to a membership of 700,000 following the demise of the International Labor Union. Women now also formed voluntary associations for mutual aid, for gaining the vote, and for social reform.

As industrialization spread, some individuals gained new personal fortunes and accumulated wealth and power. The growth of these immense personal fortunes (such as that of John D. Rockefeller, Andrew Carnegie, and J. P. Morgan) gave rise to a new notion of philanthropic giving and the development of the persona of the industrial philanthropist. There has been considerable argument about the motivations of these early philanthropists, who have been described variously as guilt-ridden or God-driven.[3] However, clearly, their personal philosophies fit in well with the ideas of Social Darwinism and survival of the fittest which became prevalent by the early 1870s as a result of the work of Herbert Spencer in England and William Graham Sumner in America.[4] The idea of survival of the fittest meshed well with an expanding laissez-faire economy and individual entrepreneurism, and provided good theoretical underpinnings for a capitalist society.

The vision of charity represented by the new philanthropists was radically different from former notions of community charity for the needy and unfortunate. It included large special-purpose donations in support of colleges, museums, and medical research. Surplus wealth, which had often been accumulated in dubious ways (morally if not legally), led to the giving of enormous visible donations to particular institutions in ways which would also give renown to their benefactors.[5] At the same time it helped to strengthen and channel energies of an emergent voluntary sector, and added scope, prestige, and power to its development.

From Charity Organization to Community Chest

In the 1870s, after the Civil War, the threads of emergent philanthropic giving, new institutions, and increased needs came together, resulting in professionalism of community charity. The numbers and kinds of agencies providing help had proliferated, along with growing needs. The economic crisis of 1873–78 accelerated an already existing interest in finding a better method for providing assistance to those who needed it, while at the same time eliminating the waste of scarce resources.

Once again America turned to Europe for its model. The Reverend S. H. Gurteen, an Episcopalian minister concerned about the suffering of workers and their families at the western terminus of the Erie Canal, went to London and studied the Charity Organization Society (COS) there. He returned home with the ideas of investigating needs on a community-wide basis and of centralized referral of the needy to community agencies, and founded what may be considered the first COS in America (1877). The COS idea spread in this country. Receptivity to a scientifically organized notion of charity led to the search for increased coordination and planning of services, and was eventually connected to coordinated agency funding as well.

From the beginning, the charity organization movement embodied within itself at least two different and not always compatible functions. These have presented dilemmas for organized charity ever since. On the one hand, there was concern about insuring that the needy were provided with appropriate assistance; on the other hand, charity was not to be given indiscriminately—it was to be given sparingly, and on a scientifically determined basis, avoiding duplication of effort. The COS established in Buffalo did not provide any relief funds directly, but served as a clearinghouse and coordinative body for community charitable activities.

Major new directions in the development of coordinated charities occurred shortly thereafter with the formation of the Charity Organization Society of Denver in 1887. This organization, considered to be the first federated fund-raising organization in America, apparently learned from a previous experience in Liverpool, England (1873). Denver's effort was the first in the United States to incorporate the notion of raising money for varied charitable agencies through one combined communitywide fund drive, rather than through multiple solicitations. Coordinated charitable giving was thus matched with efforts at organized fund raising in the community.[6]

Three attributes of the first communitywide fund-raising drive deserve particular attention. First, the Denver organization was created by a group of religiously affiliated community leaders, which included initially a Catholic priest, two Protestant ministers, and a lay leader from the Jewish community, Frances Jacobs, but which expanded its leadership shortly; second, it appears to have been affiliated with the Associated Charities, a group of twenty-three agencies, not all of which participated in the first campaign (which raised a little over $21,000); and third, it already evidenced the dual connection of institutions and lay leadership, with limited business involvement.[7] Even without professional staff, the Denver organization lasted for several years, eventually coming on hard times and changing its name twice, to "The United Charities of Denver" (1911) and "The Denver Federation for Charity and Philanthropy" (1913). Meanwhile the idea of federation emerged in other cities, such as Elmira, New York, and the Jewish communities of Boston (1895) and Cincinnati (1896).

What is called the first *modern* federated fund-raising organization emerged in Cleveland in 1913, twenty-six years after the first attempt in Denver. The founders of the Cleveland Federation for Charity and Philanthropy knew about the Denver experience and studied it. Primary among the lessons they learned was the need to provide for continuity through professional staffing.

The Cleveland organization, far more than that of Denver, was an outgrowth of the efforts of local business leadership, and the product of many years of study by the Committee on Benevolent Associations of the Cleveland Chamber of Commerce.[8] A leader of the Cleveland community expressed the ambitious aims and philosophies of the proposed organization this way:

> The proposals put before you seem . . . not only reasonable but positively inevitable if the problem of philanthropy in Cleveland is to be solved. The plan proposed differs in essential points from any devised in any other city. It is not a federation of institutions alone as in Denver, nor of givers alone, nor of both together. It is a federation for the advancing of charity and philanthropy, of institutions, of givers and citizens. It does not intend to be merely a mere collecting agency. . . . It will hope to produce its results in the way of a wiser distribution mainly through a better educated giver.[9]

The modern community chest was thus born with the rhetoric of the future. It included both business involvement and professional staff as well as the initiation of citizen-informed budgeting to agencies, and was based on the notion of an association of agencies whose main purpose was coordination of charitable efforts. In some places this group was totally independent of the Charity Organization Society, while elsewhere, as in Denver, they were closely interwoven. Many of these associations became Councils of Social Agencies, the antecedents of later planning organizations affiliated with community chests.[10]

By the end of the nineteenth century (in 1893), another fund-raising model had developed, not out of the federated fund-raising organization but out of the efforts of one specific service organization, the YMCA. The YMCA already included on its board of directors prominent businessmen, and they had developed the concept of the short-term, intensive fund-raising campaign in two communities —in Omaha, Nebraska, and in New Westminster, British Columbia (Canada).[11] These drives had been considered successful, and the concept of the once-a-year intensive fund-raising campaign soon became an integral part of the concept of combined fund raising at the local level.

In the progressive era around the turn of the century, the growth of coordinated fund raising and community organization paralleled the growth of the social work profession. In the period before the First World War, the idea of professionalism in social work developed rapidly, with a number of other schools following the establishment in 1898 of the New York School of Philanthropy (now the Columbia University School of Social Work). This was also a period when social work was divided sharply in orientation. It encompassed social reformers, such as Jane Addams, who worked in the Settlement movement (Hull House), and fought for the cause of justice in the community and in the national arena. And it was influenced by the notions of the Charity Organization Society, which considered method, orderliness, and efficiency as primary to the professional helping role.[12]

Charity Organization Societies, Associated Charities, and their sometimes distant relation, the federated fund drive, were attempts to address the need for organizing and coordinating charitable activities in the community. The growing professional emphasis of these agencies was tied to democratic notions of community, and meshed well with the exuberant spirit of the progressive era at the turn of the century. However, the contrast between the social reform orientation of the settlements and the COS emphasis on method caused strains between these two groups, even while they worked side by side. By the 1920s, the leadership in social work went to those who emphasized professionalism, including the various groups in organized charity, as the zeal of reform gave way to a new functionalism[13]

The issue of charity coordination had another side to it. After decades in which charities developed primarily on the state and local level, in a horizontally oriented direction, vertically oriented agency development began to accelerate in the early twentieth century. By the First World War the number of national voluntary agencies had proliferated greatly. Between 1906 and 1912, the Boys Club Association, the Boy Scouts, Goodwill Industries, and the Family Association emerged nationally. They were followed in 1913 by the largest national health organization, the American Cancer Society, which more than the others was organized on a top-down basis.

In 1918 there were fourteen federated fund-raising organizations, recognized as separate entities. In what was to become a pattern for the future, fund-raising activities were recognized as different from others in the social welfare field, and in fact had been criticized in a report of the social work organization. Despite opposition by some COS executives, federated organizations recognized their own separate identity, and formed a national organization with the name American Association for Community Organization.[14] This coordinating national body joined other welfare-related state and national coordinating organizations that already existed, many of which were connected to the growing profession of social work.

Finally, there was one major event which marked the importance now placed on the development of the voluntary sector in our country. In 1894 charitable institutions were specifically exempted from the income tax which was placed for the first time on public corporations.[15] Thus, the non-profit sector was clearly separated from the profit-making sector as a matter of fundamental public policy.

Community Chests, War Chests, and Federations

As America entered World War I in the spring of 1917, the focus of activities changed dramatically for organized charity. The issues were clearly joined around national agencies versus local needs, and the national concern for war-related causes had far-reaching implications for local charitable efforts.

Separate successful campaigns were carried out by some of the national agencies, using direct emotional appeals related to the war effort. Chief among these were the Red Cross and some religiously connected agencies, such as the YMCA, with activities on the national and international scene.[16] Federations were also soon confronting a new organization, the War Chest, which would encompass many causes at the local level, and which in some communities included either the Red Cross, the YMCA, or both. The idea of the combined war chest spread rapidly from about forty-five communities to four hundred by the war's end. Such was the power of the unifying emotional appeal, that all of the campaigns claimed to be successful in reaching their goals, and indeed it was stated that they were "oversubscribed."[17]

In 1917, as America was entering the war, federated fund raising was subject to criticism by a committee of social work leaders at the American Association for Organizing Charity. (Despite the similarity of names, this was not the same as the organization formed shortly thereafter by federation staff, the Association for Community Organization.) The social workers' committee questioned the effectiveness of federated organizations in raising more money for local charities. In their report these social workers also expressed serious reservations about the "immunity" clause for subscribers to the one combined drive, which meant that agencies could not go back individually to ask businesses for additional funding. Their conclusion was that non-federated cities should not adopt the federated model.[18]

On the whole, existing community charitable drives had an uneven relationship to the new war chests. They seem to have combined with them in about a dozen cities, while apparently all but disappearing in many other locations. In the meantime, the confusion resulting from multiple efforts and duplicate activities by organizations overseas led Secretary of State Newton D. Baker to encourage President Wilson to sign an order directing formation of a joint appeal of several national agencies. This joint campaign, the United War Work Campaign, was formed as the war was drawing to a close, and subsequently disappeared.[19]

One major change in fund raising which continued after the war was a direct result of the development of war chests. Fund raising, which had until then been largely directed at wealthy givers and businesses in the community, now involved a broader spectrum of givers, and also moved directly into the workplace. Funds were raised through approaches to employees in the worksite, and it became possible to reach larger numbers of potential givers.[20]

When the war ended in November 1918, the number of war chests declined quickly, and by 1919 there were only thirty-nine communitywide campaigns in the United States and Canada. These campaigns raised $19,651,334, in contrast to the over $100 million reportedly raised the year before by the approximately four hundred war chests.[21] It was not until the depression year of 1931 that approximately the same number of chests were operating, and raising that amount of money again.[22]

In 1918 the Rochester War Chest, one of the war chests that had incorporated within it a preexisting community fund drive, became the first organization to adopt the name "Community Chest." The new organization carried with it the echoes of the popular wartime appeal, and other federated organizations soon adopted the name.[23]

In the early 1920s, with a nation returning to "normalcy," the concept of local federated fund raising gradually spread, and in many communities took on the character and name of a Community Chest. Even though in many communities national agencies remained outside the federated appeal, the formation of war chests had paved the way for additional coordinated fund-raising drives, and by 1923, 203 federated campaigns existed in Canada and the United States. The prosperity of the period, along with its conservative temper, seemed highly compatible with notions of communitywide organized charity, which was appealing also to local business leadership. By 1926, a total of $66,432,072 was reported to have been raised in 308 federated campaigns.

Contributions from big business by this time had assumed more significance in the financial support of community chests. In this regard, a major event occurred in 1929, with the decision of the Corning Glass Works case. The Court of Appeals of the District of Columbia held that a contribution by Corning Glass Works to the local hospital was deductible from income as a business expense, since it satisfied the condition that "business corporations may have authority to make donations of money or property to enterprises reasonably calculated to further their general business interest."[24] Efforts which had initiated with the war chest, to solicit at the workplace, now combined with the rise in importance of organized labor, to suggest the beginnings of a new role for labor, and labor unions, in fund raising.

A continuing dilemma, however, remained concerning the influence of funded agencies. This influence was still frequently exercised through the Council of Social Agencies or agency representatives on chest boards, and raised questions about budget accountability. More broadly, there continued to be mixed opinion about the effectiveness of federated fund-raising efforts in the community, both in terms of the amounts of money raised and the quality of the allocations.[25] This was occurring at the same time as social workers were continuing to strengthen their own identity, and was undoubtedly related, since the community chest and council workers had already formed their own professional organization, the American Association for Community Organization (1918). In the 1920s social casework services also developed with increasing professional intensity in family agencies and elsewhere.

Changing Roles: The Great Depression

In the period from the turn of the century through the late 1920s, the role of the charitable institution, or what was turning into the formalized voluntary sector, again began to show signs of change. Prior to this time private voluntary hospitals and service-providing agencies had become the initiators of services, and service delivery became a larger part of the sector's activities. In the early 1920s "private" agencies still distributed charitable funds, but the essence of the sector was no longer totally bound up in the provision of financial assistance, or even services to the financially needy. By the mid-1920s the first stirrings of the private social welfare agency's "disengagement" from the poor were in evidence. Mary Richmond's ideas of professional social casework as method, together with Freudian and other psychiatric views, were helping to determine a new direction for social work. Character-building and recreational services were also emerging, frequently with the support of community federated fund-raising efforts.[26]

The depression of the late twenties and the stock market crash of 1929, however, caused a more fundamental disruption in the ways of doing business for all major institutions, and in particular for the institution which was becoming defined as social welfare.[27] Although President Hoover had been reluctant to depart from his reliance on voluntarism in the 1920s, even he had begun to recognize the sector's inability to meet the enormous demands of the depression. With the arrival of President Roosevelt's New Deal, the government first assumed temporary and then "permanent" responsibility in relation to financial assistance in major categories of dependency, including the temporarily unemployed, children, widows, the aged, and the physically handicapped. Although the federal government emerged with a new role in insuring that financial security was provided through social insurance, after the New Deal legislation was enacted all levels of government were involved in meeting a variety of categorically defined needs and providing public welfare payments to needy children. New public agencies were created to administer Aid to Dependent Children (ADC), and support was provided for services at the state and local level.

In this climate, the voluntary social welfare sector inevitably experienced a loss of purpose and major confusion about its basic role. Consciously and unconsciously, agencies began to redefine their own functions. At first, private family agencies received extensive new amounts of philanthropic funds to distribute as relief to the poor, particularly in 1931. These agencies, however, rapidly depleted their resources, and as the depression continued they proved unable to cope with the enormity of the pressures caused by the distribution of public funds. Thereafter, there was a loss of confidence in what private social welfare agencies could or should do, in light of expanding public sector activity. In this climate, and with the encouragement of local federated fund-raising campaigns, character-building agencies, recreation and group-work services, and specialized services for children assumed increasingly large shares of the voluntary or philanthropic social welfare dollar, along with mental hygiene clinics and social casework services in family agencies. (A somewhat parallel phenomenon occurred with the rise of specialized medical professionals and the voluntary hospitals, many of whom also received some support from community chest campaigns.)[28]

With unemployment and rising poverty the major problems facing the country, and with the public sector clearly taking a leading role in social welfare, it is not surprising that the community chest had a harder time garnering either funds or enthusiasm during the mid-1930s. Not only was there considerably less disposable personal income generally, but chest leaders also worried about the effect of increased personal income taxes (now graduated somewhat more to pay for new federal programs) on income which wealthy individuals considered available for philanthropic causes. Although the number of chests continued to increase, the total amount they raised decreased in the mid-1930s, and federated fund raising appeared to be in trouble.[29]

The concept of voluntarism at the local level, however, continued to have considerable appeal both for leaders of the corporate and business community and for members of the social work profession. Thus, in line with the scarcity of available resources, planning and budgeting procedures assumed more importance as local volunteers and professionally trained staff sought to stretch scarce funds, and cut allocations where they could.

In 1935, at the height of the depression, the national association of community chests, then called the Community Chests and Councils (the CCC), participated in a successful attempt at convincing the U.S. Congress to amend the income tax laws concerning corporations. New legislation allowed companies to make tax deductible contributions of up to 5 percent on their net income for charitable purposes.[30] The significance of this is plain: by 1950 corporate contributions represented over 40 percent of the amount raised in local federated fund drives. By the end of the 1930s, however, payroll deductions for charitable giving by workers had also emerged as a phenomenon which was to become increasingly widespread in the next decades.

More Changes: From Community Chest to United Fund

As the 1930s drew to a close, America reluctantly recognized that war loomed large on the horizon. Once in the war, however, patriotic spirit swept through the country, and as in the First World War, it changed the role of federated fund raising in line with the national interest. Community chests struggled with new relationships to state war chests and to the National War Fund, with added responsibility for helping to raise and allocate funds for war-related services and programs. Labor assumed a prominent role in the war fund effort, with the AFL and CIO working together with business and local communities, as well as with fund-raising professionals. In 1944 over $225 million was reportedly raised by 773 local community chests.[31] Again these campaigns were successful in raising unprecedented amounts, based on the urgency of a wartime appeal. Unlike in the First World War, however, somewhat more successful efforts were made to organize war-related services, and a USO was formed out of seven national agencies to help insure coordinated efforts with civilians and soldiers overseas.[32] The Red Cross, however, was not part of this organization, which was composed primarily of sectarian service agencies.

Once again a wartime effort changed the federal government's relationship to individual resources, in a way which also shaped the future of organized charity. On July 1, 1943, a new law had gone into effect which directly affected individual take-home pay; this was the initiation of compulsory withholding, by employers, of federal income taxes. Prior to that time, however, and subsequent to earlier withholding for social security payments, the dues checkoff by unions had already become established in several major industries. Most notable of these was the contract signed on June 20, 1941, between the Ford Motor Company and the UAW. With this contract the Ford Motor Company became the first major company in the auto industry to have a labor agreement which provided for the checkoff system of dues collection. By 1946 it was estimated that about 40 percent of all labor agreements provided for the checkoff; by 1954 about 75 percent of all agreements allowed for it.[33] Thus in the 1940s the way had already been paved for future payroll deductions for purposes defined as appropriate.

Chapter 2

From Community Chest To United Way

> The Chest had the organization and the War agencies had the appeal. As long as the War lasted, it was a winning combination.
>
> Harold Seymour, *Design for Giving*

> Something was happening in the grassroots. There was thunder in the west—from Iowa, Wisconsin, Ohio, Indiana, Illinois. . . . There was a muttering of many voices. And in true democratic fashion, the muttering became a meeting.
>
> *Community* (September 1947)

As World War II drew to a close, the mood in the country was on the whole optimistic. Nevertheless, the war left a variety of matters to be settled on the domestic front. Population shifts arising out of the wartime economy had changed the demography of our cities, and the necessities of production for war had changed our industrial technology. By the time the war with Japan ended in the summer of 1945, business and labor were already reassessing their relationship. At this point, the pent-up energies of the unions, contained during the push for wartime production, erupted in a series of strikes in some major industries of the nation, including steel and the auto industry. Unions also began reassessing their relationship with the community, a reassessment which frequently revolved around their interactions with social work agencies.[1]

In organized charity, as in other arenas, problems unresolved but covered over with wartime enthusiasms began to emerge, and the need for structured resolution of the relationship between local and national agencies, business, and labor, and of all of these groups to community fund raising, surfaced as a serious issue. Newly formed and greatly strengthened national health agencies added another wrinkle to the situation, as health became more of a factor to be reckoned with in the health and welfare complex. For the Community Chest and Council national organization (the CCC) and for most local community chests, resolution of these issues became increasingly critical.

Structural resolutions generally do not happen quickly and rarely evoke strong positive sentiment. Chest leadership, however, was aware of the continuous need to mobilize sentiment, particularly during the period of reassessment that follows wartime fund-raising successes. Thus the dramatic words of the epigraph above, from *Community*, used the rhetoric of American grassroots democracy in support of a change in fund-raising practices.[2] And, indeed, the words suggest the myth of Americana being promulgated by the community chest movement.[3] But what did they actually refer to?

The free-flowing description refers to one particular event—a meeting called by Henry Ford II on July 15, 1947, for the purpose of launching the United Health and Welfare Fund of the State of Michigan. Although the rhetoric is exaggerated, the event was actually of considerable significance in the history of federated fund raising. It marked the official birth of what would become the United Fund, a federation crated to resolve the problems caused by increasing numbers of independent fund-raising appeals and competition from the burgeoning health agencies, or what has been called the "disease of the month" fund-raising causes. And it signaled a new direction of the chest movement, away from concentration on people in their local community, and door-to-door fund raising, to a more aggressive complex and interlocking role with national agencies, labor, and the world of work.

The basic elements of the United Fund concept were not new: workplace solicitation; corporate support; labor involvement; an attempt at inclusiveness, including national agencies; and even payroll deduction had happened before.[4] But the combination of all these elements resulted in a new gestalt, which included the formalization of limited access to the workplace. Agencies that did not participate in the one-drive workplace solicitation would not be allowed to conduct their own separate drives at other times of the year. In this respect the chemistry of federated fund raising was altered fundamentally.

Multiple factors came together to create the sense of urgency that brought this new kind of federated fund-raising organization into existence. To begin with, industry, and in this case, the auto industry in particular, was tired of the time lost and the costs of multiple charitable appeals in the workplace. In addition, Ford had a particular reason for taking the lead, since it had a history of troubled relations with its workers, and in 1941 the union gained great strength through a general strike. In 1947 Henry Ford died, and his grandson, Henry Ford II, came in to revitalize the company. Regulation of charities tied to the checkoff was part of a larger plan to contain workplace organizing efforts, and at the same time to strengthen local federated fund raising.

Although many individuals and groups were involved in developing the united fund idea, clearly the interest of Henry Ford, on the business side, was matched on the federation side by the persistence and political skill of Walter Laidlaw, an executive of the Detroit organization, a former businessman, political leader, and non–social worker.[5] As a result of complex negotiations, it was initially determined that solicitation in the auto industries for local agencies would be combined with a statewide campaign for national health agencies, which could not be "controlled" in local communities. Of the local communities, Detroit was by far the largest; and in fact, the role of the state organization shortly was overshadowed by the local Detroit organization, although the Michigan Health and Welfare Fund continued to be significant. The United Foundation of Detroit was the name given to the new model for in-plant and industrial solicitation which emerged in that city, and, as one observer reported, "Detroit became a storm center" when the Foundation "invited" all the nationally organized fund-raising organizations to join, and gave notice that no other plant solicitations would be permitted.[6] The model was applicable to other industrial worksites as well and soon spread across the country, but without a state component.[7]

In development of the united fund idea with limited inplant solicitation, labor support was obviously essential, and it was forthcoming. As one labor leader later expressed it, "Our shop stewards were becoming panhandlers. . . . This had to stop. The united funds solved the problem with their simple payroll checkoffs. Furthermore, they invited labor into positions of leadership. This was important to us. . . . Labor could not be indifferent to the fact that the Detroit Community Chest fell three hundred thousand dollars short of its goal the year before the united fund was established."[8] Labor wanted to show good citizenship too; and it wanted to use its new power to join in the decision-making system. The checkoff provided a means for doing this.

From the business point of view, there was another environmental factor which made the participation of labor extremely desirable in the late 1940s. In the aftermath of the war years, excess profit taxes were reduced and the incentive for big giving by profitable corporations was reduced. In the years from 1945 to 1950 specifically, corporate giving overall declined from the high of $266 million (1945) to the low of $252 million in the year 1950, before the Korean war.[9] With reduced corporate taxes, coupled with a concern about a mild recession, corporations had added reasons for wanting to limit their contributions to local chests. By 1947 when the United Health and Welfare Fund of Michigan was created, corporate contributions to local chests had been increasing continuously, while the incentive for giving was beginning to decrease. In such a mood the big corporations could only be eager to increase the number of givers, while still keeping the corporate role of good citizen. The best way to keep that role prominent was to encourage more widespread giving by their employees. Moreover, ultimately broadening the base by increasing employee gifts would also allow corporate gifts to be diversified, away from the preponderant share that was at that time going to local chests.[10]

From the point of view of the community chests, the united fund was an effort to co-opt the opposition, and a matter of survival. But the move to a unified campaign in the workplace clearly suited the mood of the country, and meshed well with the needs of both labor and business. Moreover, it was a time when labor was seeking new allies and a new role for itself. With a more conservative spirit prevailing in the nation, business had begun the process of undermining some of the gains which labor had made under the New Deal, and in 1947 was able to secure the passage of the Taft-Hartley Act, which potentially undermined the institution of the closed shop. In this uncertain climate, the labor movement also suffered from internal conflict and questions about its own directions.

In the end, more conservative forces prevailed. In the late 1940s and early 1950s, unions developed closer, more cooperative relationships with management, and the CIO moved away from identification with the political far left, expelling its more radical affiliates. Concomitantly, the unions also developed an alliance with business management and chest professionals in efforts to limit the access of other fund-raising groups to the work place, and in promoting the united fund one-drive-for-all concept. Walter Reuther and the UAW played a significant part in this development.[11]

No matter how one felt about the creation or notion of the united fund, however, its formation could not be accurately described as from the bottom up. The process was the result of a meeting of business leaders, fund-raising professionals, and union leaders, and the most active united fund professional was not a social worker, but came also from business. It was this leadership group which in effect determined the manner of giving for large numbers of industrialized, blue-collar workers for the next three decades. Thus, the only sense in which the development of the united fund could be described as "grassroots" is by interpreting "grassroots" to mean state or local community (as opposed to the national CCC organization), and considering large industries or big cities to be "communities."

Wanting something to happen does not of course guarantee its success. While chest, business, and union leaders had reached a basic agreement in Michigan about the desirability of a unified appeal in industry, the agencies involved were not all necessarily willing to cooperate. In the pilot campaign in the spring of 1949, difficulties were already in evidence. Although eighteen agencies participated in that first state campaign, some notable agencies did not. The American Cancer Society (newly organized and renamed two years before), the Michigan Tuberculosis Association, the National Foundation for Infantile Paralysis, the Heart Association, and the American Red Cross initially remained outside. According to United Way historians, the Cancer Society and the National Foundation refused to negotiate with federated drives even after the United Fund blocked all canister solicitations in some major theaters in Detroit; the Michigan Heart Association eventually joined in the campaign at the urging of its chairman, Charles Wilson, who was also president of General Motors; and the American Red Cross eventually agreed to participate for in-plant or company solicitation.[12]

The first Michigan statewide campaign was not successful in reaching its goal, but the United Foundation–Torch Drive of Detroit in the fall of 1949 was, reportedly exceeding its combined chest-fund goal and raising over nine million dollars. Moreover, although the American Cancer Society and the National Foundation remained outside the drive, the Detroit United Foundation literature for the campaign was able to claim that their funds would help to "save lives" in relation to cancer and polio, since they included in their funding "package" the Michigan Cancer Foundation and the Sister Kenny Foundation, for care and treatment of polio. With the establishment of the United Foundation, therefore, the pattern of giving to alternative health groups, and even to creating them if necessary, was established. The pattern was copied by other federated fund-raising organizations, as the health wars escalated with the growth of united fund organizations in the 1950s.[13]

The development of the local united fund was important to all three of the groups described, labor, business, and federated fund raisers. But it certainly had the highest priority for the latter group. For the chests, the united fund as developed in Detroit was a survival issue, because it embodied three critical goals fundamental to federated fund raising. First, the fund was to be inclusive; by including the old locally based agencies of the Community Chest, and the top-down national agencies together in one campaign, it would justify the idea of one unified community appeal. Second, the fund would insure that there was only one fund-raising campaign in the workplace, and that it would be essentially a community fund drive (Community Chest/United Fund) approved by management and supported by labor. And third, it would increase the use of payroll deduction on a companywide basis, and help gain acceptance for an idea whose importance was just beginning to be fully appreciated. Moreover, the times were ripe for this idea: federated campaigns were beginning to sag by 1945, and by 1946, despite an increase in the number of chests (from 773 in 1944 to 842 in 1946), the amounts raised had decreased nationwide from $225,934,893 (1944) to $173,512,638 (1946).

Putting it somewhat differently, Carter, in *The Gentle Legions*, pointed out that the American Cancer Society increased its revenues by over 549 percent between 1945 and 1948, while federated funds in 1948 had only produced around 91 percent of the amount produced in 1945.[14] One agency funded by the Chests put matters bluntly in the Chest publication (in 1949): "The campaign had tough sledding last fall, said the chest men. . . . if Chests and Red Feather Services didn't blame everything on each other, they blamed it on The Recession."[15] In this climate, popular health causes that could bring in money to a federation might be desirable partners.

One other circumstance might have made the need for action seem urgent. This was the increasing appearance of in-plant federations, or what at that time was referred to as an "Industrial Chest." According to one authoritative study, there were at least 535 of these plant-level federations or industrial chests in existence in 1951.[16] These company-sponsored federations allowed employees to determine the manner in which their collected funds were distributed. In practice, apparently, the funds were divided between the local community fund and local branches of a few of the national health organizations, such as Cancer and Heart, or the Red Cross, with the bulk of the funds generally going to the local federated fund-raising organization. Nevertheless, as one authority expressed it, the impression was growing that the chest was just one more of many competing causes. Surprisingly, however, community chests were initially not certain about how they should handle the spread of industrial chests. An article in *Community* (1949) stated that "the employee or industrial chest idea is apparently spreading by leaps and bounds," and noted that the industrial chest idea may be promulgated, initiated in response to request, or discouraged by local staffs.[17]

The success of the Detroit campaign in the fall of 1949 offered a viable alternative to in-plant federations, or to open charity wars such as suggested by Basil O'Connor, a leading representative of the health agencies.[18] The united fund idea was consequently disseminated widely through meetings with the national CCC staff, through *Community* magazine and other trade publications and newsletters, as well as though more informal contacts among local chest staff. Corporate leaders also met to discuss the idea, and by 1955 the movement to a united fund was already characterized as positively related to leadership of the donor community. In Pittsburgh, business leaders were reported to be interested in insuring that control of the federation would remain vested with the big givers, and connected with business, rather than dominated by social workers and their agencies.[19] Thus, the idea of the united fund gained powerful supporters across the country in a direction that had implications for the future relationship of social work and community organization to federated fund raising.

Clarity and Confusion: The Health Wars

The campaign of the United Foundation in Detroit in 1949 signaled a new direction in the struggle between the proponents of federated fund raising and the supporters of independent fund raising, and in particular the supporters of the national health agencies, with their over 20,000 local branches, programs, and affiliates.[20] The problem of national agencies and state chapters had emerged during World War I, occurred again and been submerged in World War II, and spilled over into peacetime. By the spring of 1947, the fight had already been declared openly, and state federations had emerged as one solution. Sides were drawn between those who urged open competition in the charity market, and those who considered the existing conditions as chaotic and badly in need of coordination and planning. Natural and state structures raised new issues for locally organized community chests, and there was concern about the future of organized fund raising.

The Rockefeller Foundation report on health and welfare agencies (1949) had summed up the situation after the war succinctly. The authors of that study noted that, "although all agencies reported exceptionally strong financial support since 1941, they sense great uncertainty as to the national income after the war and as to the effects of taxation and new legislation upon voluntary contributions. Every organization is attempting, however, to broaden the base of its support and is looking to small gifts from many rather than large gifts from few."[21] The crux of the issue seemed now to revolve around how best to raise money efficiently from large numbers of people, at a time when changes in the society suggested turning away from the focus on more diffuse residential campaigns and there might be less incentive for corporate giving. Workplace fund raising presented one creative way to help insure reinvigorated federated campaigns.

The United Fund seemed a pragmatic alternative also to the notion of company-run in-plant federations, which were a means for coordinating charity in the workplace, but which ultimately might lead to workplace problems for employers. In comparison with outside united funds, in-plant federations did not solve issues of competing claims for support arising inside the business organization, and might lead to other workplace conflicts or organizing among employees as well as for charitable competition. The United Fund would provide one neutral third party, or desired intervening force, between the corporation and its employees, and agencies in the communities that met social welfare needs. Moreover, the Fund idea meshed with the desire of corporations to expand the giving base and take themselves somewhat off the hook as the major supporters of the community funds. This in fact occurred initially in the late forties when the excess-profits tax of wartime was removed, and some signs of recession were evident, so that corporations were feeling the burden of giving more directly out of their own profits.[22]

The Rockefeller-funded study completed in 1945 clearly reflected the concerns of big philanthropic givers about multiple solicitations from the health and welfare field. In fact, the Gunn and Platt study was only one of at least three studies to be supported by the Rockefeller Foundation, and directed at efforts to improve the efficiency and effectiveness of the non-profit health and welfare sector.[23] The notion that there was a separate agency for every disease or for every major organ of the body raised serious questions for people interested in holistic or preventive medicine, and, moreover, the accountability of many of the national health agencies was certainly questionable. The need to coordinate fund-raising drives and research efforts was addressed in the recommendations of the Gunn and Platt Report, but most of the big national health agencies flatly rejected the idea of cooperating in a coordinated or combined fund-raising campaign, and were apparently not interested in any form of cooperation. They certainly thought they could make more money alone and demanded independence.[24] When accountability emerged as a big issue in the later Hamlin study in 1960, the national agencies also were reluctant to accept the idea of more stringent reporting procedures.[25]

The story of the tempestuous relationship between the national health agencies and federated fund-raising proponents in the years 1945–1970 is told in considerable detail elsewhere. However, it is important to note here that the relationship between the health agencies and the growing united fund movement became an increasingly byzantine affair in the two decades after 1945, with moves and countermoves that stirred up considerable emotion in the field of organized charity, if not with the public at large.[26] It is therefore worth reviewing a few of the highlights of these years, for the light they shed on future events.

The American Red Cross

In the First World War the Red Cross had received considerable corporate attention, along with the Community Chest, and it was not surprising that chests paid attention to this organization after the war (see above, chapter 1). However, relations between local chests and the Red Cross were subject to stress, as dissatisfaction with Red Cross activities increased, and funds available for agency support became scarcer, during the depression. In 1936 the Red Cross passed a national policy against joint campaigning with local chests, and thereafter Red Cross chapters were not allowed to join in community chest campaigns.

If the Red Cross suffered during the decade of the emerging New Deal, it was later strengthened by the exigencies of war. As one authority stated unequivocally: "The American Red Cross collection of more than a half billion dollars in World War II will long stand as a high water mark in a people's philanthropy," encouraged by sophisticated public relations "experience, imagination, and polished performance in the art of money raising." In 1945 alone the Red Cross drive raised $231 million, in only 31 days, which was considerably more than the amount raised by 799 community chests that whole year ($201,859,357).[27] It was in this spirit that in 1947 Basil O'Connor as head of the Red Cross was able to state his strong opposition to the notion of federated fund raising. Nonetheless, in 1948 Red Cross replaced O'Connor with George Marshall, who had a more tolerant attitude about cooperation with united funds. Thus, by the first United Fund campaign in Detroit (1949), an agreement could be reached with the local chapter of the American Red Cross becoming part of a United Foundation–Torch Drive. This development was a real coup, since the biggest public relations problem for the Red Cross during the war had been the opposition of organized labor leaders who felt that their workers had not received adequate assistance from the Red Cross during the strikes of the 1930s.[28]

With the departure of O'Connor, and the return to a less emotional appeal in fund raising, the idea of a Red Cross partnership in federated fund raising was more acceptable. In 1955, the National American Red Cross, confronting declining campaign funds, finally stated openly that local units could merge with community chests to form united funds "subject to retention of certain privileges." Among the most emphatic of these conditions was the notion of a partnership in fund raising and "equal billing."[29]

In some significant respects the Red Cross relationship would seem to be the paradigm for federated fund-raising organizations in their negotiations with other large national health agencies. Even though the Red Cross has been characterized as in "a class by itself",[30] it certainly has some similarities to other health agencies with which it is often loosely grouped. These include a strong national structure, a variety of health education programs closely related to fund-raising efforts, and a broad volunteer base upon whom it depends on the local level. Nevertheless, it took more than twenty years, until well into the 1970s, before there was any widespread replication of the Red Cross–United Way model, and even then there remained some particular factors which limited its adaptability to the other health agencies. These complications will be discussed below in relation to events of the decade from 1975 to 1985 (see chapters 5, 6, and 8–10).

Other Health Agencies and Federated Fund Raising

In the years after the creation of the United Fund of Michigan, only two of the health agencies stood out continuously as noncompromisers at any point, the National Foundation, which still maintains its independent position, and the Tuberculosis Association. Both of these were popular agencies that were able to reach the giving public easily. Of the other smaller health agencies, a few either joined in local campaigns at various points in time, or were not objects of great interest to the federated fund raisers.[31] (Some, like Planned Parenthood, have been so controversial that most local United Fund/United Ways have tried to avoid involvement with them, and where they have been involved, there have often been problems for the United Way.[32]) Of the other larger health organizations, the

American Heart Association (the AHA) and the American Cancer Society (the ACS) remained a concern to federated fund-raising organizations because they continued to grow in size and appeal.[33]

In the good fund-raising years of the late 1940s and 1950s, ACS increased its revenues and organizational scope considerably, and in 1957 it established a firm national policy to "withdraw all its units from united funds and to conduct a completely independent crusade by 1960."[34] Moreover, ACS made the point explicitly that the decision was not made impulsively. Among the reasons that ACS gave for the decision was that the great majority of its more than 3,000 local units had never participated in local funds at all. During these same years AHA leadership was also fighting to preserve its "Heart Sunday" appeal in February and spoke out consistently in favor of the independent health drive. In any case, the decision to remove local units from federated fund-raising efforts had consequences for ACS. While community chests and united funds raised more money in the late 1950s and early years of the 1960s, ACS revealed in October 1960 that it "had raised two million dollars less than in 1959, and for the first time in 16 years would be unable to make all its research grants."[35]

United fund influence in limiting the access of the health funds to business and to the industrial work force had certainly been a contributing factor in the ACS decrease, and in addition united funds were successful in gaining the cooperation of the press in an extensive "blackout" of press releases and free publicity about health agencies. At the same time, across the country relationships between the United Fund and smaller health agencies such as Cystic Fibrosis or Multiple Sclerosis were generally not of great concern to most local united funds.

Overall, the union remained a supporter of united fund restrictive policies during these years. As a part of the powerful triumvirate of management, labor, and community chest, organized labor remained firm in the belief expressed earlier by Charles Livermore, who was the assistant director of the National CIO War Relief Committee (September 1943):

> Labor is not particularly interested in preserving institutions as such or in furthering sectarian interests. Rather, labor is learning that the importance of social work lies in the functions of agencies, which in their broadest and most favorable light involve planning and developing programs for health, for recreation, for family stability and the priceless dignity of the individual being.[36]

This meant dealing with people in a holistic way and raising funds for community needs as a whole, and concomitantly, it meant citizen planning for allocation of resources. Thus labor opposed a model of individual choice or preference, based upon the emotional nature of a particular health cause. It preferred the opportunity to influence the allocations to agencies made through the budget review process of the community chest or fund.

The major issues dividing local chests and health agencies remained troublesome through the next two decades. There were essentially six major dilemmas to resolve: the degree to which national organizations control the policies and actions of local affiliates from the top, as related to the theoretically more bottoms-up nature of the United Fund–United Way system;[37] the closely related issue of community involvement and local services versus research or nationally determined purposes; the single purpose of most of the health agencies versus the more broadly based "whole person" approach of most of the traditional United Way agencies; the question of proportional giving, or giving according to income, as opposed to an equal contribution by all (i.e., a dollar for the cause); commitment to the allocations process and the fund's citizen review, versus the belief of the health agencies that they are entitled to a predetermined formulaic share of funds raised, based on the popularity of their cause; and the question of whether health funds could conduct separate campaigns outside the workplace, and if so, under what conditions.

These dilemmas would not go away, and remained part of the continuous controversy in the negotiations which the United Way later faced. They were sufficiently difficult to resolve so that most of the larger and more powerful health agencies stayed outside of federated fund-raising systems through the 1970s.

By the mid-1950s the United Fund had developed momentum, and had probably gotten a "boost" from another outside event, which was the Korean War (1950–1954). War funds, now United Defense Funds, again proliferated, and at the same time Fund professionals across the country were actively promoting the notion of payroll deduction together with the united fund idea. Nevertheless, the United Fund was hardly united across the nation, if by "united" was meant "standard in its definition or broadly inclusive of the health agencies in the package of funded agencies."

At that time United Fund professionals were in fact wrestling with the operational definition of the United Fund. Ultimately, in their pragmatic fashion, they came up with the simplest format: A United Fund was defined as including, whatever else it did not include, the Community Chest agencies and one national agency, generally the Red Cross.[38] It was no wonder, however, that there was confusion in the minds of Community Chest officials, as well as the general public. The emerging united funds and councils movement now contained within itself several different, officially sanctioned, kinds of organizations: united funds; community chests; other types of federated funds, which could include a variety of health agencies and/or the Salvation Army; and the related non–fund-raising organizations known as health and welfare councils or councils of social agencies.

Finally, in 1956 the national organization of the chest movement changed its name from Community Chests and Councils of America (CCCA) to the United Community Funds and Councils of America (UCFCA). Even if the reality did not quite equal the dream of inclusiveness, the united fund idea was now blessed with the appearance of universal acceptance. Staffs in the burgeoning united fund movement were working to spread the use of payroll deduction and to protect their hegemony over the workplace in industrial America, and they had friends in high corporate offices to support their efforts. If some national health agencies would not join them, the United Fund would move ahead with agencies that did cooperate. Indeed, eventually federated funds created and gave support to their own separate health foundations, with a holistic approach to research and health care in the local community.[39]

Public Policy: Social Services and Social Action

While the UCFCA was absorbed in fighting the "health wars," a social revolution was occurring in American life. Significant new directions had already appeared even during the conservative decade of the 1950s with a series of civil rights actions and decisions of the United States Supreme Court, culminating in the ruling of *Brown v. The Board of Education of Topeka* in 1954 that racial segregation in public schools was unconstitutional. The nation was changing: the war economy in the 1940s resulted in major demographic shifts; as people began to move off the farm, blacks moved north and west, and urban areas grew, while at the same time urban whites increased their movement to the suburbs. Technological developments resulting from wartime needs also pushed America into a new high-tech era, as automation and artificial intelligence moved into industrial circles. Worker displacement became an issue for the near future, and television made mass culture a burgeoning reality. Looking back, the 1950s might be characterized as a time of passive optimism and political conservatism; but like the 1920s, this decade could also be considered a seedtime of reform.[40] And in the early 1960s the Kennedy administration embodied a new spirit in which more passive optimism was replaced by a willingness to confront the problems of our society with a renewed, active optimism about the possibilities for resolving them.

Once the events of the 1960s began, they moved quickly in ways which deeply impacted on American social policy. The civil rights movement emerged out of the demographic changes and unevenly shared prosperity of the fifties, but the ensuing legal action and legislation were both causes of, and reactions to, the civil unrest which erupted during the sixties. During this era poverty was rediscovered, new entitlements and old rights were claimed, and venerable institutions were subject to profound challenge and question. Even before Michael Harrington's book *The Other America* (1962) stirred America's social conscience and awareness of poverty, legislation had begun to address the issue of changing work and manpower needs, with the passage of the Manpower Development and Training Act of 1962.[41] Concern about the poor was joined with faith in social services as a way out of poverty, and the need to promote better public services was recognized with the passage of the 1962 amendments to the Social Security Act. In these amendments additional federal funding was made available to the states, on a matching basis, as an incentive for the provision of improved and expanded local public social services. The same amendments also established more liberal provisions for public welfare payments under ADC, including expansion of the program to cover two-parent families with an unemployed parent.[42] In 1965 the Medicaid and Medicare programs were enacted, providing increased health services for the poor, the elderly, and other vulnerable populations. In the same year additional public funding for services to the elderly was assured through the passage of the Older American's Act, and a year later the Model Cities Program was enacted.[43]

Increased welfare payments and supportive social services constituted one approach to eliminating poverty, but there were advocates for more deep-seated social reform even among the stalwarts of the social welfare establishment. Under the leadership of the Ford Foundation, a series of urban projects had been funded to demonstrate the possibilities for neighborhood rehabilitation in the "gray areas" of the cities.[44] The enthusiasm of academics, enlightened philanthropists, and social scientists was thereafter linked to the practical concerns of a democratic administration for political support in urban areas, and led to the passage of a dramatic new concept for attacking poverty. Of all the programs that formed part of Lyndon Johnson's Great Society approach, the Economic Opportunity Act of 1964 and "the war on poverty" that it represented became the most ideologically loaded of the new social welfare programs. Other Johnson programs may have started out in controversy, but did not remain the subject of such continuous, heated debate.

The Economic Opportunity Act embraced a number of varied specific programs in what might be considered a scatter-gun approach to fighting poverty; but what gave special character to Johnson's War on Poverty was probably its messiest and most controversial, if most innovative feature—the rallying cry of "maximum feasible participation" in program development.[45] This feature gave sanction to the poor to deal with their own future, to work with (or against) city hall, and to demand more benefits for welfare recipients, more responsive services and institutions, and the recognition that benefits were theirs by right or entitlement, not charity.

With this great increase in the number, variety, and scope of public social welfare programs, it is not surprising that federal spending grew sharply in the 1960s and 1970s, both as a percent of the national budget and in absolute dollars. In 1960, for example, the federal government spent $67.6 billion on social programs, an expense constituting 28.5 percent of total federal spending. By 1965, social programs were 30.2 percent of total federal spending and cost $93.5 billion. In 1970 these costs had reached $158.3 billion, or 38 percent of federal spending, and were still rising.[46] Much of the increase in social welfare spending was due to direct cash transfers to individuals, which almost doubled the welfare rolls in the 1960s and added significantly to the overall costs of social welfare.[47] But under the so-called "open-ended" service provisions of the 1967 amendments to the Social Security Act, federal expenditures for social services increased greatly as well, going from $0.8 billion in 1966 (0.1 percent of the gross national product—the GNP) to $2.7 billion in 1971 (0.3 percent of the GNP), and this does not take into account other related programs under the War on Poverty, Job Training, or Housing. The same years also saw the beginning of the sharp increase in health expenditures. Federal outlays for health were $2.6 billion (or 0.4 percent of the GNP) in 1966; in 1971 they were $13.5 billion (1.3 percent of the GNP); and in 1976 they were $31.5 billion (or 1.9 percent of the GNP) and still rising.[48] Not since the early days of the New Deal had there been such an expansion of federal government support for health and welfare programs, and moreover the states also added to the expansion.[49]

The agenda of the nation had clearly shifted in the 1960s, and for most of the decade it was moved by a positive, optimistic spirit. The economic growth of the country, combined with social welfare program initiatives, resulted in an overall decline in poverty nationwide. At the same time the civil rights movement enjoyed notable successes, including the passage of the Civil Rights Act of 1964. Poor people were participating in new ways through the programs of the War on Poverty, and new black leaders were appearing as part of the political and social scene.

Urban unrest continued to escalate, however, and by the mid-1960s it had begun erupting across the country. A series of urban disorders occurred during those years, culminating in the riots in Detroit in 1967, which profoundly shocked the nation and inescapably drew attention to concerns about a nation divided in two; one part white, and the other black; one part rich, and the other poor.[50] Domestic problems came home to roost, while on the international scene Americans were suffering from the wounds of a destructive war in Vietnam. It was a time when people said, "If you are not part of the solution, you are part of the problem," and strong stands on social issues were an expected norm. The social consensus of a more quiescent time was suffering strains, and some questioned openly the validity of a socioeconomic system which permitted deep inequities in the distribution of its resources.

In this climate the role of the UCFCA was by definition problematic. This was a decade in which old assumptions and accepted values were subject to intensive challenge, and new leaders were emerging from groups in the population which had not formerly played a part in the old elite systems of community leadership.[51] At a time when questions were being raised about the nature of community and the degree of equality of opportunity which actually existed in American society, any institution which promulgated the myth of an American consensus was bound to have trouble. And any organization, like a united fund, which supported established agencies with traditional programs, was likely to be labeled "irrelevant." Moreover, to the extent that united funds and councils were focusing their energies on the "health wars," they were also being distracted from the main themes in the environment around them.

New subgroups were forming in the community, and ethnic and racial minorities were increasingly entering into the mainstream service system and seeking leadership positions. Conflict was replacing consensus as a major concept in social work–community organization practice, and the notion of a common public interest was being challenged generally. A new ideological view of community organizing as social action-advocacy was replacing earlier views, and this was also tied closely to the movement for community control.[52] What is more, this was happening with the benefit of public money, and at the same time as services and welfare supports were increasing.

Officials of the UCFCA were not unaware of the changes going on around them, and some local funds made efforts to respond to the new environment after the Civil Rights Act was enacted in the 1950s. But the "movement" was not certain about the kind of response it should make, and controversies connected to the civil rights movement added to the dilemmas of maintaining community consensus. Thus, in the 1950s some local chests and funds responded to pressure and withdrew funding from even such a relatively establishment organization as the Urban League, because the Ku Klux Klan in some communities in the South and Southwest raised objections to it. That controversy also reached the UCFCA Board, where the question of a national stand in support of the Urban League was raised by Leo Perlis in September 1956. However, the UCFCA took no official action until August 1964, when it issued a cautious memorandum to local United Ways.[53]

In the 1960s the UCFCA was ultimately forced to confront the degree of change in the external environment. In 1963 the UCFCA Executive Committee voted unanimously to recommend a national affirmative action policy in anticipation of new rulings concerning the fund-raising campaign among federal employees. This also led to the issuance of the board's August 1964 memorandum, reaffirming a non-discrimination policy.[54] In the same period minority representation increased on the national board as well as on local fund and chest boards. Furthermore, the UCFCA could not ignore the impact of the War on Poverty on local communities. The anti-poverty program could be considered a threat or an opportunity. But one way or the other the local funds and councils would have to deal with local community action agencies and new programs being developed. A summary of events in the national journal, *Community*, took the high road in 1964, noting that "the Poverty Program represents the best opportunity the United Way has to spearhead a drive of voluntarism on some of the basic social problems of our time."[55]

In 1966–1967 the UCFCA began to work more closely with the federal government, in an effort of mutual accommodation and support. In 1966 the UCFCA was one of the signers—indeed the only one for the voluntary sector—of a joint policy announcement on "Government and the Voluntary Sector: A Statement of Consensus." The other signatories were the secretaries of Commerce, of Labor, of Health, Education, and Welfare (HEW), and of Housing and Urban Development (HUD), as well as the director of the Office of Economic Opportunity. By 1967, Lyman Ford, national executive of UCFCA, reported that Sargent Shriver was so interested in getting UCFCA leadership involved in local poverty programs that he was willing to finance a project to promote better understanding of the poverty program on the part of these leaders. Although concern was expressed about the bias of business leadership against government, particularly the federal government, a project was developed with the OEO.[56]

Thus, by the late 1960s the UCFCA was involved in an effort of accommodation with the new role of government in local affairs, and in particular, in the funding of local social services. By November 30, 1967, a report of the chairman of the Community Planning Advisory Council of the UCFCA noted that Community Planning Division staff of the national organization spent approximately 50 percent of their time in the past year "relating to the new federal programs and their local application." Nevertheless, there was no nationwide unanimity on the appropriate response to the new federal programs. Consensus and caution remained trademarks of the federated movement, while the capacity for quick response and the ability to cope with controversy and risk were requirements for the new climate.

It was no wonder that by the end of the 1960s the UCFCA suffered an external loss of credibility and internal confusion about its own role and purpose. Massive infusion of government funds had threatened the core of voluntary funding and undermined the basic mission of the fund and council movement. The poverty wars had created a new quasi-public system of local organizations to run programs or to oversee their development in the community. These organizations, local Community Action Agencies, were responsible for oversight of a wide variety of fledgling service programs and innovative approaches to special needs, such as Legal Services or Head Start.[57] In contrast, although UCFCA reported that over 40 local Planning Councils assumed the role of the anti-poverty agency in their community at some point in time, the general picture of the UCFCA was of a stodgy system with traditional programs which did not meet the needs of the 1960s.

Organized charity had to change directions in response to the increased involvement of the federal government with local services. In addition, there were already rumblings about withdrawal of support for many of the programs which the federal government had initiated, raising the question of who would pick up the pieces. The leaders of the UCFCA recognized the need for change and they hired the firm of Peat, Marwick, Mitchell to help determine the direction of that change.

In many respects the report of the consultants of Peat, Marwick, Mitchell, completed in 1969, confirmed what the UCFCA already knew operationally. Both on the local level and nationally, "the movement" was out of step with the mood of the country and had no clearly defined posture, at a time when organizational survival demanded both a sense of purpose and a willingness to adapt to a rapidly shifting environment. There was certainly little unity within the organization about what directions should be taken. And although the national organization was more forward looking than many local funds in its view of the issues, the UCFCA was limited in its ability to influence the actions of local communities. Moreover, within the same community, major differences often existed between Planning Councils and the organizations which funded them.

It was a critical time for the movement, and, as the Peat, Marwick, Mitchell study put it, "the UCFCA, like other institutions, is facing a crisis of identity."

Part II

Planning and Allocations

A Time of Transition

On January 30, 1970, the UCFCA board of directors adopted the report of the Organization and Management Study Committee of their board, and took what they described as "the final step" in a study process which had begun on September 13, 1968.[1] The study committee had reviewed the findings and recommendations of the Peat, Marwick, Mitchell report, which they considered to be a "useful tool" for the years immediately ahead. Although the study committee used cautious language in discussing the recommendations of the consultants, on the whole it accepted them. In keeping with the traditional pattern of the federated fundraising movement, the study committee took an up-beat posture, and the study committee report to the board of UCFCA recommended positively that

> ... the movement reaffirm its belief in the united voluntary way; in its future role as a viable partner and sometime critic of government; as a spokesman stressing local responsibility and local decision-making as a counter weight to pressures for national centralization and as the voice of citizen concern for human beings who are victims of developments keyed to masses rather than individuals.[2]

The emphasis in the reports was on leadership for the national organization and greater accountability at all levels. This required a more assertive public voice, and a national organization which was to be involved more intensively with government and with other national agencies, as well as with the business world. In regard to local funds and councils, the proposed thrust was also clear. Only by reaching out and taking a pro-active stance could the United Way system restore its credibility. In the language of that era, local funds and councils had to be part of the solution, or they would be part of the problem. Moreover, by this time the message was also coming from the corporate world as well.

After the Detroit riots in 1967, corporations had begun to shift some of their support to new causes and to organizations such as the Urban Coalition, which business leaders formed in response to pressures rising out of the "urban crisis."[3] Therefore, if united funds did not become more effective in their community role, and in the use of their financial resources, it was clear that fund raising would also suffer. Indeed, the uncertainties of leadership and direction were reflected in the campaign results across the country in 1970. Nationally the United Way campaign registered only a 3.0 percent increase that year, compared with 6.7 percent the previous year (1969), and considerably below the 1970 inflation rate of 5.9 percent (see below, appendix C.2).

Adoption of the study committee report in 1970 was a symbol of change for the UCFCA. Among the changes instituted subsequently were a plan for reorganization of the UCFCA structure;[4] the official adoption of a new name for the organization nationwide, "the United Way"; increased expectations of support from local United Ways for the national organization, the United Way of America;[5] the installation of the new national executive, William Aramony, who was described as "a breath of fresh air" by the president of the old UCFCA;[6] and the move of the UWA from New York to a new building in Alexandria, Virginia, close to the seat of the national government (January 1972). The United Way was positioning itself for the future.

Chapter 3

Community Planning in the United Way

There is no "magic formula" which can erase the problems facing the Council Movement. . . . But one thing is crystal clear; the voluntary social planning movement must step up to the pace of social change.

> Ronald O. Warner, Chairman
> of the Michigan Welfare League
> Board of Advisors,
> (November 1968)

The Movement should establish a clear and precise statement on purpose that goes beyond fund raising and community planning. It should reflect the intent of the Movement to address the solving of selected social problems within local communities.

> Peat, Marwick, Mitchell,
> *Report* (September 1969)

The Mission of a Fund-Raising Organization

IN its recommendations about future directions for UCFCA, the Peat, Marwick, Mitchell report concentrated on fundamental issues of structure and function, and on organizational mission. Although the UCFCA could not have been satisfied with the fundraising performance of local funds in the preceeding years, the report barely mentioned fund raising. Instead, the consultants focused on ways to improve the interaction of the system as a whole, and in particular, the community role of local funds and councils.

The Peat, Marwick, Mitchell report suggested that the United Way movement had lost its identity, and thereafter the United Way study committee explicitly stated new directions:

> The United Way movement should not limit its activity to fund raising in the narrow sense of the term. Local Funds and Councils should be problem-solvers and need-meeters rather than just fund raisers and coordinators of existing services.[1]

Local federated fund-raising organizations should become active participants in community problem solving, and a "positive force" for social change. Not articulated, but clearly an underlying theme, was the idea that local fund-raising efforts would not be successful without a more active community role. Moreover, since Aramony had participated actively in the deliberations of the study committee, these recommendations could hardly have been a surprise to him. Practical necessity meant finding an identity that would create enthusiasm and philosophical guidance for the movement, and in effect, this goal required reviving the old connections to community organization and social work activity.

There was a certain irony to these conclusions. For years the UCFCA board deliberations had been dominated by local fund executives, most of whom were trained social workers, and presumably should have been dedicated to social issues and community problem-solving efforts. These executives included Lyman Ford, the national executive of the UCFCA before William Aramony; Charles Sampson, associate executive of the UCFCA; and local United Fund and Council executives such as Robert Mabie (Des Moines) and Owen Davison (Philadelphia).

In addition, the UCFCA had for years attempted to maintain its close relationship with schools of social work. There had been a special funded relationship first with Ohio State and then la.er with Boston College through the 1950s and 1960s, and scholarships were offered at other schools (including Bryn Mawr, the University of Pittsburgh, and the University of California) to encourage entry into the UCFCA field.[2] However, in a changing world, there was a loss of enthusiasm for such training and for what some now considered an "old boys" network. By the mid-1960s the relationship between the schools and the UCFCA had cooled, and the UCFCA began to consider other alternatives. Thus, one of Bill Aramony's first acts as executive of the United Way of America was to start the new in-house training center for United Way professionals, which became the National Academy for Voluntarism (NAV).[3]

With the reports of the consultants and its own study committee in 1970 the UWA was now aware of the importance of creating a new pro-active community role. The perceived necessity for broader community involvement for local United Ways became one of the major items on the agenda of the national organization in the 1970s. In effect, the next decade became a time of laboratory work for the United Way in the field of planning and community coordinating activities. The national organization could not, however, implement this idea directly. It could only encourage local United Ways to take the notion of community planning seriously, and help them develop an awareness of the importance of community problem-solving activities. Some United Ways already were actively involved in community planning related to their fund-distribution allocation activities; but for others it was a major departure from their usual way of doing business.[4]

In many communities, the suggested new thrust for the United Way directly affected relationships with another organization, the local Planning Council. These planning councils, while theoretically autonomous, were usually dependent on local fund organizations for financial support and for authority. The councils had a parallel historical development with federated fund organizations, and by 1970 existed in some form in hundreds of communities, though most significantly in larger (Metro I-IV) cities. The nature of their interaction with local fund-raising organizations varied from community to community. Usually they performed special studies for the local United Way, and provided a forum for interagency meetings. In some communities they assisted with the allocations process, either serving as staff for the process, or providing specific analysis about community needs.

Despite the urgency for the United Way to demonstrate a social work "soul," or at least an effective community presence, the capacity of federated fund-raising organizations to undertake these activities was questionable. But where there was a community planning council, issues of authority and turf were likely to emerge. A brief review of the history of planning councils and charity organization will help to illustrate the nature of these conflicts, and the dilemmas of planning within the United Way system, including the conceptualization of planning that was developed in the 1970s, and its implications for the United Way system in the 1980s. Finally, the chapter will conclude with a case study of Toledo, Ohio, to illustrate the conflicts between the fund-raising system and its planning subsystems.

Planning and Organized Charity, 1908–1975

The earliest organizations that became councils of agencies were founded in Pittsburgh (1908) and Milwaukee (1909), with others following rapidly. Like the whole COS movement, and the related federated fund-raising organizations, these early councils grew out of a desire to coordinate existing welfare services. But they also were concerned with the study of social problems, and included from the start concepts of planning and standard-setting for agency work in the voluntary sector.[5] Initially some of the same individuals frequently supported the development of both councils of agencies and federated fund-raising organizations, including members of the local Chamber of Commerce and voluntary agency personnel. However, in keeping with their commitment to coordinate public and private welfare efforts, councils sought to involve a broader constituency, insuring representation from public agencies as well as leading political figures.[6]

The structure of councils varied, along with their functions, according to the conditions of the community in which they were formed. However, most councils were initally closely related to, or part of, an Associated Charities or COS; a few were connected to fund-raising functions; and later some more independent organizations emerged.[7]

In 1939, the function of community organization was given renewed emphasis in social work practice. In a document referred to as the Lane Report, attention was given to the aim of community organization for bringing about and maintaining a "progressively more effective adjustment between social welfare resources and social welfare needs."[8] This definition covered activities of both the local fund-raising organization and the councils to which they were increasingly related, although the focus on social work and concern about planning for community welfare was more specifically attached to council efforts.

By 1947 there were reported to be over 300 councils as compared with 878 community chests, and they existed in large cities like Cleveland, as well as smaller cities like New Haven. In those days the CCC was not precise in its definitions or its record keeping, and many of the councils listed as independent may, actually have been units of the local fund-raising organization.[9] In any case councils, like community chests, expanded in number during World War II, due particularly to their role in helping organize and maintain government-sponsored neighborhood councils.[10]

After the war, the consensus model of community organization and planning which councils represented gained prominence in programs of community organization in social work, and particularly in some schools of social work.[11] Indeed, in this period most textbooks which dealt with community organization as social work practice highlighted funds and councils as arenas for this kind of practice. Professionals in the planning and coordinating arm of the movement struggled with issues of agency interest and community need, but in a time of relative calm and affluence, planning and coordination could be treated as complementary to the fund-raising function, whether councils were actually inside or outside the fund-raising organization.[12] Even so, there were tensions, and social workers attached to the council movement felt that planning councils, and planning staff, were not treated equally either by the national UCFCA, or by local funds.[13] Nevertheless, the idea of community planning based on common interests, and for the health and welfare needs of the whole community, flourished throughout the 1950s, based on the idea that it would lead to community-wide benefits.

Unions, in their new role of community citizen, voiced this sentiment at social work meetings. In 1945, Leo Perlis, speaking at the National Conference of Social Work, said, "It would be futile to deny the basic truth that the health and welfare of C.I.O. members cannot be separated from the health and welfare of the community as a whole. This fundamental principle—that *the common good is our good* —guides us in our work."[14] Similar sentiments were expressed by other union leaders in the newly formed AFL-CIO in 1955.[15] The old ideologies seemed to have disappeared as a common view of the public interest emerged.[16]

By the early 1960s this romantic view of a common community good no longer seemed viable. Urban renewal activities which benefited the rich and hurt the poor were arousing open resentment, and poverty had been rediscovered in the country as well as the city.[17] Power differences were increasingly recognized as a fact of American life, together with a notion of competing interests and aggressive self-advocacy. The Democratic administrations of Kennedy and Johnson, and in particular Johnson's War on Poverty, changed the nature of government involvement in the city and with the voluntary sector.

Citizen involvement and community organization also took on a whole different set of meanings after 1964 when "maximum feasible participation" became a keynote of the Johnson program (see above, Chapter 2). New kinds of citizen involvement resulted, based on the participation of consumers of services, rather than elite leadership groups or professionals. Programs in the health and welfare field were connected to active constituent groups, often with anti-establishment attitudes that put them into conflict with city hall, or with traditional service-providing member agencies of the UCFCA.[18]

The multitude of government-mandated planning activities of the sixties changed the role of the local planning council. Federal government initiatives reached into health and welfare planning, including hospitals, psychiatric hospitals, manpower, and urban renewal activities, with requirements for citizen advisory committees.[19] Since these bodies were generally quasi-public, and officially sanctioned, they presented a new specialized form of competition to the old role of the community councils. Councils generally had no control over the way public funds were spent in the voluntary sector, and they were on the whole tenuously connected to the allocations process of local chests or funds.[20] Local planning councils relied on their ability to influence community decision makers through expertise and information gathering, and they also "borrowed" prestige from their connection to the more powerful boards of local fund-raising organizations.[21]

In cities where the War on Poverty took hold, the critical role of program coordination and fund distribution tended to pass around city government to the Community Action Agency. Apparently, about 45 councils served in this role for some time, and another 150 were instrumental either in creating or operating a variety of OEO–War on Poverty related projects.[22] However, as the politics of the poverty program played out, leaders emerged from other constituencies in the community, including blacks and other socially active minorities. Many of these groups became more powerful and developed close connections to city hall.[23]

Councils claimed that they could respond better to the demands, and changing circumstances of the urban crisis, if only they had more resources. Indeed, many councils did at first attempt to get a share of the new increased federal funding sources. Although nationwide the major funding source for most councils remained the community fund, by 1965 there was clearly an infusion of public money in their collective incomes.[24] These sources, however, were uncertain, and development of service contracts with government money also put councils into competition with their own member agencies, alienating some of their traditional supporters in the voluntary sector.

As councils were losing some of their old constituency base, and suffering eroding strength as a citizen-convening group, their relationship to community united funds also became more difficult. In a time of increased politicization and instant decision making, in fact, the connection to federated fund-raising was not necessarily an advantage. It tied councils to an elitist power group and a model of decision making which was slow and cumbersome and which did not generally tolerate controversy.

On the other hand, for all of the reasons discussed above, and more, the relationship with local councils also began to lose much of its value for local funds in the late 1960s. One union observer expressed concern about the situation, stating: "The final challenge faced by the United Way is to find the appropriate role for our Community Health and Welfare Councils."[25] At the end of the sixties three special factors made the councils even more vulnerable. First, with the establishment of new agencies for health planning, and particularly after the nationwide network of Health Systems Agencies created under the National Health Planning and Resources Development Act (P.L. 93-641, 1974), they lost their basic health-planning role. The health-planning role had been valuable to community funds because they were frequently battling with the national health agencies, and councils provided a more neutral connection to the medical-health system.[26] Second, the government became interested in gaining political support and funds for their programs from the voluntary sector, and this led to a connection with the UCFCA nationally. Mutual interest of the government and the voluntary sector resulted in passage of amendments to the Social Security Act (1967, 1974), which encouraged the use of private agencies, and matching voluntary funds, in the delivery of publicly authorized social services.[27]

Third, in this period, there was increased interest in priority setting related to determination of needs in the community. In the confusion which these efforts engendered, much of the responsibility, and ultimately the blame, for some significant failed attempts at priority setting was given to the local planning council, which had been assigned this activity by the United Way in the first place.

The 1970s marked a watershed for the new United Way that was forming out of the old federated fund-raising system. As the Peat, Marwick, Mitchell study had anticipated, it became strategically more important for community funds to be involved with community issues and to work directly with the public sector. Local planning councils were no longer perceived as valuable mediating influences in relationships with the government or other agencies of the voluntary sector. Indeed a local Planning Council could be an unwelcome intermediary as good relationships with the government also became more significant in fund raising.[28] Thus, local planning councils became good targets for funding cutbacks by local United Ways. Other organizational factors made them even more tempting.

To begin with, during the 1970s most United Ways were not raising enough new money to meet the increasing demands being made on them. Their annual campaign increments, which hovered between 3 percent and 9 percent (the latter reached only in 1977 and 1978), were practically meaningless in the highly inflationary climate of the period. From 1972 to 1982, United Ways increased their funding over the inflation rate only five out of the eleven years, and then only by a few percentage points (see appendix C.1). In that period agencies were also facing the effects of inflation, and the first government cutbacks were initiated. Consequently, United Ways were under pressure from their own regular member agencies to either raise additional funds, or allow member agencies to increase their own fund-raising efforts. This was occurring at the same time as the United Way system was facing pressures for inclusiveness in the funding of new and emerging agencies, subsequent to the Filer Commission Report and events of the mid-1970s.

In light of the shifting role of local planning councils in relation to government-sponsored planning activities, it was easy to question the effectiveness of councils or their ability to produce work which made a difference. Although this argument was politically convenient for local United Ways, there was certainly some truth to it. Planning councils in the voluntary sector had insufficient chips to influence the spending of public dollars, and their efforts to set priorities for the voluntary sector were frequently both politically and technically naive.[29]

Thus, in the 1970s many United Ways found themselves in the position of paying more than 50 percent of the budget of an organization that they did not believe was helping them, and with whom their relationship was at best problematic. These funds varied in amount, but amounted to over $300,000 in several Metro I communities.[30] At a time when funds were scarce, recapturing these funds for other purposes was certainly tempting. It was therefore not surprising that in the first decade after the United Way was reconstituted, the number of councils in the United Way system declined dramatically. United Ways either merged with their planning councils or cut them loose with little or no funding, after which they usually went out of business. The rationale of United Way professionals was that they could do the planning better and more cheaply themselves.

In 1982, there had been close to eighty councils in the United Way *International Directory;* by 1986 there were fewer than sixty listed. The national trend particularly affected larger councils. In 1969, thirty-six out of forty-eight Metro I communities had independent local planning councils; by 1979 they were down to sixteen; and in 1984 there were only eleven councils remaining, of which one was a hybrid organization, having the same executive as the United Way.[31] Interestingly, the decline in planning councils received little attention from the media. There was little public outcry and it was not protested greatly by the professional social work community. Corporate leaders apparently hardly paid attention to it, although the move ultimately had consequences both for United Ways' budgets and for their interactions with other groups in the community.[32]

Defining Community Planning in the United Way

In its simplest definition, planning essentially means analyzing information in the present to select strategies for a course of action to be carried out in the future. It is a rational process, in the sense that information is used to make an informed selection among possible options. It is both a problem-solving and goal-oriented activity, and as process, it involves the participation of appropriate actors and is subject to change and modification along the way. In this basic sense, organized charities had been involved in planning related to fundraising campaigns since their formative years.

By the 1970s the idea of broad-based social welfare planning was being promoted as a standard for effective local United Ways.[33] It was, however, not clear how it could best be accomplished in the United Way context. In welfare planning there is no precise bottom line, and goals always tend to be amorphous. To begin with, therefore, there was the question of defining social planning, community welfare planning, or health and welfare planning in relationship to the United Way system. What would be its relationship to the distribution of funds, or to the allocations process? Were priorities for human service funding to be determined by the planning process, and what impact would these priorities have on allocations to United Way–funded agencies? What was the role of public sector services in a planning process, or of other, non–United Way affiliated agencies?

Second, who should do the planning, and at what level was it best accomplished? If it was in a community where local planning councils existed, could they be the vehicle for United Way planning? But if they were the vehicle, would planning councils then be telling United Ways how to spend their money? Was there a state role in planning, or was there a need to consider area-wide planning, in light of the increasing importance of suburban development and the changing patterns of urban-suburban commuting and corporate locations?

Finally, did planning mean operational planning, primarily in the interests of the United Way, or should the United Way carry out more broadly-based community problem-solving and data-gathering functions, as some councils had been doing? Was it better for the United Way only to provide support for such activities, but have them carried out by various other organizations? What was the capacity of a fund-raising organization for convening agencies, forming coalitions, studying problems, developing new programs to meet community needs, handling conflict, advocating for the disadvantaged, and developing public policy statements?

While these questions were being debated, planning councils continued to lose their funding, be absorbed by United Way, or otherwise go out of business between 1970 and 1985. There also was a great deal of discussion in United Way circles about the role of planning in the United Way, formally through papers and presentations at meetings and conferences, and informally through networking of council and fund professionals. United Way executives were saying to each other privately, "Haven't you gotten rid of your Council yet?" The official United Way position was that planning could take place either in an independent planning council or within a United Way. However, if actions speak louder than words, the United Way had made its preference clear, and many United Ways began to assume a more active community planning role.

A year after William Aramony assumed the position of national executive of the United Way of America, in May 1971, volunteer leaders of the United Way met in Chicago. That conference was the first United Way national conference to bring together volunteers dealing with all three of the major United Way functions of planning, campaigning, and fund raising.[34] The conference therefore had a certain historical significance.

Typically, one of the ways that new directions for the United Way system are given credibility is through pronouncements by high-status volunteers. At this conference one of the chief speakers was Donald S. McNaughton, chairman and chief executive officer of Prudential Life Insurance, who disseminated an important message. His speech addressed concerns about the process by which funds were allocated to agencies in the United Way system, and the need to improve the process. He connected priority-setting efforts and planning to the improvement of that process.

Interestingly, McNaughton separated out two kinds of planning: one was directly related to the allocations process and to the selection of services which might be purchased by local United Ways; the other was "overall community planning . . . covering a large number of service delivery systems, many without direct connection with United Way, such as schools, courts, legislatures etc. . . ." Such a planning group would have "considerable research capacity" and "the authority to implement plans." It would have appropriate representation of community leaders, and would operate like a consulting firm. While United Way "should provide support for such a planning group," McNaughton stated that the organization should be independent.[35] The implication was fairly clear: local United Ways should do their own operational, limited planning, in relation to their allocations process. They should additionally support an independent planning group which would carry out communitywide planning activities across public and private sectoral lines.

The idea that there were two kinds of planning needed in the United Way system and that the broader function should be independent appeared frequently as a theme in the next few years. Variations of this same concept appeared in a series of papers given by staff members of the UWA, of which possibly the most well publicized was that of Paul Akana. Akana, reputedly an influential advisor of William Aramony, presented something called "Plan X" at a staff conference as early as 1970, prior to McNaughton's discussion. In his Plan X, Akana suggested two types of planning, one a "research–plan of action–results oriented operation," the other a "forum-platform–coordination–standard setting–watch dog operation." He suggested that these two types had to be independent. Plan X was greeted, however, with mixed reactions, and Akana himself noted that not much result followed.[36] In 1976, at another biennial staff conference, Paul Akana once again presented his view of planning in a United Way context, but with a somewhat altered focus. Indeed, the idea presented at the staff conference in 1976 was a decided effort to make a unity out of the three disparate functions of United Ways: planning, allocations, and fund raising. The name of Akana's talk was "United Way–1996" and it was proposed as a kind of blueprint for the next twenty years.[37]

Akana's 1976 talk attempted to move beyond Plan X, (1970), which had been "rejected by the planners" because it split the function of planning into two parts, one of which was independent of the United Way. It also moved beyond other United Way proposed plans, Plan Y (1971–1972), and Plan Z (1974), which were also controversial. The first, Plan Y (called "a plan for unity"), suggested a major change in United Way funding, away from deficit across-the-board funding of organizational structures to direct purchase of needed and high priority services. Allocators in local United Ways were afraid this would make too drastic a change in their relationship to the "core" group of United Way member agencies since it tied funding of services to priority planning. The second, Plan Z, presented a more flexible approach to the United Way–agency funding relationship, in which restrictions on supplemental fund-raising efforts by agencies would be removed, except for campaigns in the corporate workplace, where there would remain only one single, United Way campaign. Plan Y was not acceptable to many local United Ways and their campaign staff, because it gave official sanction for more agency fund-raising activities in competition with United Ways.

Akana picked up the theme of unity in his futurist speech of 1976, when he attempted to formulate an integrative approach to the various functions of United Ways (planning, allocations, and fund raising). Indeed, in this speech, planning was only one part of a "centrist" notion of the United Way, which consisted of three concentric rings. The first of these rings was essentially the centrist platform of the single workplace campaign, all-inclusive and area-wide, including the possibility of funding sub-federations; the second ring was the monitoring ring, which included evaluation of agency performance and the possibility of donor designation of funds; and the third circle was the allocations ring, which incorporated both new kinds of allocations and planning functions.

The broad scope of Akana's projections was in some ways prophetic of the future directions of United Way. In relation to planning, however, Akana stated that he "was not going to get into the question of structure," except to say that it should be regional, serving a "sub-state" region, or a multi-state region, in order to have a large perspective. This notion of regionalism was, however, objectionable to United Ways concerned about the local nature of human service delivery, and the community base of their campaign organization. The notion of regionalism, accordingly, remained controversial.

The discussion did not end there. The following fall a small group of twenty-one United Way planning professionals were called together by Akana to discuss the question further. About half of the group were planning directors in combined United Way organizations, and the other half were executives of independent local planning organizations. As Akana later stated, "Surprisingly we came to one agreement . . . to draw a clear distinction between two types of planning" which they then called "Type A" and "Type B." Type A planning was essentially operational United Way planning, and included "such functions as: consultation to allocations committees; development of agency profiles; agency income and expense information; admissions studies . . . development and maintenance of priorities plans; needs assessment studies, with special reference to . . . United Way supported agency programs; government relations, with special reference to impact . . . on United Way supported agencies; handling of inter-agency coordination activities; and development of community consensus on issues affecting United Way."[38]

Type B, on the other hand, contained the functions of data base maintenance, management consultation, program development, and program evaluation.

Although there had been agreement on the two different types of planning activities, there was apparently no agreement among the executives on what organization should perform what functions. But given the nature of the activities, Akana recommended that Type A should be the responsibility of a combined fund-raising–planning–allocations organization, while Type B could only be done by an independent regional planning organization. Akana had occasion to summarize these ideas once again. In a paper presented at a retreat of the United Way Planning Advisory Committee in 1977, he repeated that these ideas did not represent the official position of the United Way. They were his "own thoughts on planning—United Way style."[39]

Akana was considered something of an "original" within the United Way movement, but he was actually not alone in his discussion of these issues. In a paper on "Fund-Council Relationships" (March 1972) another United Way planner, Harold Edelston, recognized that "controversy is now again raging in a number of communities." His paper, based on "the deliberations" of a group of twelve executives from both United Way organizations and separate planning councils,[40] presented options which were essentially an elaboration of the Akana discussion. On the whole the assignment of "preferred auspices" was also in line with the Akana plan, although some grey areas were indicated where either fund or council could be the auspices.

Among those functions which could have either auspices he listed, for example;

> soliciting government to purchase service and to make grants; conducting an information and referral service; operating a program to recruit, orient and refer volunteers to give service to other agencies; [and], "convening groups of agency representatives to discuss common problems, learn of new developments, take joint action on an issue, or have an opportunity to . . . communicate with their peers in other organizations."[41]

During this period another actor in the "planning arena" appeared at the national headquarters. Like Akana, Russy Sumariwalla came from the local planning council in San Francisco. Hired by Akana, he became deeply involved in the planning and allocations arena at the UWA, producing among other documents an ambitious taxonomy of the human services, the United Way of America Services Identification System, UWASIS (1972, revised 1976); and a Needs Assessment Compilation (1982).[42] In 1973, Sumariwalla also wrote a paper on "Planning and Managing the Human Services in Local Communities Under Non-Governmental Auspices".[43]

Although the Sumariwalla paper was more scholarly in its approach, his conclusions were not very different from those proposed in the final (1977) model of Paul Akana. There was a need for an independent "model planning organization" (an "MPO"), which would provide a core program that included management consultation, program planning, program evaluation, and resource development (maintenance of a data base on funding and grantsmanship). Other services including "research" were considered valuable "add-ons." Following the Akana pattern, Sumariwalla also did not claim to be speaking for United Way of America, but except for Akana's expansion into regionalism, his "MPO" was undeniably close to the concept of "Type B" that was said to have emerged from the Planning Advisory Committee meeting in Chicago in 1977.

Despite the fact that both of these documents presented arguments for an independent planning council, they were not received with enthusiasm by local planning council executives. Throughout this period most council executives continued to feel beleaguered and threatened by the United Way. Even in the mid-1980s, planning council executives still revealed a strong negative reaction to the Akana-Sumariwalla proposals. To begin with, council executives challenged a basic assumption in the Sumariwalla-MPO model that planning can and should be neutral, and by extension, that advocacy is unrelated to fact-finding and technical assistance.[44] Secondly, the executives were concerned about the implications of increased separation of planning councils from allocations and operational planning for the United Way. This was suggested in all the papers, but was particularly obvious in Akana's arguments about Type A and Type B planning. Council executives must have sensed danger to their own organizations with the loss of operational planning responsibilities, including needs assessments and priority planning. They also believed that such activity would lose credibility and become subservient to political interests and power games, if done by the United Way. Finally, the discussion was taking place in a climate which included lack of trust and even open hostility. This context reinforced the fear that councils would feel in cutting the umbilical cord to the United Way.

Councils understood that having to sell planning services as consultants might make the price of independence too high. Loss of support from United Way was likely to make councils far more vulnerable to environmental uncertainties. No wonder therefore that the Akana, Sumariwalla, and Edelston papers failed to have a calming effect.

Although there was a lively debate at conferences and in local communities about planning, officially there was no United Way position to this effect. Akana even suggested that the issue was not one of high salience for the UWA:

> My position on planning is my own, it is not United Way of America's. There has been no sanction . . . for my point of view. . . . I am allowed to present these thoughts . . . because they are deemed to be harmless.[45]

However, planning councils continued to vanish during the next decade, as Type A planning became increasingly important to local United Ways. As Akana himself noted, in the twenty-five largest cities (Metro I organizations) in 1970 there were twenty-two "large, viable, well financed planning organizations" and only three combined fund-raising and planning United Ways (Cincinnati, Milwaukee, and Seattle). By 1977 there were only ten independents left, and four of those were under study. Akana in fact indicated openly his belief that eventually no local planning councils would be left in the United Way system.[46]

At staff conferences and annual volunteer leaders conferences, United Ways presented successful examples of how planning and evaluation activities were used as part of an effective allocations process. In some communities Harold Edelston and other staff from the United Way of America helped influence local United Ways in developing a stronger planning component within their own organization.[47] In many communities new staff were hired with planning interests and appropriate planning credentials, and this was accompanied by increased expenditures for planning in the United Way budget. The following case study of Toledo, Ohio illustrates this process.

Toledo: A Site Case Study

The City of Toledo is located in northwestern Ohio, sixty miles southwest of Detroit, Michigan. The City is a major freshwater port, situated at the southwestern tip of Lake Erie and the mouth of the Maumee River. It has a diversified manufacturing industry, including automobiles and automobile parts, glass, and various machinery products. Toledo is located in, and dominates, Lucas County. In 1980 Lucas County had a total population of 471,741 persons, and Toledo a population of 354,635. Both the city and county are predominantly white, with 80.11 percent of the city's population white, and the remaining group predominantly black (17.44 percent), with a few Hispanics (3.10 percent). The county is 84.24 percent white, 13.60 percent black, and 2.70 percent Hispanic.[48]

Toledo's mid-American life-style traditionally was based on locally developed industry and firmly entrenched local values. A few readily identifiable old-line families provided leadership to the community for more than a generation, and these families continue to interact frequently in their nearby suburban homes, in country clubs, at church, and in business and volunteer activities.[49] Beginning with World War II, however, divisions and branches of large corporations with new managerial personnel moved into the city. By the 1970s there was also a notable trend for members of the younger generation of Toledo's elite families to move away from Toledo after college, and young adults from the "old" families were not taking a part in building the future of the city. Members of the "new" managerial group were not usually accepted into the community's inner leadership circle, with the possible exception of chief executive officers of such major corporations as Owens-Illinois. By the 1980s leadership in Toledo seemed to be in a period of transition, with some movement away from exclusive domination by the old elites, and no one group emerging yet to replace it.

By 1982 the Ohio economy was in the third year of a recession, resulting from decline in the automobile and related manufacturing industries, and the unemployment rate rose to 12.2 percent.[50] During that time there was a major urban renewal effort which modernized the downtown area of Toledo, but did not prevent a continuing decline of corporate business in the city. In 1985–86, Champion Spark Plug was one of several local companies cutting back its work force; Owens-Illinois had reduced its headquarters staff; several companies had moved their production facilities out of the Toledo area; and Libbey-Owens-Ford had been bought out by an English company, leaving questions about its future in the area.

The United Way of Greater Toledo covers Lucas, Wood, Ottawa, and Eastern Fulton counties. This includes several wealthy suburban communities, but does not reach into neighboring Michigan formally, although some funded agencies serve Michigan residents.[51]

The United Way/Community Chest is very much a part of the Toledo community, and local leaders have generally served with enthusiasm in top volunteer positions in the organization. Payroll deduction was also a part of corporate life. In 1981 the campaign raised over $9 million for the first time, and the United Way of Greater Toledo became a Metro I community. Despite difficulties, the campaign of 1982 reported $200,000 additional funds, for a total of $9,636,379. However, it did not reach its ambitious goal of $10,200,000.[52]

In 1982 the federated fund-raising system in Toledo was still tied to a model developed by united funds in the American industrial heartland during the late 1950s. There was a community chest, which was the basic operating organization for fund raising and allocations, with a superimposed campaign organization, now called the United Way, which was formed by the community chest in partnership with the Red Cross. The partnership agreement with the Red Cross guaranteed a fixed percentage of the annual campaign for that agency, at that time set at 12.29 percent.[53] There was also an active local planning council, established in the early 1930s. In 1982 the planning council was still connected to the chest from which it received over 90 percent of the funding for its total budget of $176,000.

Despite all the tensions, in 1981 the planning council had received an increased allocation of $7,000 from the United Way for the following year.[54] But at the same time, simmering conflicts between the two organizations were coming to a head, and the United Way formed a joint committee on chest-community planning council relations. The committee was to examine the function of the local planning council and consider what the future relationship of the two organizations should be. The chairman of that study committee was Duane ("Pat") Stranahan, Jr., a former president of the council, a board member of the United Way, and a member of one of Toledo's leading families, the family that owned Champion Spark Plug. The committee met several times in an atmosphere of high feelings and tension, and in October of 1982 completed its report.[55]

As a result of the report, the council was to change its structure to reflect its mission of serving the entire community, and to include on its new board representatives of the major private and public funding sources in the greater Toledo area. It was to become more independent of the United Way. Funding was to come from a broader group, with the intention that the United Way share would decrease to no more than one-third of the total support of the reborn council, and might eventually be only by contracted services.[56] Accordingly, the planning council was no longer listed as an affiliated planning council in the 1982–1983 United Way *International Directory*, and the

United Way was listed as a Planning Allocations and Fund Raising Organization (PAF). The future of the planning council would require careful cultivation of former friends and new funding constituencies.

Relations between the planning council and the Community Chest/ United Way had been troublesome for decades. Volunteers in both "camps" indicated that they could not recall a time when the relationship had not been problematic, and particularly so from the planning council point of view. So the question is, Why did definitive action finally take place in 1982?

In order to understand what precipitated the final break between the council and chest in Toledo, it is helpful to review briefly the nature of the controversy between these two organizations in light of the difficulties between councils and chests generally. Like many other planning councils, the council in Toledo started out as a council of social agencies. It developed in the 1930s out of the need for social agencies in the depression to get together and examine their mission in a time of severe community need and changes in the role of the voluntary sector.[57] Like other community councils, the Toledo council provided a forum for local voluntary agency professionals to meet, carry out studies, and discuss common problems with the public sector. It also assisted in the allocation of funds to community chest agencies in these years. The council thus continued to thrive during World War II and in the following decade. By the mid-1950s the council was showing increased interest in broader community welfare issues and conflict was emerging between the chest and council. However the council continued to expand its role and took on new activities during the 1960s and early 1970s. Nevertheless, the structural issues continued to cause tensions, particularly around the role of the council in relation to the budget process by which funds were allocated to agencies.

In contrast with other cities, such as neighboring Detroit, Toledo did not have traumatic upheavals in the sixties. The minority community was relatively small in numbers and not as highly organized as in Detroit. Nevertheless, changes were taking place in the expectations for human service agencies, and the council was attempting to be part of the change process. In the mid-1960s the council hired a woman as its executive. Charlotte Shaffer did not have a social work degree, but she had some experience in the social welfare field, and a commitment to carving out a more activist role for the council.

Under Charlotte Shaffer the council became deeply involved in community welfare planning across the public and private sectors. To reflect this new direction and its wider scope, the council changed its name to the Community Planning Council of Northwestern Ohio, and during the next few years, the council budget grew along with its program development efforts. Among these efforts, the council became the sponsor for the local Area Office of the Aging (for five years), before that office was spun off as an independent agency. In this period, the major thrust of the council was social planning and the carrying out of studies which would have an impact on service delivery in Toledo, but it also began to develop new services. Thus in 1968 a group of services provided by the council (including the Volunteer Action Bureau) were spun off as a separate United Community Services agency, since the council did not view itself as a long-term service-operating agency. This pattern also was occurring in other planning councils across the nation, but it weakened the council.

In line with the nationwide interest in needs assessment, the planning council carried out a number of significant studies during the 1970s, both at its own initiative and in response to requests from the community chest. Among the more controversial of the studies was the Priority Determination Project carried out in 1973 under the sponsorship of the planning council, but with the formal cooperation of the City of Toledo, the Community Chest of Greater Toledo, the Economic Opportunity Planning Association of Greater Toledo, and Lucas County. This was a time when priority studies were in vogue in many communities across the country.[58] As in other localities, such as Westchester County, New York, or San Francisco, California, the study found that many United Way services, such as camping or adoption services, had a lower priority than non–United Way or public sector services such as detention (jailing), housing, or environmental health.[59] The findings challenged the validity of voluntary sector services paid for by the chest and upset the leaders of this organization in Toledo, resulting in a tension which had not fully disappeared ten years later, as many respondents revealed in retrospective interviews.

The priority study was not, however, the only study to cause ill feelings between the two organizations. Two studies of the late 1970s also continued to be sore points with agency staff and volunteer leaders of both organizations for many years. The first was a study of home health care in 1978, and the other was a study of need for credit counseling services which was carried out about the same time.[60] Both had implications which were not in the end acceptable to the chest.

The controversial finding of the study on home health care was that homemakers and home health aides essentially provided the same service, closely related to health needs. The study suggested therefore that homemaker services should be removed from the family service agency which was part of the United Way system, and become the responsibility only of the Community Nurse Service. The family service agency resented this finding, and sufficient pressure was put on the Chest–United Way board so that the recommendation was never implemented. The situation was somewhat different with the second study concerning credit counseling. This service was needed by low-income families in Toledo, and would have been run by the family service agency. However, it was not likely to be popular with local businesses, and the board somehow never voted on implementation.

After the controversy generated from such studies, by the end of the 1970s the chest issued the dictum that it only wanted facts from the council, and that future studies should not contain any recommendations concerning allocations of funds. The council was understandably restive about this charge, but even more upsetting was the fact that the council was later criticized precisely on the grounds that it was too political, and unwilling to reach hard and clear decisions. Thus it appeared to council leaders that they could not win either way: either they would be called ineffectual, or they would make trouble with agencies in the community, and, as one chest volunteer leader from the business community expressed it later, "Nothing the council ever did made things easier for us."

The council, however, saw matters differently. The executive director and her board believed that the council served as a "whipping-boy" for the chest and was deliberately used to deflect the heat from unpopular studies or actions which the chest might be considering. This seemed likely. Social planning is rarely popular even under the best of circumstances, and it was hardly likely to cause enthusiasm among agencies whose funding might be affected. Attempts to make decisions among competing groups, based on rationally determined criteria, are elusive and suspect.[61] In any case, recommendations which affect the allocation of resources or the share of the funding pie will inevitably arouse resentment among the agencies affected negatively. Therefore, any "hard" or firm recommendation by the council would weaken its agency constituency base, and simultaneously further jeopardize its relationship with the chest. At the same time, the chest used the council as a "neutral third party" and was protected from direct involvement in these controversial planning activities.

By the 1980s attempts to use planning studies as a way of bringing about social change or differences in fund allocation in the community had caused increased friction between the council and the United Way/Chest agencies. Moreover, as frequently occurs around issues which start out as structural, personalities now entered into the equation. The closely knit leadership group of old elite Toledo families that had been involved on both sides of the council-chest situation was also involved in the heated arguments. Although more powerful business interests were represented on the United Way board, wives and relatives of these same individuals served on the council as well, and on boards of United Way member agencies. Personal accusations by both factions thus were made in board room and bedroom.[62]

Despite the appearance of civility, working relationships between the council and the chest deteriorated rapidly through the informal as well as the formal network. The executives of both organizations contributed to the conflict, and also became the focus of warring factions. Political maneuvering was rampant, and the competence of the council's executive director was openly questioned.

Although interpersonal relationships and structural strains were contributing factors to the final break between the council and the chest, several critical events influenced the timing significantly. To begin with, the executive director of the United Way/Chest was getting close to retirement and he seemed to have been personally committed to putting his house in order before doing so. Putting the house in order meant solving some organizational problems which had caused internal and external difficulties for some time. Among these was the problem of the Community Chest/United Way relationship, which locked the United Way into a fixed partnership with the American Red Cross, and established a poor precedent for admission of other large health agencies into the Chest/United Way package. In addition, the two-tier fund structure of the Chest/United Way was confusing to the giving public and impeded organizational change.

In 1981 the Chest/United Way began a series of negotiations with the Red Cross to change their contract, along with an effort to restructure itself as one organization, which would include chest agencies and functions, but be called the United Way. By the end of 1982 this had been accomplished, and the chest went out of existence. In the same year funding was provided for the first time to two health agencies: the American Cancer Society ($150,000) and the Arthritis Foundation ($60,000), as well as to the Rosa Morgan Enrichment Center which provided services for senior citizens ($30,000).[63] The United Way also formed a study committee to consider including some major services of United Community Services, such as the Volunteer Action Bureau, as a part of the United Way itself.

It was, finally, financial considerations, together with the vision of a "full service" United Way, which forced the hand of the United Way in relation to the council.[64] Feelings in the community made the situation ripe for change, but ultimately the bottom line required it. Constraints came from the bottom and the top. The local organization was being pressured to give more to the United Way of America, and to reach its fair share of support for the national organization; that year it increased its dues payment to $70,000.[65] On the other hand, the local United Way simultaneously faced the necessity to become more inclusive in its service package, and to include big health agencies considered essential to the campaign, as well as newer agencies serving growing numbers of a more diverse and needy population.

All of this was happening in the context of a declining industrial economic base, while thousands of workers were being laid off. For several years in a row the United Way campaign did not make its goal, and in fact it dropped in per capita giving from fifth in its category as a Metro II city (1976-77) to fifteenth in its category for 1982. Indeed, the only way that Toledo raised additional funds in 1981 and 1982 ($200,000) was by going back to the same small group of leading families for additional support, and, as United Way staff and volunteers observed, these individuals were now beginning to say "no more." Thus, the powerful leaders of the Community Chest had strong personal and financial motivations to look for ways to cut back United Way expenses, as well as to find new sources for contributions.

The United Way of Greater Toledo committed a total of $240,000 to the funding of three new agencies, at the same time as older member agencies were in need of additional support because of tightening in government funding and local economic conditions. The agreement to take on the Cancer Society was, however, the most serious in its implications. The original agreement stipulated that the agency was to be allocated $150,000 in 1982; in 1983, it was to get $200,000; and in 1984 the amount was to increase again to $250,000.[66] Even though these amounts were supposed to be contingent upon the United Way's making its campaign goal, there was still a commitment to funding the agency at a high level, and an underlying threat that if ACS was disappointed they could pull out of the United Way. Moreover, the Cancer contract must have seemed far preferable to the United Way than the fixed percentage agreement which they had with the Red Cross, all the more so since it was expected to bring in new dollars. In addition, having Cancer in the package of agencies would provide protection from a possible rival combined health agency drive.

In any case, the $170,000 allocated to the planning council was a tempting source of funds for the United Way's increased funding needs in a time of scarce resources. Consequently, whatever the merits of the planning council, the critical issue after all was money. Moreover, the planning council was vulnerable: it had a less powerful board than the United Way, and lacked strong corporate support.

The United Way was well prepared for change. As far back as 1977 it had hired Glenn Richter as allocations and agency relations director. Richter was a social worker with credentials as a planner, with an interest in a more active United Way planning role. Thus when the United Way volunteers suggested that the planning council was ineffectual, they could also say, "we can do our own planning, and do it cheaper."[67] And of course, ultimately, the United Way used the council's own arguments against it in creating the new council's structure. The United Way argued that if the council wanted to have a community-wide planning role, across the public and private sectors, then the public and private sectors should share the bill.

By January 1, 1985 the council was incorporated as the Toledo–Lucas County Council for Human Services, with a board that included funders and representative community leaders, and with Charlotte Shaffer as the executive. There had been some hard negotiations all around, and the solution was a compromise which did not cut the council off completely from United Way funds. There was to be a two-year trial period, during which the United Way would continue funding the new council at more than one-third of its total budget, or $70,000 for 1985.[68] But in the future the county and city of Toledo, and other voluntary sources, were going to have to contribute their one-third share each. If the council was not successful in obtaining these funds the United Way would also have no further responsibility for funding the council. In the meantime, Shaffer altered her tactics. In 1985 the council prepared a paper describing its new function and objectives, "A Partnership to Serve as a Catalyst for Community Problem Solving." Given the United Way's interest in community problem solving, the title selected was provocative, and suggested that there were still some unresolved questions of role relationships between the council and the United Way.

Chapter 4

From Allocations to Alternative Funds

First, I would like to challenge a few myths, including the thought that the original United Fund concept was conceived on a myth. The myth was to "give once for all." We are all very much aware that this has never happened, and frankly, I hope it never does happen. . . . This leads to myth number two. It is the concept that the United Way can meet all community needs. This is ridiculous.

> Louis A. Werbaneth, United Way
> Volunteer, Volunteer Leaders
> Conference, 1974

". . . the great opportunity now open to private charity is the ability to fund organizations which attack the causes of social problems, rather than provide services for the victims. . . ."

> Frank Blechman, *Combined Federal Campaign*, Hearings before the Congressional Subcommittee on Post Office and Civil Service, 1979

IN the aftermath of the 1960s, the united fund and council system went through a period of considerable soul-searching about its fundamental mission and relevance to a changing America (see above, chapter 3). However, many of the issues that federated fund raising faced at that time were not unique to the United Fund, but were a part of the questioning of the role of organized charity and philanthropy in our country as a whole. Thus, not long after the report of the UCFCA self-study committee was accepted by the national board in January 1970, another far larger inquiry into the status of philanthropy in America was initiated by John D. Rockefeller III at a meeting of the Brookings Institution on August 13, 1973.[1] John H. Filer, chairman of the Aetna Life and Casualty Company, agreed to head the new Commission on Private Philanthropy and Public Needs. The commission also received significant encouragement from Wilbur Mills, chairman of the House Ways and Means Committee, as well as from Secretary of the Treasury George P. Schultz, and Deputy Secretary William E. Simon.[2]

The Filer Commission started with the involvement of corporate leaders and representatives of the national administration concerned about the general condition and financial state of the voluntary sector. Indeed, the initial agenda of the commission was based on the perception that, on the one hand, there was a need to restore vitality to voluntarism in our country, and, on the other hand, the sector might need more effective monitoring. This agenda apparently arose largely out of concerns which had emerged in connection with the Tax Reform Act of 1969, but which remained unresolved, including the increasing impact of government funding on the voluntary sector, and the connection between tax policies and philanthropic giving (the particular concern of John D. Rockefeller).[3] Early inquiry therefore focused on the impact of public tax policies on philanthropic activities generally, and on sectarian organized charities specifically, as well as on regulatory questions. However, the debates that took place soon began to recapitulate other controversies taking place elsewhere in American society at that time.

Although the blue-ribbon panel which formed the commission was later described as representing "a diversity of views and a range of experience which encompass the mainstream of American society," it was on the whole an elitist group. Research papers and studies initially commissioned included a considerable number of specialized econometric studies about the factors which influence charitable giving by individuals and corporations, as well as historical research about the role of philanthropy in American life. Thus, the major direction of the commission's efforts seemed to be on ways to develop support, justification, and restored credibility for the institution of philanthropy in our nation.

The agenda of the commission was, however, modified quickly when almost inadvertently it became an ideological battleground. Among those who criticized the commission were Pablo Eisenberg, executive director of the Center for Community Change, and Mary Jean Tully, president of the National Organization for Women (NOW)

Legal Defense and Education Fund.[4] Eisenberg attacked the commission's work program on the grounds that it was not addressing the most important issues, and did not include among its members and researchers appropriate representation of minority and social action viewpoints. He suggested that despite its name, the commission was not adequately addressing the basic question of how well philanthropy was meeting public needs, since it was not concerned with the needs of the poor and disadvantaged in our society.

The Filer Commission responded quickly to the public criticism and spotlight on its activities, and Eisenberg was among those who met with commission leadership to develop an additional set of research topics. With an Ivy League education (Princeton) and a commitment to the notion of empowering the disadvantaged, Eisenberg, was well suited for the role of "go-between," and helped in locating individuals who could carry out the proposed research agenda. In Tully's words, "a collection of social-action organizations was put together for the specific purpose of getting some non-Establishment viewpoint into the Commission's Proceedings.[5] This loose group became known as the Donee Group, because of its concern about the recipients of charitable funds, or the Donees. The group focused its attention on questions of access to philanthropic funds for the disadvantaged, including women and blacks and other minorities, and criticized philanthropy which served as a conservator of the status quo.[6] The Donee Group presented its arguments in papers written for the commission but also later wrote its own report, in opposition to the main final report of the Filer Commission.[7]

While the focus in most of the papers of the Donee Group was on the role of foundation funding in relation to special need populations, some of their studies were targeted to other issues, including corporate giving and the related institution of the United Way. Of the criticisms that were directed at the United Way, one of the most seminal was the argument by David Horton Smith.[8] Smith challenged almost every function of the United Way, including the way it distributed its money, and to whom it distributed (allocated) funds. In addition, Smith articulated the emerging question of the United Way hegemony over workplace fund raising. The issues Smith raised were soon picked up by journalists and academic researchers, and eventually became part of the platform of the new organization formed from the core Donee Group after the Filer Commission officially completed its work. This new organization became the National Committee for Responsive Philanthropy (NCRP) and was later to influence significantly the future of the United Way.[9]

Table 4.1 United Way Allocations to Thirteen Selected Agencies and Each Group's Percent of Total Reported U.W. Allocations to Agencies and Services, 1973, 1974, 1975

Agency	1973 Allocation	%	1974 Allocation	%	1975 Allocation	%
American Red Cross	$98,597,237	14.6	$102,459,430	14.8	$106,053,742	14.5
Family Service, Nondenominational	41,069,135	6.1	45,239,622	6.6	47,871,448	6.6
YMCA	39,287,733	5.8	41,587,161	6.0	43,546,215	5.9
Boy Scouts of America	34,457,151	5.1	37,166,012	5.4	38,331,890	5.2
Salvation Army	30,775,438	4.6	32,496,972	4.7	34,728,592	4.7
Settlement House/ Neighborhood Center	24,906,600	3.7	26,214,259	3.8	28,745,174	4.0
YWCA	24,136,252	3.6	25,331,588	3.7	26,159,564	3.6
Girl Scouts of the U.S.A.	20,307,902	3.0	22,259,125	3.3	23,175,334	3.2
Boys' Club of America	20,156,706	3.0	22,134,906	3.2	23,849,115	3.3
Home Health Agency	16,421,711	2.4	17,751,019	2.6	17,560,950	2.4
Family Service, Catholic	16,096,824	2.4	17,767,569	2.6	18,072,265	2.5
Hospitals	13,534,617	2.0	13,479,924	1.9	12,368,923	1.7
Urban League	10,130,202	1.5	11,165,972	1.6	11,769,046	1.6

Source: *1975 United Way Allocations, Allocations to Agencies and Services* (U.W.A., 1975).

Allocations and its Critics

What started, then, as a search for ways to support charitable giving and philanthropy in American society had ended up including a critique of the basic institutions for organized charity in America, and therefore inevitably also criticizing one of the symbols of this charity, the United Way. The philanthropic community was now forced to recognize openly a concern which had long smoldered under the surface. The fact was that the United Way was historically tied to a group of large, established agencies, with affiliates located across our country, and generally with strong national organizations.

While each United Way may have had a somewhat diverse package of agencies with its own configuration of dollars allocated, in the 1970s the names Family Service, Boy Scouts, Girl Scouts, Boys Clubs, YMCAs and YWCAs, the Salvation Army, and the Red Cross appeared in just about every United Way of significant size, and as table 4.1 indicates, a group of 13 agencies absorbed over 57 percent of all United Way allocations in the three-year period, 1973–1975. Moreover, the pattern across the country appeared to be relatively fixed. Major national agencies generally continued to receive incremental increases; few agencies lost United Way funding, and relatively few new agencies were admitted to "member" status.[10]

Although the Filer Commission drew attention to the question of

United Way allocations and the manner in which United Way funds were distributed, the issue was certainly not a new one. It had long been recognized, both inside the United Way and in the outside community, that local United Ways provided support for a traditional core of agencies which had over the years received large shares of United Way funding nationwide. This was so, despite the fact that each local United Way was in theory completely autonomous from the national organization in decision making about allocations. In fact, the United Fund system had been supporting most of these agencies for a long time. In 1932, for example, the list of agencies funded by community chest cities already included among the most dominant: Boy Scouts (125 cities); Salvation Army (122 cities); YWCA (107 cities): Red Cross (99 cities); the YMCA (89 cities); and the Girl Scouts (83 cities).[11] Moreover, there seems little doubt that both the national UWA and the local United Ways had, and continue to have, ambivalent feelings about their relationship with these nationally affiliated agencies. It may have caused United Way some problems, but the interlocking relationships and ongoing exchanges had been a source of strength and continuity over time for the federated system.

All organizations have secrets, and generally so long as they remain at least partially concealed, the organization can ignore their public ramifications and carry on business as usual.[12] However, once a problem surfaces openly, and is brought to the attention of important constituencies, efforts have to be made to cope with the problem. Indeed, the way that an organization reacts to problems that have been identified is crucial for its effective survival in a hostile environment, as the history of United Way demonstrates plainly.

Questions about fund distribution have haunted federated fund raising since its earliest days. In 1957 the authors of the comprehensive study of the Indianapolis Community Chest had observed, "we do not know whether or not budget control by United Funds restricts the growth of young agencies. We do not think anyone else knows."[13] And they continued: "At least one staunch supporter of the United Fund movement has expressed doubt about the ability of United Funds to handle new agencies." They asked publicly, "Do we freeze the individual agency and only permit growth as the funds grow?"[14] Over the years other local studies had also touched on the problem of change (or lack of it) in the allocation of funds through federated fund raising. Among the studies often cited is one by Beatrice Dinerman of the Los Angeles United Fund, reported in *Newsweek* in 1970. Dinerman was emphatic in her critique, stating that the "supposedly difficult and delicate process of distributing community chest contributions becomes little more than a charade designed to lull the decision maker into the belief that he is, in fact, making a monumental decision."[15] This criticism touched on the heart of voluntarism in the United Way.

The issue of inflexibility in United Way funding, and the need for far greater inclusiveness in the package of United Way funded agencies, had been raised in the 1960s and was part of the concerns embodied in the UCFCA self-study report of 1969 (see above, chapter 2, and chapter 4, n.15). The issue was at least partly contained through that decade, and ultimately the solutions proposed were couched in ambiguities about the definition of inclusiveness. However, after the Filer Commission reports, the issue was more openly discussed.

To understand the dilemmas which inclusiveness presents for organized charity, it is important to review the nature of the allocations process in the United Way system. Although each community differs somewhat in the specific details of its process, in the late 1970s and early 1980s there was something of a prototypical allocations process followed by most of the larger and middle-sized United Ways, Metros I–VI (and possibly even by many of the smaller ones). This process is built upon three basic factors which interact systemically: the volunteers, the United Way staff, and the agencies requesting funding. The process nominally involves year-round activity, and builds upon frequent, if informal, contacts between the United Way and its funded agencies. However, the allocations program generally culminates in one demarcated period of several weeks (usually, but not always, in the spring) dedicated to formal reviews of agency budgets and programs, and concluding with volunteer decision making about allocations to each funded agency for the following year.

United Way literature generally refers to the allocations process as the "citizen review process' and extols its virtues widely. Review of agency program and budget is presumed to be thorough and impartial; the decision making process is intended to be rational; and it is assumed that good decisions in the public interest will emerge from a consensus process of volunteer (citizen) participation. The process is managed by United Way professionals who provide staff assistance to panels of local volunteers from a variety of walks of life (union, mangement, housewives, professionals, and various types of lay people). These volunteers meet in panels which usually review several similar kinds of programs (e.g., day care, recreation services, or the "Y's")—at least to the extent possible. They study the agencies' budget submissions and program descriptions (narratives about the agency) and generally visit one or more agencies. In earlier times staff from the local planning council also assisted in "staffing" the panels, in reviewing of the agency budget and program descriptive material, and in presenting background reports or studies (including the "famous" priority studies). Many larger United Ways have taken over these functions, including the use of planning materials, but the actual impact of these studies on allocations decisions still remained a problem by the early 1980s, as subsequent chapters will demonstrate.

Site Case Example: Allocations in Corpus Christi

The United Way of Corpus Christi, or as it is titled formally, The United Way of the Coastal Bend, serves a five-county area (Bee, Jim Wells, Kelberg, Nuces, and San Patricio counties). At the time of the site visit in 1983, the five counties had a population of approximately 405,603 people, and an ethnic mix which reflected the area's proximity to Mexico: 40 percent Hispanics, 46 percent Anglo, and a 5 percent black population group.[16]

According to the United Way, the population was expected to increase to approximately 450,000 by 1986, based on a projected growth rate of 12 to 16 percent between 1980 and 1990. The United Way expected immigration to bring in people of a slightly higher income and basically not to affect the ethnic mix in the community. However, many people in the community believed that official counts underestimated the number of Mexican-Americans, which seemed to be growing daily. On the whole, the community was on the young side, with over 33 percent of individuals under age eighteen. Although there is some diversification of industry, the area depends greatly on the petrochemical industry, with oil and gas, and finance and shipping being major sources of jobs, along with the military.

Despite the recession in 1983 which affected the oil industry, the United Way of the Coastal Bend registered a "record 10 percent increase" in its 1982 campaign receipts. This increase probably reflected the energies and competence of a recently arrived new executive director, Joseph Haggerty, who had been brought to Corpus Christi by volunteers interested in turning around a United Way which was not performing well in any area, including the campaign. One example of his success was an initial pilot project at the Corpus Christi Army Depot which in 1982 resulted in a 40 percent increase in employee pledges.

The allocations program of the United Way of the Coastal Bend needed revitalization, and in 1982 improvements in the allocations process were instituted. Efforts were made to insure better training and continuity of volunteer leadership, greater clarification of stan-

Figure 4.1. Timetable of the Corpus Christi Allocations Program
United Way of the Coastal Bend
1982 Calendar—Allocations Council

February
A. Recruit panel chairmen
B. Set goals and objectives
C. Allocations council meets to make decision on 1982 allocation
D. Mail-out budget forms and instruction packet to all agencies

March
A. Recruit panel members
B. Critique prior year

April
A. Complete panel assignments by April 30
B. Set panel meeting dates and places (timetable)

May
A. Budget requests due back by May 3
B. Allocations panels have orientation and first meeting during last week of May

June
A. Begin agency visits and agency presentations
B. Panel members attend agency board meetings

July
A. Allocations panel recommendations to be completed by July 9
B. Allocations council sets tentative allocations during the week of July
C. Allocations council presents tentative allocations to the board of governors on July 28

December
Allocations will be made final

Source: United Way of the Coastal Bend.

dards and procedures, and, eventually, increased self-evaluation by agencies. An outline and timetable of the Corpus Christi Allocations program is given in figure 4.1.

This barebones timetable hardly captures the real flavor of the United Way allocations process. Countless hours of work typically go into designing the budget forms, preparing the budget package, meeting with agencies to discuss programmatic issues, incorporating priorities-related material into the process if there is a priorities system in place, and reviewing the agency budget and program information prior to the agency presentations to the panels. Agencies are generally allowed about an hour for their budget-program presentation and discussion with the panel, although this varies with the size of the agency, the number of agencies a panel is reviewing, and the frequency of reviews, as well as the total number of agencies funded by the local United Way in proportion to the volunteer manpower available. The depth and intelligence of the discussion also varies considerably, depending on a number of factors, including the use of planning studies and needs assessments/priorities; how well informed the volunteers are and the orientation the staff has provided; and the nature of the site visits paid to the agencies and the volunteer's prior familiarity with the human services. Although some very large United Ways (e.g., Boston, Seattle, Denver, San Diego) were already using, or considering moving to, a multi-year funding cycle for their core group of agencies by 1983, the Corpus Christi pattern was certainly a typical one in the late 1970s and early 1980s.[17]

Most volunteers asked about the allocations process in connection with this study expressed overall satisfaction about it. Typically, a volunteer would say, "It isn't perfect, but I don't know anything better," or "We're trying to improve it, but it works." Volunteers show an almost boundless enthusiasm for the process, remaining with allocations for more than a decade, and they are evidently flattered and pleased when asked to chair an allocations panel, or the more prestigious oversight allocations committee.

The United Way organization itself has continually touted the volunteer review process as one of the major strengths of a local United Way, and, as one local United Way expressed it,

> It's been called United Way's "best kept secret." It sets United Way apart from other charities. It's the best expression of the financial accountability of United Way. And it's evidence of how United Way executes its public trust of contributors' dollars.
>
> It's the way in which United Way distributes its campaign contributions to agencies, and it's called the Citizen-Review Process of Allocations.
>
> The basic meaning of the process is simple: it's a case of local citizens— United Way *volunteers*—making decisions for their own community.[18]

Despite the promise of the volunteer allocations process and the almost unbounded enthusiasm of the volunteers, criticism of United Way allocations persisted, as disgruntled member agencies complained they were not getting adequate funding, and groups outside the system complained that they were not able to get any funding at all; in Corpus, this included some Hispanic community agencies. The truth was that the typical United Way allocations process embodied some very real dilemmas, related to its basic assumptions. It was rooted in an assumption of accountability, which required that any agency meet certain fiscal requirements and show a stable history, generally of at least two years as a functioning agency. Newer agencies by definition had trouble complying with these requirements, and tended to have looser administrative practices as well as higher fund-raising expenses.[19] Moreover, there was another parallel assumption in the allocations process: that the core group of agencies would continue to be funded, with an incremental increase in support every year. It was largely this expectation that made United Way funding so valuable to the member agencies. But this expectation also was in conflict with the necessity that United Ways were facing to increase funding to new agencies.

When the site visit was made to Corpus Christi (January 1983), it was early to assess the effectiveness of new efforts at changing the allocations process, but some indications were already present. As table 4.2 reveals, not surprisingly, the rising tide of increased campaign revenues brought good news for all the agencies; everyone got an increase. The pattern of large dollar increases for "core" member agencies, such as Red Cross, Boy Scouts, or Salvation Army, also continued, apparently in a relationship to their large base of previous years. Between 1981 and 1982, however, when the campaign made significant growth, incremental change in allocations to identified new areas of funding or "priority needs" also seems to have followed. For example, the Women's Shelter (funded for the first time in 1981) went from $5,000 in 1981 to $20,000 in 1982; a new Information and Referral Service was funded at over $40,000 (1982); an early childhood development center went from $4,100 (1981) to $15,000 (1982); and a Community Center (Robert L. Moore) went from $55,500 to $75,000 during the same period. Additionally, the Cancer Society was held to the same amount, $75,000 (by formula) from 1980 to 1982, but was scheduled for a large increment in the next allocations period, when the Allocations Council recommended that they be given $100,000.

As table 4.2 plainly indicates, some shifts in the allocations process occurred in 1982 and 1983, and volunteers and agency professionals in Corpus Christi expressed satisfaction with the improvements that were taking place in the allocations program. However, by 1983 environmental conditions were beginning to change in ways which would have increasing impact on the allocations program and the United Way generally in the next few years. First, there was the economic climate, and the recession in the oil industry, which would undoubtedly make funds harder to raise in the near future. Second, there was the increased strength and sense of self-identity of the Mexican-American community in Corpus. Finally, there was the nature of suburban growth in the counties outside of the center of Corpus.

The United Way could do very little about the first factor, except to campaign harder and more effectively with their targeted giving

Table 4.2. United Way of the Coastal Bend Allocations—Five Year History

	1978	1979	1980	1981	1982
American Cancer Society	$	$	$ 75,000	$ 75,000	$ 75,000
American Red Cross, Bee County	7,840	8,527	9,250	9,741	10,441
American Red Cross, Coastal Bend	179,828	201,199	170,000	190,375	222,685
American Red Cross, Kleberg/Kenedy	9,850	10,620	11,000	11,625	13,150
American Red Cross, San Patricio	3,050	3,050	3,250	3,150	3,200
Bee County Four H Clubs	1,400	1,600	1,000	1,000	1,500
Bethune Day Nursery	43,866	48,252	38,000	38,900	45,000
Big Brothers/Big Sisters			5,000	20,000	24,477
Boy Scouts, Gulf Coast Council	118,000	129,000	102,000	127,000	146,000
Boys' Club, Alice	12,000	12,000		15,000	25,957
Boys' Club, Beeville			25,000	29,000	32,962
Boys' Club, Corpus Christi	60,000	68,671	55,000	60,000	71,207
Boys' Club, Kingsville	26,000	27,095	27,000	32,000	38,057
Camp Fire, Alice	10,600	11,150	12,000	13,500	16,000
Camp Fire, Corpus Christi	40,500	42,000	35,000	36,000	41,500
Camp Fire, Kingsville	13,600	14,000	14,000	15,000	18,000
C. B. Alcoholic Rehabilitation Ctr.	18,000	21,000	10,000	17,200	22,180
C. B. Council on Alcoholism	15,000	16,300	12,000	13,090	24,910
C. B. Youth City	87,700	102,000	75,000	88,000	105,000
C. C. Drug Abuse Council	16,646	21,600	15,000	20,000	22,500
C. C. Heart Assn./Cardiac Rehab.	7,766	8,200	5,000	6,893	7,002
C. C. International Seamen's Center	6,000	7,500	7,000	12,000	15,477
Early Childhood Development Center		5,000	476	4,100	15,000
Family Counseling Service	49,100	57,500	47,000	51,000	64,000
Girl Scouts, Paisano Council	61,000	65,500	53,000	60,000	74,265
Goodwill Industries	14,170	20,571	15,000	16,350	17,985
Greenwood-Molina Day Nursery	20,410	22,451	18,000	24,200	27,000
Information, Referral, Crisis Center	31,730	37,000	28,000	33,000	67,272[a]
Jewish Community Center	10,300	11,500	5,720	7,800	12,000
Kleberg County Family Guidance	17,500	23,000	22,000	22,000	26,000
Money Management Counseling and Services		3,340	3,100	6,000	20,000
Moore, Robert L. Community Center	60,710	67,500	53,500	55,500	75,000
Neighborhood Centers	66,061	70,000	55,000	62,900	66,000
Robstown Day Care Center	20,279	32,000	25,000	26,800	30,800
Robstown Youth Recreation	4,400	4,800	286		8,000
Salvation Army, Alice	4,600	4,700	4,700	5,000	5,170
Salvation Army, Beeville	3,400	3,800	3,800	4,500	5,001
Salvation Army, Corpus Christi	89,000	100,000	77,000	90,000	108,750
Salvation Army, Ingleside	1,000	1,000	1,000	1,000	1,000

	1978	1979	1980	1981	1982
Salvation Army, Kingsville	6,200	6,100	6,100	6,400	6,710
Salvation Army, Portland	1,300	1,460	1,460	1,500	1,766
Salvation Army, Robstown	2,200	2,300	2,300	2,700	3,500
South Tx Speech, Hearing, and Language	26,206	31,000	26,000	28,900	32,950
U.S.O. South Texas	32,450	38,345	38,000	38,000	45,000
United Way of Texas	4,000	3,000	1,000	1,500	4,000
Voluntary Action Center	5,000	13,056	13,000	15,033	20,655
Wells, Jim Crippled Children	2,500	2,500	1,800	2,088	2,500
Wesley Community Center	6,699	12,500	12,500	10,600	11,180
Wilson, Ada Hospital	82,520	88,500	69,000	79,200	91,250
Women's Shelter of Corpus Christi				5,000	20,000
Y.M.C.A.	58,000	62,000	51,000	53,000	59,435
Y.W.C.A.	62,100	70,000	60,000	63,000	76,000
Total	$1,420,481	$1,614,187	$1,401,242	$1,611,545	$1,980,394

Source: United Way of the Coastal Bend.
[a] Increased funding for new Information and Referral Service.

groups. However, the second and third conditions, the increased Mexican-American population and the growth of certain outlying (or suburban) counties, suggested that some changes in the allocation of funds would be necessary. This would involve more Hispanic United Way leadership (volunteers and staff), and more careful analysis of community needs. This direction was suggested cautiously in the long-range planning report of the United Way of the Coastal Bend prepared early in 1983.[20] The plan mentioned the Hispanic population, discussed priorities in a general sense, and focused on the need to enhance credibility in the community by working with a number of other organizations, including Mexican-American leadership groups, the NAACP, and the Jewish Community Council. However, it did not specifically suggest the funding of more services either run by, or targeted explicitly to, the Mexican-American community. The Mexican-American community in Corpus was on the whole officially accepting of the United Way, although some grassroots groups were more disaffected. The relationship was to a large extent shaped by the United Way's relationship to the local Catholic hierarchy, and it appeared that so long as the local church encouraged support of the United Way, empowerment did not erupt openly as a major issue.[21] However, it should be noted that by 1984 Joseph Haggerty had left Corpus Christi, and his successor as executive director was Edward J. Rivera, who was Hispanic.

In the good campaign years of 1981–1983, allocations to United Way member agencies in Corpus Christi increased across the board;

some agencies were targeted for particularly large increases, some based on *percentages* (generally newer agencies, or agencies with smaller bases of funding), while other agencies (national agencies, or those with long funding connections to this United Way) received large *dollar* increases. All agencies benefited, and the United Way was able to avoid some of the real problems connected with "The Painful Necessity of Choice."[22] Political expediency in funding services such as the Women's Shelter meshed well with newly identified community needs.

When campaigns are good it is easier for a United Way to be more flexible in funding, even if only at the margin. But as table 4.2 reveals, in tighter years allocations to agencies are at best held steady, and may even be cut. Indeed, during the stagflation years of the mid-1970s the problem of a United Way system which wished to expand its services was plainly exacerbated. In most of the years from 1972 to 1982, many local United Ways did not actually raise large increments above the inflation rate, and consequently the system was undergoing severe strain from the dual demands of inclusiveness in the funding of new agencies, and the simultaneous requirements of their member agencies for significant increases in funding every year.

These were also the years when many United Ways were attempting to use priority plans and planning methodologies to help shift funds from some more traditional programs to newer advocacy-oriented agencies, and were having problems doing so.[23] Although there began to be some shifting of the funds at the margin through new types of funding arrangements with agencies, by and large unless a United Way raised significant amounts of new money, shifting funds to newer agencies was likely to cause difficulties. Thus in the early 1980s Corpus Christi and Seattle, for example, were able to get away with shifting allocations to new agencies, while San Diego had trouble when it attempted to cut allocations to the Red Cross by 10 percent and took in Cancer with a generous contract.[24]

Public Interest and Private Concerns: An End to the Consensus View

The discussions that took place within the Filer Commission were in many respects a forerunner of controversies that United Way would face directly by the end of the 1970s. Questions about organized charity emerged from grassroots organizations across the country, and the realities of a new society began to catch up dramatically with the mythical notion of one United Way campaign that works for everyone. Indeed, The consensus view of the world seemed to be coming to an end.

To some extent the United Way system was caught in a situation which was not entirely of its own making, and with consequences that could not have been predicted at an earlier time when the basic structure of community-based organized charity was developed. The connection of community funds to local affiliates of large, powerful, national agencies was partly an historical phenomenon deriving from events of the early twentieth century. The growth of these national agencies, and the circumstances of wartime fund drives, had helped to make the connection a basic aspect of federated fund organizations.[25]

By the 1980s charitable organizations were functioning in a very different environment. New movements and expressed needs were evident in the community and the nation, and they would necessitate changes in organized charity as well. Pressures that the United Fund system had experienced previously now intensified, because they were related to other upheavals in the philanthropic arena as a whole. To begin with, the size and relative importance of the voluntary sector grew considerably between 1960 and 1975. According to one estimate, the non-profit sector's relative share of our gross national product (GNP) grew from $10.0 billion in 1960 to $45.4 billion in 1975, or twice as fast as that of the government's share.[26] Accompanying the dollar increase in the sector's share of the GNP was also a notable increase in the number of persons employed in the sector: in 1960 the non-profit sector employed 3 million persons; by 1980 the number had grown to 6.3 million persons, or an increase of over 25 percent in the relative share of employment in all sectors of our economy.[27] Much of the sector's growth was also due to the formation of new organizations; according to one authoritative study of the sector, two out of every three agencies in existence in 1982 had been formed since 1960, presumably with considerable support from the federal programs of the era. Nevertheless, despite the diversity of the non-profit sector and the great number of new organizations, it appeared that the resources of the sector were still concentrated in a relatively few large and powerful institutions. In this sense, the United Way truly mirrored the situation in the sector generally.[28]

During the 1970s the voluntary sector was also subject to considerable fiscal uncertainty. These were years in which the economy of the country underwent stagflation and even mini-recessions (1974–1975), and as corporate profits went down there were also changes in tax policies. Concern about the increasing amounts of government support for the voluntary sector was therefore coupled with a reluctance of business to assume more financial responsibility. This meant that there would have to be more of an emphasis on giving by individual donors, an interest which was apparent in the studies of the Filer Commission concerning factors, including tax deductions, which affect motivation in giving.[29] And it also meant that there would be increasing interest in workplace fund raising, where large numbers of individuals could be easily reached.

Additionally, there was a changing attitude on the part of minorities and subgroups in our society, which were growing in numbers and importance. This, too, was reflected by the Donee Group in connection with the Filer Commission. The new groups that were encouraged in the Kennedy-Johnson era were beginning to coalesce, and they continued to make demands on the mainstream institutions of our society, including the United Way. Their demands were of three different types: some wanted to have United Way funding if they didn't have any, or a larger share of the pie if they already were funded; many wanted to be admitted inside the seats of power to the United Way decision-making process, and to be on committees, boards, and in staff roles; but others wanted to be outside the system, developing their own connections to workplace campaigns, and finding empowerment through fund-raising activities.[30] The resulting dilemma for the United Way is evident: if United Way did not somehow give these groups a greater share of the pie, there would be increasingly open conflict which the system could not tolerate. But if they did so, they would be doing so at a time when they were not raising vast amounts of new money (therefore, without a greatly increasing pie), and at a time when the government was also beginning to tighten its support for the voluntary sector. By the late 1970s the United Way system was feeling pressured by the growing numbers and strength of the challengers and the alternative fund movement was emerging.[31]

The demands of accountability in this period, coupled with the effort to shift funds through the planning process, not surprisingly also put the United Way into a power struggle with some of their larger funded agencies, and with their national organizations. The concern of these agencies was understandable. For if funds were to be shifted to new programs, what was to happen to "old" programs? Although the core established agencies were often encouraged to develop new programs, local United Ways were also taking on totally new and different agencies in response to demands for more inclusiveness. In California, where the environmental pressures were particularly strong, the United Way of the Bay Area (the United Way in San Francisco) funded over seventy new agencies and programs in the period from 1970 to 1981.[32] The new agencies were at first apparently small or minority and advocacy-oriented agencies, such as La Raza and other organizations targeted to underserved population groups, but after the mid-1970s the list in larger United Ways increasingly began to include the American Cancer Society or even the Heart Association. This was expensive, and as we have already seen, finding the additional funds was not always easy.

While United Way was attempting to broaden its agency base, and at the same time increase the accountability of its planning and budgeting process, the percentage of member agencies' total budgets that United Way support represented continued to decline. Whereas in 1977 the percentage of agency expenditures from United Way was reported to be 25 percent, by 1982 United Way indicated that it was 17 percent, and it was even less by 1986.[33] The reaction of larger agencies to this anomalous situation was articulated clearly by the YMCA in an article in its national association journal (1977) entitled "King Kong Ain't No Ordinary Monkey." The author pointed out that no matter what percentage of support was provided by the United Way, the United Way would "still SEEK TO EXERCISE CONTROL OVER THE YMCA BUDGET."[34]

The Charity Wars Begin: The Alternative Funds

Although United Way often appeared to be the only game in town, across the country there had always been other groups in the fund-raising business, and this included other federated funds. Such federated funds were primarily of three types: first there were the obviously sectarian funds, such as the Jewish federations or Catholic charities; second, there were in-plant federations, which were minifunds run by employees inside corporations; and third, there were other miscellaneous fund-raising organizations in different communities, including combined health appeals such as that in Baltimore (CICHA, founded in 1959) or AID–United Givers, founded in Los Angeles around the same time.

Through the years local United Funds had coped with these other funds and generally lived peacefully with them from the late 1950s through the early 1970s. They had accomplished this by many ways. In regard to the first group of sectarian funds, there were a variety of arrangements across the country; and many United Funds directly funded these pass-through organizations. In 1982, for example, we found that many funds in our sample of 131 United Ways incorporated some method of support for other federations such as Jewish federations, allowing them to pass on their allocations to their own service agencies, e.g., to a Jewish Community Center. Although there was some effort to eliminate these "middlemen," or sub-funds, many United Ways (Baltimore, New York) still had formal agreements with religious organizations.[35]

The second group, in-plant federations, was potentially more threatening, since it involved the workplace and its corporate world. These workplace federations can affect what has become the core of the United Way fund-raising activity: the payroll deductions of individual givers at the workplace. The practice of in-plant federations has, in fact, been much more prevalent than has been commonly realized, and it appears that United Ways have long since learned to cope with them. With the help of many company executives and union leaders, United Way has been able to co-opt the leadership of most in-plant federations, across the country, with strong employee commitment to the United Way idea.

Finally, there were workplace oriented, cross-cutting funds which sprang up almost serendipitously in some communities across the country. These funds were for the most part health related, and seem to have grown out of the need for a response to the intense competition between the health funds and the united funds. In some cases they were actually created because of pressure from the local business community, or Chamber of Commerce, as with the Commerce and Industry Combined Health Appeal (CICHA) of Baltimore. In any case, these funds had usually been a concern to United Fund in the local community where they existed (for example, Baltimore and Los Angeles), but it was not until the mid-1970s that they began to be a problem to the United Way system nationwide. To understand why and how this happened, we will look first at the case of California, and at Los Angeles in particular.[36]

Site Case: California

California, once considered an anomaly within the American social scene, has in recent years possibly bypassed New York as an influential force in shaping the directions of our country. Indeed, the challenges which it presented to mainstream institutions during the 1960s are well documented. The laidback lifestyle and the glorification of independent actions based on personal preference have become deeply embedded in the new directions of American society.[37] The challenges that this change presented to the United Way had already been recognized to be of serious concern to the United Way in the mid 1970s. It was certainly not an accident that the "Charity Wars" broke out there in the late 1970s and that California subsequently became the center of United Way national attention for many years. Moreover, although the conflict escalated in Los Angeles in 1977, there had been serious challenges to the United Way earlier, in San Francisco (1972–76) and in 1970 in Los Angeles.[38]

Site Case Study: Los Angeles and the Black United Fund

To begin with, then, a relatively little-heralded event of the time was to be a portent of future events. The Brotherhood Crusade was formed in Los Angeles in the late 1960s. The early history of this first Black United Fund has been discussed thoroughly in a study by King Davis of fund raising in the black community (1975). As part of his explanation for the founding of this organization, Davis noted the size of the black community in Los Angeles, which tripled between 1950 and 1970, going from 170,000 (9 percent of the population of the city) in 1950 to over 504,000 (or 18 percent) in 1970.[39] Davis also pointed out that Los Angeles ranked sixth in the number of blacks in the population and that it numbered nearly 300,000 adults among its half-a-million blacks.

Davis argues that both the size of the black population and the long history of conflict which existed between blacks and the United Way of Los Angeles were contributing factors to the development of a Black United Fund. He states that the Brotherhood Crusade "grew out of conflict between Blacks and the United Way over the amount of resources given to Black agencies by the United Way, lack of Blacks in the United Way structure at decision-making levels, and a desire for community control on the part of Black community leaders.[40]

The idea for a black fund-raising campaign had been considered as far back as 1951 by members of the Urban League and the Human Rights Commission, and there were a variety of efforts made to establish it in the next fifteen years. They had continually met with obstacles which prevented the formation of the fund through the period of the Watts disturbances and the militancy of the late 1960s. Many of the agencies interested in such an appeal viewed the militancy of the era as a detriment to fund-raising efforts. Davis points out:

> Throughout the formation of the Black Fund in Los Angeles, public conflict with the United Way was, by design, kept at a minimum. . . . However, unexpressed dissatisfaction with the United Way was quite evident and was instrumental in the development of the appeal.[41]

The purpose of the Los Angeles Crusade in its early stages was defined as providing support for a small number of social agencies unable to get adequate support from the United Way or through individual fund-raising drives of their own. However, the purpose was modified and changed many times. By 1985, the Brotherhood Crusade had become an aggressive, large organization, with a dual stated agenda of empowerment and fund raising. But even as early as 1970, the Crusade had promulgated the notion of an ambitious dollar goal, and while it was unable to raise large funds through fund-raising campaigns, it did become the delegated agency for planning use of over two million dollars of Model Cities funds.[42] Moreover, the excitement of the City of Los Angeles Crusade, and of one leader, Walter Bremond, is credited with having resulted in the formation of a National Black United Fund. This organization was incorporated formally in 1972 in Delaware, and it established firmly the principle of a nationwide movement for local black fund-raising activities.[43]

Aid

It has been said that "most everything that's good comes out of California," but also almost everything that's bad comes out of here. . . . AID was born in the early fifties on [sic] L.A. . . . but part of the strategy . . . came out of Riverside and San Bernadino and Ventura. . . . Ventura had the courage two years ago to part with AID and that was the beginning of the end.[44]

Associated-In-Group Donors was in essence what its name implied, an organization of givers or donors, organized along a "chapter plan" within companies and joined together in a cross-cutting association. AID's stronghold was the high-tech industrial group around the city of Los Angeles. In some of its characteristics it bore a strong similarity to the theoretical model for the united funds of the 1970s: AID was donor-driven and it was organized in the workplace. But it was also different from a United Way model: it was primarily health agency–focused; it encouraged designations to funded agencies, and it did not run a community (neighborhood) campaign. Despite differences with AID, the Los Angeles United Way had maintained a contractual relationship with AID for a period of ten years.

In 1977 the contract with AID was terminated abruptly after the AID–United Givers fund announced that it was no longer going to give its undesignated funds to the United Way. It was going to distribute undesignated campaign funds directly to the United Way agencies themselves. Since the amount of undesignated funds totaled one million dollars, the money was significant, and there was also a dangerous precedent involved.[45] United Way would lose control over the funds to be allocated, which would no longer be counted as part of United Way income and allocations. Thus, the Los Angeles United Way retaliated quickly, insisting that their agencies could *not* accept funds from AID if they wished to remain connected to the United Way, and the war was on. In what was described as "unprecedented," on March 13, 1978, AID–United Givers filed a lawsuit against the United Way for attempting "to create a charity monopoly."[46] An injunction against the United Way was denied by the Court, whose position was that the matter should be settled in out-of-court negotiations. An agreement was reached on March 28, 1978, but not until the case had apparently become so "hot" that a third judge had to be brought in, because the two previous judges had disqualified themselves.[47]

The March 28th agreement was incorporated in a court order and was in effect a legally binding decision for activities in the county of Los Angeles.[48] It stipulated that the one million dollars of undesignated funds from AID would be designated through the United Way, and furthermore that in the future all such undesignated funds would be distributed the same way. The court order also stipulated that the Los Angeles area United Way would have to accept any and all undesignated funds given to the United Way by AID, but that "AID shall not attempt to distribute such undesignated funds directly to any United Way agencies or partner." While AID could list the United Way as a recipient of donations, the organization could not "state that it 'represents' United Way, its agencies, and/or partners."[49] A compromise had been reached: the United Way agencies got the money, but the United Way had protected its name, and its control over the disbursement of the funds.

In the end it appeared that although AID had come out reasonably well in the settlement, it had lost the war. The United Way battled so successfully that in one year 182 AID companies switched to the United Way and AIDs fund-raising results went from over $18 million dollars to approximately $8.5 million dollars. They considered this to be a direct result of the "volatile conduct by the United Way."[50] By 1982, moreover, United Way staff members at a United Way staff conference reported that AID was out of business as a separate organization. It had merged with the Los Angeles United Way.

The battle had not, however, been without cost to the United Way. Although United Way could continue to claim that it had never lost a lawsuit, it had come close to doing so in this case. The agreement included a precedent-setting compromise forcing United Way to recognize that another fund-raising organization could raise funds for distribution to the United Way and its member agencies. United Way thus became officially a recipient organization. Since this gave the "power of the purse" to another organization, it was potentially a real threat to the critical powers of the United Way.

In addition, the message to United Way member agencies was clearly a disturbing one. In forbidding United Way agencies to accept funds directly from AID, the United Way was forced to use power and control overtly over its member agencies; a power and control which it generally preferred not to show openly, but to use more subtly through the budget and evaluations process. Moreover, the threat of monopoly charges had a long-range impact on the United Way system as a whole. It certainly was one of the major reasons that by 1980 a donor option plan was adopted by many of the large United Ways in California (Los Angeles, Orange County, San Francisco, and Santa Clara), and even by some of the slightly smaller ones involved in the AID dispute, such as Sacramento and Ventura.

That the United Way nationwide was watching events in California closely was evident to those in the system, and was also signaled by an official event that occurred in September 1977. At that time the United Way of America's Long Range Planning Committee Report on Inclusiveness was given to the UWA executive committee. In its report, the committee recommended that local United Ways "consider a Donor Option program for agencies funded by United Way *and those that are not.* The issue . . . [is] how to balance the allocation of funds to meet community needs with the right of the donor to determine the recipient of the grant" (emphasis added).[51] Although the leadership of the UWA recognized the urgency of the situation, and some local United Ways were convinced that the situation in California was contagious, many local United Way professionals were deeply committed to the philosophy of citizen review and to volunteer participation in the decision-making process about fund distribution. Thus, there was considerable resistance to the adoption of an official Donor Option policy, either at the UWA board level or in the local community. It was not until February 18, 1982 that the executive committee of the UWA, and subsequently the board of governors, approved the following Donor Option Resolution:

Donor Option Resolution
Whereas, United Ways across the nation support and assist financially some 37,000 voluntary health and social services and are including new agencies each year;

Whereas, local United Ways are already developing relationships with agencies and organizations not in the regular campaign appeal through Management Assistance Programs, venture project funding, and through voluntary and professional training:

Whereas, a single campaign is essential for effective fund raising at the workplace;

Whereas, donors need to understand how money is distributed to the most urgent community needs through the citizens review and allocation process; and

Whereas, generous voluntary giving is a by-product of commitment—and commitment is generated by understanding community needs, and through personal volunteer involvement, now therefore be it

Resolved, that United Way of America's Board of Governors hereby asks United Way organizations to consider ways to provide Donor Option programs in a manner appropriate to their community which can be integrated with the ongoing citizens review and allocations process.[52]

The realists within the system, and the urgencies of the environment, had been convincing. Better a banner with holes in it which could withstand the breezes, than no banner at all.[53]

Site Case Example: Philadelphia

Guns were fired in California, and the United Way responded by overcoming the opposition on the one hand, and by altering its own position on the other. In adopting new donor plans in 1978-1979, United Ways in California made a significant symbolic change in their posture toward community fund raising, and did so with the approval of the national United Way organization. Although the exact structure of the plan to be used and the financial significance of the change to the United Way system remained to be determined, at the very least, a donor option plan in the new era meant that donors could designate funds to organizations outside of the United Way system. As later defined by the UWA, Donor Option was

> a program that allows the contributor to designate all or a portion of the contribution to any tax-exempt, volunteer-run, health and social services agency in addition to agencies funded by the United Way campaign; and which is in some way publicly communicated to the potential donors.[54]

The purists within the United Way system, however, continued to resist the new form of donor option. They were concerned that any encouragement of donor designation would inevitably weaken the allocations process and would furthermore send out mixed messages to the community. Many of the more enlightened United Way professionals were committed to rational planning and to citizen review, which they believed an open donor designation system would undermine, and their position was, "It can't happen here." Meanwhile, the pragmatists within the United Way pointed to California and asked, "Who's next?"[55] They found out in January 1980, when a story broke in the Philadelphia newspapers concerning the relationship between the United Way of Southeast Pennsylvania, the Archdiocese of Philadelphia, and an emerging advocacy organization, Women's Way.

In its barest outlines, the issue which exploded in Philadelphia was similar to other sporadic outbreaks across the country, including Corpus Christi and San Antonio.[56] The issue revolved around funding of abortion services provided by some agencies which were under the umbrella of the Women's Way, services that the Catholic Archdiocese of Philadelphia did not want to be associated with. But the specific course that the opposition took, and the long-range impact it had on the local United Way, gave the event special significance for the United Way systemwide.

Philadelphia is a large metropolitan region with a diverse racial and ethnic population of over four million people. The Philadelphia area has a varied industry; it has been losing some of its major home office centers in the core center and older urban areas, but there has been some growth in new high-tech industries in the surrounding suburban counties. Philadelphia is characterized by its many health-related and university-related activities and by a mixed religious influence, which includes a well-known Quaker center, but also a dominant Catholic gentry and an established Jewish community. With all of this, Philadelphia is considered a quiet and fairly staid community.

The United Way of Southeastern Pennsylvania (the United Way in Philadelphia) is a Metro I organization; it covers most of four counties (Philadelphia, Delaware, Chester, and Montgomery) and a population of 2,667,582 (1980).[57] The 1980 campaign raised $29,251,031, of which $23.5 million was reported to have been available for funding of services.[58] At the time that the Women's Way was applying for admission, the United Way campaign had raised an increase of about 10 percent over the preceding year, but did not raise an outstanding per capita amount. It had just completed a long-range planning process, with a report, "New Directions for a New Decade," which discussed a variety of donor option formats generally, but did not explicitly take a stand on using any of them.[59]

ALLOCATIONS TO ALTERNATIVE FUNDS

In the late summer of 1979, Women's Way, a coalition of womens' organizations, applied to the United Way for funding. Women's Way, which had been in existence a little under four years, had been having difficulty raising funds, and had been turned down by a number of corporations. Several controversial agencies were included under the Women's Way umbrella, and at least one that performed abortions.[60] It was several months before the United Way arranged the meeting, but when it was held, it was cordial. The United Way, however, pointed out that while they were receptive to the idea of funding of some of the women's agencies in the group, they were not eager to fund another coalition as a whole. Moreover, United Way had an agreement with the Catholic archdiocese "not to finance any agencies, such as the Elizabeth Blackwell Center [which was one of the Women's Way members] that provided contraceptive counseling, abortions and other services that ran contrary to Catholic teachings."[61] Subsequently Women's Way held a special board meeting, and after a heated discussion (and by a 7–5 vote), agreed to keep in its application, as a coalition.

In January 1980 the United Way wrote to say that Women's Way could not be considered for funding as a coalition, and cited the agreement with the archdiocese specifically. This letter, and the reasons given, became a major news story (January 23, 1980) and subjected the United Way to severe criticism for its hidden policy concerning allocation of funds.[62] Women's Way got a great deal of publicity, and the United Way was subject to controversy which it could not tolerate. As the executive director succinctly expressed it:

> I think most of you would agree that the best climate for fund raising is a calm climate. The rough seas which create unrest, turbulence, controversy are not what we look for each fall.
>
> In Philadelphia, 1980 was the exception to the calmness doctrine.[63]

By June 1980 the United Way had officially adopted a donor option plan, which it announced just before the Women's Way annual fund-raising dinner. In the first year of the Philadelphia donor option program (1980–81), the United Way raised approximately $3 million over the year before (an 11 percent increase) and the Women's Ways fund-raising campaign brought in a total of $206,000, compared with the $130,000 it raised in 1979–80. Donor option was installed in Philadelphia, but the United Way's troubles were far from over.[64] By the fall of 1981, campaign designations in Philadelphia were over $4 billion dollars, or 12.73 percent of the total raised.

Philadelphia became one of the top cities in terms of percentages of designations and the highest in percent of funds going to agencies outside the regular United Way system of agencies. Moreover, in the next few years, alternative funds in Philadelphia continued to grow. In addition to the Women's Way, a CHAD (combined health agency drive) began to make some inroads into fund raising in high-tech companies in suburban areas, and a Black United Fund emerged. In addition, ferment resulted from the efforts of a "gadfly" organization, led by a social activist who was influential in the alternative fund movement nationwide as well—Nan Steketee, executive director of the Center for Responsible Funding.[65]

The Philadelphia story provides a vivid illustration of the way organizations adapt to turbulence in the environment. In this case the cycle began, as it frequently does with the United Way, with denying that there was a problem, and in fact, United Way initially resisted even meeting with Women's Way to discuss admission of the organization into the United Way. Thereafter, the United Way attempted to negotiate a compromise, and offered to admit some agencies of the Women's Way into the United Way, which, in effect, would also have split up the Women's Way and diluted its strength as a powerful force. When this was unsuccessful, and controversy broke out into the open, the United Way made a major effort to avoid further conflict, and to develop a solution—donor option—which would offer an immediate palliative, without making too great a change in the systemic order.[66] Eventually, when the Women's Way and other social action groups continued to push for open access to the workplace and for increased designations, the United Way tried to co-opt and absorb the opposition by inviting the leaders inside, even asking them to sit on United Way Donor Option committees.

Although co-optation is often an effective strategy, in this situation it had only limited success, and the struggle in Philadelphia continued. Increasingly large amounts of monies were designated outside the United Way system of funded agencies in Philadelphia and the local United Way's choice of donor option was ultimately seen only as a necessary compromise, barely preferable to an open workplace fund-raising drive. The United Way continued to resist direct competition by alternative funds in the workplace, on the whole successfully in the private sector, but far less successfully in the public sector. In 1985 the competitive health agency drive, CHAD, lost its executive director and at least temporarily was driven into a state of eclipse.

As the figures demonstrate, in Philadelphia the Donor Option Program was planted in receptive soil. What started out largely as the problem of one organization, Women's Way, found a solution that allowed the funding of a variety of social action funds, nurtured in a city used to a Quaker ethos which valued independent thinking and social causes. Thus, in the early 1980s Donor Option channeled increasing amounts of donor's into new causes outside the United Way system, and became a source of support for more advocacy-oriented social change organizations, and particularly for Women's Way, which later demonstrated a remarkable marketing capacity.

Part III

Whose Pie Is it? Voluntarism and Big Government

Chapter 5

Donor Option and Controversy in the Combined Federal Campaign

> While the voluntary sector and the rest of the country have been changing significantly over the past two decades, the CFC has remained frozen in its concept of the voluntary sector: trapped in a 1961 time warp.
>
> Statement by Robert O. Bothwell before
> the Congressional Hearings on the
> Combined Federal Campaign, 1979.

> The Combined Federal Campaign (CFC) has become a source of intense controversy because of admission to the campaign of organizations whose principal purpose is other than the providing of direct human care services, or health research, to persons and families in need of such services.
>
> United Way Position Paper
> September 1982

By the end of February 1982, the United Way of America had officially adopted a donor option policy, and by the following fall, forty-five donor option programs were in place or under consideration, with more to follow.[1] Many of the largest United Ways continued to struggle with the question of donor designation, but by February 1986 no more than eighty local United Ways actually had donor option in place. Only twenty (less than half) of the larger Metro I communities were included. If donor option was becoming more accepted, it was reluctantly, even though it was being pushed by the UWA as an effective response to the increasingly insistant charge that United Ways funded primarily old-line traditional agencies and at the same time limited access of other groups to fund raising at the workplace.

Donor option, however, had some powerful supporters. Donor designation would satisfy some major corporations such as AT&T, since it offered an effective, if minimalist, solution to the question of open access to the workplace.[2] In many respects donor designation was the least difficult solution for a United Way system faced with charges of monopoly in the workplace, because donor option was essentially not a new idea to the United Way. Federated fund-raising organizations had practiced some form of donor option throughout most of their history. That is, they had allowed donors to contribute to, or to earmark funds for, one or more specific agencies in their "package" of funded agencies. These contributions would then be passed, theoretically, through the United Way (Fund/Chest) to the agencies so designated.[3] If this was indeed the practice in the past, why were many United Way professionals so reluctant to adopt a donor option plan?

The answer lies in the fundamentally important place of the citizen review process and of allocations in the United Way system, as well as in the actual way that the donor option dollar was handled in its earlier form. In fact, under the previously existing practice of donor option, the designated dollar generally did not go to the agency, and it had essentially no impact on the amount of money that the agency received.[4] In the decades before the new thrust in donor option, monies which were designated were considered first dollars in a pot of money whose distribution was determined through the citizen review process. Whether or not contributors earmarked funds for a particular agency, let us say the Red Cross, the Red Cross would in fact get the same $100,000 that the allocations committee and the United Way board allocated to it. Thus, although thank-you notes were often sent to donors who designated to a particular agency, this essentially only contributed to a fictional notion of a gift relationship.

In short, the old form of donor option was on the whole more a matter of appearance than substance, and it was generally minimized in use, and even discouraged by local United Ways. Moreover, the old system of donor designation was on the whole applicable only to agencies within the United Way system already, or to other United Ways to which employees felt connected, for example, by residence. The system was not set up to allow for designations to agencies which were not already members of the local United Way "family" of funded agencies. The new donor option system, on the other hand, was developed in order to allow for designations outside the United Way group of funded agencies and, therefore, was intended to serve as a release valve, at a time when there was pressure over the limited number of choices in giving at the workplace. In these early days, it was not clear how it would affect the overall pot of money raised.[5]

The donor option program which emerged in the late 1970s was more complicated in practice than the old system, and involved a quantitatively as well as qualitatively different intention. Designations to agencies outside the United Way systems of affiliated agencies were to be allowed, and would be administered by the local United Way. This form of donor designation was expected to coexist alongside of the old practice of donor designation to regular United Way agencies, and the citizen review process, and was intended to provide for a real donor option. It was developed with different specific policies and variations in administrative procedures in different local communities (table 5.1).

As table 5.1 demonstrates plainly, the new donor option idea took a variety of different forms depending on the following factors: the way that the plan was developed (i.e., Was it set up under great duress?); the way that the plan was actually promulgated or publicized; the amount of money that was charged for administrative costs; the question of whether or not negative designations were permitted; and the manner in which designations were actually handled, whether, for example, any 501(c)(3) organization could be written in by a donor, or whether the agency had to be chosen from a list of pre-approved agencies.[6] However, although the chart demonstrates procedural differences among United Ways, and variations in the form of donor option, the extent to which its usage was encouraged, and the depth of commitment to it are not equally obvious from written comparisons. Yet the manner in which a donor option plan was implemented clearly had major implications for its effectiveness in offering real choice.

In Philadelphia, as an example, the donor option plan continued to be a subject of considerable controversy even after it was formally established. As in San Francisco, the Philadelphia plan was put in place rather hastily, and some wrinkles remained. Thereafter, the advocates for aggressive promotion of the donor option plan maintained a vigilant and activist stance toward making the plan meaningful. Women's Way and the Center for Responsible Funding in Philadelphia provided aggressive leadership in the drive for greater visibility for the donor option plan, and donor choice eventually became a major company issue.

Table 5.1. Metro I Donor Option Communities: Comparative Policies

	Eligible Recipients (besides Non-UW)	Geographic Area	Donor Awareness
Baltimore	Other UWs; "CR Process"; Negative desig.	State	Fully publicized
Columbus	Other UWs; "CR Process"; Negative desig.	United Way	Solicitor training
Dayton	Other UWs; "CR Process"; Negative desig.	No limit	In brochure; verbally by solicitors
Indianapolis	Other UWs; "CR Process"		If asked during solic.
Los Angeles	Other UWs	USA	In brochure; verb. by sol.
Miami	Other UWs	State	In brochure; verb. by sol.
Milwaukee	Other UWs	United Way	Sol. training
Orange, Calif.	Other UWs	USA	Sol. training
Philadelphia	Other UWs; "CR Process"	PA; NJ; DE	Fully publicized
Pittsburgh	Other UWs; Negative	United Way	In brochure; verb. by sol.
Providence	Other UWs; "CR Process" Negative	State	Fully publicized
Rochester	Negative; "CR Process"	United Way	In brochure; verb. by sol.
San Diego	Other UWs	State	In brochure; verb. by sol.
San Francisco	Other UWs; "CR Process"	State	In brochure; verb. by sol.
Santa Clara, Calif.	Other UWs; "CR Process"	State; USA UWs	If contributors ask

Source: UWA, 1985.

1) Pledge card format—all United Ways use separate designation cards, furnished on request (except San Diego—separate cards furnished automatically to all).

2) Dollar minimum—all United Ways have $24 or $25/year limit (except Baltimore, Indianapolis, Milwaukee, Orange, Philadelphia—*no* limit).

3) Number maximum—all United Ways allow unlimited number designations (except Columbus, Providence, and Rochester—1; and Dayton—3 United Way agencies, 3 non-United Way agencies, 1 negative).

Recipient Promotion	Distribution to Non-UW	Costs/Who Charged	Shrinkage/Who Charged
Written prohibition; widespread promotion	<$1,000 < Ann. Quart.	7.2% to non-UW + UW "overbase" $	7% to non-UW + UW "overbase" $
Written prohibition; some promo.	Quarterly	5% to non-UW + other UWs	7% to all
Written prohibition; some promo.	< $1,000 < Ann. Quart.	11.2% to *all* designations	8% to non-UW & other UWS
Some promo.	Annually; except neighboring UW (large $) quart.	$2.53 per designation to non-UW	6.84% to non-UW
Written prohibition; no problem	Quarterly	10% current actual to non-UW	Varies by account to non-UW
No problem	Quarterly	6% to non-UW	Varies by account to non-UW
Written prohibition; no problem	"Periodically"	6% to *all*	6% to *all*
No problem	Biannually	No charge	Based on last audit—to *all*
No problem	Quarterly	5.6% actual (policy being reexamined) to all	9.9% (some accts. vary) to all
Written prohibition; some promo.	Monthly	8% current actual to non-UW	Varies by act. to non-UW
Some promo.	Quarterly	7% to non-UW	10% (on P.D. + bill direct) to non-UW
No problem	<$500 < Ann. Quart.	6.5% to non-UW	4.5% to non-UW
Written prohibition; some promo.	Quarterly	10% to non-UW	12% to non-UW
Written prohibition; some promo.	Quarterly	9.8% to *all*	Varies by acct. to *all*
No problem	< $500 < Ann. Quart.	9.8% to non-UW	9.5% (on P.D.) to non-UW

4) Criteria—all United Ways require agencies to be 501(c)(3) and health & welfare (in addition, Pittsburgh allows 501(c)(4); Dayton allows health and welfare *programs* of churches, schools, government units; Philadelphia requires provision of local service).

5) United Way agency designations—11 United Ways treat as first-in $ toward allocations (except San Francisco—outside income).

Despite their presence on donor option committees of the United Way, Nan Steketee and Lynn Yeakel continued their protests about inadequate public notice and media advertisement, about the insufficiency of informative materials distributed in campaigns through 1985, and about the eligibility rules for inclusion. In addition, the Center for Responsible Funding was instrumental in organizing informal educational promotional procedures using post cards, flyers, word of mouth and other means to insure that information about choice in giving was available and knowledge about donor designation was disseminated to workers.[7] Leaders in this campaign were convinced that the United Way was not encouraging use of the donor option, and that donor choice was underplayed in advertisements of the campaign and made difficult through the use of such devices as special locations for the required signatures, or an extra card to be filled out to validate donor designations. Even with the obstacles, however, the continuous efforts of the local alternative funds seem to have paid off. As appendixes F.2a and b indicate, Philadelphia reported large amounts of donor designations to non–United Way agencies in the years 1983–86, with a continual increasing trend.

It could be argued that donor option was a fairly modest modification of an already existing practice within the United Way system. However, the moment that the donor designation idea was promoted officially for widespread application, it would also be problematic. The notion of active donor choice was philosophically incompatible with the citizen review process, in which decision making was supposed to be based on a priority-setting process, or rational system of needs assessment. Even if the fact of rational allocations was short of the commitment to it, and if politics and history resulted in maintaining the status quo in distribution of most United Way funds, the idea of rational planning and citizen review was a basic underpinning of the United Way.[8] Individual choices were not considered informed choices in the same degree, and the principle of individual freedom to choose suggested a weakness in the fabric of the United Way myth of community decision making on the consensus model. Indeed the long-standing quarrel with the national health agencies from the 1950s included arguments against their system of distributing funds according to donor preferences, as contrasted with the United Way allocations process, planning principles, and need determination (see above, chapter 3).

From the United Way vantage point, there were serious pragmatic difficulties in the wholesale use of donor designations, which would ultimately undermine the fundamental concept of citizen involvement in determining allocations. The use of volunteers for allocations is critical to the whole United Way system, since volunteers become excited by the idea of United Way and committed to it through the allocations process. They then go back to their communities and workplaces as givers, fund raisers, propagandists, true believers, and future leaders of the campaign. Participation of volunteers in citizen review is essential to the continuation of the United Way, as well as to maintenance of the myth and the machinery of informed community decision making. It also appears to lead directly to greater giving on the part of the volunteer.[9]

In addition, there are some serious structural dilemmas in the implementation of any kind of donor option plan. These dilemmas include the problem of containing its scope so that it will not endanger the essential middleman role of the United Way in the allocation and distribution of funds. A true donor option plan could eventually eat into the basic funding provided for traditional United Way–supported agencies. Therefore, unless significant amounts of additional funding are raised in the campaign each year, donor designations could result in shifts in funds to newer added-on agencies, and less for the old members of the United Way "family." This would of course endanger the important relationship of the local United Way with a major constituency group, that is, its traditional family of funded agencies.

Donor Option and the CFC

There was another structural dilemma inherent in the use of donor option in some local communities. In these communities, including Baltimore and San Diego, for example, where there was both a donor option plan in place and a large Combined Federal Campaign (CFC) for federal employees, the United Way faced the necessity of coping with two competing principles in relation to the use of designations and the allocation of undesignated funds.[10] In order to understand this structural dilemma it is helpful first to understand the basic concepts of undesignated and designated funds in federated fund raising.

In the regular United Way or Chest campaign, typically the bulk of funds could be considered undesignated because money was given to the collecting federated organization for distribution to other organizations. The federated fund-raising organization served as the decision maker and agent for the allocation and disbursement of all funds it received. The CFC, on the other hand, incorporated elements of several separate campaigns, run at different times, and by different organizations. Thus, as late as 1963, the United Fund and

Community Chests ran their campaign in the fall, the National Health Agencies group (the NHAs) and the International Service Agencies group (the ISAs) ran their campaigns in the winter, and in communities where the Red Cross was not part of a United Fund, it ran a spring campaign. Prior to 1964, funds in the CFC not actually designated to specific agencies in the National Health Agencies or International Service Agencies campaigns could be divided among those two groups of agencies as they saw fit. The United Way did the same through its citizen review process, and the American Red Cross was either a direct designee or part of the United Way campaign.

With the formation of one unified federal campaign in 1964, the problem of how to distribute undesignated funds emerged. Each of the competing combined groups in the campaign (United Funds, NHAs, or ISAs) had a different system for distributing undesignated funds to its own agencies, and more importantly there was the immediate question of which group should get how much of the total pot of undesignated funds resulting from the overall combined campaign.[11] It was ultimately agreed that each of the separate groups was to be allocated a portion of the undesignated funds based on their previous share of the designated funds. This plainly gave the United Fund the advantage, since in the period which became the base period, they had run the most aggressive campaign and had the largest share of designated funds.

The question of equity in the distribution of undesignated funds in the CFC became more serious as the CFC grew in dollar amounts and in symbolic significance. Throughout the period 1973–1982, the United Way share of the total of undesignated funds remained fairly constant and actually increased from 85.8 percent (1973) to 89.9 percent (1982). At the same time, however, the overall proportion of designated funds in the CFC increased more dramatically, from 33.7 percent of the campaign in 1973 to 64.8 percent of the campaign in 1982. (see the tables of CFC trends in appendix G). During this time the health agencies "thought better of the deal struck in 1964" and increased pressure on the federal government from a variety of national agencies to change the basis for distributing undesignated funds so as to make current donor preference more of a factor.[12] In this period there was also continuing pressure to allow new organizations into the CFC, and therefore to increase competition generally in the workplace. These pressures eventually resulted in a series of changes in the procedures and policies of the CFC which by 1985 had turned into a donor designation campaign. Furthermore, this happened at the same time as the United Way was beginning to receive a decreasing share of the designated funds (see appendix G).

Consequently, by 1985 local United Ways were facing a real dilemma. They were being forced into the position of encouraging designations to themselves in the CFC, while they were at the same time trying to prevent increased use of donor designations in their own United Way campaign. In their regular community campaign increased use of donor designation was discouraged because, as already discussed above, it undermined the citizen review process, and perhaps even more importantly because it resulted in funds going outside the regular United Way system of funded agencies.[13]

In summary, what started out in the 1960s as concern about equity in charitable fund distributions began in the 1970s to turn into philosophical questions about open access to the workplace and the effectiveness of donor designation as a way to insure this, both in the private and public arena. Although donor option was possibly the least disruptive solution to the nagging charge of monopoly from the United Way viewpoint, and probably from the corporate viewpoint as well, it was not accepted with equal enthusiasm by all members of the alternative fund movement. There were those who thought it might work and should be pursued aggressively, as in Philadelphia; and there were others who thought of it only as a palliative which should never be accepted, since it was really a way to "cool the mark." Robert Bothwell of the NCRP was firmly established as a leader in this latter camp.[14]

In any case, while donor option was not entirely welcome, any of the likely alternatives seemed far worse to the United Way. At the extreme, alternatives included either total breakup of the United Way hegemony at the workplace under substantiated charges of monopoly, or permitting alternative funds to actively solicit in side-by-side competitive campaigns with United Ways in the workplace. Employers, as well as United Way, resisted the latter solution, and would be embarassed by the former.[15] It is moreover not only corporations that wish to perpetuate a unified fund-raising system at the workplace. Any large employer concerned about public image and productivity seems likely to conceive of a unified campaign as a way to enhance morale, cut down on wasted time, and strengthen unity in the work force. As the discussion of the CFC below plainly demonstrates, this concern about loss of productive work time from competitive campaigns was not unique to the private business sector, but was shared by government as well.

The Combined Federal Campaign to 1980: Power in the Smoke-Filled Room

The Combined Federal Campaign (CFC) is the workplace fundraising drive for federal employees, both civilian and military. It evolved essentially out of the various fund-raising drives conducted in governmental work sites during World War II. Notably in World War II, separate campaigns had been allowed for chests in the fall and the Red Cross in the spring (see above, chapter 1). In those years, however, the campaigns were run by these organizations themselves in the government work site, and other selected groups also had access to the public workplace.

Concern about the lack of control over fund raising in federal installations had surfaced by the late 1940s. However, it was not until Dwight D. Eisenhower became president that rules and regulations for government oversight were first seriously promulgated.[16] On June 27, 1956 President Eisenhower established a new "Federal Service Fund Raising Policy and Program" which like United Fund organizations was at least in part created to address the problem of competition among fund-raising efforts, and pressures placed on the giver. As with the United Fund in the 1940s, the announcement was made with some flourish, and the president stated:

> We who work in the government want to assume our full citizens' share of voluntary support of the many worthwhile private health and welfare organizations.
>
> The new program will make available to everyone in the government the opportunity to give his full measure of support to these efforts.[17]

Several specific features of these initial policies about a federal employees fund-raising program were significant. First, under the program, "a single solicitation" would be conducted when the local community had "a United Fund" with an open-door policy toward the admission of recognized and approved national voluntary agencies and when it was the consensus of the local federal employees that they want a United Fund. Second, it allowed for several separate campaigns (two for the Community Chest and the Red Cross if no United Fund existed in a given community; plus one for any recognized national health agencies that did not participate in the local federated campaign; or one combined United Fund (Community Chest and Red Cross campaign) with one other campaign for any recognized separate national health agencies campaign. Third, different time periods were established for the various campaigns with some flexibility, so long as there were not more than three solicitations annually. Provision was also made for employees to contribute to some organizations, like Crusade for Freedom, which did not fall into any of the three major categories of defined groups.[18] Fourth, an administrative structure was established which allowed for the inclusion of the "key man" typically connected with the Community Chest, United Fund, or the American National Red Cross. In addition, fund-raising committees were established as continuing organizations within the federal program. And fifth, there was the clear intention of having the program based on "Acceptability to Givers." This included the preservation of donor's choice, by providing that the gift goes "intact to the agency of his choices" and the option remains with "the individual giver of disclosing his contribution or keeping it confidential."

The new Federal Service Fund Raising Policy did not establish one single federally-run charitable campaign, but it did set down administrative rules for oversight of fund raising in the federal workplace. The response of the United Fund was not positive, however. A resolution of the UCFCA board of directors (December 7, 1956) suggested that the "real potential threat" from the Federal Policy Statement was "not in the loss of contributions but in the fact that the White House has by certain passages in the Federal Policy Statement implied that quotas, use of pledge cards, payroll deductions, and the practical application of what we call 'Fair Share Giving' in some way violates the spirit of what is called 'True Voluntary Giving.'"[19]

In its statement of the issues, the UCFCA said, "This proposed federal policy if it spreads elsewhere could result in a substantial reduction in the services provided by all the agencies that depend largely upon United Funds and Community Chest allocations for operating funds." The UCFCA was already worried that limitations on fund-raising practices which this policy would impose on the campaign could be deleterious to the fund-raising efforts of United Funds generally, if it were to spread to the non-public sector. On February 11, 1957, John S. Hayes, chairman of the UCFCA committee on the federal solicitation plan, wrote a letter expressing these concerns and thus initiated what subsequently became a constant interchange over policies and procedures of the campaign for charitable contributions from federal employees. In any case, Executive Order 10728 of September 6, 1957 established the president's committee on fund raising within the federal service (including both military and civilian employees) with responsibility for monitoring the federal fund-raising program.

The next major step in the development of the current model of a combined federal campaign took place on March 18, 1961. President

John F. Kennedy issued Executive Order 10927 abolishing the president's committee, and transferred responsibility for the federal employee campaign to the U.S. Civil Service Commission in an effort to secure "the broadest possible participation in and support of private voluntary agencies by the federal community." This order also stated that "the Chairman of the Civil Service Commission shall make arrangements for such national voluntary health and welfare agencies and *such other national voluntary agencies as may be appropriate* to solicit funds from federal employees and members of the armed forces." (emphasis added)[20] However, there was still no single federal service campaign, since the united funds and community chests still campaigned in the fall; the National Health Agencies group and the International Service Agencies group in the winter, and some Red Cross chapters in the spring.

The prototype of the modern Combined Federal Campaign was finally established in 1964, with payroll deduction and the idea of one campaign fully implemented in six cities.[21] However, as soon as the chairman of the U.S. Civil Service Commission proposed his experiment with one community, the UCFCA again responded with protest. This time the protest was even stronger: "The UCFCA Board recommends that the local United Funds and Chests in the communities chosen for the demonstrations decline to participate." The problem, according to the UCFCA and local united fund communities, was that the plan was an attempt "to combine agencies that accept the disciplines of United Fund raising as well as the benefits, with organizations that are unwilling to do so . . . , namely, the national health agencies."[22]

In the next few years the UCFCA continued to argue that united funds should be treated as privileged participants in a separate campaign, locally based and run separately from the campaigns of the National Health Agencies and International Service Agencies. Consequently, many united funds actually chose not to join in the newly organized CFC. But campaigners are basically pragmatists, and by 1970 there were approximately 200 locations participating in the CFC. In that year also a major revision was made in the CFC formula. A "dollar base was established for each participating group (UW, NHA, ISA, and Red Cross) equal to the receipts for the preceding year's CFC."[23] According to the United Way, this system allowed distribution of undesignated funds in such a way that it minimized the potential impact of designations. In a letter to the United Way, Robert E. Hampton, chairman of the United States Civil Service Commission, stated: "Overall, Combined Federal Campaigns have proved very successful. . . . CFC has met the wishes of federal managers and employees for one on-the-job campaign and has yielded a significant benefit in economy to the government." Mr. Hampton indicated that a return to separate campaigns was "not feasible from the standpoint of the government," and that the government did not wish to keep the system "as it is with participation at the option of the local United Fund." Hampton stated further that "we have been disappointed at the amount of controversy which the optional method has generated."[24]

Ultimately the UCFCA agreed to endorse a single campaign in the federal establishment, but apparently only so long as it was coupled with a "national and local fiscal and program review process to validate national social and health agencies' requests for funds." The importance of local review for allocations was stated emphatically by UCFCA leadership, stressing that "only provision of local decision making on allocations by a broadly based national committee and broadly based local committee . . . makes possible our full and complete support of the single campaign."[25] This principle of both "a national review process to validate" the requests of national agencies and a local community allocations process remained as a compromise throughout the next decade.[26]

Problems continued while the CFC continued to grow. By 1977 there were already 535 locations, and CFC campaigns raised $78.5 million, with over 5 million federal personnel involved. Four voluntary groups were authorized to participate in the single campaign: National Health Agencies, International Service Agencies, the American Red Cross, and United Way.[27] Among the major criteria for the CFC were the requirements that agencies must be non-profit tax-exempt charitable organizations; they must demonstrate that they are national in scope, "with a national association . . . representative of its constituent parts . . . and earned good will and acceptability throughout the United States, particularly in . . . communities [with] nearby . . . large numbers of federal personnel"; and they would be expected to spend less than 25 percent of the total support and revenues for administration and fund raising.[28]

In the same year a new formula was introduced for determining "distribution of undesignated receipts" based on a minimum of 90 percent of the contributions raised in the previous year's campaign. This total dollar base would then be distributed among the four participating groups in the same percentage ratio as each group's average receipts from the past CFCs had been to "the total receipts reported at the close of these campaigns."[29]

The situation, however, became increasingly volatile during the late 1970s, and by 1979 a series of congressional hearings were held to review the CFC. These hearings were held partly in response to particular problems but also in the context of changes resulting from the Civil Service Reform Act of 1978 (P.L. 95–454). This act reorganized major governmental administrative functions, including some formerly assigned to the old Civil Service Commission. The newly created Office of Personnel Management (OPM) was given responsibility for managing the CFC.

In discussions surrounding authorization of appropriations for newly created government agencies, Congresswoman Patricia Schroeder showed concern about the role of congressional oversight. She suggested that under sunset legislation passed by the House, Congress would be forced "to scrutinize the operations of . . . [the new] agencies on a periodic basis."[30]

In October 1979, therefore, hearings were held by the Subcommittee on the Civil Service of the Committee on Post Office and Civil Service, which was chaired by Congresswoman Schroeder. She called the hearings "because the Combined Federal Campaign is a significant feature of the federal civil service. Virtually, every civil servant is solicited for contributions once a year." In her description of the atmosphere surrounding the CFC Congresswoman Schroeder said: "In calling these hearings, I was aware of the controversy in this area; I was, however, unaware of [the] profound paranoia with which these hearings would be greeted."[31]

The congressional hearings of 1979 addressed questions about the CFC which had been raised with increasing intensity in the preceding decade: which charities should be included in the CFC; how undesignated funds should be distributed; whether undue pressure is exercised in CFC solicitations; and the underlying question of the role of the United Way in the CFC. The hearings were held in a heated atmosphere in which United Way mustered support from its local organizations and leadership across the country, and the alternative funds and supporters of a more open campaign did the same. When the hearings were over, they filled a large printed volume, and rules for the 1980 campaign had been modified significantly, if not sufficiently for everyone, including Congresswoman Schroeder.[32]

Among the modifications in the regulations for the 1980 fall CFC were the following: First, the criteria for eligibility in the campaign were broadened and made more flexible. Agencies could be admitted at the local level, the limit of 25 percent on administrative costs was defined as preferred rather than absolute; and national agencies could be admitted, even if they did not have local chapters throughout the country. Second, all agencies would still have to be admitted through groupings, but a new group of agencies, the National Service Agencies, was established, which would allow for participation of minority organizations such as the National Black United Fund (NBUF). Third, local federal employees were guaranteed a right to serve on the local coordinating groups or committees that had responsibility for deciding which agencies would be admitted at the local level. Fourth, high-pressure tactics and coercion were officially denounced, and the campaign was limited strictly to a six-week period in the fall. And fifth, the old dollar base formula for distribution of undesignated funds on the pattern of old designations, which had favored the United Way greatly, was done away with. For the campaign of 1980–1982, new systems for distribution of these undesignated funds were to be tried experimentally, based on the four old agencies' groups' shares of *undesignated* funds in the past five campaigns.[33]

Sources of Change—Institutional Case Study: The CFC and the Courts

The congressional hearings under congresswoman Schroeder were successful in focusing attention on the CFC and the need for change in the manner in which it was conducted. The hearings were largely the result of an increasing number of legal actions being brought against the federal government in connection with the federal fund-raising campaign. These actions were part of the general questioning of organized charity and the United Way in particular in the 1970s, but they took on a special urgency when related to a campaign in the federal workplace. Since they affected personnel practices of the federal government, they were the charge of the Subcommittee on the Civil Service and therefore the responsibility of Congresswoman Schroeder from Denver, ironically, the declared birthplace of the federated fund-raising idea.[34]

The most pressing and immediate cause of the 1979 congressional hearings on the CFC was undoubtedly the charge of coercion which was raised in the case of *Riddles et al. v. the Department of the Army*, with the background of issues concerning the rights of employees generally raised in relation to the passage of the Hatch Act.[35] Benjamin T. Riddles and other plaintiffs alleged that they had been subject to undue coercion by their superiors in the United States Army Band, in their effort to insure that there was 100 percent participation by the band in the campaign, and that every band member would contribute a defined fair share. Riddles, who testified at the CFC hearings, claimed that the requirement to give in this manner violated his fundamental religious principles, and he also refused to give or to allow others to give for him. He was joined in his suit by a group of sixty-five other members of the Army Band who claimed that they were subject to abuse for not giving, and that their names were publicly posted on a list of non-contributors placed on the unit bulletin board. As Riddles expressed it, "This was the last straw . . . we simply felt that we had to resist such a flagrant example of coercion."[36]

By the time of the hearings, the Riddles case had already been settled by a consent decree (March 1979). This consent decree prohibited one-on-one solicitations and multiple solicitations of an individual, and required that there be protections for individuals from knowledge by his superiors about his giving or non-giving. In addition, the Army was not allowed to establish 100 percent participation goals or to take account of the participation percentages of units. There would be no more lists of non-contributors, and the Department of Defense was to undertake a study of the feasibility of extending those safeguards throughout the military service.[37] But the issue was of concern also to federal civilian employees and, therefore, to the Subcommittee on the Civil Service, which had responsibility for oversight of personnel practices for civilian federal employees.

Constitutional Issues, 1970–1982

If the Riddles case was the immediate and proximate cause for the CFC hearings of 1979, there were also a number of other reasons for them. Even more important perhaps than the *number* of legal actions in this period was the *nature* of the court decisions and the fundamental issues they were raising. Among these issues were First Amendment rights of freedom of speech and the question of equity of treatment, or fairness of government. Both of these issues were raised in connection with the limiting of agency access to the campaign, and they involved fundamental rights guaranteed under our constitution.

The major opening gambit in the round of legal challenges to the CFC had actually begun early in the 1970s, when the United Black Fund (UBF) of Washington, D.C. applied for solicitation privileges in federal installations in the area on January 28, 1971. The UBF request was denied in a letter dated March 31, 1971, on the grounds that the greater Washington area was a "federated community," meaning that a community chest or United Fund in the United Way system was the umbrella group for any local agencies wishing to receive funds from the campaign.[38] In his reply to the rejection of the application, Calvin Rolark, president of the UBF, stated that the "cited regulation was discriminatory" because United Way had been "under attack" in several cities other than Washington for discriminatory disbursement policies, and that the United Givers Fund, or UGF (the United Way of the Washington area), had recently released a task force report of its own which "highlighted" past failures of UGF in meeting certain community needs. Mr. Rolark emphasized the UBF's rights to solicit alongside UGF rather than to supplant it.

Additional correspondence and meetings took place between the chairman of the Civil Service Commission, Robert Hampton, and Rolark, with investigation into the composition of important policy bodies within the allied Health and Welfare Council (HWC), the United Way (UGF), and the Red Cross.[39] It was stated that Hampton analyzed "the percentage of funds allocated by HWC to black persons" and HWC regulations concerning the racial composition of member agency boards. He reported that there was "no genuine evidence" of discrimination, and denied the request of UBF for "injunctive and declaratory relief with respect to charitable solicitation privileges within federal installations." The court held that Hampton was correct in determining that the discrimination charges against groups in the CFC were "not sufficiently well-founded to warrant altering arrangements for participation of local health and welfare agencies in the drive."[40]

Although the decision was based on narrow grounds, it had important future ramifications for the CFC. The court noted that UBF had not applied for solicitation privileges as part of the United Fund (UGF) for 1973, and therefore had not exhausted administrative remedies available to it at that time. This finding put pressure on the UBF to talk with UGF about joining the United Fund campaign before it could come back to the courts.

Second, the court decided it was beyond its jurisdiction to determine whether UGF was "at present" discriminating against black agencies. The court recommended that UGF bring factual evidence of such discrimination to the attention of the chairman of the Civil Service Commission as it had sought to do for the 1971 campaign.

Third, and perhaps most significantly, the court determined that the government did not have sovereign immunity from legal action in this case and could be sued. In addition, the judge agreed that the chairman could make national fund-raising arrangements applicable to all communities. This was a mixed blessing for the United Way, which had always argued for local determination in regard to campaigning. At the same time, the decision put the government on notice that it would need to guard its house carefully against further litigation. Finally, the judge noted that one of the factors which influenced his decision was that the governmental function involved in the CFC was that of a proprietor.[41]

Thus, despite the fact that the case was decided against the UBF, United Way had good reason to be concerned about its many ramifications. The decision left matters of fact which could at any time be decided against the United Way (UGF) and affirmed the principle that the federal government could be sued for actions in local campaigns. But on the other hand, UBF clearly had to try to deal first with the United Way if they ever wished to contest the decision. The result was that by the fall campaign, the UGF, now known as United Way of the National Capital Area, and the UBF had become partners in the first joint campaign for the Washington area.

UBF may have entered into the joint campaign because it would benefit from the partnership arrangement with the United Way, but for concerned black leaders of the BUF movement nationwide, the partnership between a local black fund and a United Way could certainly not have been greeted with any joy.[42] A partnership in the United Way even for CFC purposes meant losing the struggle for independence which black leaders in the BUF movement nationwide considered essential.

In 1976 the National Black United Fund (NBUF) raised the issue of separate fund raising again, moving the case from the local Washington level to the national level. NBUF applied for admission to the CFC as a "national voluntary agency."[43] The NBUF application recognized that "several organizations concerned with health, energy relief and international service had satisfied the criteria for this status" and were thereby eligible to "participate in the CFC in any community in which they are active." While local welfare agencies participated in the campaign by virtue of their participation in a local community, or United Fund umbrella, the national agencies were exempted from this requirement, even though they received designated funds in the community and gave these funds to their members.[44]

NBUF's application for admission to the CFC was denied by the Civil Service Commission on two major grounds: that it did not meet the "national-in-scope" requirement, with chapters in all or most states; and that it did not meet the administrative expense limitation (25 percent or less). Again, following the pattern of the earlier UBF case in Washington, the chairman of the Civil Service Commission suggested that NBUF should make arrangements to participate in the CFC through local United Ways in communities with NBUF chapters.[45]

NBUF brought the case to court, and on July 1, 1980, the U.S. District Court for Washington, D.C. concluded that the national-in-scope and administrative expense requirements of the CFC impaired NBUF's protected interests and did not serve compelling state (that is federal government) interests through the most narrowly tailored manner (i.e., by least limitations on the interests of NBUF). Moreover, the district Court made a precedent-setting decision in relation to another more fundamental issue. It concluded that the denial of national status to NBUF substantially impaired the NBUF's First Amendment rights by prohibiting the organization's protected speech in a "public forum."[46] The potential implications of this decision for all of United Way were enormous, if the doctrine were to spread to the private sector as well. The United Way therefore mobilized quickly and entered the case as an appellant along with the chairman of the Civil Service Commission.

The decision of the District Court was subsequently overturned by the U.S. Court of Appeals for the District of Columbia in a decision on October 20, 1981. The court concluded, first, that the CFC case did not have to be considered as a "public forum" issue, but only involved possible unequal treatment of would-be speakers; and second, that NBUF provided insufficient evidence (or "specific predication") of "how its activities would be affected" (negatively) by affiliation with the United Way. The appeals court determined that it did not have to renew the matter of whether or not "the criteria for 'national' status served compelling state interests through the most narrowly tailored means."[47] In short, the judge did not consider the issue of whether or not exclusion of NBUF was essential to the running of the CFC.

Issues once raised take on a life of their own, however. By the time of the court decision, the issue of NBUF admission to the CFC was moot; changes in the CFC Manual had already allowed for admission of NBUF into the 1981 campaign. These changes were partially the result of the congressional hearings of 1979 but also reflected a response to court decisions being made elsewhere. Specifically, two cases were significant: the first was the *Village of Schaumburg v. Citizens for a Better Environment*; the second was *Big Mama Rag v. United States*.[48]

The Schaumburg case struck down an absolute limitation on the allowable costs of fund raising and administration in relation to agency budgets (the 25 percent used in the CFC as well) and thus forced greater flexibility in determining an acceptable relationship of costs to total expenditures. This decision had an immediate impact on the fiscal eligibility of new or struggling advocacy–public interest groups, and also raised a broader issue. It connected soliciting for charitable causes to the constitutional right of freedom of speech. Thus, it was not surprising that OPM subsequently considered making the CFC a totally designated campaign. Only United Way's "last moment intercession" appeared to prevent this from happening. United Way believed strongly that an all-designation campaign "would . . . do substantial monetary damage to United Way . . . and was in opposition to their strong belief in a citizen-based community allocations process.[49]

The pressure to open up the federal campaign continued through the late 1970s and into the 1980s. On January 19, 1981, another significant decision was made in the courts in regard to the *NAACP Legal Defense and Educational Fund et al. v. Alan Campbell* (director of the Office of Personnel Management), when the NAACP and other complainants won their case about the nature of agencies that could be admitted to the CFC.[50] The issue revolved around the eligibility rules for admission to the CFC, and specifically whether the CFC could limit admission of agencies only to those which provide direct health and welfare services. The judge determined that the condition that a charitable organization must provide "direct services" to persons in the fields of health and welfare was "constitutionally vague in putting limits on First Amendment activity" and was not acceptable. In short, the CFC Manual could not delimit the eligibility to a group of agencies which provided direct services in the health and welfare field, because such a regulation would deprive agencies such as the NAACP-Legal Defense and Educational Fund and other funds (the "Legal Defense Funds" or "LDFs" as they became known) of their protected first Amendments right to free speech, and also of a related right of due process under the Fifth Amendment.

It was not surprising, therefore, that in June 1981 the Office of Personnel Management indicated that it would allow twenty additional national charities to solicit its employees in the fall campaign. Included on the list for the first time were many social action and advocacy litigation oriented organizations, including the Black United Fund, the NOW Legal Defense and Education Fund, and the Native American Rights Fund. These agencies were not admitted wholeheartedly. Simultaneously with the memorandum listing the agencies eligible for the fall campaign, including the new ones, OPM sent another memorandum indicating that ten applications were denied for admission based on "severe departure from the regulations." This memorandum emphasized that the regulations lacked precision, but that because the timing was so tight, there was no choice but to apply the regulations liberally for the 1981 campaign. The director of

OPM plainly stated that although there was considerable question about some of the organizations admitted, "they must be allowed to participate" for 1981; but that some agencies would be reviewed for the next campaign. Among these agencies were those which did not meet the "direct services" requirement, and Planned Parenthood–World Population, on a series of "procedural questions."[51]

Although the rules were interpreted liberally for the 1981 campaign, the June memorandum suggested that the new flexibility might last for only one campaign. However, between the promulgation of the new CFC campaign rules of April 11, 1980 and the campaign of 1981 with its broadened eligibility rules there was a change in the National Administration, and President Ronald Reagan chose Dr. Donald J. Devine to replace Dr. Alan Campbell as director of the Office of Personnel Management. The CFC June memoranda were among his first acts but were followed immediately by other documents reflecting this position.

Among the papers issued before the campaign had concluded was the draft of an Executive Order concerning the CFC. This draft Presidential Order proposed to limit membership in the CFC to organizations defined as actively conducting health and welfare programs and providing direct services to individuals by meeting of one or more common needs within a community. Devine was attempting to narrow the scope of eligibility to the campaign and to do it within the boundaries of the court decision which had stated that the original "direct service" provision was too vague. Thus the proposed Executive Order was to be precise. It stated that "organizations providing counseling or referrals to abortion and abortion-related services" are ineligible for the campaign, as were organizations that carried out political and lobbying activities "on behalf of any person other than itself."[52]

There was an immediate reaction to these regulations. Among the leaders of the opposition was Congresswoman Schroeder, and in the end the proposed order was not issued. Instead, on March 23, 1982, President Reagan issued Executive Order No. 12353, "which essentially reenacted the Kennedy order of twenty-one years earlier," allowing in theory for a broad latitude of interpretation of "appropriate organizations" in the campaign.[53]

The Executive Order of March 23, 1982 laid the groundwork for extensive revisions of the CFC Manual, and the Revised Manual was thereafter published in the *Federal Register* on May 11, 1982. The degree of interest in the content was manifest in the over 6,500 comments on the published notice. According to OPM, most of the commentors (70 percent) were supportive of the proposed regulations, another 7 percent were supportive but had some suggestions for changes, and the majority of the other responses indicated concern that the "proposed regulations were being considered too late in the year" for an effective CFC campaign that fall. Congresswoman Schroeder found the new regulations disappointing because they did not live up to their "advance billing" in openness.[54] When the new regulations were finally issued in the *Federal Register* on July 6, 1982, they contained these basic features:

> The criteria for eligibility were made somewhat more precise, and broadened to include, for example, services which included "Delivery of legal services to the poor and indigent, and defense of human and civil rights."
>
> Local community federated fund raising organizations were to be selected (from among the existing charitable groups in the campaign) to serve as Principal Combined Fund Organizations (PCFOs) to manage the campaign under the direction of the local Federal Coordinating Committee and the Director of OPM.
>
> Designations to specific charities would be encouraged and contributors would be given clear notification that contributions not designated to a particular charity would be *deemed designated* to the PCFO.
>
> There would still be both national eligibility and local eligibility determination for national voluntary agencies, but for a one-year period only, local *unaffiliated organizations* could participate in the campaign. After the one-year grace period, these organizations would have to join in one of the major existing groupings of agences in order to participate in the CFC. (emphasis added)
>
> Federated groups had separate status and did not need to apply under the usual National Agencies requirements. The term, "Federated groups" was defined as including the American Red Cross, United Ways (including local chests and funds connected with the United Way of America), the National Health Agencies, the International Service Agencies and such other federated groups."
>
> Information about the agencies was to be available through CFC brochures, and pledge cards were to provide (mandated but limited) space for designations.[55]

In many respects the 1982 regulations were a compromise between the competing interests of three groups and their constituencies: the big national agencies, the United Way, and the non-traditional advocacy-oriented groups generally outside the mainline charitable stream. In effect the government was attempting to buy time, by proposing that the challenging organizations be allowed in the 1982 CFC, but under circumstances that would change after one year.

The new regulations did permit some smaller advocacy funds with local bases to be funded in the 1982 campaign, but after the year of grace, the price tag for their continuing in the CFC would be high. Local organizations would either have to join with major national groupings (apparently including the United Way as a national federated system) or they would have to form a national organization of their own in order to meet the national scope requirements. With the exception of NBUF for local black funds, there was really no national organization with which local advocacy groups could join, and most of these local groups were too small, too disparate, and with too few resources to support a national organizing effort. Thus, despite appearances of more openness, the new regulations still gave a great advantage to the larger traditional agencies, already affiliated with one or another of the major groupings, and to the United Way system as the gatekeeper for organizations in the community.

The United Way was also the principal beneficiary of the 1982 regulations in another significant respect. In establishing the PCFO as the local federated fund organization with responsibility for managing the campaign, the description for the PCFO was so tailored to the model of a United Way organization that in any CFC community it was unlikely that there would be any other organization better able to qualify for this role.[56] The importance of the managerial role of the PCFO was evident. Under the new rules undesignated funds were to be considered as designations to the PCFO, which could then distribute them to its participating agencies in any manner agreed upon locally. In addition, the managerial role would allow for greater influence on the campaign as a whole, particularly since descriptions of agencies in the brochures were to be limited to about thirty words and donor contribution cards would also only allow listing of a few choices.[57]

Although perhaps no group was entirely satisfied by the compromise regulations of 1982, it is unlikely that anyone could have anticipated the actual outcome of the campaign that fall. Not only was the controversy surrounding the campaign not resolved by the new rules, but actually the conflicts erupted even more violently. In addition, the crossover between the two campaigns, that of the CFC and the United Way "Community Campaign" caused problems for regular local United Way campaigns. Conflict centered around three agencies in particular: the National Right to Life group, the Planned Parenthood organization, and the National Right to Work organization. Problems that emerged in connection with the latter were by far the most serious, and resulted in an official boycott of the campaign by two groups of federal employees—the National Association of Letter Carriers, and the National Treasury Employees Union, as well as by the International Association of Machinists. The latter group had a separate serious impact on regular United Way community campaigns. Many campaigns were already having trouble that fall due to the depressed state of the economy and the related decline in manufacturing. Union boycotts were, however, a real concern, given the importance of contributions by blue collar union members to the United Way campaign.

Over the summer the problem of union opposition surfaced across the country.[58] As a result, the executive committee of the board of governors of the United Way of America was compelled to take action. On September 8, 1982, it passed a resolution requesting that President Reagan clarify and amend Executive Order 12353 in order to limit the campaign to "charitable agencies, providing direct, human care services in the fields of health and welfare, including health research."[59] This was followed a week later by a letter which made explicit the connection between the United Way request and the union opposition roused by the inclusion of the National Right to Work Legal Defense Foundation in the CFC. The letter was signed by Donald V. Seibert, chairman of the board of governors of the United Way of America and chief executive officer of J. C. Penney.[60]

The flood of letters to OPM and the president continued through the fall and winter of 1982–1983, as local United Way organizations and their supporters protested the inclusion of controversial agencies in the campaign generally, and most particularly the National Right to Work organization. Communities like Seattle, which had generally been solid United Way communities, integrally related to the community, had not made their goal that fall for the first time in decades. In Springfield, Missouri, the local United Way board noted that corporate profits were down nationwide, and also added that there was considerable questioning about the United Way campaign by local union members. Indeed, as the memo below indicates, union members did not always distinguish between the CFC and the regular United Way campaign.

October 5, 1982

TO: Officers and Stewards

FROM: Stephen R. Losh, President

Several members have been inquiring as to the legitimacy of accusations being made charging that the United Way is funding the national Right to Work Legal Defense Foundation.

I want you to let our members know that the charges are totally false. I have information from several reliable sources disclaiming the charges. I also have talked to Tom Brown of the United Way here in Springfield and he has assured me that none of the money from the local United Way funds have gone to any organization that is anti-union.

The United Way solicitations will begin in about one week. I urge you to give your fair share and encourage other members in your office or work locations to do the same.

*Memo from: Stephen R. Losh, President, Local 6512
Communications Workers of America
to: officers and stewards
October 5, 1982

Subsequently the board determined that it would be wise to ask local labor leaders to join the United Way board.

Despite all the opposition, the CFC campaign of 1982 was described as a success. Although it reported a slight drop-off in the rate of participation, overall campaign contributions increased by about 6.6 percent and the campaign raised a total of $101,195,318 with something over two million contributors.[61] At the same time, the United Way campaign nationwide increased about 6 percent over the preceding year, but according to a statement made later by the public information officer, Steve Delfin, United Way agencies lost three million dollars during 1982 because of the controversy generated by the CFC.[62] In any case, many United Way campaigns had trouble that year due to problems in the economy as well as the union boycott.

As the CFC got underway in 1982, seven categorical groups were recognized as federated organizations and 115 individual charitable organizations were included in the campaign. This number included the controversial organizations already noted above and others which were not traditional health and welfare agencies, such as the U.S. Olympic Committee and the Sierra Club (one of several environmental agencies). However, even under the seemingly open admissions policy, considerable local option had remained, and an organization like the Native American Rights Fund (NARF) reported that it was turned down by over 210 of the 550 local CFC campaigns to which it applied.[63]

Whether or not the 1982 campaign was defined as a success merely for political reasons was debatable, along with the question of the impact of controversy on the campaign. Some trends, however, seemed evident in looking at the campaigns from 1979 through 1982: the rate of participation had dropped significantly (from 72.8 percent in 1979 to 59.4 percent in 1980, back up slightly in 1981 and down again slightly in 1982 to 57.96 percent), and, concomitantly, the amounts designated to particular agency groups had increased steadily (from

40.1 percent in 1979 to 64.8 percent in 1982). Thus, while the overall amount raised in the campaign increased from 1979 to 1982, the increase was due to larger amounts given by fewer individuals to designated organizations rather than to increased numbers of contributors generally. This was true for 1981 and 1982; however, it was not true for 1980. In that year the amount raised in the campaign actually dropped, going from $60,306,856 (1979) to $59,480,299 (1980) (see below, appendixes G.1–4 for the complete listing of CFC statistics for these years). Since the sharp decrease in the participation rate for the CFC of 1980 preceded the entry of many major controversial agencies into the campaign, it was at least partially due to the changes in the rules and procedures of the CFC, which in that year (following the decision in the Riddles case) explicitly included prohibitions against the use of coercion and discouraged 100 percent participation goals in military installations.

In any case, the campaign of 1982 was at best a mixed success: the rate of participation declined, but only slightly, and the overall amount raised also rose slightly, along with the increased average gift (up about $4.00 from 1981). Since the increased amount raised occurred together with a more open campaign, it suited the groups who favored an open CFC to define the 1982 campaign as a success. They focused on the over 6 percent increase in the amount raised, while underplaying the factor of inflation and the absolute decrease in numbers of individuals contributing, as well as the decreased rate of participation. Since local United Ways generally served as PCFOs and therefore as managers of the campaign, they also would be reluctant to describe the campaign as a complete failure. Indeed, Donald Devine had suggested that there was no drop-off in funds raised in the campaign, precisely because diligent efforts (on the part of the PCFOs) were made to insure its success. Nevertheless the decline in the numbers and rate of participants had to be a source of concern for both OPM and the United Way.

By the time the campaign of 1982 ended, competing principles of organized charity in the workplace were plainly in evidence. First, there was the concept of federated fund raising in the community, based on a commitment to consensus and a centrist philosophy, in contrast to a campaign with open access to a variety of agencies. The notion of consensus represented the rock upon which federated fund raising was founded, and incorporated the strongly held belief that controversial agencies, and the controversy they inevitably caused, were detrimental to community fund-raising efforts. Second, there were the competing groups of powerful national agencies, and the international service agencies, which were excluded from the "local presence" requirement.⁶⁴ Third, there were the principles of an open workplace and freedom of choice for the contributors, which suggested that any 501(c)(3) agency should be able to participate in the campaign, whether or not it was not a health and welfare service agency and whether or not it was controversial. Thus, even though many non-direct service agencies were not in fact admitted under the 1982 rules, in theory the campaign boundaries had now become almost limitless.

In the next few years these issues were to be debated vociferously. the United Way of America found itself caught between the competing demands of its many constituencies and the issues raised by the CFC.⁶⁵ Meanwhile the political aspects of fund raising and allocations were magnified and tied to the agenda of a conservative Republican administration, raising questions about the implications of court decisions for activities in the workplaces of the private sector.

Chapter 6

From Charitable Controversy to Congressional Action (1982–1985)

An all designation campaign would clearly do substantial monetary damage to United Ways, and would stand squarely in opposition to United Ways' belief in the need for a citizen-based community allocation process.

> "Key Issues Confronting United Way in the Combined Federal Campaign," United Way file document, May 5, 1981

A major issue of controversy has been the methods used to distribute contributions that federal personnel contributed but did not designate to particular charities. GAO does not believe that any method OPM prescribes for distributing undesignated contributions will be acceptable to all charities. The charities will not support a method that would cause them to receive a smaller share of undesignated contributions than they currently receive.

> Milton J. Scolar, Acting
> Comptroller General of the United
> States, in a letter to the Honorable Jack Brooks,
> Chairman, committee on Government
> Operations, House of Representatives,
> June 24, 1984

When the Combined Federal Campaign of 1982 was over, almost universal dissatisfaction was expressed about the process. Many new organizations were accepted through the relaxed criteria for national eligibility, but admission at the local level for many of these organizations was far from easy. Unlike United Ways or the International Service Agencies (ISA) group, agencies in the National Service Agencies (NSA) and National Health Agencies (NHA) categories still had to meet double standards of national eligibility and local admission, which required demonstrating "local presence" in each of the community campaigns in which they wished to participate.[1] Since there were over 500 campaigns in the country, this could amount to a considerable effort, without much success.

The "local presence" requirement was particularly difficult for advocacy organizations that did not provide human services directly in a community. Most of these organizations were in the National Service Agencies category. A survey of organizations in this category found that twenty-four NSAs had made a total of 5,612 applications to local CFCs, and were rejected by 1,842 CFCs, or over 32 percent of the campaigns to which they had applied. This rejection figure was conservative, since in many cases the organizations had received no notification of any decision at all. In addition, it was reported that only 48 percent of the appeals made by these agencies resulted in the agency being granted admission at the local level.[2]

Local United Ways complained about controversy harming the campaign, citing particularly the Right to Work Legal Defense fund and union boycotts. They also contacted local leaders, elected officials, and congressional representatives asking for support of the United Way position.[3] While it appeared that the CFC campaign as a whole was not harmed by the conflict, the more open and controversial campaign did seem to have an impact on the United Way system in two major ways. First, the controversy around the new advocacy-type agencies attracted attention to the campaign generally, but more specifically to individual causes involved in the controversy, rather than to the consensus-based federated fund. Consequently, donors were more likely to contribute to particular organizations that attracted them, and whose causes they wished to support. Second, the proliferation of new agencies meant that the donor had a greater choice in designating contributions, which consequently resulted in a decrease in the amount of funds that were available for the pot of undesignated funds as a whole, the pot which was the largest share of funds for the United Way. Thus, no matter what the United Way claimed about the nature of its objections to the 1982 rules for the CFC, the bottom line seemed to be that the middle-of-the-road, consensus mode of federated giving was threatened far more than the overall campaign.

Of the original groups in the CFC prior to 1980 (the NHA, ISA, American Red Cross, and United Way) only one group, the National Health Agencies, could actually have been pleased with the results of the 1982 campaign. That group had increased its contributions by about $2 million, or up 17 percent from the previous year, while the Red Cross agencies in local communities and the United Way both received a smaller amount than they had the previous year, losing nearly $3 million and $85,000 (4.3 percent and 17.9 percent respectively). The ISA group gained, but only a small percentage (1.7 percent) (see appendix G.1). The big gainers in the 1982 campaign were obviously the NSAs, which received greatly increased contributions, going from over $1.7 million in 1981 to slightly more than $7 million in 1982, and the local nonaffiliated agencies group, which grew by over 37 percent, from $956,871 to more than $1.3 million in the same year. Much of this increase was apparently due to the numbers of new agencies admitted, rather than to increases in amounts received by individual agencies. In any case, despite the complaints of many of the groups aligned with the advocacy groups and by Congresswoman Schroeder and Bothwell of the NCRP, the alternative funds, local health agencies, and the more social action NSAs were clearly benefiting greatly from the opening up of the rules. And this was so even though the United Way system retained control of the undesignated funds by serving as the PCFO in at least 90 percent of the local campaigns.[4]

Almost from the time the regulations were promulgated, and certainly from the initiation of the campaign, United Way of America had registered its opposition to the new rules. As already noted, the president of the United Way, Donald Seibert, had written to President Reagan in September 1982, protesting the inclusion of agencies which did not provide direct health and welfare services. Floods of letters also were sent by local United Ways and their supporters (volunteers and member agencies) across the country, as well as by staff of the local CFC campaigns, protesting the rules and documenting their unhappiness with the controversy surrounding the campaign that year. In the naval base at San Diego, for example, officers involved in the coordinating campaign found themselves concerned with new kinds of problems and an unwelcome, more active, interaction with the OPM in Washington over issues related to the admission of new agencies.[5]

It was hard for the administration to ignore the protests of an organization as formidable as the United Way, which could muster elite local leadership in communities across the nation, and which included among its volunteer leadership chief executive officers of many of the nation's leading companies, such as General Motors, Aetna Life and Casualty, the Prudential Insurance Company of America as well as J. C. Penney. At the same time, the conservative Reagan government would be reluctant to provide for support of liberal, politically active advocacy organizations in a CFC under its administrative aegis. Eligibility restrictions had already been proposed in the earlier draft Executive Order in March 1982; these had met great opposition. In January 1983 another parallel effort emerged out of the Office of Management and Budget (OMB) in the form of a proposed revision of Circular A-122, "Cost Accounting Rules for Non Profit Organizations Receiving Grants from the Federal Government."[6] This proposed revision of Circular A-122 caused an even greater uproar than the previous draft Executive Order of March 1982. And although the administration claimed that most of the more than 48,000 responses were favorable, even business organizations objected to it, and the broader, more objectionable limitations on lobbying activities which it contained were omitted when the circular was revised again in November of 1983.[7]

In the meantime, in February 1983, the president issued another Executive Order, which embodied some of the same restrictions for the CFC which had been incorporated in Circular A-122. The similarity of the language and content between Executive Order 12404 and Circular A-122 in fact led Congresswoman Schroeder to ask Donald Devine specifically whether the two documents were related, although she apparently never received an answer to her question.[8] In any case, with the issuance of Executive Order 12404 the issue was again raised openly: should the federal campaign be open to non-traditional agencies and advocacy organizations? To what extent should organizations other than health and welfare agencies be part of a charitable drive such as the CFC, or was charity to be defined only as meaning direct-service organization? Should environmental funds, or organizations such as the Olympic Committee (or an arts fund) be part of the CFC? Since the line was frequently difficult to draw between the various types of organizations which could be considered charitable organizations for the purpose of helping people in trouble, the issue of *how* the decision should be made was also critical. What role should the various branches of government have in this kind of decision, and how much should be left either to the local federal coordinating group on behalf of OPM, or the participating groups themselves—not to mention the special role assigned to the PCFO?

In regard to both the issue of direct health and welfare related service provision, and the question of political advocacy, Executive Order 12404 was unequivocal in its language:

> Eligibility for the Federal Campaign shall be limited to voluntary, charitable health and welfare agencies that provide or support direct health and welfare services to individuals and their families. . . . Agencies that seek to influence the outcome of elections or the determination of public policy through political activity or advocacy, lobbying, or litigation on behalf of parties other than themselves shall not be deemed to be charitable health and welfare agencies and shall not be eligible to participate in the Combined Federal Campaign.

This presidential order appeared to de-emphasize the idea of "national agencies" as a basic eligibility requirement. At the same time however, the order also signaled a return to a more restrictive campaign, and away from more permissive interpretation of President Kennedy's position in establishing the CFC in 1961.[9] Even United Way requested a modification in the order. Donald Seibert, chairman of the Board of Governors of the UWA, again wrote the president, this time expressing support for his "meritorious action" in issuing Executive Order 12404, but also expressing "some concern that one provision of the order (the part dealing with advocacy) might be construed to prohibit even such limited advocacy as is explicitly permissible for charitable agencies under existing 501(c)(3) regulations of the I.R.S."[10]

In order to implement Executive Order 12404, administrative rules and regulations were still needed, and OPM had the responsibility for providing them in a timely fashion before the start of the fall campaign. But, at the same time, there was ongoing litigation before the courts, and, in addition, congressional concerns once again surfaced, first in a series of hearings held by the Subcommittee on Civil Service of the Post Office and Civil Service Committee (Congresswoman Schroeder's subcommittee), and thereafter in a series of hearings held by the Subcommittee on Manpower and Housing of the Committee on Government Operations, chaired by a liberal Democratic Congressman from Massachusetts, Barney Frank.

In the hearings of the Civil Service Subcommittee in March 1983, the CFC was only a small part of a larger concern about federal employee-related issues generally. The subsequent hearings of Congressman Frank's committee, on the other hand, were entirely dedicated to the CFC, beginning on March 24th and concluding with hearings in June and July.[11] Although the reasons for a change in committee jurisdiction were not made explicit, Congressman Frank's committee had a broader legislative mandate, and Barney Frank came from former President John Kennedy's home state, where constituents still might have an interest in preserving Kennedy's idea of the CFC.[12]

In any case, Congresswoman Schroeder appeared to be less willing to compromise on the nature of the CFC. However, since she apparently had by then succeeded in meeting some of the needs of her own constituency, both in the Civil Service and in the health agencies, there may have been less of an incentive for her to lead the fight.[13] At the same time, one of her causes, Planned Parenthood, had taken its struggle to the courts, where it would have a better chance of prevailing than in Congress.[14] Most importantly, there were other more crucial issues facing the Subcommittee on Civil Service, since federal personnel were facing cutbacks and major reorganization by the Reagan administration.

While the hearings continued in the spring of 1983, and regulations were being drafted, the NAACP and other Legal Defense Funds (LDFS) again filed a legal action against OPM, challenging Executive Order 12404 and seeking to prevent the administration from blocking their participation in the next CFC.[15] Indeed, on June 24, 1983, OPM issued proposed new regulations for the campaign which were designed to implement E.O. 12404, and spelled out the criteria for "direct" provision of support of health and welfare services, as well as delimiting the nature of political activity.[16] OPM evidently hoped by this means to answer criticisms in the earlier decision of Judge Gesell which found the direct services requirement "too vague" and therefore in violation of First Amendment rights under the constitution.[17]

In the discussion of these rules in the *Federal Register*, OPM stated: "In the wake of judicial findings that the ground rules of the Combined Federal Campaign inadequately and imprecisely distinguished among kinds of philanthropies, OPM was persuaded a few years ago to experiment with a relaxation of its standards of eligibility for the Combined Federal Campaign." "Pursuant to the President's instructions," OPM was with the current rules seeking to resolve "problems caused previously by the admission of advocacy, legal defense and other groups to the Combined Federal Campaign" . . . [being] careful not to discriminate against any particular viewpoint but to excluded advocacy groups evenhandedly, confining participation in the campaign to traditional health and welfare charities."[18] Some supplemental lobbying activities on the part of health and welfare agencies was also to be allowed.

By August 1, 1983, when the final CFC rules were adopted, the national eligibility rules had been tightened. The "numbers of local combined campaigns in which a national federated group must have at least 10 local voluntary presences" had been increased from two hundred to three hundred. The "number of local chapters, affiliates or representatives an agency must have promoting its campaign if it is to demonstrate national scope" also increased from seventy-five to two hundred.[19] Both of these rule changes clearly favored the larfjger national agencies and federations. OPM claimed that the local eligibility criteria and the direct service requirements were more precisely drawn, but this so-called clarity seemed to be more rhetoric than reality,[20] and also of great benefit to the United Way. At the same time, the national-in-scope requirement was no longer to apply to all organizations, so that local agencies could apply and be admitted to individual community campaigns, even if not part of a local united fund or federation. However, there was a limit to this open admissions policy. Organizations that received less than three thousand dollars in designations in a given year could be dropped from the campaign for the next few years (three maximum).[21]

While the debate continued in the congressional hearings, another court decision was handed down. On July 15, 1983 Judge Green of the District Court for the District of Columbia held that the CFC could not exclude LDFs without violating constitutional rights. The court found that in regard to designated contributions, the directive in Executive Order 12404 "seeking to reinstate a direct service requirement is contrary to plaintiff's first amendment right to engage in charitable solicitation in a limited public forum." The court continued to distinguish between designated and undesignated funds, stating that since regulations had not yet been promulgated for the CFC, the claim related to undesignated funds would be dismissed "without prejudice."[22]

During the congressional hearings in June and July of 1983, an interesting discussion took place. Devine initially equivocated about the actual effect of the latest NAACP-LDF decision on OPM's new regulations, stating that he was consulting with the Attorney General about the effect of this decision and the possibility of an appeal. In his words, he was concerned about the philosophy of the campaign, as well as the pragmatic implications:

> Are we simply to open the Combined Federal Campaign to everyone or can the government set priorities of need. . . . The whole health and welfare apparatus of the Federal government is nothing other than a declaration of choices favoring particular social enterprise at different levels of *public* expenditure.[23] (emphasis added)

This latter statement opened up a real Pandora's box, since the federal government's official position in relation to the CFC had generally been that the government did not wish to make choices among charities in the campaign, but sought only to regulate the campaign sufficiently so as to insure that the campaign was run efficiently and equitably.[24] Indeed, that was behind the reasoning in support of the use of the PCFO for distribution of "undesignated" funds.[25]

The attorneys for the LDFs highlighted the rights of employees to give to the charity of their choice. As one attorney expressed it, "the ultimate beneficiaries in Judge Green's decision are not the plaintiffs or other public-interest organizations; the real beneficiaries are the thousands of Federal employees who contribute to the Combined Federal Campaign [who] will be able to give to the charities of their choice.[26] Thus, the issue was openly defined as one of employee rights.

The OPM and the congressional leadership continued to be bombarded with letters in favor of Executive Order 12404. Much of this correspondence came from United Way agencies and related groups or individuals, who would be likely to gain by regulations favoring the more traditional health and welfare organizations. This gave OPM some of the political clout that it needed, even while articles in the press clearly sympathized with new charities trying to get into the campaign, or remain in. Alternative funds and the supporters of advocacy-oriented charities used the press effectively during these years, building on the often controversial remarks of Donald Devine.[27] The congressional hearings also served to register the concern of Congress about the management of the CFC, and provided a general atmosphere in which the courts could make decisions contrary to presidential orders and in favor of a more open CFC.

The final CFC regulations published on August 1, 1983, differed very little from those proposed earlier in June. Despite the congressional hearings and the recent court decision in the NAACP-LDF case, OPM made it plain that it intended to use the new rules to implement Executive Orders 12353 and 12404, almost ignoring the incompatibility of these two executive orders.[28] It would appeal the NAACP decision, but in the meantime the LDFs would be admitted to the 1983 campaign, and other organizations "similarly situated" would be allowed to participate on an exceptional basis that year. This included Planned Parenthood, which Devine kept trying to keep out on technicalities.[29]

That spring the National Health Agencies case was also decided. Essentially, the court held that there were no grounds for the complaint of the NHAs and no need to change the practice of distributing undesignated funds through the PCFO. The United Way would be the principal beneficiary of this decision, since the criteria for the PCFO were so closely matched to the qualifications of local United Ways. Indeed, Congressman Frank, in an apparent attempt to reach a compromise, later referred to the undesignated funds as going directly to the United Way when he suggested with reference to the NAACP decision of July 15, 1983:

> I note . . . that Judge Green explicitly states that the right of all the eligible groups to receive an equal share of undesignated funds is less than their right to be included in the solicitation for undesignated funds. I believe . . . that it would be perfectly proper for the CFC card to contain a notion to the effect "Any undesignated contributions will be distributed to the local United Way according to the needs of the community." So long as the United Way did not discriminate on racial or sexual grounds.[30]

When the 1983 CFC was completed, the United Way had received a 5.1 percent increase in dollars raised, largely due to control of undesignated funds. The CFC had grown overall, along with a notable increase in the amounts designated, while United Way's share of the designated funds had continued to decrease from the preceding year, going from 46.5 percent (1982) to 44.3 percent (1983) (see appendixes G.1 and 3).

The seesaw of action back and forth between different parts of the government continued. What had started out as a quarrel between charitable partners in the CFC had escalated into a full-scale war involving the three branches of our national government. While congressional interest centered around the functioning and use of the OPM by the President, the NAACP-LDF case went up to the U.S. Court of Appeals for the District of Columbia Circuit. The court again ruled in favor of the LDFs on the grounds that the government's plan, under Executive Order 12404, interfered with their First Amendment rights to free speech in a public forum.[31] Big government, voluntarism, and civil liberties were joined as issues.

Institutional Case Study: The CFC (1984) and the Supreme Court (1985)

On April 13, 1984, new rules were proposed for the CFC which now were vastly different from those of the preceding years. They eliminated the national eligibility process; they removed all restrictions on eligibility for advocacy-type agencies, as well as the 15 percent cap on advocacy activities for health and welfare service agencies generally; and in fact they opened up the campaign broadly. The proposed rules essentially made the CFC into a donor option campaign.

Under these rules, any 501(c)(3) organization that wanted to be in the CFC could apply to local communities on a community-by-community basis, and if it satisfied the "local presence" requirement, the agency would be admitted in each community. At the same time, however, there was to be no requirement for a listing of agencies or publicly printed brochure of the type that had formerly contained the brief thirty-word agency descriptions. The campaign therefore was to be designed as a full designation campaign, based on choice by write-ins, with one notable exception. Any funds which were not actually designated were to be defined as "deemed designated" for distribution by local PCFOs as they saw fit, and therefore in practice as designated to the United Way federation in the community.[32]

The United Way of America was by now deeply involved in promoting donor designation for local United Way campaigns and it was likely to look favorably on these rules with their fail-safe provision for "deemed designated" funds to the PCFO. Indeed, the United Way board of governors subsequently passed a resolution in favor of the proposed rules, while the alternative fund movement, or at least its leading spokesperson, Robert Bothwell, was upset by them.[33] The plight of these agencies was described in the press by such headlines as "Minority Charities Could Lose $2 Million".[34] NCRP helped to publicize the situation, and an official of the organization was widely quoted as saying:

> On the surface these rules sound pretty good. Employees can write in the name of nearly any charity they want to get their money. But the problem of charities under this system is similar to the problem of political candidates who run a write-in campaign: unless you have a massive name identification, you are going to get very few votes or dollars . . . less well established, smaller, minority charities will be devastated.[35]

As dramatic as the new rules were, they had not come out of the blue. On February 17, 1984, the U.S. Court of Appeals for the District of Columbia had affirmed the District Court's decision in favor of the LDFs, agreeing with Judge Green's opinion that excluding these organizations interfered with their rights of free speech under the First Amendment. This decision in essence forced the OPM to open up the campaign to this group of agencies and other organizations "in similar situations".[36] Many United Ways were already prepared with a donor option plan which allowed them to cope with an open campaign. In many local CFC communities also either cancer or heart agencies were already under the federation umbrella, so that the local United Way would be credited with designations to these agencies (see below, chapter 9).

Hearings were held again in the spring of 1984 by the Congressional Subcommittee on Manpower and Housing of the Committee on Government Relations.[37] The CFC was also the subject of discussion in the Senate, where specific recommendations regarding the CFC were incorporated in the Report of the Committee on Appropriations. These recommendations addressed the major complaints of other groups and urged that some listing of agencies involved in the campaign be required, along with a brief description of the agency services.[38]

In the voluntary sector, the United Way now stood relatively alone in support of the proposed new rules for the CFC of 1985. The nontraditional agency groups, and other allied organizations, expressed fears that the campaign would work against them and that the campaign would be more difficult to run with the wide-open admissions policy, and, in particular, the lack of a list of agency description.[39] Even the International Service Agencies and the National Health Agencies spoke against the proposed regulations. James A. Fitzgerald, speaking for the National Health Agencies made the problem explicit when he stated, "We must face the fact that under proposed CFC regulations the PCFO is the surrogate fundraiser for the rest of us."[40]

At the 1984 hearings, Pat Schroeder complimented the OPM on opening up the campaign, but said the new changes did not go far enough and would eventuate in a "much worse campaign" than that of the previous year. She asked that local eligibility requirements be eliminated and suggested that the campaigns be run entirely by federal employees.[41] The reply to her suggestions appeared later in some detail when the final CFC rules were promulgated in the *Federal Register*, stating that "the President and OPM have long decided that Federal officials . . . should have no role whatsoever in deciding how gifts are distributed. The CFC should be operated on the principle of full-designation."[42] This appeared to represent a reversal of the statement made earlier by Donald Devine in the congressional hearings in the summer of 1983.[43]

The final set of new rules was printed in the *Federal Register* on August 16th with only a few changes, while the administration was still "evaluating its avenue of review of decision of the Court of Appeals, and weighing whether and how to pursue them." The OPM argued that the court orders had virtually eliminated meaningful eligibility criteria short of recognized status under 26 U.S.C.

501(c)(3). The CFC was to be "guided by the principle of self-certification" for agencies which were not affiliated with federated groups but sought admission at the local level.[44] Where a local federal coordinating committee elected not to provide a list of agencies itself, the local PCFO would provide the list of all organizations that received funding from the preceding year's CFC. This meant including a brief (twenty-five-word) description. The United Way stated that the new rules reflected "a significant unprecedented shift of the basic philosophy, structure and organization of the Combined Federal Campaign." United Way of America was "on balance" prepared to move ahead with the new rules, which still left United Ways in the favored position for being the PCFO.[45]

The campaign by most standards had to be judged a great success. The percentage of participants increased (if only slightly) from the previous year, and the number of contributors increased from 2,337,223 to 2,414,254.[46] More notably, the total amount raised increased by 11.25 percent to $122,670,076, due to the larger amounts given by those who contributed, while designations increased from around 67 percent to over 74 percent in one year. Dollar amounts to United Way as a part of the campaign, however, only increased by 1.7 percent, while the National Health Agencies and the International Service Agencies registered increases of 10.7 percent and 22.8 percent respectively.

The alternative funds and advocacy groups had done their job well, printing brochures and taking advantage of the publicity generated by the media to get their message across to federal workers. The National Service Agencies (which incorporated most of the LDFs and national social action groups), the local non-affiliated agencies, and the new category of "write-ins," all registered significant increases. The NSAs continued their large increases of the preceding four years, and received $9,980,921 (up 19.9 percent from the preceding year), while the local non-affiliated agencies were given $3,233,524 (up over 68 percent from the preceding year) and the new write-in group received over $3 million. Although no listing was distributed by the OPM, in 1984 the write-in category apparently included local animal leagues and humane societies, with programs of churches among the frequent recipients.[47]

The United Way may not have been happy, but by now the evidence was clear: an open campaign, with more choice, certainly brought in more money, but not necessarily to the United Way system. The United Way, however, was, as always, adaptable. United Ways were now officially reporting all the monies raised in United Way–managed CFC campaigns as part of the amount of their total campaigns. Inclusion of money going to other designated organizations made the United Way campaign look more successful than it was, and it established the principle that money raised for the CFC was indistinguishable from United Way money. As more than one United Way professional expressed it, "We do the work anyway."[48] Nevertheless, this idea that United Way funds and CFC contributions were one total pot of monies was not entirely in keeping with earlier statements of Aramony and others that the CFC was *not* a United Way campaign.[49]

It took almost a year, but on July 2, 1985, the Supreme Court of the United States finally handed down a decision on the case of *Cornelius v. NAACP Legal Defense and Educational Fund*. The court found in favor of the administration.[50] In a court which was plainly divided along ideological grounds, the conservative majority ruled that the exclusion of LDFs and related organizations did not violate First Amendment rights, since "the CFC, rather than the federal workplace, is the relevant forum." The court argued that unlike the federal government itself, the CFC could be defined as a non-public forum. Moreover, the government's decision to exclude the respondents from the CFC appeared to be reasonable in light of disruptions caused by controversial agencies. In a non-public forum, such reasonableness was an adequate standard for judging the exclusion to be permissible. The court left open one major issue, and that was the question of whether "the purported concern to avoid controversy excited by particular groups" concealed a bias against the viewpoint of the particular speakers excluded. On this question, the court remained neutral and stated that "respondents are free to pursue this contention on remand."[51]

Despite the open-ended question of "concealed bias," the Supreme Court decision was a blow to the open access movement in the CFC and left the administration with a powerful weapon. While the government did not have to run a closed campaign, our nation's highest court had ruled that it was *permissible* to do so on legal and constitutional grounds. The OPM and President Reagan had won a major victory in the conservative battle to suppress social action and advocacy activities in the voluntary sector. In fact, after the Supreme Court decision, the administration made an attempt to change the rules for 1985, and once again exclude the advocacy groups and nontraditional charities from the CFC. At the last minute, on August 22, new rules were promulgated to exclude these groups and favor the direct-service traditional health and welfare agency groups.[52]

The war, however, was far from over. While the LDFs were regrouping for litigation in the lower courts, congressional concern mounted. "A bipartisan array of legislators" with legislative appropriations power over OPM was mobilized by a coalition of non-profit organizations opposed to the Supreme Court decision.[53] They argued successfully that although the Supreme Court had ruled that the OPM *could* exclude the action-oriented groups from CFC, nonetheless, *it did not have to do so*. Such influential senators as Mark Hatfield, chair of the Senate Appropriations Committee, were now involved and openly committed. Senator Hatfield wrote to the OPM, saying, "The CFC is too important to become a political football, and your decision to implement the 1984 regulations (will) help to avoid turning it into one."[54]

An opportunity to prevent the rule changes presented itself most fortuitously that summer at the confirmation hearings of the proposed new director for OPM, Constance Horner. The forces for an open CFC used the hearings to discuss the CFC, expressing their opposition to implementing any new rules which would limit eligibility for the campaign.[55]

Victory for the non-traditional charities and donor choice was finally assured when the chair of the hearings, Senator Theodore Stevens, a Republican conservative from Arkansas, sided with the majority, and warned Horner that it was "too late to change the rules of the game" for the 1985 campaign. Horner was confirmed, and on August 19, OPM announced that the 1985 CFC would be run under the old 1984 rules, thereby allowing for an open eligibility process. Subsequently the Senate Committee on Appropriations congratulated the OPM for its wise decision. Nevertheless in the report accompanying the Treasury, Postal Service, and General Government Appropriation Bill, further protection was included to insure that this decision remained in effect throughout the entire 1985 campaign:

> To avoid any disruption in the timely orderly implementation of an effective 1985 fall campaign, the Office of Personnel Management is directed to operate the campaign accordingly, and to postpone making any changes to applicable regulations until completion of this year's Combined Federal Campaign.[56]

The trend of the previous years continued. The campaign in 1985 raised approximately $130,000,000 and rates of participation rose slightly as amounts designated continued their increase.[57] However, although the overall amount raised was about 6 percent higher than in previous years, United Way's total receipts were reported down by 6.7 percent. The amount of designations to agencies not under the United Way umbrella increased, while designations to United Ways themselves declined. In that year contributions to the National

Service Agencies, the general category used for the more activist, advocacy organizations, also declined, while the local non-affiliated agencies group and the category of write-ins both grew dramatically, up a reported 173.8 percent to $8,853,000 and 24.2 percent to $11,739,000, respectively. Complete nationwide listings of agencies in these two categories were not made publicly available, but from the increased amounts raised, it was evident that choice influenced the way donors contributed. By comparison, the United Way system as a whole raised $2,330,000 (up approximately 9 percent from the previous year), including amounts raised through CFC campaigns.[58]

Not only United Way had reason to be unhappy with the results of that year's CFC. It appeared that as the number of designations grew, the amounts contributed to local organizations and to popular causes, such as selected health agencies, also grew, while the amounts given to organizations in the national alternative funds movement, and activist groups in the NSA category, began to show some decline. As United Way could probably have told everyone earlier, in a competitive fund-raising drive, locally known "pet" charities and emotionally appealing causes, such as cancer and heart, or church-related programs, are likely to benefit from what becomes essentially a local popularity contest. In that kind of campaign, the United Way, with its more amorphous image, was likely to show continued losses in designation, but national activist groups would also suffer from lack of broad-based appeal, and, indeed, ironically from lack of local presence. In short, in United Way terms, "large gains in 'market share' were achieved by local non-federated agencies, 1985 write-in agencies, and 1984 write-in agencies," which altogether in 1985 gained 10.6 percentage points in the total CFC, or 13.4 percent of the designated portion of the campaign. The United Way, the NHAs, the ISAs, and the NSAs (which were the groups defined by the OPM as federated groups), all lost "market share" in 1985, as the nationwide campaign became more localized. Average gifts also continued to increase in amount (from $50.81 in 1984 to $53.05 in 1985).[59]

The increase in designations to the non-federated groups was a complex phenomenon. To begin with, the amounts of contributions going to the category of local non-affiliated agencies was inflated over the previous years as an almost-accidental result of the way that the rules concerning the listing of agencies worked. Under the rules of the 1985 campaign, either the local federal coordinating committee, or the PCFO, had to issue a listing of agencies for the CFC, and this list was to include all agencies funded in the previous campaign. Over 90 percent of local CFCs printed brochures with PCFOs, while some alternative funds and activist organizations also did so separately.[60]

The result of this ruling was that any agency with write-in funds in one campaign moved into the category of local non-affiliated agencies the next year, and out of the category of write-ins. This process remained in place under the mandated continuation of the old 1984 rules. If continued indefinitely, it would certainly result in an unwieldy list of agencies, including some admitted by "self-certification" that groups on both sides would consider of dubious quality. On the other hand, it appeared also that some branches of the American Heart Association and the American Cancer Society withdrew from federations, receiving funds as local non-affiliated agencies.[61]

Meanwhile, the NAACP-LDF litigation against the CFC had not been concluded. It had gone down to the lower courts for further consideration on the issue of "concealed bias," leaving the threat to both sides that another court decision might be worse. Therefore, congressional concern continued actively. The CFC also was not problem-free administratively, as a series of reports, written at the request of the Congressional Committee on Government Operations had demonstrated.[62] Administrative costs were rising, along with the broadening of choices and increased numbers of write-ins. Although these costs were shown to be a relatively modest amount, in 1985 they amounted to 4.7 percent of the total raised, in contrast with the under 3 percent they averaged in the years before 1980.[63]

During this period advocacy groups involved in the NAACP case asked for an injunction against the CFC on the grounds of hardship caused by viewpoint discrimination. On May 30, 1986, Judge Green of the U.S. District Court, District of Columbia granted a preliminary injunction enjoining the OPM from excluding these groups from participation in the 1986 campaign, and stating that there would be further hearings starting on September 24, 1986.[64]

Before these hearings were held, Congress took action which would render any injunction moot. An amendment was developed by Congressman Steny H. Hoyer in the Treasury, Postal Service and Government Appropriations Subcommittee of the House Appropriations Committee, and a parallel action was taken in the Senate Appropriations Committee by chairman Senator Mark Hatfield, a liberal Republican from Oregon. The two "amendments" were reconciled and passed into law quickly as part of the Supplemental Appropriations Bill for Fiscal Year 1986, as a definitive response to further the OPM moves to change the rules of the campaign for that fall. The amendment which was finally incorporated as part of the Supplemental Appropriations Bill for Fiscal Year 1986 stated:

> None of the funds appropriated by this Act or any other Act shall be used for preparing, promulgating or implementing new regulations dealing with organization participation in the 1986 Campaign other than repromulgating and implementing the 1984 and 1985 Combined Federal Campaign regulations, unless such regulations provide that any charitable organization which participated in any prior campaign shall be allowed to participate in the 1986 campaign.[65]

Congressman Hoyer's responsiveness to the pressure from the advocacy groups was not hard to understand from a political point of view. Hoyer came from Prince George's County, Maryland, a largely minority district, with a strongly activist, Democratic constituency. Numbers of his constituents were also employees of the federal government. His constituents were likely to be interested in an open campaign and particularly in non-traditional or minority-oriented charities such as the Black United Fund, the NAACP-LDF, and the United Negro College Fund. Even the United Negro College Fund, hardly a controversial organization, might not qualify for eligibility of the CFC were to be limited to health and welfare service-providing agencies only. As evidence that the Reagan administration might attempt to do so again surfaced, another security measure was built into the 1987 Appropriations Bill. To insure that there was no gap between campaigns, "Hoyer 2" covered both the 1986 and 1987 fiscal years.[66] The OPM had been threatening to hold off start of the 1986 campaign until the original "Hoyer 1" Amendment would expire at the end of fiscal 1986 (September 30, 1986), and thus the new action, covering both Fiscal 1986 and Fiscal 1987, was clearly needed.

Congressional action then served to keep the heat on the administration and prevent any changes in the rules while the case remained "active" in the lower courts. There was also some feeling that with the departure of the more ideological and controversial Donald Devine, compromise might become more possible. Despite difficulties, the CFC was after all raising new money at a time when other sources of money, public and private, were drying up. The implication was not lost on the United Way or other actors involved in the CFC, and efforts were intensified to arrive at a compromise which would protect the interests of the more powerful parties. These included the traditional health and welfare agencies and the United Way, as well as some of the larger national advocacy groups and alternative funds such as the BUFs, while excluding numerous little organizations in the local community admitted under the self-certification procedures and write-in categories of the CFC. Otherwise, as one of the leaders of the alternative fund movement expressed it: "The whole campaign is in danger of exploding and caving in under itself."[67]

Part IV

The Corporation and the United Way

Introduction to Part IV

DESPITE the efforts of a conservative national administration (or possibly in reaction to it), in the years 1980–1985, vast changes took place in the fund-raising campaign of the federal workplace. In effect, the CFC in those years became open-ended, and turned into a marketplace, in which popular emotion-laden causes, such as health related organizations, or animal serving programs, competed for funds with civil rights advocacy groups and traditional social welfare agencies in the local community. The United Way meanwhile increasingly served as the administrator of a campaign in which it was actually receiving a smaller share of the total contributions each year. Moreover, similar although somewhat less dramatic challenges and changes were occurring, parallel to the CFC, in local public sector campaigns in cities, counties, and most notably in the State Employee Federated Appeal, known commonly as SEFA.

The story of the CFC has focused on the intertwining of two major sectors in American life, the voluntary sector and the government or "public" sector. Indeed, the CFC presents the anomaly of big government increasingly involved in defending, protecting, and defining a role for organized charity, presumably based on its commitment to more voluntarism and less government. But there is a third sector involved in American life, and that is the sector which defines itself as most private—the business or corporate sector. Although the power of the corporate backing of the United Way was occasionally invoked openly in the events, for the most part corporate leaders remained outside the fray, as the social welfare agencies and the government fought the battle.

The next question therefore seems to be, To what extent do the issues in the government workplace relate to organized charity in the private sector and more specifically to fund raising in large corporations? Is the model of the public sector campaign applicable to organized charity in the private sector and more specifically to fund raising in large corporations? And if it is not, what is the nature of the difference between a fund-raising campaign in the private, profit-making sector, as contrasted with that in the public workplace?

The answer to these questions concerns fundamental issues in the mythology of corporate America and the United Way. It also involves consideration of the pragmatic interests of the various constituencies of the United Way, including the corporation, its stockholders, employees, and management; the social agencies; community residents; and American society more broadly.

The argument in this section begins with the history of corporate involvement in philanthropy, and with federated fund raising in particular. The discussion focuses on corporate philanthropy in relation to the United Way, and the implications of that relationship, in the context of a turbulent environment.

Chapter 7

Corporate Responsibility and the United Way

The Bell System fulfills its primary obligation to society by providing high quality tele-communications services at reasonable costs. In addition, it has a corporate citizen's responsibility to be concerned for and to act in support of the well-being of the communities in which it operates. One way in which it fulfills these obligations is by contributing financial and other material support for charitable, educational and general welfare programs which benefit these communities.

AT&T Contributions Report, 1981

Prudential supports the United Way in many ways. In addition to an outright corporate grant from The Prudential Foundation, we conduct a 'Fair Share' campaign among employees. We also lend key executives to United Way so that these loaned executives can share their talents and expertise with the organization during the busy weeks of the annual campaign and throughout the year.

The Prudential Insurance Company of America
Newark, New Jersey

THE peculiarly American phenomenon of business involvement in community charity developed together with the growth of the voluntary sector in America in the late nineteenth and early twentieth centuries. Business interests were identified with support of the YMCA as a residence for workers on the railroads even before federated fund raising emerged. The move toward federated fund-raising efforts, however, involved other motivations as well. By the turn of the century, interests of local businessmen in coordinated, more efficient support of local charities began to coalesce, frequently through chambers of commerce in their community.[1] This early stage of exploration in coordinated welfare efforts and joint fund raising reached a high point with the formation of the Cleveland Federation for Charity and Philanthropy (1913), later dubbed the first "modern" federated fund-raising organization.[2]

The institutionalized connection between corporate contributions and community charity accelerated greatly during World War I, following the rise of the corporation in American life. In connection with the war effort, companies increased their giving to national voluntary social welfare agencies, particularly the American Red Cross and the national board of the YMCA, along with other patriotic fund drives, which included the war chests. Corporations, however, were wary of stockholder opposition to charitable donations, and some utilized a "Dividend Plan" particularly for giving to the Red Cross, by means of which stockholders signed off their dividends as gifts.[3] During this period it was not unusual for companies to make a joint contribution to a chosen charity in the name of their employees and the company, and by the end of the war, direct giving by the corporate "entity" had become an established practice.[4] When the war ended, the war chest in Rochester, New York, became the first of the local war funds to convert to a community chest under the influence of the president of Eastman Kodak.

The connection between business and fund raising continued to develop in the 1920s, as fund raising itself became a more businesslike activity. Apart from the community chest movement, fund raisers generally began to use more formalized techniques, and identified themselves as a separate group of professionals. In the prosperous era of the twenties, fund raising thrived and fund-raising firms were formed, crossing occasionally with social workers, through interaction in community chest campaigns. Both groups were involved with voluntary agencies, and chest fund raisers apparently learned from the organized efforts of the professional firms.

Although there was some permissive state legislation passed in response to the fund-raising realities of World War I, the issue of the corporate gift remained unresolved. Corporate officers continued to worry about stockholders' concerns, and contributions to local agencies such as the YMCA or a local hospital were reported as business expenses for the "direct benefit" of the corporation and its employees.[5] Although corporations were now required to pay income taxes, they were not allowed to take income tax deductions for contributions, even after the 1917 tax law allowed individual givers to do so.[6]

The pattern of reporting corporate contributions as business expenses, related to employee needs in the community, continued throughout the 1920s and persisted thereafter. The narrow interpretation of "direct benefit," formulated by the English courts in 1883, continued to determine the parameters of corporate giving, and influenced legal interpretations of the rights of stockholders. However, during this period, corporations began to ask more questions about the conditions of their giving, and expressed increased interest in the idea of income tax deductions for their contributions, in line with federal income tax policies favoring the contributions of individuals. Meanwhile, the decision in the Corning Glass case (1929) established a broader interpretation of contributions as business expenses, when the gift was to a particular health and welfare service agency, in this case a hospital. Shortly thereafter, in the American Rolling Mill Co. case, a contribution by a company to a civic improvement fund was also held deductible as a business expense; but it was *not* held to be allowable as a tax deductible charitable donation.[7]

Thus, while corporations were now generally in the practice of considering contributions as allowable business expenses, contributions to the local community chest remained in a more ambiguous position than those to other charities. Chest concern about corporate giving was already signaled with the undertaking of the Croxton study completed in 1930, and by 1931 (after the two cases noted) the different position of the chest versus other charities was state explicitly:

> It will appear that corporations must be careful to *designate* the particular agencies in the chest to which they wish their contributions made if they are to deduct their contributions [as business expenses] on income tax returns.[8]

By 1934, the United States Supreme Court had ruled that a corporate contribution to a community chest was not deductible as a business expense,[9] and thereafter chests and corporate leaders rallied their forces to lobby effectively for a change in the tax laws (1935).[10] Thus, starting in 1936, deductions for corporate contributions were allowed —up to a maximum of 5 percent of the corporation's pre-tax income.

Although figures for this period are not considered complete, it does appear that corporate giving did not show any sharp decline in the early depression years (1929–1932). Thereafter the amounts raised by community chests from all sources did decline, from $78.7 million in 1932, to a low of $69.7 million in 1934. By 1936, however, the overall amounts raised by chests rose to $81.7 million and in the next decades continued to rise.[11]

In the years 1936–39, with more accurate records being kept, corporate giving was reported to have hovered around $30 billion nationwide. An analyst of this period noted the gap in chest data during the depression years (1931–33), but reported that corporate giving increased from an estimated $16.1 million (331 chests) in 1929, to an estimated $28.5 million (452 chests) in 1937.[12] Corporations evidently wished to maintain the voluntary sector during the Roosevelt era and, after the passage of favorable income tax provisions in 1935, once again seemed to view community chests as a prime means for doing this. Thus, community chests garnered nearly all reported tax deductible corporate contributions during the years 1936–39. This fact ultimately caused tensions in the relationship between corporations and chests, and led to the attempt by some corporate leaders to develop a formula for giving which would provide for a more equitable distribution of the burden.[13] At the same time, however, chest staff also attempted to insure that any formula would allow for more incentives for giving.

Encouraged by rising profits and high tax rates, corporate giving flourished once again in World War II. In addition, workplace solicitation provided generous support from employees for the numerous war chests, fund drives, and war bond collections. By the end of the war, workplace solicitation had been widely instituted and, subsequent to the mandating of additional federal withholding taxes in 1943, payroll deduction for employee giving became a recognized phenomenon.

At the end of the war the changing industrial scene led to a brief period of intense labor unrest, and to passage of the Taft-Hartley Labor Law (1947). The more conservative elements in the CIO prevailed, and took leadership in the auto industry, joining with corporate leaders in support of the United Fund model developed in Detroit in 1947–49. One federated campaign was convenient for all involved. It meshed well with conditions of the Taft-Hartley Law concerning limitations on solicitation in the workplace, and the requirements that such limitations be value neutral. Definitions of acceptable workplace fund raising thus were connected to limitations on the activities of other organizations during work time, including union organizing as well as competing charitable activity in the workplace.[14]

The united fund movement spread rapidly during the 1950s as chest professionals worked energetically, and corporations welcomed the idea of instituting one fund drive for all causes. Limitations on fund raising became attached to National Labor Relations Board (NLRB) interpretations of no-solicitation rules for the workplace, and were delineated as one of the few exceptions to these rules.[15] Rhetoric, however, was once again different from reality. A study of corporate giving in 1952 noted that when united funds were not successful in bringing branches of the national agencies, such as Red Cross or the Cancer Society, under their umbrella, corporations often formed their own in-plant federations to deal with the situation. By dividing monies raised themselves, these company employee federations enabled employers to avoid the necessity of considering separate workplace access to chests and health agencies not incorporated in the same fund-raising drive.

During this period, corporate philanthropic policies and practices generally underwent considerable reappraisal and modification. In 1953 the landmark decision of the New Jersey Supreme Court in relation to a gift to Princeton University loosened the narrow interpretation which had been used concerning direct benefit and allowable business expenses. The decision in the *A.P. Smith Mfg. Co. v. Barlow* case paved the way for a far broader view of corporate self-interest, and set a precedent which led specifically to increased giving by companies to educational institutions.[16] Moreover, early in the same decade (in the high profit–high tax years of 1950–53) 620 new foundations were established, and by 1965 the number grew to 1,472 foundations, many of them established during the 1950s.[17] The device of a foundation afforded individuals and companies additional protections from taxes, and flexibility in allocation of their funds. Although there were abuses reported over the years in the organization of foundations, eventually the development of the corporate foundation led to a separate force of corporate contributions experts within the corporations with new ideas about the distribution of corporate contributions.[18]

From the viewpoint of chest-corporate relations, the major phenomenon of the 1950s certainly had to have been the turn-around in the balance between the corporate gift and the employee contribution to the fund-raising effort. As noted earlier, in 1956 for the first time corporate support became a smaller percentage (38.1 percent) of the total raised by united funds and chests than support from employees (39.6 percent).[19] Just about the same time the federal government, under Dwight D. Eisenhower, made its first real effort to put some order in the apparent chaos of the peacetime federal workplace campaign, where multiple appeals competed for employee dollars. In any case, the pattern of increasing shares of employee support and a diminishing proportion of corporate funds in the chest campaign continued through the 1970s. It then appeared to have stabilized at the end of that decade when the percentage of corporate support dropped to 25 percent and corporate employee giving reached approximately 50 percent of the total amounts raised.

The conflicts of the 1960s resulted in considerable pressure on national corporations to pay more attention to the needs of minorities and disadvantaged urban groups. Although United Ways continued to be the primary beneficiary of business contributions even after the 1960s, thereafter corporations began to increase their funding in other arenas, including civic and urban/community causes, in addition to education and the arts.[20] A potential rival for business involvement was created with the founding of the Urban Coalition (1968), but this organization never developed into the powerful force that seemed possible when it was started.

Overall, health and welfare organizations continued to receive an increasing percentage of total corporate contributions through the early 1970s. Health and welfare organizations received 42 percent of all corporate contributions in 1972, and as part of that trend federated organizations received 26.6 percent. However, from the United Way point of view, there were some disquieting signs. Corporate contributions as a whole had decreased relative to a number of other significant measures—as a share of the total of all contributions in America (including individual giving), and also as a percentage of corporate pre-tax income.[21]

After years of steady increases, in 1970–71 corporate contributions declined, both in absolute dollars and as a proportion of pre-tax income. The decline was particularly dramatic in 1970, when corporate contributions dropped to $797,000,000 (1.06 percent of net income before taxes) in comparison with the year before (1969), when contributions had been reported at $1,055,000,000 (or 1.22 percent of net income before taxes). The percentage of corporate giving to profits dropped to around 1.00 percent in 1972, although total dollars contributed went back up to over $1 billion.[22]

The decline in corporate contributions occurred during a time when most of the country's traditional institutions were under attack, and after serious questioning of corporate tax practices and corporate foundations in congressional hearings. These hearings preceded the passage of the Tax Reform Act of 1969, which placed severe restraints on the operations and tax status of foundations, including corporate foundations. Thus, the bottom line of costs of contribution, rather than disillusionment with the functioning of the voluntary sector, was probably the major reason for the decline in corporate giving, although the general atmosphere and loss of institutional confidence may have compounded the problem. Moreover, this was occurring at the same time as the government was beginning to question its own expanded funding of programs in the voluntary sector. In addition, rising costs were beginning to be a factor, since the private sector could not increase its income directly by "hiking up" prices to match inflation, while trends in individual giving were also beginning to shift downward.[23]

These events resulted in concern about future support for the voluntary sector and eventually led to the creation of the Filer Commission. In that vein, commission findings highlighted the fact that of 1.7 million corporations filing an income tax return in 1970, only 20 percent had claimed a charitable deduction, only 6 percent gave over $5,000, and nearly 50 percent of corporate giving that year came from fewer than 100 large companies.[24] Studies for the commission also documented decreasing trends in absolute levels of individual giving. By 1972 the downward trend of the relative share contributed by individuals was clear after increased use of the standard deduction in income tax returns.[25] Finally, the commission also noted the increased percentage of support being provided for voluntary agencies by government funds relative to other sources, a trend which the commission suggested was detrimental to the future of voluntarism in our nation. Indeed, in this case, it appeared that a Republican administration and corporate leaders had common cause: neither wanted the government to increase its influence over the voluntary sector.

The Aramony Era Begins

The reorganization of the national United Way in the early 1970s was designed to increase corporate leadership on the UWA board, with renewed attention to the role of corporations in every aspect of the United Way. William Aramony was chosen as national executive because of his evident energy, but the choice certainly reflected the fact that Aramony, more clearly than most other United Way executives at the time, recognized that strengthening the relationship between corporations and the national organization had become the essential ingredient for the survival of the United Way system. This was true, of course, because corporations and their employees provided major financial support, but also because corporate leaders provided the authority which enabled local United Ways to walk with confidence in the halls of power, and make an impact on public policy at the local, state, and national level. Indeed, the need for a powerful national voice for United Way in dealings with the federal government was one of the reasons for the reorganization of the national organization and removal of professionals from board positions.[26]

As they had in past decades, after 1970 corporate leaders continued to speak out on United Way policies at volunteer leaders conferences and elsewhere, and to be available for critical meetings where their presence added weight to the deliberations. They made phone calls and sent letters in support of the United Way position when this was needed, as in the case of the CFC (see above, chapter 5). And as corporate involvement became both more critical and more difficult to maintain, Aramony spent increasing amounts of time in cultivating corporations, and in maintaining their commitment to United Way, through such programs as the National Corporate Development Program and through more informal contacts.[27]

By 1980, however, the environment around the United Way was undergoing a kind of metamorphosis. The American work scene was changing dramatically, from a predominantly blue collar, unionized, and heavily industrial workplace, to a service-oriented world with low-paying jobs, punctuated by some high technology industries with highly educated workers. There were serious questions about the future of corporate America, as large industrial sites such as automobile factories and steel plants closed their doors, and multinational corporations increased in significance. These changes resulted in loss of jobs, and were bound to have an impact on the United Way system as well, testing the commitment of business to continue the relationship with the local funds, and the ability of the United Way system to raise new dollars.[28]

The Nature of United Way Corporate Relationships

The events of the 1960s had the effect of unfreezing an old system of charitable fund raising and corporate relationships, but it was the pressures of the 1970s which ultimately demanded a restructuring of a system which was resistant to change. By the end of the decade, and in the early 1980s, the corporate world would have to deal with a series of issues raised in the context of the CFC, including the issue of pressure, or even coercion, on employees to give in the workplace; the question of limited access to the workplace and, concomitantly, exclusionary United Way funding practices; freedom of choice for the giver; the distribution of funds to old line United Way member agencies; and the method by which the campaign was administered.

In the aftermath of the Filer Commission report the sharp delineation of these issues, along with the evident breakup of a consensus viewpoint, seriously threatened to undermine the bonds between the corporate world and the United Way system. Corporate response to this new situation would depend upon how corporations defined their relationship with the United Way specifically, but within the context of their motivation for corporate philanthropic activities more broadly.

Corporate motivations for support of United Way organized charity has been considered well suited for business purposes, and over the years federated fund-raising organizations became the primary vehicle for corporate participation in community social welfare activities. This was so both in terms of direct dollar contributions, and in terms of company involvement in workplace fund raising, or agency volunteering. In addition, many companies viewed the United Way as a place to give rising corporate executives experience in community leadership.

It must be recognized, however, that social welfare and community interests are ancillary to the business of the corporation, and have not usually been a primary concern of the corporate world.[29] The need to limit their attention in this area is certainly one major reason why corporations have welcomed the United Way as a convenient way to be involved in community affairs. Indeed, this involvement served for many years as a way of delimiting the scope of corporate social responsibility which, in its broadest interpretation, could have been taken to include examination of the impact of corporate products and externalities (e.g., waste dumping in the community), and labor practices, as well as provision for the general well-being of members of the community. This latter idea was clearly most attached to a commitment to the United Way.

Despite the rhetoric about corporate interest in philanthropy generally and some explicit emphasis on involvement in organized community charity, corporations have not been generous givers, and have never reported corporations anywhere near the maximum percentage allowed for tax deductible contributions (5 percent prior to the 1981 Tax Act, 10 percent thereafter).[30] Corporate foundations on the whole function differently, but most other corporate involvement in philanthropic activity in recent years seems to be stimulated more by initiatives of the grant seekers and fund raisers than by long-range planning of the corporation. Even United Way professionals have long admitted privately that it often takes a great deal of effort on their part to get into a corporation at all, to get a large increment in the corporate gift, and most of all to get a company to allow a United Way employee campaign for the first time.

Although corporations are not in the business of philanthropy, the connection between the corporations and federated fund raising has certainly been of utility to many corporations. The United Way has served as a "middleman," or neutral party, between multiple appeals and management and owners. United Way funding of its member agencies has served as a protection to corporations from multiple appeals by human service agencies, ever since the days of the "Immunity Clause" in Cleveland in 1913. In fact, United Way has been called a "protectionist" society for the corporations. Linkage to the United Way is supposed to guarantee that a corporation will not be approached by a United Way "funded" agency, either for a direct corporate gift or for a workplace campaign. In reality, many United Way agencies (particularly the large and powerful ones such as Salvation Army or Boy Scouts) have been allowed to break the first rule of a direct approach for a corporate gift, but not the second. It appears that for United Way "companies," the second principle, of limited access to the workplace, is far more significant because it relates to fundamental issues of labor relations and the "private" nature of the corporation. The implications of this connection will be discussed below in chapter 8.

The linkage with federated fund raising has at the same time served other latent purposes. It usually insured that corporations had little or no direct corporate exposure to any controversies involved in choices about giving, and were protected from responsibility for any bad choices. Given the absence of time necessary to make wise decisions among competing causes, the use of the federated fund-raising organization seemed to be an effective way of insuring good stewardship of the donor's dollar, and accountability was presumed assured by means of an allocations process in which employees of the corporation could actually participate. In addition, the relationship with this one organized charity has provided an important bridge to the community. It enabled a company to project an image of corporate good citizen, participating actively in a kind of consensus-driven community good, and also helped to insure some minimum awareness of corporate social welfare responsibilities, even when there was little internal motivation for this effort.[31]

Corporate Interaction with United Ways

Corporations interact with United Ways at the community level in three principal ways: first, through the involvement of their employees, including CEOs, on local United Way boards and committees; second, through internal decisions about gifts or corporate funds to United Ways, and exchanges around philanthropic functions; and third, through United Way–company fund-raising campaigns. This may mean using the corporate workplace for a United Way fund-raising effort, or through a more company-driven employee campaign, run as an in-plant federation or employee club, which makes choices in designations to organizations, including the United Way. In addition, companies are involved with local United Ways by supplying loaned executives and in staff deployment for campaigns. Less directly, corporations also connect to the United Way through participation on the boards and committees of other voluntary agencies, and therefore interface with local United Way personnel in different roles.[32] Involvement of corporate employees in local United Way activities serves a variety of specific corporate needs, such as providing a training ground for some employees on their way up the corporate ladder, and occasionally a way to "outstation" employees for whom there is no future in the company.

Finally, companies are involved with the United Way of America on the national level through membership on UWA committees and task forces, as well as through company involvement in the National Corporate Development Program. This program, which was initiated in 1977, by 1987 was credited with having increased corporate contributions from the over 300 participating companies, and served to keep companies committed to the United Way appeal.[33] This program, moreover, is another sign of how hard United Way works to integrate corporate involvement in the United Way system, starting with the top corporate executive, and to maintain the linkage between the two worlds through constant interaction as well as through direct contributions of money.

On the local level, the corporate call and the corporate case are the two critical connecting points for corporate involvement in the campaign. The "call" is the moment at which the sales pitch is made—either in relation to the corporate gift, or more broadly, including also the permission to run a new campaign, or to establish the basic ground rules for the campaign of the coming year. Although the first contact is in theory made by one corporate executive to another corporate executive, in fact not infrequently corporate calls are handled in some part by United Way staff, and they make the "corporate case" or sales pitch, leading to a determination of how much a company will contribute and other matters concerning the outlines for the campaign.

The corporate case will usually include a statement about the local United Way and community needs, and a justification of the campaign goal in terms of community needs as well as an indication of how the corporate gift relates to that goal. Generally the case will also include a past history of the giving of the particular corporation, or the particular worksite or plant location (if different from that of the corporation as a whole), with a comparison between that company's gift and other companies in the same category (i.e., other firms of comparable size, or product, such as chemicals). This of course has special significance if the corporation lags behind its peers by some significant measure, such as overall size of gift, gift per employee (based on numbers of employees), or gift as a ratio of pre-tax income.[34]

The Employee Campaign

Corporate time is precious, and the initial corporate call is expected to be very brief. United Way staff generally indicate that a half-hour with a CEO is considered a generous amount of his time. A significant part of this first corporate call is usually concerned with the employee campaign. After this the campaign will be turned over to some assigned staff person who may serve under a top management person. The relationship between that top staff person and the local United Way is important, but the most critical factor is considered to be the attitude of the CEO toward the campaign, which is passed to this staff person.[35] In most large companies, additionally, a campaign committee or team will be formed; and a loaned executive may also be assigned by the local United Way to work with the company team, instead of, or in addition to, United Way staff.

In regard to involvement with the United Way, original policy discussions and major decision making usually take place at the highest levels, including the CEO and senior offices of the corporation charged with community relations and public affairs. It is at this level that the amount of the corporate contribution is decided. However, the corporation's involvement with United Way is in other respects bifurcated below this level. In most large companies operational responsibility for a workplace campaign rests in the specially appointed group which involves on the one hand community affairs personnel, and on the other hand high-level executives (vice-presidents) responsible for personnel functions in the corporation. Payroll deduction is after all a personnel issue as well as a community relations matter.

Companies vary in the way they organize the campaign overall, how much interaction there is with United Way staff or loaned executive supplied by the United Way, and how much of United Way–supplied promotional material they use. Sophisticated companies like IBM may assign two or more middle-management headquarters staff people to work all year round on the campaign, basically full-time, and they expect department or unit heads and staff from other areas, such as public relations, to work closely with the leadership

CORPORATE RESPONSIBILITY AND UNITED WAY 165

staff. In branch and division locations, management teams will also work closely with employee clubs which are involved in the campaign. Most large companies like IBM appear to do their own promotional materials and pledge cards, although they may use United Way models and information extensively.

Many companies use the same kinds of internal debriefing procedures they use for any significant corporate activity. If the top corporate management (and particularly the CEO) is committed to the campaign, complete reports will be compiled, identifying weaknesses and including suggestions for improving performance in the next campaign.[36] Thus, after the 1985 campaign in IBM, the leadership staff that ran the campaign (reporting to a top IBM executive) carried out a thorough review of their own process, and concluded that the team leaders needed to be appointed at least a year before they took over the campaign, so that they could observe one complete campaign and learn from the process, and in order to have sufficient time to organize the team and assign responsibilities.

In many past IBM campaigns, United Way staff spoke to employees in group solicitation at some corporation work sites. At other times, IBM preferred that only IBM employees be involved in the internal campaign, with United Way providing background materials, such as a solicitor training film; advice on possible strategies; and information to the IBM in-house group running the campaign. Limitations on outside participation in the early 1980s may have been the result of increased concern over a company's legal ability to protect the idea of limited (selected) access to the workplace after renewed challenges to that concept.

In most companies, and particularly in companies with long, intensely visible connections with the United Way, the campaign is taken very seriously, and corporations compete with each other here as elsewhere. A specific company goal, or dollar amount to be raised, is set based on the previous year's experience, changes in the corporate climate, and in light of pressure from the United Way corporate campaign's leadership. Division or unit goals are then determined, and an entire campaign strategy is developed as carefully as it would be for any other activity of the corporation. Employees attend United Way briefings and are informed about the United Way through site visits to its funded agencies and through brochures, movies, and site visits to member agencies. Even where there is an employee club or in-plant federation (as in IBM nationwide or in Boeing's Good Neighbor Fund), and therefore, theoretically, a more open, broad-based campaign, United Way material and information about United Way agencies has traditionally dominated these workplace campaigns.

This has apparently been done through the variety of formal and informal exchanges already discussed, and relationships which are carefully cultivated and maintained by the federated fund-raising organization.

Once the campaign is accepted, a special kick-off event inside the corporation will generally be planned, separate from the United Way's own communitywide kick-off event. In the corporation, once again the personal involvement of the CEO is essential. His personal word, preferably delivered at the internal kick-off and also through a letter of encouragement to employees, is usually considered the most critical factor in insuring a successful campaign.

Thereafter the results of each unit (branch, division, department, etc.) are reported frequently, and in-house competition among units is either deliberately inculcated or treated with benign neglect and permitted as part of the campaign spirit. Special prizes and rewards are offered, and these are frequently tied to fair share giving, as the sample notice from Seagram's in figure 7.1 indicates. A unit which has achieved 100 percent giving may receive a day off as a reward, and individuals who give at the defined fair share level may become eligible for a raffle with a new car as the top prize.[37]

It was still not an unknown practice in the mid-1980s for supervisors in some units to cover up for a non-contributing employee. By giving a small amount—even one dollar—in the non-contributing employee's name, the supervisor enables the unit to show 100 percent participation in the campaign, and therefore to be eligible for a reward. Staff responsible for the campaign usually become invested in its success and work hard to insure that there is full participation by all employees in their division. Less than 100 percent participation is disappointing for competitive unit leaders.

When all the funds are raised, and the campaign is closed, a check is sent to the United Way by the company. Procedures for sending the check, however, vary. It appears that not infrequently, companies still send one check representing the contribution of both the corporate entity and the gifts from the contributing employees. Indeed, in many places, prior to the 1980s, it was often difficult to distinguish the amount given by the corporation itself from the announced corporate gift at the "victory dinner" held at the end of the campaign. Increasingly, however, employees, and unions most vocally, have pressured to have the labor gift highlighted apart from the company corporation, and consequently the distinction is becoming more apparent in the presentations. This kind of separateness, however, can present a dilemma for corporate leaders who certainly

October 27, 1982

TO ALL EMPLOYEES:

Once again, the employees of Joseph E. Seagram & Sons, Inc. came through in their usual generous manner during our United Way of Tri-State Drive. As of today, 85% of all employees contributed fair share. This is truly a remarkable performance considering today's economic climate.

The Grand Prize drawing for the Subaru automobile will take place at 12 noon, this Friday, October 29, 1982, in the Fourth Floor Conference Rooms at 375 Park Avenue. All J.E.S. employees are cordially invited to attend. Each person who contributed their fair share will receive one chance on the car, and those who contributed double their fair share will receive three chances.

A Second Prize of dinner for two at the Laurent Restaurant will also be drawn.

Again, on behalf of my Co-Chairman, Bill Putnam, and my Campaign Co-ordinator, Coleen Raftery, I extend to you my sincere thanks and appreciation for a job well done.

Sincerely,

James P. Spillane
1982 Campaign Chairman

Figure 7.1

wish to have the employee campaign function as a unifying company experience.

In regard to who is providing the support for United Ways, corporate rhetoric is not entirely clear, and corporations seem to like it both ways. On the one hand, they stress the separateness of the employee campaign and the employee contribution from the company's own gift; and on the other hand they use such terms as "our company's total United Way effort" to include both the company contribution and the amount contributed through payroll deduction. This has been the case whether or not the company runs an official United Way campaign, or there is some other version of such a campaign, including United Way plus donor option, or even an in-plant federation, where the employees theoretically control the campaign dollars.

In-Plant Federations

Subsequent to the events in Detroit (1947–49) and continuous efforts in the 1950s, the idea of one unified charity campaign in the workplace has been connected with the United Fund–United Way concept, and the public certainly gave little consideration to what form it took. Until the attack on the workplace campaign as a United Way monopoly, structural differences in the organization of workplace campaigns were either not noticed or not considered important. Consequently, the development of in-plant federations received relatively little attention outside the United Way system, and their implications for worker choice in giving were not widely recognized.[38]

Since the 1960s there has apparently been no in-depth study of the phenomenon of in-plant federations—why they exist, how they function, and what their implications are for open or closed workplace campaigns.[39] Even their exact numbers and location are generally unknown. Understanding of in-plant federations has been maintained as a deep organizational secret of the United Way, whose professional staff share this knowledge, but are not likely to discuss it openly, and certainly not with outsiders. Moreover, it has also been convenient for the opponents of United Way to underplay this phenomenon. The existence of "in-plants," as United Way staff refers to them, suggests that employees in many companies seem to have the possibility of choice in to whom to give, since these federations, or employee contribution clubs, as they are often defined, are structured so as to be able to make decisions about the allocation and distribution of funds.[40]

In this sense, therefore, one of the most interesting and surprising findings revealed by our survey of local United Ways was the extent to which in-plant federations remain a factor in local community campaigns across our country, and in some major corporations. In our sample of 131 local United Ways, nearly half (56) indicated that they received some support from a total of 200 company federations. Moreover, the amount contributed by in-plant federations was significant, and occurred in all Metro size groupings. The total amount that these 56 United Ways received from this source in 1983 was $6,369,280.

The preponderance of company federations were located in mid-America (where almost 20 percent of the United Ways reported three or more in-plant federations among their companies). Using the conference board category of America's breadbasket, (Minnesota, Iowa, Missouri, Kansas, Nebraska, South Dakota, and North Dakota), 37 percent of United Ways reported from three to ten in-plant federations, although the amount that they contributed to United Way varied considerably. The median reported contribution from these in-plant federations was $24,000. The highest median amount for a single size-grouping of United Ways was reported by Metro II United Ways, which received a median amount of $72,963 from in-plant federations.

The continued functioning of large numbers of employee clubs or in-plant federations reflects the history of the united fund as well as corporate culture concerning employee relations. This is particularly evident when it is realized that these company clubs exist system-wide (if in different forms) in such major companies as Boeing Aircraft, General Electric Manufacturing Company, and International Business Machines (IBM).[41] (Indeed, typically, in-plant federations are found in specialized high-tech industries, including aerospace and electronic equipment.) However, if, as it appears, most of these in-plant federations continue to give most of their money to local United Ways year after year, then the issue of who controls giving at the workplace needs to be given a somewhat different perspective from that usually attached to it.[42] Thus the question about United Way control of workplace giving may now be reframed. It can be asked: how is it that, when United Way does not run the campaign, and when employee-run organizations (with formal structures, rules, or by-laws) are actually making decisions about fund distribution, United Ways across the country are still the single largest beneficiary of these contributions, and in most cases apparently get most of the money? The answer which seems to mesh with corporate practices is also expressed by United Way professionals and corporate personnel. Employee contribution clubs and in-plant federations involve employees in the decision-making process, but the campaign nevertheless continues to be defined as a company campaign (and in fact frequently also as the company's *United Way campaign*), and management generally controls the rules and procedures under which such campaigns operate. Thus, ultimately company leadership (which may include union leaders as well as management) has a strong influence on the pattern of fund distribution.

Institutional Case Study: Boeing Employees' Good Neighbor Fund

A closer look at the Boeing Employees' Good Neighbor Fund in Seattle will illustrate how employee clubs actually function. The Boeing Employees' Good Neighbor Fund (BEGNF) was started in 1951 as an in-plant federation at the time when some companies (in communities where there was no united fund) were using that device to circumvent the complications of competitive campaigns between the community chest and national health agencies (see above, in chapter 2). In 1986 the BEGNF was still functioning, and celebrated its thirty-fifth anniversary with enthusiasm.

The BEGNF is incorporated and operates under formal by-laws, operating rules, and procedures. The board of directors consists of eight persons, divided equally between hourly employees and salaried employees. Board members are elected for staggered two-year terms. In order to insure continuity and time for learning, the chairman serves one year as chair-elect prior to assuming the chairmanship, and by an informal understanding the position rotates between hourly and salaried employees, or, in other words, between management and non-management employees. Procedures for the distribution of funds (raised through payroll deduction) are reviewed and adopted each year for the coming year.

For many years the amount of funds given to local United Ways by the BEGNF has been 85 percent of the total amount raised by the employees, with the remaining going to a variety of other causes, particularly Cancer and Heart. By the early 1980s (and subsequent to the admission of more health agencies, including Cancer, to the United Way of King County), the remaining 15 percent, the funds that were not distributed through United Way, were allocated for capital fund needs of agencies in the community. These apparently included, but were not limited to, United Way agencies. When questioned about the reasons why the amount contributed to local United Ways remained so constant, members of the BEGNF board and United Way staff were somewhat vague, but suggested, first, that there was always some risk that this would change; second, that the choice of the chairman was very significant in this process; and third, that management (apparently with the assistance of union leadership) may have influenced the practice in some subtle but continuous ways.

BEGNF membership grew in the early 1980s and the enthusiasm of the campaigners seemed unbounded, even in a time of uncertainty about job security in Seattle.[43] The percentage of participating Boeing employees continued to grow, and by 1982, in the time of the Reagan cutbacks, over 76 percent of Boeing employees were members of BEGNF, and therefore, by definition, contributors to the campaign. The campaign was clearly identified as a Boeing employee campaign, despite the high percentage of money given to United Way, and even though the United Way had at one time called itself the United Good Neighbor Fund/United Way of King County. BEGNF operates throughout the Boeing system, but the state of Washington has the largest concentration of Boeing employees, and within the state Seattle is by far the most dominant location. Thus, in 1985 and 1986 respectively, BEGNF gave United Ways in the state $7,647,733 and $9,023,634, and in the same years, the United Way of King County received nearly 90 percent of the funds raised in the state.

At the time of the site visit to Seattle, many United Way professionals considered the United Way of King County to be a model, if special, "fund." It had a defined role in a community which had a central place in the Puget Sound area. Seattle represents more than one-third of the population of King County, or 498,000 out of 1,256,800 people. In 1982 Seattle was considered on the whole a homogeneous and somewhat insular community, in which social change was just beginning to take place. King County had a small but growing minority population; according to the 1980 census, nearly 90 percent (88.89 percent) of King County was white, 4.35 percent was black, 4.94 percent was Asian (and Pacific Islander), and 1.05 percent was Native American. In 1980 the numbers of each group were still relatively small, with the approximately 54,500 Asians the largest of the subgroups.[44]

Seattle itself had a readily identifiable elite leadership group, and a few business and social clubs where these leaders meet on a regular basis, formally and informally. In addition, for most of the 1970s through the mid-1980s, the United Way of King County had had only one United Way executive, Charles Devine, a social worker who was skillful in working with people, and particularly with his corporate constituency, with whom he was comfortable, if respectful.[45] The United Way had a history of campaign success, and in 1983 had raised almost $23 per person in its campaign area, or one of the highest per capita giving amounts in the country.

The United Way had an established leadership position in the community. It had incorporated within itself a powerful planning council, the Council of Planning Agencies (COPA), which included public and private agencies in the area. COPA frequently took strong public policy positions, and its semi-autonomous stance caused internal tension within the United Way, among volunteers as well as

Table 7.1. United Way of King County
Boeing Contributions, 1976–1986

	(1) Pledge Corp	(2) Pledge Employee	(3) Actual Employee	(1+3) Total	Total Amount Raised UWKC	Boeing %
1976	$ 510,588	$2,728,937	$2,479,800	$2,990,388	$11,212,144	27
1977	630,000	2,582,176	2,815,965	3,445,965	12,381,116	28
1978	825,000	3,073,545	3,529,644	4,354,644	14,055,019	31
1979	935,000	3,700,910	4,189,395	5,124,395	16,306,633	31
1980	1,200,000	4,372,003	4,968,453	6,168,453	18,626,506	33
1981	1,380,000	4,836,202	4,898,747	6,278,747	20,805,807	30
1982	1,670,000	4,640,713	5,163,742	6,833,742	23,032,559	30
1983	1,668,000	4,965,728	5,418,472	7,086,472	23,517,000	30
1984	1,732,000	5,803,542	6,038,609	7,770,609	25,461,000	31
1985	1,686,000	6,854,339	6,992,711	8,678,711	28,212,000	31
1986	1,866,651	7,308,566	N/A	9,175,217	31,052,000	30

Source: Boeing Corporation.

campaign oriented staff.[46] Thus, although many United Way professionals had come to Seattle to study the COPA mechanism, apparently none had actually copied it, presumably because there was some risk involved in doing so. The United Way of Seattle also prided itself on having a high level of support for its funded agencies relative to the United Way system as a whole.

Perhaps most significant in shaping the culture of this United Way was the fact that Seattle was essentially a one-company town in these years. Although there were other major companies in Seattle, including the SAFECO Corporation, the Ranier Bancorporation, and Weyerhaeuser Corporation, the Boeing Company certainly dominated the local employment scene. The only other group to come close to Boeing in number of employees apparently were federal and local government employees.[47] As table 7.1 shows, for most of the decade after 1976, the Boeing Company, including the corporate gift and the employees contribution, accounted for a consistent percentage of the United Way campaign, after 1977 hovering between 30 and 31 percent. By far the largest amount of this was the employee share. In 1985 out of a total of over $28,200,000 raised by the United Way of King County, Boeing Company and its employees gave $8,678,711, of which $6,929,111 was contributed by Boeing employees through BEGNF.

In this context of a tightly knit community, clearly dominated by Boeing and with the careful guidance of Chuck Devine, support for United Way had been consistent throughout the 1970s and early 1980s. In more difficult times, such as the recession of 1971–72,

United Way had even succeeded in mobilizing additional support and developing special programs for workers laid off by Boeing and other companies.[48] In 1981, United Way took an active part in a coalition of public agencies and other private funding sources and raised over $1.5 million in contributions for funds to be used for special programs of agencies (not all United Way affiliates) to help displaced workers in the community. Despite some initial resistance, corporate leaders agreed to continue special funding to this project through 1983. Although the project included others, United Way seized the opportunity to participate in efforts to mobilize new resources and help provide services to displaced workers through a variety of purchase-of-service agreements with non–United Way agencies. United Way continued to push its buffer role between the local corporations and community problems, and therefore maintained a valuable visible stance in the community as well.

In the early 1980s the alternative fund movement made an appearance in Seattle. Challenges to United Way's hegemony in the workplace occurred from environmental funds, the Black United Fund, and the Women's Funding Alliance, a federated group of women's organizations. In this relatively homogeneous community, where United Way was strongly tied to corporate and community leadership, these funds had difficulty getting started. However, by 1986 the BUF group had emerged in Seattle, and in keeping with developments elsewhere, the Women's Funding Alliance under Dyan Oldenberg was making progress in gaining entry to municipal and state employee campaigns.[49] However, neither of these organizations was funded through BEGNF and they did not fall into the regular priorities for Boeing company contributions, which, other than United Way, were then focused on education and the arts.

Seattle is noted for a liberal "underlining," and in private one member of the BEGNF board and other community sources suggested that liberal political forces in the community (the mayor for example) might influence change within BEGNF's policies as well, to make them more sensitive to women and to minority issues (including greater responsiveness to the gay and lesbian community). However, at least one Boeing official connected with the campaign indicated that the company would be unlikely to consider requests from any small new agencies outside the United Way, stating that Boeing would use its influence to insure that they were included under the United Way umbrella.[50]

One acid test for the United Way–BEGNF relationship occurred in 1982 during the boycott of the United Way campaign by the International Association of Machinists (IAM) referred to in an earlier chapter.⁵¹ At that time, BEGNF had 44,000 members, of whom 13,000 were members of the IAM and 11,000 were members of other "bargaining units" or union locals likely to be supportive of IAM action. Given their numbers, if these workers had joined the boycott, they could have caused considerable damage to the United Way campaign. However, even in this situation of potentially conflicting loyalties, the United Way–Boeing relationship was protected.

During the summer of 1982, an "informal" arrangement was made, working around the nationwide IAM prohibition against giving to United Way. An agreement was negotiated with BEGNF leadership that contributions would be raised for the agencies of the United Way, and distributed directly to the agencies, in the same manner as they would have been distributed had the money been given to the United Way. In an even more complicated second step, the agencies then returned the money to the United Way, which in turn, immediately distributed the same money back to them. Thus the United Way was able to count the funds as part of its receipts that year, and the allocations process was not violated.

These arrangements were made with the active involvement of union leaders, and the encouragement of the Boeing top management. Success with the complicated negotiations was credited particularly to the efforts of John Andrews, chairman of BEGNF that year, and Chuck Devine, but would not have been possible without the support of Tom F. Baker, president of IAM Local 751, who was described by one Boeing manager as "a real statesman and an enlightened leader." Thus, although the campaign that year was not easy, and the United Way of King County did not reach its goal ($24,023,000), campaign receipts in 1982 increased to $23,032,559, or an increase of about 13 percent over the funds raised in 1981.⁵² Moreover, this occurred at a time when Boeing sales were down and workers were being laid off.

The BEGNF story involves management and leadership of a blue collar union, where United Way has traditionally had its strongest grasp on payroll deductions. It also involves a situation with an in-plant federation, where, in theory, the employees could have voted almost any use of the funds collected. However, it is apparent that local union leaders in Seattle followed their own instincts in a time of recession, rather than following the command for a boycott of the campaign urged by a union leader far from their community, William Winpisinger, international president of the International Association of Machinists and Aerospace Workers. At the same time BEGNF and its union members, in arguing against Winpisinger and the proposed boycott of the United Way campaign, found themselves arguing against the inclusion of any advocacy group in the United Way campaign, not just the National Right to Work Legal Defense and Educational Foundation, which had been Winpisinger's official target. Indeed, the circle between the public campaign of the CFC and the private campaign in Seattle appeared to have been closed with the following words from the president of the BEGNF board of trustees:

> It is recommended that advocacy groups be eliminated from the Combined Federal Campaign. We do not believe that the support of political advocacy groups should be permitted to impact our much needed ability to support human services.[53]

Finally, in considering the nature of in-plant federations it must be recognized that not all such employee groups are composed of blue collar, or unionized, workers. IBM employees, for example, are not unionized. The company prides itself, however, on its employee relations and is generally recognized for its careful attention to personnel practices.[54] Thus IBM contribution clubs, which are presumed to be decentralized in operation, might be expected to have a different attitude toward United Way dominance in their fund distribution. Yet as late as 1985 IBM indicated that all but 5 percent of the money raised by its employees and distributed through IBM employee contribution clubs was given to local United Ways, and, in fact, the IBM campaign was generally identified as a United Way campaign.

Chapter 8

Changing the Rules of the Game: Corporate Response to Challenge

> I see many communities where real change initiative is coming from the business leadership.
>
> Executive Director of a Local
United Way (1976)

> Public sector challenges have ranged from an American Civil Liberties Union (ACLU) suit challenging the singular focus on United Way to legislative activity questioning a United Way–only campaign. Directly or indirectly, events in the public sector affect the private sector. We must develop tactics to deal with these and other threats and carry out these tactics on time.
>
> "Single Community Campaign at the
Workplace," United Way of America,
Long Range Strategic Planning
Committee, October 20, 1983.

I T is not easy to pinpoint an exact time when the corporate world might have begun to feel particularly concerned about its relationship to the United Way during the debates over charitable contributions in the late 1970s and early 1980s. As critics of the United Way pointed out frequently, even in the aftermath of the Filer Commission report, companies seemed as a whole to remain closely attached to the United Way. Nevertheless, there were some perilous moments.

Among the earliest of these events were those that occurred in California, revolving around the CHAD suit in Santa Clara County (1977); the AID controversy in Los Angeles (1976–78); and the situation in San Francisco, which was both volatile and long-lived (from the late 1960s through the mid-1970s). Corporations in California were involved directly in these events, but how did corporate America react to them?

Site Case Study: The California Charity Wars

It is frequently claimed that California, with its varied constituents and special climate, is a kind of bell-weather for the rest of the nation. In the United Way of the late 1970s, this indeed became a crucial question—the extent to which happenings in California were representative of systemwide issues that would spread to other United Ways and which they would also have to face.

To begin with, the "Charity Wars" around the competitive donors federation, Associated In-Group Donors (AID), was the most publicized and inflammatory of a series of California events concerning the United Way. Here, however, it seems that companies acted quickly in support of the United Way in Los Angeles as one after another switched their employee campaign away from the donor-driven AID group and to the United Way campaign.[1]

By the time the "war" was officially ended by the court-mandated settlement, the relationship of the United Way to corporations in that area had been strengthened. Even though the settlement did not appear to put United Way in the most flattering light, the United Way in fact had made new inroads into the corporate workplace Los Angeles. Indeed, Robert J. Flour, chairman of the United Way campaign (1976–77), was reported as having praised the "outstanding contribution" made by United Way's Future Funding Division in winning over firms with AID chapters to the United Way. Flour pointed out that "142 companies and organizations were added to our roles," giving more than 325,000 employees the opportunity to participate for the first time in the United Way company campaign.[2] Thereafter corporate support for the United Way of Los Angeles was actually to prove remarkably constant. This was so even when internal troubles emerged in the mid-1980s around the administration of the organization and activities of the local United Way executive. At that time a *Los Angeles Times* reporter was subjected to considerable pressure from corporate leadership of the United Way for his reporting of the story and was eventually removed from coverage of philanthropic issues.[3]

Next, there was the Combined Health Agencies Drive (CHAD) litigation against four United Ways in northern California, filed in Santa Clara County in late 1977. The case centered around charges of unfair business practices, monopoly of payroll deduction, and interference with CHAD's relationships with businesses, and was eventually decided in favor of United Way (June 1978).[4] This case, however, seems to have influenced United Way's relationship with health agencies elsewhere.

Corporations might have been expected to have more tolerance of the concept of a separate CHAD, in line with the approval given to the formation of the Commerce and Industry Combined Health Appeal (CICHA) by business and the Chamber of Commerce in Baltimore in the 1950s, and the continued interest of their employees in health related issues. But neither the corporations nor the United Way really wanted side-by-side campaigns. Unions apparently also maintained their stance against drives by health agencies in the workplace. In a confidential memorandum which was reported as circulating around that time, it was stated:

> The AFL-CIO has traditionally been and continues to be, opposed to a national health agency federation limited to "place of employment" campaigns employing payroll deductions. This is primarily due to the fact that such an effort does not eliminate their residential, direct mail and special event fund raising in the community.[5]

The document then goes on to point out that CHADs, unlike United Ways, rely on donor choice for fund distribution, rather than the use of citizens in a rational allocations process.

In any case, CHADs did continue to grow, with uneven success, across the country through the mid-1980s, and even formed a national organization (separate from the NHA group of the CFC) during this period, claiming to have local organizations in seventeen cities. In several cities, including San Diego, Baltimore (the CICHA), and Hartford, local CHADs were uneasy partners with the United Way during the late 1970s and early 1980s. In Hartford, some big companies, including the Aetna Life and Casualty Company, and Pratt and Whitney, as well as the Chamber of Commerce, encouraged the United Way and the local CHAD to develop a working partnership, maintaining the one-drive idea, while also preserving the identity of the two different groups in the workplace drive.[6]

Between 1980 and 1984 many United Ways across the country continued to woo the American Cancer Society and the Heart Association with attractive partnership contracts. Some of these United Ways, such as Baltimore and San Diego, were also faced with CHADs in their communities. The ACS and the AHA were the strongest and most popular of the health/disease agencies, with the Cancer Society particularly a big winner in employee donor designations everywhere. Thus, getting them somehow under the United Way umbrella considerably weakened CHADS in their struggles against United Way hegemony in the workplace. Cancer and Heart also had health education programs which were attractive to employees, and therefore of interest to corporate employers as well. Consequently, once again the company and the United Way had common cause in bringing Cancer and Heart into the United Way workplace campaign, where they provided health education (prevention) programs, while at the same time promoting the campaign—of which they were a part—as worthy of support.[7]

By 1984 there were over one hundred agreements in place with ACS units, and at least fifty-five communities were reported to have raised an average increase in their 1982 campaigns of 3.4 percent more than those that did not have ACS in their package. (According to United Way figures, the group with ACS contracts showed an average increase of 8 percent in their campaigns that year, while those without them showed only an average increase of 4.6 percent.) Since the contracts often guaranteed shares of the campaign as high as 10 percent, it seems that weakening the position of a threatening CHAD was more of an incentive for forming partnerships with Cancer and Heart than the actual expectation of dollar gain.[8]

The situation in San Francisco was even more complex. This city had been a center of conflict in the 1960s when emerging counterculture groups in Berkeley and newly identified minority groups in Oakland (particularly blacks) had dramatically challenged traditional institutions.[9] These groups openly confronted the United Way about its lack of responsiveness to their needs. Consequently by 1970 the United Way had embarked on what became a traumatic "quick-fix" attempt to change its priorities and related funding patterns. After that attempt, efforts were made to heal some of the wounds with the core group of United Way–funded agencies, but considerable damage had been done. There was also a renegotiation of the United Way's relationship with its local planning council, which had been involved in the process of setting the United Way's "New Directions." The council was subsequently defunded.

In the tumultuous climate of San Francisco, labor groups were not solidly behind the United Way, and given the conflict and problems involved, corporations were also showing less than enthusiastic support for a United Way campaign in the workplace. Many companies in the San Francisco area had in-plant federations which gave money outside the United Way system, and overall the employee per capita gift was low in comparison with other Metro I United Ways. Subsequent to the AID problem in Los Angeles, in the winter of 1977-78 the United Way of the Bay Area carried out a donor option study, and a new executive was hired to implement the plan, which was put in place that June. The new executive was Joseph Valentine, a social worker who was open in manner and comfortable dealing with corporations and agencies, as well as with dissident groups. But even he was not able to turn the situation around easily. It was several years before the United Airlines campaign became a United Way campaign, with donor option, and it was not until 1984 that Crocker Bank, itself now under a new CEO, finally abandoned its in-plant federation for the United Way-donor option campaign.[10] By this time, San Francisco's offering to the donor was a complicated series of choices. There was a fully open donor option plan, but there were also other "competitive" causes involved in various forms of contractual partnerships with the United Way, including the Black United Fund, the ACS, and the Heart Association.[11]

Change from Without and Within

While all this was going on, the Black United Fund (BUF) movement had also emerged on the scene and was gradually growing, first in California, and then elsewhere. In Los Angeles where it originated, BUF remained totally independent of the United Way, while in San Francisco it joined with the United Way in a partnership arrangement in 1982. It will be recalled, however, that a separate black fund (a UBF) had developed in Washington around the same time as the Los Angeles BUF and before the official incorporation of the National Black United Fund (NBUF). This was the UBF in Washington, headed by Calvin Rolark, which had sought entry as a separate agency into the Washington area CFC. The UBF had lost its case in 1972 when the District Court judge held that there was insufficient evidence to support a charge of discrimination against minority groups in the local CFC.[12]

Although IBM's loyalty to United Way is generally accepted as a firm tradition, in 1971 IBM employees in the Washington Metro area were already giving funds to this UBF. After the court decision against it in 1972, UBF, however, moved away from the nationally emerging more militant BUF movement. The name "United Black Fund" was retained, in contrast with the Black United Fund name, which became identified with the more separatist national BUF movement. Moreover, after the Washington, D.C. united fund was reorganized, the local UBF joined the new Metro area United Way in a close partnership arrangement. IBM employee funds thereafter flowed through the United Way system in a pattern that was repeated elsewhere in the next decade.

During the 1970s and early 1980s the activist BUF movement grew sporadically, while it retained some of the militant feeling of the black power movement of the 1960s. BUF had been energized initially by the national leadership of Walter Bremond and Professor King Davis, who provided a philosophical framework for the movement, as well as by several dynamic local leaders, most notably Danny Blakewell in Los Angeles. Other activist leaders emerged later, including Kermit Eady in New York City and Dana Alston, who left NCRP to become the executive of the National BUF (NBUF) in 1982.[13] In general, the BUFs continued to have their greatest success in government workplaces, including the CFC, municipal, and state campaigns, where exclusionary rules could not usually be defended. Meanwhile they continued to press for entry into the corporations, on a basis of equal access with the United Way.

One of the first major salvos in the direct battle for choices among charities in the corporate workplace occurred when a law suit was initiated by black workers in the Chrysler Corporation. This suit, *Lew Moye v. Chrysler*, was brought in 1977, around the same time as the California CHAD initiated action against four United Ways in California. Black employees of Chrysler wanted the right to contribute over $600 through payroll deduction to the United Black Community Fund of St. Louis, and they charged that Chrysler's refusal to grant payroll deduction to that organization was motivated by racial prejudice. The lower court decided in favor of the corporation, dismissing the case for lack of grounds to sue. This decision was in turn upheld by a U.S. Court of Appeals on the grounds that a payroll deduction plan in favor of the United Way was not actually a contract, under United States statutes affecting labor relations.[14]

Although Chrysler ultimately was vindicated in the outcome of this case (November 1979), by that time it was evident that corporations would continue to be challenged by BUFs and other groups wanting access to the workplace fund drive, as well as by employees who felt that they had a right to choice in charities. In the next few years charges of coercion in connection with the United Way campaign were raised frequently. This was a time of increased litigation around employee rights generally, including cases concerning affirmative action and equal opportunity for minorities. Thus, despite the Chrysler decision, corporations with large numbers of black employees might well have worried about future vulnerability to charges of discrimination if they did not permit BUFs to have access to payroll deduction.

The CHAD suit filed in California in 1977 had already raised issues about limited access to the workplace. Although the local United Ways eventually won the case, the antitrust and monopoly charges raised were potentially volatile if pursued in other contexts. Moreover, after the final decision in the AID case (1978), United Ways were required to keep one critical feature of the former AID campaign, namely donor choice, when corporations switched to running United Way campaigns. Given these circumstances, it was not surprising that the United Way in San Francisco adopted a donor option plan in 1978. Indeed in some respects it is more surprising that other United Ways were so slow to follow this pattern, or that more corporations did not insist on it, as a prerequisite to their employee campaigns. To some extent, the existence of in-plant federations provides an explanation for the lack of concern, since those companies nominally offered employee control of the campaign funds.

It appears that in the 1970s some corporations were feeling skittish about running United Way campaigns. Indeed, in the summer of 1976 Roderick DeArment, attorney for the United Way of the National Capital Area (the Washington, D.C., United Way) apparently speaking for the whole United Way system, wrote to the National Labor Relations Board (NLRB) about problems that local United Ways were encountering in regard to workplace solicitations in industry.[15] DeArment noted that in recent weeks, United Ways had "encountered considerable resistance to their request for permission to conduct on-the-job solicitations." He stated furthermore that "this resistance reflects employers' expressed concern that if they permit on-the-job solicitation by United Way they may be unable to enforce an otherwise valid no-solicitation or no-distribution rule in the context of a union organizing effort."[16]

The purpose of DeArment's letter was to seek "an opinion by the General Counsel [of the NLRB] that would convincingly dispel the misconception on the part of a growing number of employers that their cooperation with a United Way fund-raising campaign on their premise will endanger an otherwise valid no-solicitation rule." United Way was seeking NLRB confirmation of the special status of local United Ways, which allowed them to be explicitly excepted from the "no-solicitation" rules during work time that corporations were entitled to establish and maintain under the regulatory provisions of the NLRB and the statutes regulating labor relations.[17] This exception meant that corporations could post rules limiting solicitations for all kinds of causes including organizing, loitering, and meeting during work hours, and still permit a United Way for charitable purposes to be an exception to the "no-solicitation" rule.[18]

The special exception was certainly an essential factor in corporation attitudes toward a United Way campaign, since it allowed a corporation to limit the amount of time lost through "beneficient" appeals, while at the same time also limiting labor activities, or union organizing, at the work site. Thus, the exclusionary status for the United Way, as a consensus charity model, had particular importance for corporations concerned about potential union organizing or other political efforts of labor (such as Political Action Committees) where there was a union in place.[19] This group then could include even such corporate giants as IBM, which was not unionized, or AT&T, with significant numbers of non-unionized professional employees—companies which could also be considered paternalistic in their attitude and treatment of their "family" of employees.[20]

Although most business leaders are apparently not highly concerned about philanthropic activities, many companies do have active involvement with organized charities, including employees' campaigns. These campaigns are required to serve the interest of the corporation both externally, in regard to the company's community image, and internally, in relationship with its employees; in short, charitable activities must be subservient to other company needs. The DeArment letter to the NLRB in 1976 requesting a ruling concerning the United Way status as an exception to the no-solicitation rule has to be understood in this context.

According to United Way's attorney, Leo Benade, the immediate precipitating factor for DeArment's letter to the NLRB was concern over an interpretation of an NLRB ruling in a case decided by the NLRB, as reported by a "well-known and widely read labor reporting service."[21] In connection with the C.G. Murphy Company decision, the reporting service stated:

> The Board has ruled employers can bar union reps from their premises if the company has a valid no solicitation rule. To be valid, the rule must prohibit all solicitation—not just union solicitation. Furthermore, the rule must be enforced against all solicitation. A company that relaxes its rule for a charity but enforces it against a union would be discriminating.[22]

The United Way of America considered this to be a serious misstating by the reporting service, and in his affadavit to the NLRB, Benade noted that not until the Hammary case did the NLRB actually "suggest that a company's sponsoring or permitting a single once-a-year on-the-job charitable campaign would invalidate an otherwise enforced no-solicitation rule."[23] Nevertheless, the UWA acknowledged that "the Board has cited a United Way or other charitable giving campaigns as one of many permitted solicitations that, when considered in their totality, cast doubt on the employer's stated company policy of keeping work interruptions to a minimum." Consequently, since 1974 some "private employers" have "expressed reluctance to sponsor or permit annual United Way campaigns in their plants or offices because of a fear that their rights to enforce their no-solicitation rules would be impaired."[24]

Another factor may have influenced the timing of the DeArment letter to the NLRB, and this was a case before the Supreme Court in 1976. Although the case before the court dealt with union dues and public sector employees, the case had ramifications for corporate–United Way relations. The case of the *City of Charlotte et al. v. Local 660 International Association of Firefighters et al.* raised issues about employee rights and equal protection, which also had implications more broadly for the issue of access to the checkoff for BUFs and other alternative funds. In this case, the court ruled that

> a city's refusal to withhold from its firefighters' paychecks upon request dues owing to a union which represented only part of the uniformed members of the fire department is not violative of the equal protection clause of the Fourteenth Amendment, notwithstanding that monies are withheld from city employees' paychecks upon request for payment to various entities and organizations when such withholding is required by law or is available either to all city employees or all employees within a particular department, since the city's practice must meet only the relatively relaxed standard of reasonableness to survive constitutional scrutiny.[25]

In making its decision the court took into account the fact that "employees can participate in the union checkoff only if they join an outside organization—the union," and consequently "the classification challenged in this case is not invidiously discriminatory, and does not . . . violate Fourteenth Amendment rights."[26] In his opinion in this case, moreover, Chief Justice Thurgood Marshall suggested that there were no hard-and-fast rules concerning the line-drawing in regard to payroll deductions. The cost of withholding monies and of administering the process could be taken into account, and denying one group of employees (in this case the firefighters) the use of the withholding process for a contribution to the union was not necessarily a violation of Fourteenth Amendment rights (equal protection under the law) so long as the standards used in doing so were fair and reasonable.[27]

The Supreme Court decision regarding the case of the *City of Charlotte v. Local 660* came at a sensitive time for the United Way and for the use of the checkoff for charitable deductions. The Filer Commission papers were being circulated, along with the Donee Report, raising critical issues about philanthropy and the United Way. Moreover, employee rights were receiving increased support from a variety of sources. Nevertheless, although the *City of Charlotte* decision left some ambiguities to be resolved about the use of the checkoff for various organizations, overall the decision was in line with United Way and corporate interests in preserving limited access to the workplace. The court also made another significant point for United Way in relating its non-discriminatory finding about selective use of the checkoff to the fact that the checkoff which could be denied was being used to fund an outside organization, namely, the union.

From the mid-1970s on, employee rights became an increasingly salient issue. Interpretations of the National Labor Relations Act by the NLRB suggested that there would also be more continued attention paid to questions of consistency of application and dissemination of information to employees about the nature of the rules.[28] Therefore, after 1976 there was to be more difficulty in enforcing the no-solicitation rule disparately, for example, by allowing United Way and flower fund solicitations on work time, while employees were not permitted the same privilege in regard to union-related activities or choice of other charitable recipients. In fact, despite the generally favorable, if cautious, response of the NLRB attorney to DeArment's letter in 1976, the issue of the status of the United Way "exception" did not disappear. Indeed, it often surfaced as part of the argument in cases of unfair labor practices which were not decided in favor of the corporation, but where the decision was made on grounds other than that of the United Way sole exception.[29]

On September 31, 1981, the issue of the "no solicitation" rule came to a head dramatically. In the Hammary Manufacturing case the NLRB held that a company's no-solicitation rule was unlawful to the extent that the rule permitted a sole exception for the United Way campaign. The United Way was apparently unprepared for this emergency, which they were convinced represented "a distinct departure from prior decisions of the NLRB and the courts" practice in the past.[30] The offending ruling by the NLRB actually appeared, almost hidden, as a footnote in the NLRB decision which otherwise generally affirmed an administrative law judge's decision that would not have affected the United Way status. The footnote, however, stated unambiguously:

> We find Respondent's no-solicitation rule invalid to the extent that it sets out the annual campaign for the United Way as the "sole exception" to

the rule's restrictions on solicitation. This exception does nothing less than sanction the rule's disparate application and therefore is unlawful.[31]

The United Way of America recognized the "serious adverse implications" that the ruling would have for United Way organizations, whose campaigns were based precisely on the point that they were generally considered to be at least limited exceptions to the no-solicitation rule.[32] As usual, United Way mobilized powerful supporters, and after a series of discussions with Hammary officials and its parent company, U.S. Industries, Hammary agreed to file a motion for reconsideration. They were also successful in getting the general counsel of the NLRB to file a Supplementary Motion for Reconsideration strongly in support of the United Way position.

On October 8, 1982, after many months of serious concern within the United Way system, the ruling in footnote 2 was finally rescinded.[33] It had taken one year of effort and continued pressure on the NLRB, but the unique nature of the United Way–corporate workplace connection was preserved. It does not, however, appear to be entirely coincidental that it was during this year (1981–82) that significant gains were made by the alternative fund movement in regard to employee campaigns, which included some major corporations. NCRP and the press announced major breakthroughs in IBM and AT&T, and it looked like other corporations might follow suit.[34]

Institutional Case Study: AT&T

In 1982, headlines pronounced changes in the campaign in part of what was then the Bell system. The situation developed first in an AT&T subsidiary in Murray Hill, New Jersey, in one of the Bell Laboratories facilities which carried out research and development for the larger Bell system. In the fall of 1979, an employee group known as ABLE, Association of Black Laboratories Employees, petitioned management to extend payroll deduction to include the National Black United Fund. Leaders from ABLE explained that they wished to raise funds through BUF to help the NAACP pay for a major loss it had incurred through a lawsuit that year, but the request certainly was made in the context of the broadening organizing efforts by NBUF.[35] In theory, it should not have been hard for Bell Laboratories to implement such a request. In effect, Bell already had a kind of donor option plan in place with over thirty-four possible designations on the payroll card, so that a thirty-fifth should not have been difficult administratively. The options on the card, however, were of a different nature. In the traditional United Way pattern they included only other local United Way fund-raising organizations located in geographic areas where Bell employees lived and to which, accordingly, they might wish to give their money.

The inclusion of an alternative fund, not in the regular United Way system, and tied to a social action minority group cause, presented other dilemmas. Thus it could hardly be a surprise that Bell management allowed the matter to continue unresolved through the 1980 campaign. In fact, according to a Bell spokesperson, they were still considering the request after that campaign, in December 1980. Clearly Bell was in no hurry to take on this controversial issue.

During the following months, there were a series of discussions involving black employees of Bell Laboratories, other management representatives, leaders of the local (New York and New Jersey) BUFs and the NBUF, and representatives of the Greater New York United Way and the national UWA. A consulting firm, Clark, Phipps, Clark and Harris, was brought in to study the situation and to help facilitate the discussions.[36] The consultants recommended that the "black employees of Bell Laboratories be granted the right to have voluntary deductions earmarked for the National Black United Fund" in time for the coming (1981) campaign; that this initial permission be granted for a two- to three-year experimental period; and that the period be used to determine ways in which the executives and management of AT&T and Bell Labs could "facilitate positive, constructive and mutually advantageous working relationships between NBUF and United Way."[37]

In August 1981 permission was finally given for the inclusion of NBUF as an option for giving in the campaign, but on a trial basis. A letter was sent to all public relations vice-presidents of the Bell system informing them that AT&T had approved a trial period "in which Bell Laboratory employees in New Jersey may donate to the Black United Fund through payroll deductions" but with strings attached. The company made it plain that the option was to be limited to Bell Lab employees in New Jersey only; the trial decision did not represent a change in the company's basic fund-raising philosophy; there would be no expansion of the trial scope during the trial period; and that "all attempts would be made to assist and encourage the inclusion of BUF into the United Way single-drive structure."[38] These conditions were accepted, albeit with some reluctance, and seventeen black managers of "BTL" (the Bell Telephone Laboratories) noted their objection particularly to the fact that the option was restricted to Bell Laboratory locations in New Jersey, and thus that other black employees of the Bell system were prevented from participating "on an equal basis in designating their donations."[39]

After this first campaign was concluded, the results were studied by the Clark consulting firm, and they found "very clear evidence of success." In their report they noted that "of the 1628 black employees at the Bell Laboratories in New Jersey, 778 chose to make payroll deductions . . . for BUF." Moreover, the report pointed out that of the total of 1,159 BTL employees contributing to BUF, one third (381) were white, or non-black; in addition, the campaign that year raised $60,303.56 for BUF alone.[40]

The Clark report, issued in January 1982, while the Hammary motion for reconsideration of the NLRB decision was still pending, recommended that AT&T should remove existing restrictions and expand the right of all Bell system employees to have the choice of making deductible contributions to NBUF for the next campaign. The report suggested that Bell Laboratories and AT&T should help NBUF and United Way work out a mutual accommodation. Thus it was not surprising that meetings continued around this issue during the spring of 1982 involving high levels of AT&T management, NBUF representatives, and representatives from United Way, including Lisle Carter, Dennis Murphy, and William Aramony. Other meetings were held in the summer of 1982, and it was reported subsequently that a vice-president of AT&T had promised that BUF—in this case the New York City BUF—would be treated as an equal partner, campaigning in the workplace alongside the United Way in the fall campaign.[41]

Although AT&T officials later denied this statement, in the uncertain climate of the Hammary decision and CFC litigation, the idea of other funds having equal access to the workplace might well have been considered. In any case, in the spring of 1982 AT&T commissioned another study, "Employee-Donation Philanthropy," and this study by Chester Burger, completed in June 1982, suggested that "the concept of the in-plant fund raising organization is attracting growing interest among corporations."[42] In light of the initial Hammary ruling, indeed, companies might well have considered running their own campaign, and the existence of computer technology for payroll deductions and agency payouts made this seem feasible. Thus, it was very likely that AT&T could have considered establishing an employee club, or its own in-plant federation, to which BUF would have access in a way similar to the United Way.

In the end, it was the more passive system of listing BUF on the card as a potential designee, in a limited form of donor option, that was utilized in the 1982 campaign. The matter, however, did not end there.

By December 1982, another report was issued on the question of employee philanthropy in AT&T. This time it was written by an in-house committee of AT&T personnel. The "Report of the AT&T Working Committee on Donor Option" reviewed the previous consultants' reports (those of Burger and Clark), met with representatives from the United Way and the national BUF organization, and worked from late September through December 10, 1982. By the time the report was finished, it embraced two major objectives which might have seemed incompatible. First, the single campaign at the workplace was to be maintained; and second, the New Jersey and New York affiliates of the Black United Fund were to be included as options in the 1983 campaign.[43] These two somewhat disparate objectives were to be resolved through donor option, and in fact, through an open form of donor option in which employees could choose to designate to any 501(c)(3)-approved organization. The report made it clear that this decision was based on a statement of consensus agreed upon by all the major United Ways in the greater New York metropolitan area, at a meeting at Woodcliff Lake. The meeting was arranged by the United Way of America, and included both partners and non-partners in Tri-State, the regional campaign organization of thirty-two local United Ways in southern Connecticut, New Jersey, and the New York City region.

The Woodcliff Lake Agreement was negotiated during the weekend of October 1, 1982, one week before the original ruling in the Hammary Manufacturing Case was overturned by the NLRB. The statement was shared with the AT&T working committee, suggestions were presented to the United Way of America, and on November 19, the United Way of America released its "Amended Statement of Consensus" governing a donor option service for United Ways serving the work and home communities of AT&T employees.[44]

As the Statement of Consensus made clear, the United Way of Tri-State would henceforth be acting as a kind of collection agency for the AT&T campaign in the tri-state area, and would bear the total costs for distribution of funds designated under the plan. AT&T officials apparently considered this a satisfactory quid pro quo. If the United Ways of Tri-State wanted to keep control of the AT&T employee campaign, and the monies that flowed through it, they could bear the expense. Thus the report was able to reconcile the objectives of one unified campaign (under the United Way umbrella) with access for local BUFs and other organizations, through an AT&T donor option plan to be utilized throughout the tri-state area.

Figure 8.1 AT&T Donor Option Plan Model Card

Donor Designation Form Exhibit and Instructions

The United Way of Tri-State Donor Designation form (a four-part form allowing only one designation per form) shown below, should be completed as follows:

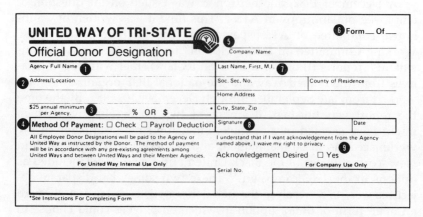

- ❶ Agency Full Name: Enter complete name of the designated agency.

  Examples: American Diabetes Association of New Jersey

  Black United Fund of New Jersey Inc. (BUF/NJ)

- ❷ Address/Location: Enter number and name of street, city and state. (If street address is not known, at least include the Town, State, and Zip Code.)

  Examples: American Diabetes Association of New Jersey
  345 Union Street
  Hackensack, New Jersey 07601

  BUF/NJ
  24 Commerce Street
  Newark, New Jersey 07102

However, even this plan was not without limitations. As the model card (fig. 8.1) shows, the card which was to be used under the new plan bore the insignia of the United Way, and the system for donor designation was such that a separate card had to be filled out for each of the agencies to be designated (up to a maximum of four). The model card, with a sample of directions to the donor, suggests that the process was not simple.

What happened in the Bell Laboratories and AT&T campaigns is illustrative of the power of choice, but is also complicated by other changes in the company's environment. In 1982, with the BUFs listed on the card along with local United Ways, the amount of funds going outside the United Way system (to the BUFs) in the Bell Laboratories was reported to have increased by 14.5 percent, with a slight drop in the number of givers (from 10,229 to 9,986) and a marked increase in the average gift per participant (from around $73.00 per participant to just over $84.00 per giver). In the following year (1983), however, the number of givers was reported to have dropped more, along with the total pledged, both to United Way ($555,884.55 in 1983 compared with $777,151.97 in 1982) and to the BUF affiliates (down to $70,867.83 in 1983, from $81,493.25 in 1982).[45] Conclusions from these figures are somewhat problematic, since the campaign of 1983 took place shortly before the announced divestiture of AT&T was actually to be accomplished, and when employees of the Bell system were already worried about the consequences of the system's break-up for their own jobs.

By 1984 designations were a major factor in the AT&T campaign, and, as table 8.1 shows, of $5,059,628 pledged that year in the AT&T Tri-State campaign, $1,186,287 was designated by employees but only $391,240, or less than half of the total designated, was indicated to be going outside the United Way, or to "non-funded" agencies. In June, 1984 New York Telephone employee designations were reported to have been over $2 million of their total pledges of $5,658,674.[46]

The AT&T employee campaign in the Tri-State area increased on the whole steadily, if slowly, from 1983 to 1986. Despite some initial decreases in the number of employees in the AT&T system overall as systemwide changes occurred, by 1986 the number of Tri-State employees involved had increased. However, as table 8.1 reveals, the amounts designated did not show a consistent pattern. The total designated decreased by over 34 percent from 1984 to 1985, and the campaign of 1986 reported an amount of $1,081,927 designated, but the amount still had not returned to its earlier 1984 high. The available figures suggest that perhaps fewer employees were giving more, and designating more, but do not prove this for certain. Although designations increased in 1986, a trend could not yet be determined. Table 8.2 shows that designations to BUF from AT&T employees, including both BUF/NY and BUF/NJ, however, fluctuated from 1983 to 1985, going from $112,276 reported for the campaign of 1983; to $142,191 for the 1984 campaign; to $78,445 for the campaign of 1985.[47]

As table 8.2 indicates, amounts designated in the top ten non–United Way category generally decreased in 1985, except for funds to the United Negro College Fund and a slight increase to Covenant House. Since this was also the period after divestiture (January 1, 1984), when people were moving about in the company, with the

Table 8.1. Donor Option Designations by AT&T Participating Companies (Headquarters, Communications, Technology and International) by Campaign Year (cy)

	(1983–84) cy 1983 [a]	(1984–85) cy 1984	(1985–86) cy 1985	(1986–87) cy 1986
Total Employee Pledges [b]	$4,116,209	$5,059,628	$5,238,104	$5,345,503
Designated:				
Partner U.W.'s	$ 138,671	$ 341,489	$ 163,356	$ 274,363
Non-Partner U.W.'s	4,905	26,175	17,271	22,283
Funded Agencies	388,334	427,923	285,308	465,970
Non-Funded Agencies	379,387	391,240	303,262	319,310
Total	$ 911,297	$1,186,827	$ 769,197	$1,081,927

Source: United Way of Tri-State.
Note: Campaigns are conducted in the fall of the year given, e.g. "cy" 1983, with pledges collected and paid in the following calendar year, 1984. "Campaign 1983–1984" means conducted in 1983 and paid in 1984.
[a] 1983 excludes technology; technology joined in 1984.
[b] Includes participating donor option companies only.

transfers and departures of workers, many pledges could have been misplaced, lost, or dropped by departing employees. Moreover, the figures made available do not include numbers of employees and therefore have to be interpreted with caution.

While designations decreased in the 1985 campaign, the overall amounts of money raised in the AT&T campaign reportedly increased. This suggests the possibility that whether or not employees actually used donor option, the availability of choice may have increased their giving. In fact campaign receipts grew in 1985, although it appeared that designations were not encouraged.[48] Even local United Ways were designated fewer dollars in that campaign.[49] A number of factors could have influenced decreasing designations, including changes in the format of the donor designation card, and the way that options for designation were presented to the employees of the various AT&T divisions. Several respondents suggested that donor designation was not explained clearly and might even have been discouraged in some AT&T units. In any case, designations went up again in 1986, along with an overall increase in amounts raised in the campaign.

Figures for designations to the BUFs (New Jersey and New York) and the United Negro College Fund for 1986 do not appear as non-funded agency designations in table 8.2, but for different reasons. In that year, United Way began to fund directly some programs of the popular United Negro College Fund, under some of its special program funding, and thus it would be considered as a United Way–

funded agency. Simultaneously, after much negotiation with BUF-NJ, AT&T adopted a new practice, distributing designations to the New Jersey and New York BUFs directly and not through the United Way of Tri-State system, and thus they are not included in United Way designation figures. Once again, however, it appears that to some extent outside events may have brought about this change; the Black United Fund of New Jersey undertook and won litigation against the State of New Jersey in 1985, successfully challenging United Way's exclusive status in the State Employee Campaign.[50] This eventually gave the BUF direct access to that workplace campaign.

In the fall of 1986 the New Jersey BUF appeared to have won another major victory. Both the New Jersey BUF and the New York BUF were now to be paid their designations directly by AT&T, without passing through the Tri-State United Way. And interestingly, in the same year and thereafter the amounts designated rose again, after what was considered a real effort by BUF to reach employees directly through pamphlets and through word-of-mouth. The networking that the BUFs used to reach black employees and their friends seemed to have paid off. For the campaign year 1983–84, final reported designations to BUFs by AT&T employees (including Bell Laboratories) were approximately $114,000; in the campaign of 1986 they rose to $205,200; with the campaign of 1987 these designations went up to a new high of $297,371. Meanwhile it seemed as if the company might continue to develop an in-house alternative-choice plan, if agreement could not be reached between the United Way of Tri-State and the BUFs. In effect, AT&T might have eventually considered treating the United Way as merely one of a number of competing funds in the workplace. When asked about this possibility, a contributions official in the AT&T Foundation said essentially that it was not impossible that they would make a similar arrangement with another fund, but that the other group would have to make as strong a case as the BUFs had done.

The situation in AT&T was in some respects similar to that faced by United Ways in California, where donor option was used as an alternative to in-plant federations, and where the implications of the suburban-urban arena also had to be factored in. But there also were differences. Events in AT&T were taking place primarily in the East; and while they were limited to one company, it was the largest corporation in America; therefore, it was not just any company. Additionally, the pressure was coming primarily from a well-organized single interest group, the black employees in the corporation and the BUF outside to whom they were linked.

Table 8.2. United Way of Tri-State Campaign Top Ten Non-Funded Agencies Selected by AT&T Employees Ranked by Total Amount Designated During Campaigns 1983, 1984, 1985, and 1986

Rank	1983	1984
1.	Black United Fund of New York $62,002.00	Black United Fund of New Jersey 93,270.00
2.	Black United Fund of New Jersey 50,274.00	Black United Fund of New York 48,921.00
3.	City of Hope/Cancer and Major Diseases Center 41,787.65	Covenant House 15,807.00
4.	Covenant House 12,228.00	United Negro College Fund 12,620.00
5.	United Negro College Fund 9,689.84	American Cancer Society of Morris County 9,243.00
6.	American Cancer Society of Morris County 7,561.00	United Way of Ocean County[c] 6,268.00
7.	American Cancer Society of Somerset 5,910.00	American Cancer Society of Somerset 5,740.00
8.	Matheny School 3,747.00	United Way of Kansas City 4,686.00
9.	Sickle Cell Disease Foundation of New York 3,440.00	First Aid Squad of Passaic Township 3,421.00
10.	Planned Parenthood of Essex County 3,155.00	Planned Parenthood of Northwest, NJ 3,364.00

Source: United Way of Tri-State.

[a] United Way of Tri-State began funding United Negro College Fund in 1986. Black United Fund of New York and New Jersey were paid directly by AT&T in 1986.

[b] Includes designations to United Negro College Fund/Atlanta (6,781.37) and to United Negro College Fund/New York (6,737.21).

[c] In 1984 United Way of Ocean County was not funded by United Way of Tri-State.

1985	1986[a]
Black United Fund of New Jersey 66,210.00	Covenant House 22,860.00
Covenant House 16,765.00	United Way of Bucks County 10,761.00
United Negro College Fund[b]	Hale House for Infants
13,519.00	8,263.00
Black United Fund of New York 12,235.00	Children's Specialized Hospital 6,166.00
American Cancer Society of Morris County 3,550.00	American Cancer Society of Morris County 4,524.00
Young Life	Young Life
3,176.00	4,469.00
American Cancer Society of Somerset 3,156.00	Matheny School
	3,888.00
Sickle Cell Disease Foundation of New York 2,870.00	House of New Beginnings 3,790.00
Little Village School for the Dev. Handicapped 2,762.00	Deborah Hospital/Brown Mills Chapter 3,463.00
National Down's Syndrome Society of New York 2,460.00	American Cancer Society of Somerset 3,385.00

Institutional Case Study: IBM

During the early 1980s, the National Black United Fund and New York BUF put continuous pressure on leading corporations to permit payroll deduction for the BUFs, but no other company responded in the same way as AT&T, and most made almost no response at all. Typically, either letters were not answered, or the BUFs were told that they should deal first with the United Way.[51] Before considering why this was so, it will be helpful to discuss what happened in one other major corporation that did at least make an effort to respond to BUF. That other corporate giant was IBM, where somewhat parallel precipitating events occurred.

In the fall of 1980, 100 IBM black employees affiliated with the Black Workers Alliance (BWA) signed a petition similar to that of the employees in the Bell Laboratories, asking for the possibility of giving to a BUF through payroll deductions.[52] The employees involved initially worked in Bedford-Stuyvesant area of New York City but seem to have been joined early on by other employees in White Plains and Poughkeepsie, New York. With the apparent direct encouragement of organizers in NBUF, and an IBM employee who was later assigned to work with the BUF organization, they asked to have BUF designated as an organization to which any member of an IBM employee club could contribute.

As in the case of AT&T the management of IBM did not react speedily, and again there was an attempt to localize any decisions in regard to funding of the Black United Fund. In this case, the employee group was told that decisions about the campaign were made at each work site, and involved participation by local IBM management with the local IBM employee club. Nevertheless, compared with the process at AT&T the decision was made rather quickly, and on July 18, 1981, IBM announced that its employees in the New York/Tri-State area could give to the Black United Fund through payroll deduction.[53] BUF was to be listed on the payroll deduction cards as an option, along with local United Ways and the American Cancer Society. Moreover, in these initial years, designated funds were distributed directly to the local New York or New Jersey BUF by the company itself—not passed through the United Way system.

This opening up of the Tri-State IBM workplace was of course potentially of enormous consequence to the United Way. Although IBM does not release figures for its employee giving, interviews with IBM employees and United Way professionals indicate that in 1983 IBM employees nationwide gave over $18 million in contributions, and a substantial part of that was raised in the Tri-State area. Moreover, all but about 10 percent of the amount raised by IBM employees went to local United Ways. However, despite the bally-hoo attached to the announcement, particularly on the part of the BUFs and NCRP, the happening did not really represent an extraordinary change in IBM's charitable practices. As we have already seen, in 1971 IBM had already allowed employee contributions to a local Black Fund; and by the 1980s, local employee groups were already, *with management permission*, involved in United Way–sponsored donor option plans in numerous communities. For example, there was one such donor option plan in place in San Francisco. Nevertheless, as with the case of the Boeing Good Neighbor Fund in Seattle, it appears that IBM employees across the country continued to earmark their funds primarily for local United Ways.

In keeping with IBM's stated policy of decentralization and local choice for its employee clubs, the relationship between BUF and IBM was apparently kept localized.[54] Listing of BUF on the payroll deduction card in the Tri-State area was treated as a local response to a request by employees in the Tri-State area, and BUF staff clearly did not have the kind of access to IBM leadership in national headquarters which United Way enjoyed. Indeed, there was a kind of dilemma in IBM's relationship to NBUF. For despite the fact that beginning in 1981 IBM ran a nationwide campaign focused on giving to the United Way, and NBUF viewed itself as a nationwide organization, inclusion of BUF was apparently limited to only a few locations across the country. Moreover, although for several years an IBM employee was assigned to work with the New York BUF, relationships with IBM remained problematic for BUF, and the New York BUF had questions about its receipt of funds from IBM employees in the Tri-State region.[55]

IBM's strategy of localism in regard to NBUF served effectively in containing employee's responses to the inclusion of BUF in the Tri-State campaign. Certainly in these initial years only small amounts were contributed to the New York BUF, and these amounts did not increase overall in the first three years. For the 1981 campaign, IBM reported $27,854.86 in designations to the New York City BUF; for the 1982 campaign, it rose sharply to $62,568.42; but for the 1983 campaign the reported figure was down to $60,438.86.[56]

By the 1986 campaign, designations to BUF were down, and the New York BUF was informed that henceforth all contributions made to the New Jersey BUF would be collected by the Tri-State United Way and thereafter passed to BUF. The message seemed clear by that time: IBM employees in the Tri-State area would be able to give to BUF, but IBM supported a United Way approach. Moreover, another interesting event occurred during this period; on the payroll deduction card for the Tri-State area, along with Cancer and the New York BUF, another black charity organization was listed prominently. This was the Associated Black Charities (ABC) formed with United Way's assistance and part of an earlier, but continuing, effort to deflect competition from an independent Black United Fund in New York.[57]

IBM's move to distribute NBUF-designated funds through the United Way was a victory for the United Way, and differed from the procedure established by AT&T that same year. AT&T had moved in the opposite direction to distribute employee designations to BUFs directly, by-passing Tri-State. The United Way was acting as the one central collection agency for the IBM campaign, and in effect serving in a similar capacity to that of the PCFO in local CFC campaigns for IBM (see discussion of United Ways as PCFOs above, chapter 7). It was not quite the same as the AT&T situation, where BUF's continued demand for equal access to the workplace seemed to be given greater credence. IBM's decision to pass BUF funds through the United Way of Tri-State could be interpreted as a further step away from this possibility. The principle of one charitable campaign in the workplace was being preserved, while at the same time both BUF and the ABC were listed on the payroll deduction card and therefore visible. Thus, choice was maintained, even if it was also contained.

Although it could be argued that funds going to BUF were not United Way funds, they would in the future be counted as monies collected by United Way, as they were in the CFC. At the same time, designations to BUF, like designations to unaffiliated Cancer organizations, or other non–United Way agencies, were directly competitive with the United Way. IBM recognized this, and seemed to accept this as a challenge to the marketing capacity of the United Way. Indeed in the winter of 1986, IBM held an intensive marketing seminar for the Tri-State United Way, and helped United Way prepare for the increased marketing needs it would be facing.[58] The company, and United Way, accepted the idea that there would be a different future in workplace fund raising and it would be competitive. IBM was, in turn, being helpful in the process.

Changes in the Air

Changes in the IBM and AT&T employee campaigns in the early 1980s appeared dramatic and were so announced to the world in the press, and by NCRP. However, the degree of change that actually occurred remained debatable. There was an apparent change in the practice of AT&T with its open form of donor option, but nevertheless it could be argued that the change was less than startling. Donor option, even in its wide-open form, was not new. At least seventy United Ways had donor option in place by that time, and this included those in Philadelphia and San Francisco, where such big companies as Crocker National Bank and United Airlines already had such plans. Moreover, in the case of IBM it could be argued that they simply extended to BUF in the New York area privileges which BUF, or ACS, had had elsewhere within the IBM system.

The changes in the AT&T campaign and the Tri-State IBM campaign were not totally without precedent, and also left United Way in the leadership position. Nevertheless, these changes had to be taken seriously. They were indeed compromises, but compromises of significance for the United Way–corporate relationship with big business. To begin with, they did appear to be "cracks in the dike." The change in AT&T particularly amounted to a real change in the practice of a major American corporation—changes which were negotiated with some degree of power on the part of the BUF, and with considerable discomfort by the United Way. At the same time, the more minor change in IBM practice was also taken by a company that was ostensibly a stalwart supporter of United Way. Although these changes were accommodations made reluctantly in response to new employee attitudes and demands, they plainly resulted in new groups becoming part of the workplace campaign. Employees could now actually contribute not only to traditional health and welfare agencies but also to other social action or advocacy agencies in AT&T, and to BUFs, in particular, in IBM.

The situation was paradoxical. While the changes were being implemented, these companies continued to proclaim their support for United Way. Indeed, IBM was a leader in the United Way National Corporate Development Program during this period and these were the years in which IBM involvement with the United Way campaign increased dramatically. The rhetoric of company loyalty to United Way was basically undiminished even in AT&T, and the changes which took place in the employee campaign were fit around this pronounced loyalty. However, in the meantime, other organized charities now had potential access to payroll deduction, and they would be competitors for employee dollars, even if these dollars passed formally through the United Way system.

Although the modifications in the charity campaign adopted by IBM and AT&T were not unique to these companies, they were unusual in the New York area. Other companies headquartered in New York had been approached by NBUF in these years, and had not responded in the same way. Among the list of those approached were such giants as Mobil Oil, Texaco, Ciba-Geigy and Pfizer Chemicals. Indeed, when asked about the letter he had received in 1984, a high official in one company stated that he was glad to be reminded about it; he had forgotten to pass the letter from NBUF to his CEO and would subsequently do so.[59]

Some companies simply did not respond to NBUF or the New York BUF's approaches. Others, like Exxon, met with BUF and informed leaders of the New York BUF that they would either have to deal with the company through United Way or gain greater credibility through a stronger, more prominent board, and a greater activity level. Indeed, in those years, the New York BUF was struggling, and it could hardly show either the kind of leadership or track record in funding organizations that a local United Way could muster.[60] Moreover, in order to show its unique nature for the CFC, the NBUF was actually promoting a program of economic and social advocacy, which would make the BUF idea less palatable to conservative corporations if they knew about it.[61]

The question, however, still remains—why did these two major companies, IBM and AT&T, respond differently to requests for more open access to the workplace than other companies did? Once again, responses to organized charity were affected by other factors in the environment which did not appear to be directly connected to charitable campaigns, but which made both companies more open to employee-initiated changes in the campaign than other major companies in the New York area. Moreover, of the two, it would seem that AT&T was in the more sensitive situation.

To begin with, in both companies the demand for choice emerged from a group of technologically trained, highly educated workers, and at the same time was spearheaded by an increasingly self-identified black employees group connected to forces in BUF or on the outside, indeed originally to Walter Bremond himself. Although the identified black group was more significant numerically in the Bell system, both companies had a group of concerned black employees. Moreover, highly educated workers or professionals generally do not have the traditional pattern of contributing easily to United Way campaigns, in the manner that blue collar workers in Detroit, for example, or even Bell Telephone affiliated factory workers would.

Second, and closely related to the first condition, both companies prided themselves on their good employee relations. But at the same time both companies had been subject to questions of fair employment practices. There were issues of affirmative action and equal opportunity in both companies, which were likely to make each in turn particularly sensitive to the demands of black employees. In 1973, a judge had strongly upheld an AT&T affirmative action plan, and in the next decade the ABLE group had grown in strength within the company. Even more immediately, IBM was actually in the courts during the early 1980s, facing charges of discrimination brought by the Equal Employment Opportunity Commission on behalf of a group of minority employees. Although the company eventually won the case in 1984, nevertheless IBM certainly must have been concerned about any complaint brought by black employees during the period when the case was being argued.[62]

Third, during the time when issues about BUF were being raised at AT&T and IBM, there were also problems occurring in New York City with the United Way municipal campaign. It began first with the question of continued payroll deductions for contributions not authorized on a yearly basis, and resulted in Mayor Koch's refusal to allow the 1979 and 1980 city employee campaigns. When this campaign was reinstated, the major municipal employee union, District Council 37 of the Association of Federal, State, County and Municipal Employees (AFSCME) passed a resolution in favor of BUF participation, and subsequently a wide-open donor option plan was adopted for use in the municipal campaign. Thus, events in the public sector must have had some influence on the attitude of black workers in AT&T and IBM and affected the position of management toward their demands at the same time. This action also may have been at least partially the result of the 1980 decision in the *Mama Rag* case, which raised a serious issue about discriminating against charities based on any kind of questionable or vague grounds under public law. Although the decision in *Mama Rag* concerned tax exemption, the court held that the definition of "educational" (in relation to educational or charitable organizations in the tax code) was unconstitutionally vague, in violation of the First Amendment, stating that "explicit guidelines" are needed "in order to avoid arbitrary and discriminatory enforcement. . . . Laws are invalidated if they are wholly lacking in terms susceptible of objective measurement." If applied by extension to all publicly regulated charitable relations this might also apply to the workplace solicitation "exceptions" provided by the NLRB.[63]

Fourth, events in the CFC and with the federal government might have affected reactions of AT&T and IBM to employee demands for options in giving. Just about a month before the IBM agreement to permit payroll deductions to BUF (July 1981), the government had announced that it would allow NBUF into the CFC.[64]

In addition, there was something special about the nature of the business that these two companies engaged in, that might have made them feel particularly vulnerable to any attack which could be related to the issues of monopoly or restraint of trade, even if only in regard to access of charitable organizations to the workplace. Both AT&T and IBM were involved in legal challenges concerning their reputed monopoly status in the business world, and could be expected to be particularly sensitive to any publicity which would cast a negative light, even tangentially, on this issue. This was undoubtedly so, even though in the end both companies appeared to have come out reasonably well, with AT&T accepting some less advantageous trade-offs in the process.

Certainly IBM won a major victory when the anti-trust case against it was finally dismissed in January 1982.[65] On the other hand, the decision in regard to AT&T seemed more of a compromise, allowing AT&T deregulated business in some product areas, but not in its long distance telephone service. Nevertheless, the AT&T monopoly in regard to the telephone system was broken up as a result of the court decision, which mandated divestiture by the AT&T parent company in January 1984. In any case, both companies were in the courts on these issues during the late 1970s and early 1980s, and at the same time both companies were facing employee questions on affirmative action as well.

Fifth, and closely related, at a time when employees everywhere were becoming more militant about their rights, IBM and AT&T would have each felt particularly vulnerable. Both companies prided themselves on their company "family" spirit based on good employee relations. Protests had originated among professional workers, including highly expert engineers and researchers. In addition, in the early 1980s, employees in AT&T were subject to a particularly turbulent environment, since the imminent divestiture had already begun to cause rumors about plant relocations and employee lay-offs. The initial negotiations around funding of the BUF were also being carried out around the time when the United Way nationwide was having trouble with the unions, typified by the attempted boycott of the 1982 campaign led by Winpisinger of the IAM.

Finally, during these years, there was a peculiar relationship developing between these two companies which might well have made them more sensitive to each other's actions. These were the years in which the headlines noted that with the breakup of AT&T, and the increasing convergence of the activities of the various aspects of the telecommunications industry, AT&T was gearing up for its challenge to the hegemony of the "big blue" in the computer-communications industry. Thus, in opening up their employee campaigns, each was certainly watching the decisions of the other, although in the end each took a different route. In any case, AT&T would have to be even more careful than IBM in its actions in the charity arena, because as a public utility AT&T was still subject to regulation in a way that IBM was not.[66]

In the end there were significant differences in the way that IBM and AT&T dealt with the BUFs. Although IBM allowed BUFs to be listed as an option on their cards in several localities, on the whole they treated BUF in a more stand-offish, removed manner than AT&T did. At AT&T headquarters, after the initial pressure from BUF was recognized, there were a series of relatively open discussions of the issues involved. Ultimately, this culminated in the decision by AT&T to pay employee designated funds directly to the New Jersey and New York BUFs, by-passing the Tri-State "collection" system entirely.

By the time of this decision, it appeared that the United Way of Tri-State had had considerable difficulty in carrying out the administrative role in managing donor option in a company undergoing vast internal changes, and the New Jersey BUF and New York BUF were raising serious questions about the accuracy and timeliness of their payments.

A Different World: Minneapolis–St. Paul Site Case

The late 1970s and early 1980s were clearly sensitive times for the United Way–corporate relationship, and yet corporations appeared reluctant to move away from involvement with the United Way. Indeed, in the cases that we have considered, Boeing, IBM, and AT&T, went to great lengths to maintain this involvement. Even AT&T, while changing the form of the campaign so as to allow a system for "open access" to payroll deduction, still proclaimed the hegemony of the United Way in the process through these years, certainly until the move to pay designations to BUF directly in 1986. There were, however, other "cracks in the dike" which represented serious challenges to the United Way system, and these had to do with the possibility of a cafeteria choice of funds, in the manner first proposed for the CFC in 1981 and 1982. A good example of this situation occurred in two companies in the Minneapolis–St. Paul region, the St. Paul Companies and Ecolab, Inc.

Minneapolis–St. Paul is considered a progressively oriented community, with a strong university and a relatively homogeneous population. The population of the Minneapolis–St. Paul SMSA was 1,787,564 at the time of the 1980 census, and was largely white

(1,685,257). The largest single minority was blacks, who numbered only 49,506 in 1980.[67] The dominant population group socially and numerically are northern Europeans, whose families immigrated from Sweden, Norway, and Germany. The area is considered liberal politically, with cultural activities influenced by the presence of the University of Minnesota, and a progressive philanthropic community, characterized by a very active grantsmakers group to which the growing number of new corporate philanthropy officers belonged in the late 1970s and early 1980s.

In this tradition of taking corporate philanthropy seriously, the Minneapolis United Way was extensively examined by a local newspaper in 1978. Although a reporter followed the United Way executive around for several days and monitored United Way activities closely, the newspaper articles basically found little serious fault with the United Way.

In the early 1980s, General Mills, and national corporation headquartered in Minneapolis, undertook a study of the users of social services in the area, focusing on the demographic characteristics of individuals who used United Way services.[68]

The study surveyed a sample of 2,000 households in the Greater Minneapolis area, and found that the bulk of United Way services were recreational, or athletic, and were used predominantly by suburban residents, and by people whose income was over the median income ($24,000) for the United Way area. The United Way responded in typical organizational fashion, playing down the significance of the findings. Officials pointed out that the study was methodologically faulty, since it over-counted time-consuming services like swimming or gym use, and services of the YMCA or Boy Scouts.[69] On the other hand, the situation was also paradoxical for General Mills as well, since it suggested that people like their employees would be likely to use United Way services described in the study, and these services might therefore be a benefit to company employees.

Once again, however, circumstances seemed to converge and cause change in 1982. This was the time when the CFC was undergoing rapid change, and opening up to competing groups of agencies and cooperating federations; it was also the year when the Hammary case was still under consideration by the NLRB. In this unsettled climate, and while the study for General Mills was being carried out, the St. Paul Companies granted permission for the Cooperating Fund Drive to solicit its employees in a side-by-side campaign with the United Way in the fall of 1983. The Cooperating Fund Drive (CFD) had begun to emerge as a strong, if fledgling, alternative fund in the area,

CORPORATE RESPONSE TO CHALLENGE 205

with success particularly in public sector campaigns, under the leadership of two driven and dynamic women.[70]

Although the Cooperating Fund Drive was a small fund, it was professionally organized, and actively involved in the nationwide movement of alternative funds, connected to the NCRP. In fact, by 1984, in listening to the campaign director of the fund talk about campaign techniques, it was hard to distinguish her approach from that of a regular United Way "campaigner."[71] In any case, CFD was permitted to carry out a side-by-side campaign with the local Arts Fund and the United Way in 1983. All three funds were on the pledge card, and allowed to give their own campaign pitch. Although the two competing funds raised $15,883 (Cooperating Fund Drive) and $22,318 (the Arts Fund), by the campaign of 1985, CFD had been locked out of the St. Paul Companies.[72]

Different explanations were given for this occurrence. Apparently, however, in permitting the Cooperating Fund into the workplace, the company had been influenced by the fact that the local United Way had been badly managed in previous years. A new young executive had since arrived, Joseph Haggerty (from Corpus Christi), and the United Way was now doing its homework. Officially, this meant that the United Way was making an effort to become far more inclusive in its funding of agencies, and more responsive to community needs. Unofficially, this meant that the United Way leadership met with the top management of the St. Paul Companies, in a successful attempt to change its position.

The Cooperating Fund Drive also recognized that it had been admitted to the St. Paul Companies during a time when the United Way was in disfavor, and conceivably it had served as a means to put pressure on the United Way to improve its own performance. In addition, however, staff of the Cooperating Fund Drive might have made a mistake in strategy in their approach to the St. Paul Companies. They had gone through the corporate philanthropy officer and middle management level to reach the CEO of the company, rather than through the employees. Thus, when the top leadership of the company was undergoing change, and a new CEO came in, there was not enough employee pressure or support throughout the company to keep the Cooperating Drive as an option.

Finally, an official of the company suggested a different reason. In addition to implying that admission of the Cooperating Fund Drive might have helped make the United Way more responsive, the official noted that the company was reluctant to be involved with advocacy organizations, or organizations which are controversial and likely to make trouble. The Cooperating Fund Drive included agencies that

Table 8.3. Dollars Raised From Employee Contributions Ecolab Campaigns,
1984–1986
Corporate Headquarters, St. Paul, Minn.

	United Way	United Arts Fund	CFD[a]	Total Giving Increase
1984	$81,000*	$ 6,300	$ 6,300	17%
	+1%	N/A	N/A	
1985	83,800	10,800	12,400	14%
	+3.4%	+96%	+71%	
1986	89,200	13,600	18,900	15%
	+6.5%	+25%	+60%	

Source: Ecolab, Inc.
[a] Cooperating Fund Drive.
*All figures are rounded.

supported women's causes, and protected gay and lesbians, which the official said were "non-consensus type organizations." By implication the CEO in 1985 was not sure that these were organizations to which the company might want to give its *imprimatur* by permitting an employee campaign.

An interesting comparison exists in close proximity to the St. Paul Companies. In the same city, while the St. Paul Companies was closing its gates, Ecolab Inc. was opening them. In 1984, Ecolab, a middle-sized company whose major business was chemical specialty products, systems for cleaning and sanitation, opened its headquarters workplace drive to the Cooperating Fund Drive and the United Arts Fund. It did so under the concept of the community giving campaign, with the primary goal of increasing "overall giving in the community." According to one philanthropic officer, the company was successful in achieving that goal.[73] As table 8.3 demonstrates, overall giving increased 17 percent in 1984; 14 percent in 1985; and 15 percent in 1986. In the same years, giving to United Way went up also, but far less than giving to the other competing organizations: 1 percent in 1984; 3.4 percent in 1985; and 6.5 percent in 1986.[74] The question remained, however, whether United Way would continue to have increasingly large shares of a growing pie, or whether the increases in these years were the result as much of special attention to the campaign (a kind of "Hawthorne effect") as they were of increased competition.

In the meantime, the philanthropic officer in Ecolab indicated that the company continued to be dedicated to increasing the rates of employee participation and the amounts of money collected through the employee campaign. Moreover, she made the point that, as of 1986, donor option was being offered through CFD and that this was attractive to the company. Consequently, it seemed possible that if donor access were made available through the United Way, the company might actually consider going back to a unified campaign in the workplace, under the aegis of the United Way.

Conclusions

Corporations move in and out of philanthropic activity, as they do with other activities, according to company need and self-interest, albeit if it is defined as enlightened self-interest. However, since philanthropic activity is generally considered ancillary to all other activities, there is always the risk that if it becomes problematic, companies will drop these activities entirely. Nevertheless, as we have seen with IBM and AT&T, companies, once committed, are unlikely to drop their relationship with United Way, and may even go to great lengths to maintain it. Even when challenged by strong environmental forces, they maintain their loyalty in their actions and in public statements and protect the myth of United Way's importance in the charitable arena. Thus, the companies we have looked at modified campaign procedures, and with the possible exception of Ecolab, were clearly reluctant to give up the notion of the one United Way–dominated campaign. This was the case even with Boeing and IBM, which had in-house employee clubs, and apparently was reflected also in the case of AT&T.

However, since company campaigns are sensitive to corporate interests, conditions in the environment will inevitably affect the way that workplace campaigns are run. In the case of AT&T employee concerns forced the use of systemwide donor option, and resulted in United Way bearing the expense of the donor option plan, in a period when there were major issues facing the corporation. Moreover, the company ultimately made real changes in the campaign in order to lessen internal conflict at a time when the company was already suffering from severe external and internal stress.

Thus, even while the principle of one unified, efficient workplace campaign is being maintained in theory, it is being altered in practice by a variety of submodels, which include in-plant federations and various new forms of donor option. Indeed, it seemed as if by the mid-1980s, the time had come for increased experimentation around different kinds of employee participation in decision making concerning their gifts to charities. If companies like AT&T were to become the model, there could by extension be more of a move away from a United Way donor option plan to a company donor option which also allows for giving directly to alternative funds, and which therefore might ultimately lead to more use of company-employee involvement in allocation systems; in short, to some form of in-plant federation. But in actuality it seems that many of the experiments are time limited, and aimed primarily at changing the United Way.

In any case, while United Way continues its major role as distributing agency for company campaigns, it may also take on the additional new role of collecting agency, and, in the model of the CFC, count all designated funds as United Way–raised monies. At the same time, local United Ways will certainly be increasingly involved in more intense competition in more open workplaces. Here some corporations are likely to be particularly helpful. They can practice their own expertise, as United Way faces market competition from health groups such as the Cancer and Heart organizations, from newer rivals such as the BUFs, or the arts funds, as well as from other smaller, more localized social action funds. And while the battle is being waged for the employee dollar, the increased use of donor option and rising demands from alternative funds must result in increasing strain on the allocations system, and in particular, on allocations to the larger traditional member agencies. These are the agencies that over the years have been strongly identified with the United Way, and that have continuously received the bulk of United Way contributions.[75]

Chapter 9

Company Choices and United Way Agencies: The Bottom Line

> Major community issues such as employment, economic development, health care, and housing may receive more thoughtful attention as their importance becomes apparent. . . . Corporate support could well become an essential factor in achieving new approaches and solutions to social problems.
>
> William F. Symes, president of Monsanto Fund and director of the Corporate Support Program of the Monsanto Company

> Although the Foundation's scope is national, emphasizing support of higher education, health and social action, and arts and culture, its staff and board members seek to fund institutions . . . and projects that help improve the quality of life on the local level as well, particularly in those communities where AT&T has a major presence.
>
> AT&T Foundation

IN the world of organized charity in which the United Way, voluntarism, and corporations come together, it is often difficult to distinguish fact from fiction, at least partly because the role of myth has been so significant in maintaining the United Way–corporate relationship. Indeed, business leaders understand that the appearance of support for voluntarism and the myth of corporate commitment in themselves lend validity to the United Way system. As the case studies suggest, corporations with a strong tie to the United Way have been reluctant to change their involvement, and they continued to proclaim their loyalty to the United Way even when they did actually modify their relationship to it. Therefore, as the United Way centennial celebration drew closer in 1987, the question remained unresolved as to what degree these modifications represented a major trend of the future, or whether they were simply temporary responses to pressure with little long-term implication for organized charity.

The rhetoric of ideological positions compounds the difficulty of interpreting the long-range implications of the events of the early 1980s. According to NCRP, there had been a "virtual revolution" in five years (1982–87), and the "giant United Way's stranglehold on workplace donations" had been broken. The NCRP newsletter proclaimed the "explosive growth in workplace donations to 'alternative charities' " and cited the over $100 million raised by alternative funds in the 1986 campaign.[1] However, most of the amount raised by the alternative fund movement continued to come from public sector campaigns, federal (CFC), state, and local government employees, while the corporate workplace remained largely closed to the alternative funds.

In fact, most national companies approached by the Black United Fund in those years still refused to permit BUF to have a separate campaign in their workplace (see above, chapter 8). Moreover, they continued to back up their rhetoric of support for the United Way with such valuable resources as loaned executives, public relations and campaign material preparation, and participation on United Way boards and committees, as well as through the participation of over 300 companies in the National Corporate Development program. Nevertheless, for the United Way, the true measure of corporate support is the actual amount of dollars contributed by the company itself, and by its employees, and the measure of success is a constant increase in both. Analysis of changing corporate giving patterns is therefore critical to understanding of future directions in the United Way–corporate relationship.

Corporate Contributions and the United Way Campaign

Complete, comprehensive, and specific figures for charitable giving by individual companies are difficult to obtain, since they are not widely disseminated and are usually subject to ambiguities of interpretation.[2] The best figures available have generally been considered those compiled by the Conference Board, a corporate-sponsored research and information center in New York City, with the Council for Financial Aid to Education.[3] The Conference Board utilizes data from a variety of sources, including the Internal Revenue Service of the federal government, and the Council for Financial Aid to Education with its own survey data, and data supplied by the United States Department of Commerce. Conference Board data are utilized here, along with data from other sources including a survey of United Ways carried out for this study and data supplied by the UWA, which present an overview of corporate giving generally, and corporate and employee giving to United Way specifically in the years after the Filer Commission (1975–1985).[4]

Corporate Contributions, 1975–1985

As a whole, corporate giving in our country increased steadily between 1975 and 1985, going from $1.202 billion in 1975 to an estimated $4.3 billion in 1985.[5] Corporate giving increased by over 250 percent in a decade, growing from 0.91 percent of pre-tax income (1975) to 1.61 percent of pre-tax income (1984), down very slightly from 1.62 percent in 1983 and up to 1.89 percent of pre-tax income in 1985. Although corporate giving in those years never approached the amount permitted as tax deductible under the income tax regulations after 1936 (5 percent prior to the 1981 Tax Reform Act, 10 percent thereafter), contributions did rise after 1975, coming closer to the 2 percent figure recommended by the Filer Commission.

In the early 1980s corporate contributions continued to rise as a percent of pre-tax income, and companies even increased their gifts in the recessionary time of 1981–1982 when corporate profits declined. Thus corporate contributions rose to $2.906 billion (and a high point of 1.76 percent of pre-tax income) in 1982, as compared with $2.514 billion in 1981 (or 1.14 percent of pre-tax income).[6] Although the higher percentages of giving to pre-tax income certainly reflected *decreases in the base of the actual amounts of pre-tax income* (down to $166.5 billion in 1982, from a reported $221.2 billion in 1981), nevertheless there was at the same time an *absolute increase in dollars of reported contributions.*

Despite disclaimers by some corporate leaders, it appears that the increase in corporate gifts was at least partially a result of the pressure placed on corporations by the "less government" lower tax policies of President Reagan, and his emphasis on "private sector initiatives." Either evidence of greater need, or a desire to support the policies of a pro-business administration, seemed to have influenced corporations in 1982 to continue the practice begun in 1980 of taking more dollars out of their foundations for giving than they put into those foundations.⁷ In 1983 and 1984 corporate contributions continued to rise, going to an estimated $3.3 and $3.8 billion respectively.

Despite the apparent steady increase of corporate giving, the picture for the voluntary sector was not quite as positive as it appeared. Although corporate contributions tripled in absolute amounts in those years, so did the CPI, the inflation index. Overall, in fact, corporate gifts hardly kept up with the increased rate of inflation in the country.⁸ Moreover, as already suggested above, rising figures of corporate giving as percentages of pre-tax income can be misleading, since this rise is affected by decreases in corporate income as well as by increases in giving. In addition, the nature of the corporate gift began to change somewhat in this decade, with the total contributions figure including larger amounts of non-cash contributions such as services, company products, or property, such as land, instead of dollars.⁹ This kind of gift is more limited in usefulness to agencies and their clients than straight cash contributions. In any case, even including non-cash gifts, the total amount of corporate contributions only rose 2.3 percent in 1986, as compared with over 10 percent growth the previous year.¹⁰

The problem was compounded for the voluntary sector, and particularly for human service agencies, because of cutbacks in government funding during these years. The impact of the cutbacks varied from community to community, and agency to agency, but they were estimated to average over 5 percent from 1981 to 1983.¹¹ With the reductions in government support, voluntary agencies had to find other sources of funds just to maintain their own programs, as well as to help fill additional gaps in community services. In theory this money could have come from the corporate world, and some money in fact was given in different communities for special projects directed at meeting emergency needs.¹² However, losses in government funding during those years were actually replaced primarily by growth in entrepreneurial activities. A major study by the Urban Institute of a large sample of agencies in the voluntary sector documented increased sales of products and materials (up 23 percent) and service fees (also up 23 percent), while private giving, which would also include the United Way, only increased by six percent.¹³ This move into entreprenurial activities raised further issues about the tax status of some non-profit organizations, but was generally accepted as a necessity.

Corporate Contributions to United Ways

As the table in appendix C.3 demonstrates, corporate dollars to United Ways continued to increase during the years 1975 through 1985. Despite the pressure on corporations to diversify their contributions to other causes, the absolute dollars they contributed to the United Way system still increased, going from $281.3 million in 1975 to an estimated $554.5 million in 1985.[14] In absolute dollar amounts corporate support showed continuous growth, but once again the figures bear closer scrutiny.

To begin with, corporate contributions to United Ways increased at a slightly lower rate than increases in the United Way campaign overall during this period. Corporate contributions increased by about 87 percent, while the United Way campaign as a whole more than doubled in the same period, going from $1.039 billion in 1975 to an estimated $2.4 billion in 1986. Thus, it appears that corporate gifts were a somewhat smaller part of the total raised by the United Way in 1985 in comparison with 1975. This circumstance is somewhat disguised in general reporting and in charts showing distribution of contributions to the United Way, possibly due in large part to the frequent changes in terminology and in composition of what is included in the categories of givers over the years (see appendix D).

Second, during the period 1975–1985 corporations began increasingly to diversify their giving. Health and social welfare causes generally, and the United Way in particular, continually received a declining share of corporate contributions during those years. As table 9.1 indicates, in 1975 health and human services were receiving over 41 percent of all corporate support tracked by the Conference Board, and by 1984 this percent had decreased to only about 27.7 percent. By comparison, as the table also reveals, giving to civic and community causes had risen from 10 percent of the total reported contribution (1975) to over 18 percent (1984), and fell again in 1986. Culture and arts increased slightly, from around 8 percent in 1976 to nearly 11 percent in 1980, and hovered around 11 percent through 1986. Education rose from about 36 percent of the contributions pie in 1975, to almost 41 percent in 1982, leveled off at around 38 percent by 1984, and increased again slightly by 1986.

The drop in the market share of the corporate contributions pie going to health and human services in this period reflected a decrease in the United Way share specifically. As the Conference Board survey indicated, in 1975 giving to federated campaigns amounted to almost 25 percent of contributions of the reporting companies. By 1984, however, although the United Way was still "the largest beneficiary" of the reporting companies, United Way and other federated

Table 9.1. Percentage of Corporate Contributions Given to Health and Welfare, Education, Culture and the Arts, Civic and Other Activities, 1970–1986.[a]

Year	Health & Welfare[b]	Education	Culture & Art	Civic	Other
1970	38.6%	38.3%	5.3%	8.1%	7.4%
1971					
1972	42.0	36.9	4.1	9.1	6.6
1973					
1974	38.5	36.0	7.3	10.4	7.7
1975	41.2	36.2	7.5	10.3	4.6
1976	39.3	37.3	8.2	11.0	4.2
1977	38.3	37.0	9.0	11.5	4.2
1978	36.9	37.0	10.1	11.4	4.5
1979	35.0	37.7	9.9	11.6	5.8
1980	34.0	37.8	10.9	11.7	5.6
1981	33.6	36.7	11.9	11.7	6.1
1982	31.0	40.7	11.4	11.7	5.2
1983	28.7[c]	39.0	11.4	14.8	6.1
1984	27.7	38.9	10.7	18.8	3.9
1985	29.2	38.3	11.1	16.5	4.9
1986	28.0	42.9	11.9	13.2	4.0

Source: *Annual Survey of Corporate Contributions, 1982 Edition*, pp. 30–31; *1984 Edition*, pp. 32–33; and "Advance Tables from the Annual Survey of Corporate Communications, 1986," Table 2 (New York: The Conference Board).

[a] Note, however, that there are a different number of companies reporting each year, and in the 1980s there was a decrease from 534 companies (1982) to 370 companies (1986).
[b] Includes federated campaigns.
[c] Health and Human Services (1983).

campaigns were now receiving only slightly more than 13 percent of the total, and this pattern continued through 1986.[15] Although contributions to United Way still represented about 99 percent of reported corporate contributions, by 1986 the Conference Board survey was beginning to ask about giving to other federations. Thus, it noted that over 40 percent of the companies reporting contributions to other federated campaigns in 1984 did not report contributions to United Way, which seemed to suggest that these donations to other federated campaigns were in place of, rather than in addition to, contributions to United Way.

In addition, the median dollar value of corporate giving to federated campaigns was also reported down in 1984, to $179,000 as contrasted with $192,300 in 1982. Interestingly, this was happening at the same time that corporate contributions (that is, the company gift) to federations on a per employee basis increased from a median of $22 (1981) to $26 (1984), or from $20 to $26 on a sum-by-sum basis (the total amount given by the company divided by its total number of employees).[16] These higher figures of giving on a per employee basis, however, may reflect decreases in the base for the calculations (the number of employees in companies) as much as increases in corporate giving in absolute dollars. These were after all years in which many major companies were laying off employees, due to mergers, plant closures, and other economy measures.

Although the corporate community as a whole continued its financial support for the United Way during the critical decade of 1975–1985, the *share* of company contributions dollars going to United Ways declined, even while the *absolute amount of dollars* continued the slow but steady increase typical of previous decades (see appendix C.3) The trend to broaden the scope of corporate support for other causes was evident. Contributions to culture and arts, and education, increased proportionately during this period, along with gifts in the civic and community category. This category was defined in the Conference Board Report of 1986 as including support for a broad base of national organizations in public policy research as well as national justice and law organizations, or local community organizations.[17] In short, it covered a wide range of national and local organizations, which could be considered as advocacy focused, as well as neighborhood development groups which were apparently not funded by local United Ways.

Nevertheless, the health and human services category and United Way still remained a major area of corporate giving in 1983–1984. The Conference Board noted that this sector still received the highest median dollar value ($345,000) and the largest median percentage of total contributions (40 percent). Total dollars to this category, in fact, increased by $62 million between 1980 and 1984,[18] although its share of total charitable donations was down. Only the subcategory of national health organizations increased as a proportion of the total. However, given the history of United Way involvement with the health agencies, this factor was bound to be a matter of serious concern for the United Way. In addition the Conference Board report noted what has already been discussed in previous chapters: corporate giving to health and human services has traditionally been locally oriented and funneled through federated campaigns in the community,[19] but many corporations may now be interested in branching out to new initiatives.

Giving by Industry Size and Type

Health and human service organizations generally receive a major *portion* of the contributions made by smaller companies. Companies (and particularly non-manufacturing companies) with contributions budgets that were under $500,000 gave a median of nearly 48 percent of their budget to health and human services, in contrast with a median percent of over 28 percent for companies giving a total of over $5 million. As a group, the median *dollar value* of corporate gifts reported by the Conference Board as going to health and human services was larger by far for manufacturers ($419,000 for manufacturers as contrasted with non-manufacturers, $251,000). Companies giving the largest gift per employee were the oil companies (petroleum and gas) at a sum-by-sum figure of $53.00, followed by pharmaceuticals at $40.00. In non-manufacturing, the highest were the banking companies ($48.00) followed closely by the utilities ($43.00) and financial firms ($40.00).[20]

In its survey of company giving for 1984, the Conference Board reported that non-manufacturers gave a greater proportion of the total given to United Way campaigns than did manufacturers (17 percent and 12 percent respectively). Greatest percentages were reported for companies in the rubber and miscellaneous plastic products industry (31 percent); retail and wholesale trades (25 percent); and utilities (22 percent). The leading industry on a sum-by-sum basis was banking, followed by petroleum and gas.

The findings of the survey we conducted for this study covering the year 1983 were somewhat different from those of the Conference Board. This was not surprising, since our sample was 131 local United Ways and not of corporations, and we asked a somewhat different question.[21] For our group of responding United Ways, there was no reported statistically significant difference between manufacturing and non-manufacturing categories as a whole. Within the two categories, there were some similarities and differences in comparison with Conference Board findings. For the manufacturing category, the mean gift of primary metal industries was the highest ($139,566), followed by petroleum and gas ($122,207); chemicals ($93,193); electrical machinery ($92,816); and rubber and plastic products ($89,040). For the non-manufacturing category, insurance ranked the highest with a mean gift of $110,183, followed by personal services ($90,333), banking ($88,927), and utilities ($85,085) (see appendix C.4).

In our survey of contributions to United Ways, banks were reported as the highest group of givers in absolute dollars; and in the Conference Board findings, banking organizations were the highest reported giving group to the United Way on a per employee basis, followed by petroleum and gas, which was also the second largest of the givers by totals in our listings. Utilities were also among the biggest givers in absolute amounts, and on a per employee basis, in the Conference Board surveys. It should be noted, however, that in terms of overall assets or dollar volume of business, utilities and petroleum and gas industries are not labor-intensive industries, so that once again the figure for the company gift on a per capita basis is inflated by the fact that such companies have relatively fewer employees than do other kinds of companies.

Overall, our findings appear to be consistent with other research findings about community-related giving by corporations. To begin with, they are consistent with the notion that banks, as locally invested companies, would have a major stake in their communities. Consequently, they may be expected to give generously to United Way at least partially as a way of helping to maintain good community services, and hence good communities—in short, as a protection for their investments.[22] But there are at least two other reasons why banks are involved in both giving to and participating in United Way charity, aside from the general high status involved in such leadership activities. For bankers, volunteering in a prominent local charity brings them into contact with other businesses and individuals who in turn may bring their money directly to the bank. And, in addition, the United Way, as a large cash business, also puts its money into banks, and in fact, to the greatest extent possible, attempts to make money on its money, through certificates of deposit and other investments offered by banks. In this case, therefore, relationship building is good business, and enlightened self-interest is visibly demonstrated in community investment (see above, chapter 7).

To some extent this same principle of community investment and community involvement by locally based companies also explains the relatively high corporate gift of the utility companies to United Ways, even if the principle does not apply to them as directly as it does to local banks. However, with the utilities there is an additional factor involved. For many utilities, such as those of New York State, the corporate contribution to United Way is charged off directly to the consumer, by being included in the rate that is set for the consumer cost of the utility's service. Thus it may be questionable philanthropy.[23]

In any case, the community investment also applies to insurance companies, with their large local commitments. However, personal relationships between executives of insurance companies and the United Way generally have a more subtle impact on direct business transactions.

Second, the findings of our survey, carried out during a recessionary period, appear to be consistent with the notion that geographically immobile industries would tend to invest more heavily in local philanthropy generally, in time of recession.[24] Thus banking, utilities, and oil companies, as well as insurance companies, all ranked high as givers to our sample of local United Ways. The ranking of some other manufacturing industries, including steel (and despite the cutbacks in that business), also suggests that immobility may be a factor in encouraging company support for local health and welfare, and particularly, federation activities.[25] However, the contributions of one major company, IBM, included in the electrical machinery category, affect the high total amounts of support in that category.

Finally, the Conference Board also reported that in the period from 1980 to 1984, several industries made significant changes in the proportion of their giving allocated to health and human services. Among the industries which reported major decreases in percentages of their giving to health and human service agencies were textiles (decreased from 46 percent to 16 percent), insurance (decreased from 40 percent to 20 percent), and the telecommunications industry (from 40 percent to 21 percent). Large increases in the proportion of total giving going to health and human services occurred only in business services (from 30 percent to 47 percent) and pharmaceuticals (from 22 percent to 36 percent).[26]

Given the number of factors that influenced these changes, and the fact that individual companies are not identified in the Conference Board reports, the particular cause of each indicated change cannot be pinpointed precisely. However, some possible connections between external factors and corporate giving seem likely. For example, in regard to textiles, textile manufacturing outside the country was expanding, and there were problems between United Way and some of the textile-related unions in the South. In regard to the telecommunications industry, the turbulence of the AT&T break-up may be reflected in these figures. But in addition, the decreased share of giving to the United Way from this industry appears to reflect deliberate changes in AT&T giving patterns through its newly created foundation (1984), which in 1985 gave $6,513,165 to United Ways out of a total of $24,886,140 (or about 23 percent), as contrasted with $6,251,495 out of $16,122,872 for 1984 (or over 38 percent), a significant proportionate decrease.[27] It also appears that corporate contributions staff in the insurance companies have begun to influence the use of foundation dollars in this industry as well, since there seems to have been a wide-spread effort at diversification of their contributions portfolio. Corporate contributions officers also suggested that they watch national average percentages of corporate contributions going to United Way, to insure that their giving is "in the ball park" of national averages. Where their company's giving to United Way is a higher share of their total company giving than the general reported averages, they evidently try to bring it down to scale.[28]

In regard to the companies that have increased their giving to the United Way, it should be noted that the business service category includes construction and engineering companies, businesses that could be considered at least relatively immobile, and which would in any case be concerned about community relationships and conditions. In the other category that showed an increase were the pharmaceutical companies. This is not surprising, since several large pharmaceutical companies were also in the National Corporate Development Program, including Ciba-Geigy Corporation, Merck and Company, Johnson and Johnson, and Pfizer. In particular, during these years Edmund T. Pratt, Jr., Chairman and CEO of Pfizer, served as chief volunteer officer for the United Way of Tri-State (1982–1983), and during these years his company's contribution to the United Way increased about 20 percent.[29]

Company-Employee Choice and Agency Funding— Signs of Change

In the decade from 1975 to 1985, corporate contributions to United Way increased, but less slowly than the overall growth in the United Way campaign. During this decade corporations began to diversify their giving, including new recipients in such areas as arts, education, and civic and community causes. In addition, after 1980, non-cash contributions, which were less useful to cash-dependent United Ways, became an increasing share of corporate giving. Thus United Way in the mid-1980s was facing the future with an increasingly smaller share of a slowly growing amount of corporate contributions. This was at the very time when, because of government cutbacks in human services spending, more demands were being placed on the voluntary sector. Moreover, at the same time, the United Way system was also facing continued pressure to diversify its funding package, and therefore to spread its slightly increasing funds to an ever-larger group of agencies, in order to respond to the challenge of employees who were demanding the opportunity to give to a variety of charities of their own choice.

The trend to increased diversification in corporate giving consequently was at least partially paralleled by the same phenomenon in the United Way system. Both the corporate world and local United Ways were being challenged to allocate funds to newer agencies, emerging groups, or advocacy organizations which had not been previously included in their preferred funding streams, and the IRS was questioning whether support of such organizations qualified as a charitable deduction. The most visible aspect of this challenge had occurred in the debates around the CFC, and in the famous OMB Circular A-122. In retrospect it was clear that on the whole the advocacy groups had emerged victorious from that battle, but not without scars.[30]

Funds distributed through the United Way campaign were being diversified in two major ways. First, changes were being made in the United Way allocations process, and the distribution of monies, to allow for increased admission of new agencies and more extensive use of targeted funds or venture grants to new agencies and programs. And secondly, funds collected through the combined United Way campaign were being dispersed though the use of donor option plans. In this second category, the activity of fund raising and the issue of employee interests crossed over directly with the nature of the end product of fund distribution or allocations to agencies. Employee contributions to United Way, like corporate contributions, continued to rise in the 1980s, rising to $1,463 billion in 1985.[31] But employees were increasingly being given the opportunity to make their own determination about the ultimate recipient of their gift through the use of donor options and other choices. In the end, with all the new options available, the United Way system was being subject to continual strain, as a variety of disparate centrifugal forces threatened to pull apart what had been a consensus-dominated movement.

Employee Giving and Donor Option
Precise data about the use of donor option in companies is difficult to obtain. However, as the case studies suggest, many workers will take advantage of donor designation, and in both Ecolab Inc. and AT&T they made substantial use of donor options when encouraged to do so. Indeed, donor designated funds increased throughout the United Way system in the period 1982–1984. Moreover, although a large part of the rise clearly reflects increased use of designations in the wide-open donor option plan of the CFC, it was not only in the CFC that the rise in designations was taking place. As the tables in appendixes F.3 and 4 indicate, by this time the United Way campaign was marked by extensive employee designations (both positive and negative) in a variety of industries.

These tables also give some idea of the relative strength of designations in various trade groups. Caution must be exercised in interpreting these data, but the relatively large numbers and amounts of designations in the communications industry plainly stand out. This undoubtedly reflects the situation in AT&T and New York Telephone, already utilizing donor option extensively in the Tri-State area in the period 1983–1984 (see chapter 8 and appendix C.6) The data also suggest the increased success of the alternative funds in opening up state and local government campaigns.

The tables of designations by industry do not indicate what amount of designations went outside the United Way system of affiliated agencies, and how much remained internal to the system. These data are, however, provided in the aggregate in the table in appendix F.6. As table F.6 indicates, in 1984, out of a total of $48,227,382 reported as designated positively in all campaigns, $32,941,417 went to local United Ways and their member agencies; $15,285,965 went to agencies either unaffiliated with the United Way or affiliated for donor option purposes only.

Increases in the amounts of designations in the United Way system in the early 1980s and through the CFC raised critical questions about future directions for the United Way, and whether an extremely open form of donor option like that used in the CFC, San Francisco United Way, or even the New York City municipal campaign, would spread through the corporate workplace—and if it did, whether such designations would increasingly go outside the United Way system of affiliated agencies, or could be contained inside the United Way system through more aggressive marketing programs. The signs suggested that specialized causes like Heart and Cancer everywhere, Women's Way in Philadelphia, the BUFs in some communities and workplaces, and even some local communities like Morris County in the Tri-State area could muster strong separate appeals. They were consequently a continual threat to the consensus idea and to system-wide campaigns.

By the 1980s the UWA was typically trying a number of ways to prevent the dam from breaking, and to hold the federation together. United Ways tried to woo the most popular causes, such as Cancer and Heart, into the United Way system through sweetheart contracts and partnership agreements; in the New York area, special arrangements were made to fund a particular program of the United Negro College Fund. In some communities, even services of Planned Parenthood were funded through targeted funds. With strong corporate urging the UWA continued to push the idea of inclusiveness in the 1980s, and tried to gain as many affiliated agencies from among the threatening agencies as possible. However, it could not win over those who, like the BUFs, or the CFD in St. Paul-Minneapolis, considered it fundamental to their basic mission to stay outside the United Way; and in some case, they could not co-opt organizations like Women's Way, or some affiliates of Planned Parenthood, which believed they could make more money on the "outside."

In the early 1980s, the one notable exception to the BUF external relationship policy occurred when the San Francisco BUF formed a partnership with the United Way. That BUF was subject to criticism on ideological grounds by other BUF leadership. Later the same BUF also claimed that the United Way had not treated it fairly as a campaign partner, restricting its access to the corporate worksite, and limiting its base in the campaign receipts.[32] By 1986 it had, in fact, broken off partnership with the United Way. As a whole, despite the adaptive policies of the United Way, United Ways were unable to co-opt some of the major alternative funds, and these challengers successfully continued to remain outside the United Way system by choice, including women's organizations, general social action funds, many CHADs, and most of the BUFs (see appendix J.2).

United Way Responds—Changes Through Shifts in UW Dollars

The Health Agencies

In the years between 1976 and 1983, generally the term "inclusiveness" in United Way circles meant different things to different people and was shrouded with a certain amount of ambiguity. It covered admission of new programs and agencies with social action orientations and minority leadership, as well as the traditional United Way rivals, national health agencies. However, from the words and actions of Bill Aramony, and the allocations pattern typical of most United Ways, its primary meaning in practice during those years clearly meant inclusion of the health agencies—first, local Cancer Society affiliates, and then later the Heart Association. Indeed, with the increased use of donor option by 1983, the United Way was actively pursuing the very marketable health agencies, including, among others those two big national agencies. An internal United Way document noted that the United Way's relationship to health agencies was "One of Our Best Kept Secrets," and partial listing of local United Way allocations to selected national health agencies reported that health allocations to represented health agencies represented 18.5% of local allocations, with the American Cancer Society alone receiving $22,500,000.[33]

By 1983 approximately seventy-six local United Ways had agreements with ACS chapters and approximately forty-eight local agreements had been signed with affiliates of the AHA. These arrangements usually guaranteed these organizations a large base amount of money, or percentage of the campaign, for a period of years, and the organization was not required to go through the allocations process. The official justifications for adding Heart and Cancer as partners in the campaign was that they would bring in more money than was paid out to them in campaign receipts. As suggested earlier, however, the major reason underlying the avid pursuit of these organizations was undoubtedly to keep them out of the corporate workplace in their most pernicious form: as participants in rival fundraising organizations, that is, in local CHADs. In any case, in the 1983 campaign, United Way figures indicated that United Ways with Cancer contracts did better than others without them, (9.6 percent campaign increase compared to a 9.1 percent increase), but those with Heart contracts apparently received a smaller increase (9.1 percent compared with 9.4 percent).[34]

Given the numbers of variables affecting United Way campaigns, it could not be proven definitively that Cancer contracts were the reason for any increases, or that Heart contracts caused decreases. It would also seem that most Cancer contracts cost more to the United Ways than they could be proved to bring into the system. However, there was no doubt that health agencies, and cancer-related causes in particular, were big winners in the donor-designation popularity contest. For example, in the years 1983–1986, Memorial Sloan-Kettering Cancer Center (a cancer treatment hospital in New York City) was among the top ten "funded" designees for AT&T employees in the Tri-State campaign, ranging in those years from $8,451 in designations (1983) to over $11,500 (1986). ACS units in the non-membership category ranked consistently among the top ten for the years 1983–1986, and ACS received substantial designations nationwide also in campaigns where partnership agreements existed (see tables in appendix F). Thus United Way's decisions about the health agencies, and ACS participation, were clearly appropriate business decisions for dealing with powerful and popular competitors.

Other New Admissions and Special Grants

In the period of 1980–1985 many corporate leaders made it plain that the price for continued support of the United Way campaign by their company was an enlarged, more inclusive group of affiliated agencies within the United Way system. Inclusiveness, however, meant different things for different companies. Thus, in Hartford, the local Chamber of Commerce, as the lead for the large companies involved, was instrumental in forcing a United Way–CHAD partnership in the early 1980s. In Minneapolis–St. Paul, progressives in the corporate philanthropic structure placed pressure on the United Way to shift its allocations to more high-priority needs, through studies such as that of General Mills, and through funding of the Cooperating Fund Drive. IBM funded the New York BUF directly, and then succeeded in forcing BUF to receive funds through the United Way. AT&T and Crocker Bank required donor option.

At the same time many local United Ways actually appeared to be making some changes in their own funding patterns, by adding new kinds of agencies and programs to their roster of affiliated agencies. Our survey indicated that for our sample of 131 local United Ways (Metros I through VII), 19 new agencies (or programs of new agencies) were added in 1975; 34 agencies/programs were added in 1980; and 42 were added in 1983, with a funding amount ranging from $100 to $500,000 in 1983. In the period from 1980 through 1983, more specifically, 30 United Ways in the sample added a total of 72 new agencies classified as social action or non-traditional services, either because of their target group (minorities of color, women), or because of their defined social mission, such as employment and job training.[35]

In comparison, the Yale study of eight local United Ways reported that in the five-year period from 1976 to 1981, 176 agencies were added by the sample group. But without including San Francisco, always the exceptional case, only slightly more than one new agency was admitted, on the average, each year by each United Way in the study.[36] Overall it appears, therefore, that local United Ways in 1983 were adding slightly more new agencies in a four-year period, with some agencies in the social action or minority dominated category. However, agencies admitted in this category received far less money than was being funneled generally to health (Cancer/Heart) agencies through the partnership agreements of the early 1980s. Unfortunately, the United Way does not publish consistent data for allocations to "new" agencies or new programs. In the 1985 United Way *Allocations Profile* a more complex system for indicating new funding patterns was used, including the following categories: seed money, targeted funds, agency contingency funds, and combined funds, to participating and non-participating agencies, but there was no way to determine from these listings which funds went to new agencies. In line with a presumed emphasis on funding programs rather than agencies, there was no actual category of "new admissions," nor can it be determined from the figures in the tables how many new, non-participating agencies were actually funded or how much money they received, since the categories are overlapping, and the bulk of funds set aside for new purposes were for "all" agencies, including both categories of participating and non-participating agencies.[37]

The actual amounts set aside by local United Ways for funding of new causes, new agencies, or even new programs of "old" affiliated agencies varies greatly but is not large. For example, in Metro I, the minimum set aside in 1984 by a United Way for "new programs" was $8,315, and the maximum was $500,000.[38] Considering that most Metro I United Ways raise considerably over $9 million, and the largest raised over $80 million that year, the amount of money set aside clearly was "at the margin" of regular allocations for most of these United Ways. Moreover, it appears that most of this money in the end may have gone to regular participating or affiliated United Way agencies, and certainly some of it went to the national health agencies, AHS or ACS. Moreover, United Way's own figures suggest that increases in United Way dollars to advocacy causes are small, because the dollar base from which they start is generally so low (see below, chapter 10).

Nevertheless, campaign funds were now being allocated to agencies or programs formerly outside of the United Way system, no matter by what terms the United Way described this category of long-term affiliates. Even if the amounts included a large percent going to the popular health agencies, and if most of the money set aside in various reserve funds still went to long-affiliated agencies, a variety of previously non-funded programs were being added at the margins of the United Way agency list. Consequently, the question has to be asked, where was the money for these programs coming from? Were enough new funds being raised by United Ways during this period so that they could both increase allocations to old affiliated agencies and at the same time provide any significant amounts of funding for new program grants, partnerships, or long-term affiliation with new agencies? This question will be addressed in the next chapter.

Part V

The United Way as a National Organization and as a Charitable Enterprise

Chapter 10

Structure and Function

> The amount-raised figure . . . represents the total amount of money raised by a local United Way organization. Regardless of the final use of funds, total amount raised includes dollars donor-opted in the community through United Way and all monies raised as the PCFO within the Combined Federal Campaign.
>
> *1984–85 UWA International Directory*

ALTHOUGH the United Way had not attained its earlier stated goal of $3 billion, the amount of dollars raised through the United Way system continued to grow to an estimated $2.4 billion in 1986. However, even with the continued increases in funds, strains in the United Way system were threatening its core functions as an organized charity. On the one hand, the United Way was being forced to broaden the base of agencies that it funded through the allocations process, and to be more inclusive; on the other hand, new demands of American society and decreasing government support, suggested that it should also be giving more funds to its long-supported, core group of "member" agencies. In addition, in order to maintain its hegemony in the workplace, United Ways were responding to corporate pressures, and demands for one campaign through a variety of donor designation systems and new organizational structures.

The only way that United Ways could fund new organizations

230 NATIONAL ORGANIZATION AND CHARITABLE ENTERPRISE

without loss to any of the traditional affiliated agencies would, of course, be by raising a continually larger amount of money. If there was enough growth in the pie overall, even with new programs added, older affiliated agencies could at least theoretically maintain their share of the pie.[1] However, the amounts raised by the United Way system did not actually keep up with the inflation rate for most of those years; new charities were demanding a share of workplace funding; and at the same time cutbacks in the government sector caused further pressures on the voluntary human service system.[2] Thus United Way responsiveness to environmental demands became a major issue, at a time when scarcity of resources was evident, and friends and foes alike were examining the United Way closely to determine if there had been real changes in the system since the Filer Commission report.

It was not, of course, likely that funds would ever be distributed in a way that would satisfy all the stakeholders: the older traditional agencies, the newer social action causes, traditional corporate leaders, emerging corporate contributions officers, unions, and community groups. But change was called for. By the mid-1980s even longtime corporate supporters of the United Way were expecting changes in the basic structure of the system, in the processes by which it operated, and in the outcomes of these processes.

Distribution of United Way Dollars—
A Paradox of Outcomes

By the early 1980s many United Ways had begun to set aside funds for new programs and agencies, and had responded to pressures for inclusiveness in their allocations process or for use of donor option. Nevertheless, the distribution of United Way funds to member agencies in the aggregate appeared to be changing only slightly during these years.[3] Indeed, at United Way's centennial celebration (1987), it was, surprisingly, claimed that "forty percent of United Way money goes to 12 national charities. . . . The American Red Cross received $170 million last year."[4] The United Way of America appeared proud to announce that over 40 percent of its money was going to a group of only 12 largest agencies—an announcement which highlighted continuity of funding for "old line agencies," while they were still proclaiming the need for inclusiveness, and donor choice was in fact resulting in more dollars leaving the United Way system.

The apparent paradox of these two positions can be explained by a closer look at the figures. To begin with, prior to the early 1980s the total amount of monies collected by the United Way system officially counted only those funds raised for the United Way system of local United Ways and their member agencies. Thus, for example, the relatively small amount of money going out of the United Way system through the CFC and some SEFAs was not considered United Way money. After 1983, however, all funds raised in campaigns run by local United Ways began to be officially reported as United Way monies, even if they were earmarked from the start for non-participating agencies or other funds such as the BUFS or CHADS.[5] By the mid-1980s this included a larger amount of funds being raised through the CFC and SEFAs as well as through some companies.

The effect of this reporting of all donor-designated funds as part of the United Way campaign total can be demonstrated in several ways, starting with the CFC. In that campaign in 1985, $67 million, out of the total of $130 million raised, was designated to non–United Way organizations. Since the $67 million was raised in campaigns where the local United Way was the PCFO, that $67 million would have been counted in the total of $130 million raised in the CFC in 1985 and finally counted also in the $2.33 billion reported as raised by the United Way system that year.[6] Nevertheless, the $67 million would in fact not be available for allocation to regular United Way–affiliated agencies.

Another way of looking at the situation is to consider the total amount reported as raised by alternative funds in the 1985 campaign. As table 10.1 demonstrates, almost $101 million was reported as raised by the alternative funds and unaffiliated charities from employee contributions, and this in effect would have been about 6.5 percent of the reported total raised by United Way from employees nationally, if certain conditions were satisfied. These conditions included: funds were raised, and designated, in a United Way–managed or administered donor option campaign;[7] and money in a workplace campaign went to new agencies or alternative funds which, while not connected to United Way through a traditional membership arrangement (i.e., involving their participation in the allocations process), had partnership agreements with local United Ways; or the funds were raised in a company-run, United Way–influenced campaign, such as an in-plant federation, in which the local United Way had a donor option plan in place.

Most workplace campaigns met at least one of these conditions, since United Ways had donor option plans in most of the communities where there were large public sector campaigns (CFC or SEFA), or major challenges from alternative funds such as the BUFS, or Women's Way.[8] They also had partnership agreements with several

Table 10.1. Total Employee Contributions to Alternative Charities, 1985
By Unaffiliated Charities and Types of Alternative Funds
Also Alternative Funds by National or State/Local Base

	1985 Total Employee Contributions	# of Alt. Funds Soliciting through Payroll Deductions	
		National	State/Local
I. ALTERNATIVE FUNDS			
Health Funds			
National Health Agencies (NHAs)	$ 29,284,235	1	19
Combined Health Appeals (CHAs)	8,009,428	0	20
Social Justice Funds			
National Service Agencies (NSA)*	8,696,000	0.9*	0
Black United Funds (BUFs)	2,453,405	1	7
Social action funds	1,236,119	0	20
International Funds			
International Service Agencies (ISA)	10,817,602	3	0
United Arts Funds	1,685,338	0	12
Environmental Funds			
National Service Agencies (NSA)*	1,018,000	0.1*	0
Environmental Federation of Calif.	91,000	0	1
Subtotal of all Alternative Funds	$ 63,291,127	6	79
II. UNAFFILIATED CHARITIES**	$ 37,328,521	na	na
GRAND TOTALS	$100,619,648	85	

Prepared by NCRP
April 1987

Source: National Committee for Responsive Philanthropy, *The Workplace Giving Revolution: A Special Report*, Spring 1987.

*The NSA is but one alternative fund with 59 member agencies including six conservative organizations (such as Capital Legal Foundation) as well as eight national environmental groups whose workplace revenues are separated here for purposes of better understanding.

**These include all types of charities (such as health, social justice & others not listed above), not affiliated with any of the alternative funds. Also they are mostly traditional charities.

of the major CHADS and they seemed to garner large continuous percentages from most in-plant federations such as those of BEGNF and General Electric Company. There were only a few significant places where cafeteria-like choices among alternative funds actually existed, such as the case with Ecolab in St. Paul, Minnesota. There the United Way did not have a donor option plan in place and since Ecolabs allowed a separate side-by-side campaign which included the United Arts Fund as well as the Cooperating Fund Drive, United Way could not count all funds raised in that company. This was clearly one of the exceptions in the nationwide counting system, although another exception was created in 1986, when AT&T decided to pay designated funds directly to the BUFs.[9]

Consequently, by the mid-1980s there seemed to be some double counting, or duplication, in the counts of the United Way and the NCRP. Much of the $101 million which NCRP claimed was being raised by and for the alternative fund movement was also being claimed as United Way money. United Way recognized this, but United Way campaigners pointed out that since they did all the work in raising the money for the campaign, why shouldn't they get the credit for it?[10] Indeed, why not, if it was a United Way donor option campaign?

This argument finally makes explicit the reason why the use of donor option was so significant for the United Way system. So long as funds raised went through a donor option program managed by a United Way or in a campaign where the United Way controlled the distribution of the money, the funds counted as United Way–raised funds–even if they could not be United Way–allocated funds.[11] This was particularly obvious if the funds raised were designated to individual agencies, but was stretched by United Way even to include designations to other alternative funds like BUF/NY or Women's Way, so long as the money was collected in a donor option plan. Moreover, control of donor option was tied to overall control of the campaign. Donor option in any case was a method of co-optation by absorption, although it was not without problems when untraceable or questionable agencies were included.[12]

As we have seen, however, some major organizations resisted donor option, and wanted equal access or at least equal visibility in the workplace, including most BUFs and the CHADs in many communities, as well as individual social action funds like the CFD in Minneapolis, or the powerful national health agencies. Consequently, with the encouragement of corporations, many local United Ways used partnership agreements as another strategy. This was the case with some local units of the big national health agencies, AHS and ACS, and also with some of the alternative funds as well, including BUFs in San Francisco and CHADs (Baltimore, Hartford, and San Diego). There was even a brief period when United Way explored actively the possibility of entering into partnership arrangements, or utilizing donor option plans, for other kinds of non-profit organizations, like the United Arts Funds, which were not in the traditional health and welfare domain of the United Way.[13]

United Way apparently felt that it needed to show constantly increasing collections, even more than it needed to show growing allocations. If monies came from a single workplace campaign, administered by the United Way, or by an in-plant federation which gave a large percentage of funds to the United Way, the funds counted as United Way–raised funds. If, on the other hand, an alternative fund was allowed to enter the workplace as a separate fund, the United Way could not count this as money raised by the United Way system. In the end, therefore, whether or not the money went to the United Way "family" of affiliated agencies, and whether or not the money passed through the United Way allocations process, seemed to be less important than making the largest possible nationwide counting of monies raised in the campaign. Undoubtedly, corporations initially were not concerned about this reporting system. In the recessionary years of the early 1980s, and with a conservative national administration touting voluntarism, corporations also had been making every effort to keep up both the reality and the façade of increased philanthropic dollars.[14] Moreover, companies were still interested in maintaining the myth of United Way as working "for all of us," and the fact of a one workplace campaign.

United Way reports nationally in its press releases the gross amount of money that the system claims to have collected or administered nationally. Total dollar amounts allocated to agencies on a nationwide basis are not published, although local United Ways usually publish their own community-based allocation figures. Aggregate allocation figures, or figures about specific groups of agencies by name, have not generally been publicly tallied or disseminated. Such figures undoubtedly would expose the real gap between total dollars raised and dollars allocated. They would also have pinpointed the exact nature of support (e.g., percent of totals, trends in dollar amounts) going to specific agencies, arousing controversy over whether too much is given or too little—something the United Way has always wanted to avoid.

Typically, UWA public information releases report percentages of allocations and not dollar amounts, or they relate dollar amounts to categories of agencies, such as youth-serving agencies, rather than to a particular agency or agency group like Boy Scouts or Boys Clubs.[15] Nevertheless, the UWA collects detailed figures on allocations, including the dollar amounts to affiliated agencies, nationwide, by name. The figures become part of the United Way data base, and are analyzed also as percentages of total allocations for the group of agencies that respond to the national allocations survey.[16] These percentages of total allocations going to national agencies or groups of agencies, like Boy Scouts or YMCAs, are available internally through the United Way allocations books distributed to participants in the United Way data collection survey. (see, appendix E of this book)

Strains on the Federation Dollar

Allocations figures have been collected and analyzed by the national organization for many years, although there have been changes over the years in the way that figures are collected and measured. With the coming of the computer age, there has been a major effort to keep figures with greater accuracy, but changing numbers of reporting local United Ways, and the use of different terminology and definition, still suggest that conclusions from any trend analysis are somewhat tenuous.[17] Nevertheless, two kinds of figures have always been important to the human service community. The first is a measure of the overall percentage, or share, which United Way dollars represent of the budgets of the agencies they fund. The second is the amount of the total allocations pie which each agency receives, and, nationwide, which each agency group receives. In both cases, changes in the percentages are paid attention to, although the first set of figures is more widely cited in public discussion.[18]

The percentage of support received by United Way agencies in relation to their total budget is considered a significant factor in defining the relationship between local federated fund-raising organizations and their agencies. Federations were, after all, originally formed to provide support for their particular member agencies. Also, agencies joined a federated fund-raising organization presumably so that they would not have to do extensive fund raising on their own, and many executives still cite this reason. Federations have been viewed as providing a kind of pass-through for corporate support to the human service world, and agencies were to be limited in their own independent ability to raise funds from the business world directly.[19]

The extent to which agencies complied with fund-raising limitations and the kind of accountability which was accepted has always been recognized as variable, and a problem for the United Way.[20] Some studies of the subject have suggested that agencies that receive larger percentages of their funds from United Ways have tended to be more compliant with United Way regulations in both the area of general accountability and fund-raising restrictions. But some large and powerful agencies, by virtue of their independent connection to power bases in the community, are well-known violators, who have fought over these issues with local united funds for decades.[21]

Thus, the Boy Scouts, with their close connection to many corporate CEOs, have frequently subverted the rule against corporate fund raising; the Salvation Army raises funds—in periods that are considered closed for fund raising—through their Christmas kettles and letters to community residents; and they also resist many of the accountability tools of the United Way, without stating the obvious reason, their special status as a religiously related institution.[22] Agencies like the Red Cross, or Family Service Agencies, in the past received a high percentage of their budgets from United Ways, and also had a more consistent pattern of compliance. Overall, that higher percentage of United Way support for its core agencies certainly gave a cohesive sense to the federated fund-raising system. This was true even after it was recognized that the federated idea had become part of the United Way myth, and that the actual share of agencies' budgets represented by United Way funds ranged from almost 100 percent for some agencies to just above zero percent for others, and included many points in between.

In this respect, the trend was clear. If federated organizations in their early years raised a large part of operational income for their member agencies, this situation did not last. By the time of the United Fund (in the 1950s) agencies were relying greatly on other sources of income, and federated organizations utilized a combination of community volunteers with staff support to make decisions about allocations of funds raised. With increased interest in direct corporate participation, the idea of the donor as the decision maker about fund allocations and the Fund as steward of the money prevailed. Community-based fund-raising organizations began to consider themselves as "funds," concerned more about wishes of the donor than demands of the agency. Concomitantly, the percentage of support to "member" agencies began to drop. By 1970 it was down to 27 percent of agency total budgets; by 1985 United Way reported that it was down to 11.3 percent. It should be noted that this figure applies only to the universe of United Way–supported human service agencies. A lower figure reported by the Urban Institute around that time, of United Way support as 5 percent of the budget of a sample group of agencies, reflected the fact that the sample included agencies which did not receive any United Way funds.[23] Nevertheless, even at around 11 percent, the United Way was certainly not providing the bulk of agency support for its affiliated core agencies.

The second point of interest about percentages of support con-

Table 10.2. United Way Allocations to Selected Agencies
1973–1983–1985

Agency	1973 (%)	1983 (%)	1985 (%)
Amer. Red Cross	14.6	12.1	11.9
Family Serv. (n.d.)[a]	6.1	7.0	6.9
YMCA, YMCA-YWCA	5.8	5.6	5.3
Boy Scouts	5.1	4.5	4.3
Salvation Army	4.6	4.8	4.7
Settlements/Neighbor. Centers	3.7	5.0	4.7
YWCA	3.6	3.2	3.0
Girl Scouts	3.0	2.9	2.8
Boys Clubs/Boys-Girls Clubs	3.0	3.8	3.6
Home Health Agencies/ Visiting Nurses	2.4	2.6	2.5
Family Services/Catholic Charities	2.4	4.1	3.9
Hospitals	2.0	0.9	0.9
Urban League	1.5	1.7	1.8

Source: UWA, *Allocations Profiles* (1975, 1983, 1985).
[a] n.d. refers to non-denominational, or what used to be called non-sectarian.

cerns agencies' shares of the United Way allocations pie. As table 10.2 demonstrates, in the period from 1973 to 1985 as a whole only minor changes took place in the percentages of dollars reported as going to a top group of thirteen major agencies (those already highlighted by United Way allocations reports for the period of 1973–1975). Minor fluctuations in percentages occurred with a number of these agency groups, with the most noteworthy downward (or negative) shifts occurring in allocations shares to the American Red Cross, which went from 14.6 percent of the total reported allocations pie (1973) to 11.9 percent (1985); the Boy Scouts, 5.1 percent (1973) down to 4.3 percent (1985); and hospitals, which went from 2.0 percent to 0.9 percent of the pie in the same period. Upward (or positive) shifts of some significance are indicated for four groups of agencies: Family Service Agencies; Settlement Houses; Boys Clubs; and Family Services/Catholic Charities.

Overall, given the length of time covered (1973–1985), changes in the percentages of allocations are small, even if some are statistically significant. Moreover, the ordering of highest shares to lowest shares changed very little, with some real downward shifting occurring only for the Boy Scouts, and upward movement for Catholic Charities. The apparent large change in the Red Cross share of allocations dollars certainly reflects renegotiations or discontinuance of some of the old contracts that had existed with local chapters of this organization, such as in Toledo, Ohio, but still left the Red Cross with a hefty share of United Way allocations nationwide.

Although small, increases in funding shares in this period were generally in the line with the thrust of United Ways to allocate funds more responsively in terms of minority groups and emerging community needs. Moveover, all the major declining percentages were for agencies subject to criticism either for being recreation and middle-class oriented, i.e., the Scouts and the YMCAs, or because public sector funding seemed to make United Way dollars superfluous (i.e., home health care, hospitals).[24]

In the years from 1973 to 1983 the trend is somewhat clearer, however, than it is for 1983–1985, when some of the directions become fuzzier. In the three-year period, 1983–1985, none of the core agencies indicated had a decline in percentage, and only the Scouts essentially stayed with the same market share. As the table in appendix E.3 indicates, only planning organizations (down from 1.00 percent of the reported allocations in 1983 to 0.90 in 1985) and USOs (down from 0.20 to 0.10) showed declining percentages in the period from 1983 to 1985. In that period again for 446 matched agencies, UWA reported that the high-growth agencies in market share for the period were women's crisis agencies (150 percent), information and referral (I&R; 66.7 percent), child welfare (54.5 percent), cancer (53.9 percent), and volunteer services (50 percent).

Once again, the figures need closer scrutiny. United Ways had in fact reacted to environmental demands by giving significant increases to child welfare and women's crisis services. However, the very large percentage increase in the case of women's crisis services was from a relatively small base ($4,934,825 in 1983).[25] Furthermore, as already noted, cancer agencies, particularly ACS units, benefited from large contracts with local United Ways. Finally, volunteer services and I&R services are services which are believed helpful in the campaign and which are frequently provided by United Ways themselves. Therefore, these figures may include self-serving increases in budgeted amounts to local United Ways for their own activities. Reporting them as separate services masks their relationship to United Way–budgeted expenses.[26]

Aggregated figures based on large numbers of reporting United Ways do not reveal trends within specific communities. Thus, in the 1980s there were communities in which some older core member agencies suffered particular declining market shares of United Way funds as a result of generous health contracts and declining growth

Table 10.3. Family & Children's Service of Pittsburgh
United Way Allocation Compared to Other Income (%)

Year	Other Income	United Way	Total Income	UW %	Other %
1977	$1,027,330	$1,138,935	$2,166,265	52.6%	47.4%
1978	1,175,457	1,149,000	2,324,457	49.4	50.6
1979	1,358,570	1,230,000	2,588,570	47.5	52.5
1980	1,436,215	1,353,000	2,789,215	48.5	51.5
1981	1,798,426	1,438,250	3,236,676	44.4	55.6
1982	1,683,196	1,551,352	3,234,548	48.0	52.0
1983	1,787,276	1,386,440	3,173,716	43.7	56.3
1984	2,378,551	1,359,000	3,737,551	36.4	63.6
1985	3,502,318	1,400,000	4,902,318	28.6	71.4
1986	4,220,813	1,461,000	5,681,813	25.7	74.3
1987	4,988,432	1,387,950	6,376,382	21.8	78.2

Source: Family Service of Pittsburgh, 1987.

in United Way revenues. One typical example is that of the Family Service agency in Pittsburgh, whose income history is given in table 10.3.

As one agency executive said plainly: "United Way is losing its luster for many of us—and, regretfully, we may have to go out and do our own fund raising like other agencies have begun to do."[27] A consequence of slow growth or no growth in tight economic times, and increased spreading of funds raised through inclusiveness, is that some agencies, like Big Brother in Pittsburgh, health agencies, or Planned Parenthood in many communities find it more profitable to be outside of the United Way than inside.[28] Popular agencies believe that they can garner more funds through their own public relations efforts and donor designations than they receive from United Way membership, since designations count as the first dollars they receive through the allocations process (see above, chapter 5). Moreover, when outside the United Way, they are free of restrictions on fund raising and can approach corporations directly for contributions. Corporations, however, may have other ideas in this regard.

Centrifugal forces from donor designation were also affecting member agencies' relationships to the United Way. In 1986 donor option was in existence in some form in over ninety United Way campaigns, and the United Way system was facing increased internal strains. Designations to United Way *agencies* were actually rising, going from $86.79 (1985) to $94.35 (1986), while at the same time average amounts of positive designations to United Ways themselves fell from $220.12 (1985) to $142.53 (1986). The future of "one gift" giving, and the concomitant citizen decision-making process, seemed imperiled, even though these dollars to member agencies were under the old donor designation rules, and, therefore, first dollars in a "pot" which would be filled by the United Way allocations process.

Regional Structuring of the United Way: The Changing Nature of Communities

Underlying the myth of American federated fund-raising organizations is the idea that their roots are in the community, and that decisions about services should be made in the localities out of which they developed. These local connections have been a source of strength for federations. A local constituency for charity organization certainly existed since its earliest days, even though professionals in federated organizations often came from outside the community and could be considered "an invading army" whose purpose was to control the voluntary sector in the community.[29] Nevertheless, the myth of the "community campaign," and the community-based organization, persisted.

After the 1970s the local connection and the community roots of federated fund-raising organizations were increasingly eroded by changes in modern American life. Challenges came from three different sources: the changing nature of the American community as people moved out of the inner city and into the suburbs, often working in one place and living in another; corporations moving their headquarters or part of their operations out of one location to various suburban locations or to other cities, in dizzying new complex patterns of centralization-decentralization; and corporations merging with other companies, and takeovers and consolidations which made companies a part of larger systems, less locally related, even including international conglomerates. Door-to-door solicitation disappeared with the change in our cities and the increased employment of women outside of the home. Thus, the workplace campaign for most larger United Ways almost completely replaced the old residential community campaigns.

The workplace campaign, however, did not solve the fund-raising problem of workers living in one place and working in another, or of corporate mobility generally. In fact, the consequence of shifting workplaces and home communities meant that workers increasingly wanted to designate their contributions, but often the designation was to their own home community, where they expected to benefit from United Way services, rather than to the community in which the corporation was located.[30] Many companies committed to the idea of one community—defined as a community of their workers, the town around them, and the company itself—now also became concerned about the withering away of the spirit of community. The dispersal of workers and corporations also left the United Way with specific problems of dropped pledges and incomplete payments from changes in employment structures and payroll systems.[31]

With the encouragement of the UWA, and the support of major corporations, many United Ways regionalized their United Way campaigns in order to deal with the new work environment, and created "area-wide" United Ways. Among the most notable, largest examples of this development by the late 1970s were: the United Way of Massachusetts Bay (Boston); the United Way of the Bay Area (San Francisco); the United Way of Chicago–Crusade of Mercy; the United Foundation (Detroit); United Way Services (Cleveland); and the United Way of Tri-State (greater New York and suburbs). Although dealing with some similar problems, in typical United Way fashion, each of these arrangements also represented a different pragmatic response to particular circumstances.

The Case of Tri-State

Each of the regional United Way organizations had to deal with some fundamental problems of distribution of resources. Large Metro I United Ways particularly faced the movement of many corporate headquarters to new suburban areas, leaving inner cities with less resources and greater need. However, only the United Way of Tri-State attempted to weld a large number of autonomous and powerful United Ways into a closely interwoven group for corporate fund raising; and only Tri-State was established across three state lines, with major corporations located throughout the partner communities, including Westchester (New York), Bergen County (New Jersey), Stamford (Connecticut), and metropolitan New York.

In all of the area-wide arrangements noted above, and in others, local United Ways have attempted to solve problems of urban-suburban separation, workplace-home separation, and corporate mobility. But they have also run into serious questions about equitable allocation of resources. Each of these area-wide arrangements included local communities with differential growth rates and service needs, where some communities had marked declining financial resources, while others had expanding corporate and personal income bases. Determining how to distribute resources to the communities involved, for allocation to local agencies, is therefore extremely difficult.

None of the area-wide arrangements is more complicated than the Tri-State United Way, the partnership that started in 1977 with twenty-two autonomous member United Ways. Its sheer size would be expected to make it powerful in the United Way system: in 1976 when it was being planned, the Tri-State region encompassed 8,456 miles, a population of approximately 18 million people, total employment of approximately 8.4 million, twelve hundred corporations employing 500 or more people, and over a thousand human service agencies.[32] There was no other organization of its size within the United Way system. Aside from the problem of dealing with a larger complex metropolitan area, a financial challenge faced the new organization. The total dollars raised by the area United Ways amounted to $66,763,000, or a per capita giving amount of $3.68, which was considerably lower than the average $7.90 per capita raised by other area-wide organizations it was compared with—Chicago, Detroit, San Francisco, Cleveland, and Boston. In the words of one of Tri-State's first publications:

> It is hoped that the tri-state area's contribution will be significantly increased. If, for example, the United Way of Tri-State attains no more than the average of the major area-wide groups, it will raise 76 million new dollars.[33]

Thus, the formation of this new United Way organization was plainly tied to the desire to increase dollar amounts raised in the Tri-State area.

From the start there were difficulties within the Tri-State organization. Aside from issues of scale, the United Way of Tri-State was not considered a regular United Way organization by the UWA, because it was composed of autonomous local United Ways joined for fund-raising purposes only, and indeed with the specific aim of conjoint approaches to major companies or corporate accounts in the area—what came to be called CSAs, or corporate system accounts. The executive of the United Way of New York City was to serve also as the executive of the United Way of Tri-State. This added to the ambiguity of the status of each organization. In addition, the haste with which the Tri-State area-wide was put together meant that it did not have time for a process of "bringing along" board members and volunteers of local United Ways, with the result that they never felt any ownership of the organization.[34] The Tri-State board was to be composed primarily of illustrious corporate executives, although there was to be some representation assured for partner United Ways throughout the structure. Indeed, many United Way professionals considered the organization essentially a creature of Bill Aramony, with the expectation that Tri-State might become a feeder of corporate CEOs to the UWA board.

On the whole the urgency of creating agreements among all the partners meant that details which were worrisome or more problematic were left to be smoothed out later, and this included some important accountability matters. From the start hard negotiations went along with efforts to woo partners to joining, and autonomy, particularly in regard to allocations, was an issue. Again the Tri-State magazine stated emphatically: "Despite centralization, local autonomy and community decision-making remain intact. . . . They continue to plan, budget and allocate resources to community agencies, and have total control over residential and small business fundraising drives."[35] But finally, and increasingly in the years after the formation of Tri-State, the distribution formula itself became in issue. This formula was relatively simple in its formulation:

> The United Way of Tri-State assures each partner a base allocation equal to the total raised the previous year, plus a percentage of all new dollars produced by the single United Way of Tri-State campaign. For example, if Fund A enters into United Way of Tri-State with 20 percent the total dollars raised the previous year, it would receive that base allocation plus 20 percent of the increase.[36]

In effect this meant that United Ways which produced greater than system-average growth in a campaign would not receive any special benefit from their success, whether the success was due to an expanding economy or because they had a more effective campaign. As one active Tri-State volunteer told me: "The formula reduces all incentive for partners to be entrepreneurial in their campaign activity." Furthermore, geographic designations were expressly discouraged. A special fund which was developed later, while allowing for special incentives for new members, and rewards for one year for extra-large campaign increments (which with special arrangements could be kept by the local United Way), still did not fully satisfy most of the more aggressive partners. Moreover, it attempted to address the issue of incentives, but did not attempt to address the issue of communities with the greatest need. In the meantime, over ten local United Ways remained sufficiently restive that during the years between 1983 and 1986 they partially moved out of the partnership into what Tri-State euphemistically referred to as "transition status."[37] In this status, "partners" were able to retain their own growth in earnings and therefore benefited directly from the amounts they raised.

Feelings run high in relation to area-wide organizations generally, but nowhere perhaps so high as among the partners of the Tri-State United Way. Earlier ambiguities have come back to haunt the partners, and structural dilemmas remain to be resolved, exacerbated by interpersonal conflicts. Moreover, the business approach of the organization, increasingly emphasized in the mid-1980s, has interfered with the all-important motivation of community sentiment in the United Way. The campaign did increase revenues, growing to $146,023,046 in 1985–1986, with thirty-two partners and a per capita amount of approximately $8.00 that year.[38] However, although campaign increments were realized every year it was claimed that a large part of this growth after 1980 was due to the addition of partners rather than new money raised. Moreover, operating expenses for Tri-State also were high, with an increase of between 17 and 20 percent in its operating budget for each of the three years 1984–1986.[39]

Meanwhile the arrangement continued to be challenged for being too large, too impersonal, and not producing the anticipated economies of scale. By the fall of 1987, the United Way of New York City was again made a separate entity within the Tri-State system. The president of Tri-State was no longer to serve as the executive of the New York City organization, and the partners were still working out differences of opinion in relation to local autonomy and formulaic-fund distribution. As one long-time community loyalist from the corporate world expressed it in a widespread memorandum:

> The autonomy of the Partners' Boards is increasingly illusory, as they lose all control of how their own fund-raising efforts affect their annual TS (Tri-State) entitlements.
>
> The nature of the DF (distribution formula) makes the use of "community," "at home," "your town," etc., in public advertising . . . fundamentally misleading to many givers.[40]

Community feelings had not yet been assuaged. The Tri-State organization was growing, but serious structural problems remained.

Chapter 11

United Way as a National Organization: The Aramony Era

> Over the years, our generous and inventive people have created an ingenious network of voluntary organizations to give help where help is needed.
> United Way gives that help very well indeed, and truly exemplifies our spirit of voluntarism.
>
> Ronald Reagan, presidential proclamation, December 10, 1986

CHARITY organization in our nation has local roots and has been identified as a community-related movement since its inception.[1] Indeed, the United Way makes a concerted effort to preserve its definition as a community-based federation, protecting this status in the CFC, and maintaining, even advertising, its continuing relationship to a core group of affiliated agencies. However, at the same time, although less well articulated, federated fund raising has always been loosely connected to some national organization, such as the National Association of Societies for Organizing Charity (1911) in the late nineteenth and early twentieth centuries; the American Association for Community Organization (1918); the Community Chests and Councils (CCC) and the Community Chests and Councils of America (CCCA) in the 1930s and 1950s; the United Funds and Councils of America (UCFCA) in the 1950s and 1960s; and finally the United Way of America (UWA) after 1970 (see above, chapter 1).

Ever since its formation, the role of the national organization has been important, and at certain times has assumed critical significance, such as in wartime, during the 1930s when the CCC lobbied for changes in tax policies affecting corporate contributions, and in the 1960s when it seemed imperative to have a stronger national organization as a counterbalance to an increasingly powerful federal government.

In 1970 William Aramony was charged with developing a strong central organization which would insure the United Way system a voice in the public policy arena. However, by the 1980s some United Way professionals were saying that the UWA had been too successful and taken too dominant a role over local affairs. By the 1980s there appeared to be uncertainty about the role of the national UWA in relation to its local organizations in the public's eyes. It was in fact frequently difficult to distinguish the identity of local United Ways from the UWA in critical discussions of the "United Way." Analysis of the interaction between local organizations, and of the interaction between these organizations and the national organization, will shed further light on the nature of the dilemmas facing the federated fundraising system in the Aramony years, as well as adding to our understanding of how these dilemmas were dealt with.

The Nature of Federation

When the United Way system defines itself as a federation, it is using a term which implies a structure of autonomous local community member agencies, tied together with an understanding of continuing relationship and mutual obligations. Although the agencies originally may have made decisions about allocations, over the years, these agencies have generally agreed to yield some degree of autonomy in regard to their own fund-raising efforts, and also to submit themselves to some form of annual accountability review, or citizen's review process, in connection with their allocations. This pattern continued, even though after the 1960s, United Ways increasingly seemed to act more like funds than federations, making a variety of special funding arrangements with non-member agencies including one-time grants, partnerships, and funds passed through by donor designation (see discussion above, chapters 9 and 10). Therefore, in some sense it could be argued that the idea of federation was more a part of the United Way myth than an empirical fact in the 1980s. Because of the looseness of the affiliation, and the degree of autonomy maintained by member agencies from the start, it might in fact be more accurate to consider the United Way system a confederation, rather than a federation.[2] However, it appears that with new funding arrangements, the United Way is increasingly less a confederation of member service-providing agencies in the local community, and more a centrally influenced federation of local United Ways tied to a national organization.

Essential to the core of the United Way myth has been the notion that the United Way is a community-based, bottoms-up movement. The corollary to this concept would be that the national organization followed the lead of the local United Way organizations, and was in a sense subservient to them. However, as the case studies make clear, the national organization has not always played the follower role and took assertive action in regard to corporate funding as far back as the 1930s. By 1970 the UCFCA board, which included considerable professional representation prior to that time, recognized that the federated fund-raising system needed more prestigious leadership. It was thereafter restructured to develop a stronger national organization. In turn, the strengthening of the UWA as a national organization inevitably caused new dilemmas of influence and control, with internal structural tensions following from centralized efforts to create change.

Sources of Change and the National Organization

United Way professionals frequently argue that each local United Way is unique, warning those who attempt to study the United Way that generalization across the United Way system is almost impossible. If there were no commonalities or causal interactions among United Ways, or between local United Ways and the national organization, then indeed it might appear that each United Way reacts idiosyncratically, developing its own unique structure and facing its own challenges in its particular, individualistic way. However, our case histories suggest the contrary. Not only do all United Ways carry out similar functions (campaign, planning, government relations, and allocations), but events that happen in one United Way are also known to other United Ways. Information about them is transmitted across the country with great rapidity. This is true whether it is problems that occur, new approaches to doing business, or particular successes. The extensive commonalities among United Ways in basic structure and operations seems proof that United Ways learn from each other. Moreover, "war stories" such as that of San Francisco and Philadelphia are traded with the assistance of the UWA in order to encourage some special learning.

The United Way of America has developed a variety of means to insure that interchange between local United Ways occurs, and it also attempts to help influence both the nature of these interchanges and their outcomes. It does this in some obvious as well as subtle ways, which include formal organized conferences, national training programs, socialization of volunteers and corporate executives of national organizations, professional advisory groups, shared reports and digests of activities, an information center available to all local United Ways, and continual communication with local United Ways through memoranda and newsletters. It also influences local United Ways through participation in their hiring and promotion process.

The United Way of America uses these activities to influence local United Ways. But how does this actually work, and to what extent does the UWA actually control local United Ways?

Sources of Influence

Among the many sources of influence exercised by the United Way of America, the training programs at its national headquarters in Alexandria, Virginia, and the national conferences are probably the two most visible and dominant in terms of numbers of United Way staff involved. In 1979, a survey of local United Ways indicated that there were 3,500 professionals employed by the 579 United Ways responding. In addition the survey indicated that over the years 9,437 professionals had attended UWA courses.[3]

By 1986, the professional staffs of local United Ways apparently had expanded considerably. A survey in that year reported that there were 4,500 professional positions in 600 reporting Metros (I–IV). In 1986 United Way reported that 2,000 people participated in one hundred "courses" every year. However, course attendance figures also include volunteers and some professionals from allied human services and other agencies. Courses were also defined to include round tables, workshops, and seminars.[4] Still, a large number of United Way professionals have certainly passed through the National Academy of Voluntarism (NAV) in the years since it was founded; indeed so many courses have been taken by the senior professionals in the field that NAV has run out of regular courses to offer this group.

All new United Way professional staff are expected to take an introductory course at NAV within their first year of joining the United Way, and if possible, even sooner. Thereafter most United Way professionals, particularly in Metros I–IV, take at least one, and possibly two, seminars a year. It is considered both a responsibility and something of an honor to go to Alexandria, and although United Way staff may occasionally gripe about the inconvenience of leaving their home base for a week, or question the content of the courses,

THE ARAMONY ERA 249

by and large they seem to enjoy them, and express particular enthusiasm about the sharing that goes on with their colleagues.

Although United Way does not offer solutions to problems discussed in the classroom, the NAV program serves as a staff development program with two major purposes. It provides on-the-job training for United Way professionals, with particular benefit for those professionals who entered the system with less expertise or professional experience, or who find themselves in smaller or more rural communities and are therefore isolated from their peers. It also helps to socialize newcomers to the United Way system, and to inculcate in all staff members an awareness of the organizational culture and expectations. NAV accomplishes this through shared experiences of junior professionals with experienced instructors selected from within the system and occasionally from without.

In principle NAV instructors are expected to be good role models. Thus, local United Way executives who were considered "gurus," such as Ted Moore of Rochester or Alan Cooper of Baltimore, would be chosen from within the system to be instructors for management courses. Peter Schoderbeck, a professor in the Business School at Iowa State University, and a disciple of management expert Peter Drucker, was used extensively as a course instructor in the decade 1976–1986.[5] The same principle was generally applied to selecting course instructors in other areas, with mavens in allocations or communications expected to preside over courses in their respective areas of expertise. However, as in all organizations, not infrequently other factors entered into the decision, and it appeared that some instructors were given this opportunity as a reward for loyal support of organizational policies. On the whole, between 1975 and 1986 the NAV provided the primary means of socializing United Way professionals, first into the organizational norms of the United Way system, and secondly into the potential for using more sophisticated tools of the trade, including needs assessment techniques for planners, computers for the fiscal administrative staff, campaign techniques, and management techniques for United Way executive staff. Thus, it was a serious attempt to upgrade the United Way professional organization.

The second major means of creating team spirit and improving quality among United Way professionals has existed far longer. There are a variety of conferences including biennial staff conferences, alternate year regional staff conferences, annual Volunteer Leader Conferences (VLC), and other smaller meetings or specialized conferences. These conferences provide another opportunity for spreading the United Way gospel, and at times take on the aura of a great theatrical performance, particularly when volunteers are included. Nobody puts on a show like the United Way, unless it is the Scouts or the Salvation Army, as anyone who was present at the United Way centennial celebration in Washington (April 1987) can testify. When all the singing of the national anthem and "America the Beautiful" was done, there had to be few dry eyes in the audience, either in the ballroom of the Washington-Sheraton or at the spectacular open-air ceremony at the Lincoln Memorial.[6]

Both the VLC and the annual staff conferences provide a means for developing United Way espirit de corps as well as for showcasing the special efforts of particular United Ways in one or another area of importance—new allocation procedures or campaign involvement, for example. In this regard, the United Way staff conferences have a serious working purpose. Typically, a new United Way planning professional exposed to a presentation of an evaluation method by another United Way would return home enthusiastic about the possibility of such evaluations of agencies in her home community. Thereafter, a volunteer committee would soon be at work considering how to implement a similar system in another United Way. Similarly, the executive director of the United Way of the Bay Area (San Francisco) talked about the installation of donor option, and in a later conference, the executive of the United Way of Southeastern Pennsylvania (Philadelphia) discussed with considerable openness the problems which led to their adoption of a donor option plan.[7] Although there may have been a certain amount of exaggeration in some presentations, for example, oversell of campaign successes, key professionals certainly served as catalysts for change for other United Ways. Where local communities had progressive executive and volunteer leadership, exposure to these presentations became a source for innovation within the United Way system.

Commercial Franchise

The United Way system has often been compared to a business for the obvious reason that United Ways are concerned with a bottom line figure of more dollars every year, and also because of the more subtle ways in which they act like a business, making business-like decisions even in regard to agency affiliations,[8] and paying large salaries to their key executives, where they can. The United Way of America, however, is different. The UWA, unlike local United Ways, does not raise money through its own campaigns, but rather acts like a franchising agent for local United Ways. Thus, local United Ways pay a formula-fixed fee to the national organization in return for privileges and advantages they receive. Among those privileges are the use of the United Way logo; listing in the UWA *Directory;* reduced fees and charges for the activities run by the national organization (including NAV and annual conferences); newsletters, memoranda, and other informational mailings from the UWA; access to lease/ purchase of a variety of public relations/communications materials prepared by the UWA and its communications division; and technical assistance.[9] In this sense, therefore, local United Ways can also be considered franchise operations of the national organization, and as such are expected to measure up to the standards of performance it promulgates.[10]

Local United Ways are expected to pay one percent of revenues raised through their campaign in dues to the national organization. However, although in the late 1970s the UWA put additional emphasis on the need for local United Ways to meet their required assessment, many United Ways continued to give less than the formula assigned to them. Pressure continues to be placed on local United Way executives to meet these dues expectations. In the meantime they are still considered to be member organizations of the national organization, and even if below the formula amount, are among the approximately 1,200 local United Ways United Way reported as official members of the UWA in the mid-1980s. It should be noted, however, that the dollar figure given for the amount that United Ways raise nationwide includes projections based on the larger number of about 2,200 United Ways. Thus the reported total is to some extent an informed estimate, including calculations of what many smaller United Ways would be likely to produce in the campaign.[11] In any case, it is from the member United Ways that the UWA generally solicits its data, and on whom it exerts pressure for compliance in terms of inclusiveness and accountability. Much in the same way that Ford expects its dealers to provide adequate service, or MacDonalds expects local franchise operations to meet organizational standards, the UWA has also promulgated its own "standards of excellence."

Control

The UWA does not have the capability of controlling its local member organizations, but it has a number of structurally impressive means of influencing them. In a sense the United Way of America employs its own expertise and its ability to reward particular local United Ways (and their executives) as a power-wielding measure over these local organizations. Another aspect of this power is conferred by United Way's relationship with major corporations and their chief executive officers (CEOs).

Keeping CEOs of national corporations committed to the United Way has in fact been a chief priority of Bill Aramony. It appears that he has expended considerable time, effort, and even financial resources to do so, through formal entertainment and informal contacts on the tennis court and elsewhere.[12] Few, however, would doubt that this has also been a business decision which has paid off for the United Way. Certainly, support by CEOs and major companies is essential to the continued corporate involvement for local United Ways, both through direct corporate contributions and through the access provided to employees in the corporate workplace. It also helped the United Way at the national level to deal from a position of strength with the federal government. The relationship also accounts for such special treats as the hosting of the United Way centennial celebration at the National Gallery for over 3,000 guests; or the participation of President and Mrs. Reagan in United Way's centennial celebration.[13] And finally this influence certainly helps to explain why the federal government gave United Way a central role in delivery of emergency food and shelter under the Job Stimulus Bill which established the Federal Emergency Management Agency.[14]

Connections with corporations also helps the bond between the UWA and local United Ways, assisting the local organizations with their own campaigns, as well as making them aware of the power of the national organization. At the same time, the involvement of corporations with United Ways in the local community is also important for the national organization. Thus there is at once reciprocity in the exchange and a tension in the relationship between local organizations and the national organizations, even around corporate involvement. Nevertheless, the National Corporate Development program has certainly resulted in increments in giving, which are of direct benefit to local United Ways.

The same reciprocal dependency, or shared power, is evident also in relation to the CFC. In 1982 the UWA helped to organize a letter-writing campaign and testimony at congressional hearings to protect the CFC (see above, chapters 5 and 6). Ultimately local United Ways were protected from a worst-case scenario in regard to the CFC direct option plan by the work of the national organization. The UWA used its influence to make sure that the definition of a PCFO organization matched closely that of a United Way federated organization. This lesson is not lost on local United Ways.

For United Ways with major issues or problems to deal with, one of the most significant forms of UWA influence is through its provision of technical assistance and consulting in connection with special studies for local United Ways. During the late 1970s this frequently occurred through MACSI studies focused on the relationship between planning councils and the United Way planning function, or on planning needs in the community, where self-assessment was carried out with outside assistance (see above, chapter 3). In the 1980s these studies began to take on the broader dimension of strategic long-range planning for the local organization, in the context of environmental scanning. Among the prime examples of communities carrying out this kind of study were the United Foundation in Detroit, and the Tri-State United Way. Staff came from the MACSI group in the United Way, and included the director of long-range strategic planning, who by 1984 was Dr. George Wilkinson.

The influence of these studies includes transmitting preferred models for action from other local United Ways. For example, in one of the major Tri-State reports the subject of uniform giving guidelines for corporations was raised, with several possible options listed. All of those selected were predictably from more successful United Ways, those with high per capita giving. A quotation from this report will illustrate how this is done:

> Experience elsewhere clearly indicates that the adoption of a tailored corporate guideline is a major ingredient in the promotion of corporate leadership support of the United Way. Several options are available. In Los Angeles, the guideline is 1% of pre-tax profits. Cincinnati, Pittsburgh and Cleveland use a combination of a responsibility factor (x per cent of pre-tax profits). For example, the Cincinnati guideline in 1980 was $26.50 per employee (responsibility factor) plus .4 of 1% of pre-tax profits (ability factor). Other communities differentiate when calculating pre-tax profits between corporate headquarters and other locations. . . . Details of these guidelines are available to Tri-State staff.[15]

The report was developed out of a process which included influential and powerful corporate volunteers from the Tri-State area, and was well circulated.

Other concrete examples of how the national organization often influences, but rarely controls, local United Ways have been given throughout this book. Obvious cases concern the admission of the health agencies, ACS and AHA, and the adoption of donor option plans, beginning with California. After the AID situation broke out, the UWA anticipated more problems with charges of monopoly in the workplace, or violation of employee rights. Since companies would not be willing to take the risk of charges of unfair labor practices, the UWA was convinced that donor option would have to be offered employees (see above, chapters 4 and 8).

Despite continual communication and frequent meetings with executives of the big city United Ways, donor option plans were resisted across the country. United Way professionals really did not like them because they eroded the fundamental notion of citizen review and were risky financially.[16] It was not until after the Philadelphia story was widely known that the United Way was really able to get serious consideration for the plan from some of the more influential Metro I United Way executives in the East, such as Ted Moore in Rochester. Thus, it was not until 1982 that the UWA board adopted an official statement of support for a donor option, and it was only finally adopted after Bill Aramony had convinced the professional advisory group of United Way executives (NPAC) to propose it first. It was, however, not adopted systemwide or even by all larger United Ways.

UWA as a Federation of Local United Ways

Although it is a playful dictum of United Way professionals that Bill Aramony "walks on water," the relationship between local United Ways and the UWA is hardly unilateral, and indeed influence goes in both directions. In particular the top Metro cities, the Big Ten and other executive groups of large Metro cities, have had an important power base in the United Way, and have used it to resist UWA policies, and, at times, personal pressure from Aramony. The reality is, of course, that the UWA needs the larger UWAs as much, if not more, than they need the national organization. The sheer amount of money they raise would suggest this. For example, in the 1984 campaign, the top twelve Metro I United Ways (Boston, Chicago, Cincinnati, Cleveland, Detroit, Houston, Los Angeles, New York, Philadelphia, St. Louis, San Francisco, and Washington, D.C.) alone reportedly raised over $586 million or more than 25 percent of the total $2.145 billion reported as raised in the total United Way campaign nationwide. Consequently, if they all gave their mandated one percent of campaign revenues to the UWA, they would be providing over $5 million to the UWA, or a significant proportion of its total budget.[17]

In addition, by virtue of their location, many local United Ways have their own corporate power bases. To name just a few examples: historically, the United Foundation in Detroit has been the major link to the automobile companies (Chrysler, Ford, and General Motors); Rochester (New York) has had a close relationship with Eastman Kodak; Aetna Life Insurance Company has been involved with the Hartford United Way; and the Tri-State area has been noted for its major companies, including Texaco, IBM, and General Foods (Westchester); Xerox (Stamford); Johnson and Johnson and Lipton Tea

(New Jersey); Exxon Corporation, Pfizer, and headquarters of AT&T (New York City).

Over the years United Way executives have formed their own support groups which have operated almost like secret societies, leaving out the uninvited. The Big Ten group (which actually had increased to thirteen among the largest Metro I organizations) has been the most powerful, but at least one other group has been significant, and that is the Select Cities group.[18] Select Cities was formed essentially as a rump group to which individual executives are invited as much by personal preferences as city size. Bob Mabie, executive director of the United Way of Des Moines from the late 1960s through the 1980s, was one of those who attempted to use Select Cities as an instrument of change in the UCFCA. In any case both organizations are taken seriously, and by the 1980s top UWA staff members, such as John Garber (group vice-president) or Dick O'Brien (chief operating officer of the UWA) were attending meetings of Select Cities. Bill Aramony was also careful to meet frequently with the Big Ten, who often held their meetings close to regular United Way conferences. In addition, Aramony brought top professionals frequently into the United Way of America decision-making process through extensive use of Professional Advisory Committees (PACs).

Changes in United Way Staff

During the Aramony years, United Way personnel systemwide were trained and indoctrinated through attendance at conferences and NAV courses. The NAV program in effect replaced the social work schools for training, and in particular three social work schools, Ohio State, Boston College, and the University of Pittsburgh. Indeed although both Bill Aramony and Dick O'Brien had social work degrees from Boston College, by the 1970s this close connection had already eroded.

By the time Bill Aramony became chief executive officer of the United Way, there had already been board discussion about establishing a United Way training program, and Aramony brought this idea to fruition in 1972 (see above, chapter 3). United Way had been having trouble recruiting community organizers from schools of social work, and concomitantly the UWA began to push a business model in its own operations. NAV therefore began to implement business training techniques in its courses. By the late 1970s, senior executives in major United Ways were being rewarded for years of service by participation in either a business certification program (Harvard), or an MBA granting program (University of Miami).[19]

Training in the United Way was given a high priority in these years along with recruitment. By the end of the 1970s United Way (like other organizations) was facing concerns about renewal of personnel. Many executives of major United Ways were men in their fifties who had a great deal of United Way experience and training. There were also some "Young Turks" who were beginning to feel boxed in because their mobility ws limited. Some had come into the United Way with a social work orientation, and had gotten locked into planning-allocating positions. After rising to the associate executive director level, they were now uncertain about their future in the system. Without extensive campaign experience they could not go on to United Way executive positions in large United Ways, and they were too senior to take campaign positions in smaller organizations.

Moreover, if United Way was to be able to react to environmental demands and adapt to changing conditions, it would need new personnel with new ideas who would be capable of responding flexibly to these changes. This flexibility did not exist within the old UCFCA, either at the national or the local level. Traditionally, the federation system tended to be protective of its staff, and professionals generally had a long career which limited change in the United Way.[20]

As a counter-action to new community demands, however, in the 1970s the United Way began again to recruit actively from the outside, from local communities, and from a variety of educational and career backgrounds. In a period when United Way professionals were being encouraged to act more like businessmen, and to use corporate executives as their models, the United Way social work identity, which had never been exclusive, was diluted even more.

The NAV training program was therefore utilized to create a unified identity for United Way professionals by inculcating new ideas in older executives and spreading the United Way philosophy to newcomers.

Through the 1970s the United Way continued to have the reputation of being a white male, white Anglo-Saxon (including Irish) dominated organization. There were no women or minority (black or Hispanic) executives in large Metro I and II United Ways, and relatively few women or minorities in any Metro I–IV United Way, although by the end of that decade more women were moving into higher United Way professional positions, particularly in the areas of planning and allocations, or communications. Indeed, in 1974 United

Way had begun an internship program aimed at recruiting young people specifically from targeted populations, including women, blacks, and Hispanics. By 1979 that program had shown considerable success, including 29 minority personnel, and 54 women, among its 107 trainees for the United Way field.[21]

By 1986, the intern program was reported to have started 207 individuals in United Way careers, of which 56 were minorities of color, and 118 were women. Overall, the picture of women and minorities in the United Way continued to be a mixed one. United Way claimed to have made a major change in the participation of minorities and women in professional positions, noting that a survey of the top 600 United Ways (Metro I–IV) reported that of 4,500 professional positions, 587 (or 14.2 percent) were held by minorities, and 2,238 (54 percent) by women, of whom 184 served as executive directors or chief professional officers of their organizations. However, of the now over 50 Metro I communities in 1986, only two were headed by women (Miami, Houston), and one by a black man (Pittsburgh). Women, moreover, considered themselves to have limited mobility in the United Way system.[22]

At the same time United Way was suffering the effects of another critical dilemma. In order to renew itself, the organization had to have new people with fresh ideas and insights in its own structure. It had to seek a more diverse group of professionals, including young people, who would not be likely to accept the Aramony-UWA culture and old operating procedures and policies. The United Way was actually forced to hire new people with different value systems, and thus to sow some seeds of dissension within its own work force. This happened through its hiring of people committed to more responsiveness in the United Way, a post-1960s generation, who wanted to see real change take place and more rapidly, and who were also assertive about their own professional demands.

In fact, of course, there had always been dissenters in the United Way system. Prior to the mid-1970s these individuals were generally planners, who remained out of the inner sanctums of the United Way system. Their ability was recognized and their expertise admired; but they were often the token representative of social work values, who did not seem headed to the top rank of key United Way executives. In effect, the bifurcated structure of most local United Ways insured that this would happen. If they came in as planners, and never had experience as campaigners, how could they become the CPO of a large United Way, with major campaign responsibilities?

In the late 1970s, however, necessity once again brought change to the United Way system. Positions had to be found for the Young Turks who had come into the United Way with social work orientations and had held planning and allocation positions. These people in a sense had now come of age, and the question was, Where could they go within the system? Consequently, positions were created in some large United Ways, somewhere between the campaign side and the planning side, and under the chief executive, which allowed planning and allocation professionals to get broader exposure to the campaign as well as managerial advancement. The creation of these positions also helped bridge the bifurcated United Way system (i.e., the campaign/allocations divisions). In addition, training programs in business, developed at the University of Miami and Harvard, offered a new excitement for both the elite "old" United Way professionals in danger of "burn out" and also for younger professionals. Although this did not work universally, two eloquent representatives of the Young Turks (both males) made the transition to chief executive in the mid-1980s—Richard Aft, who became the executive director of the United Way of Greater Memphis, and Gerry Lewis, who became the president of the United Way in Nashville—both of them in Tennessee, and by 1986, both of them Metro I organizations.[23] On the other hand, Geneva Johnson, another leading planning professional who was also a black woman, accepted a high position at the United Way of America but eventually left the United Way system for the position of chief executive of Family Service America, the national organization of family service agencies.

The handling of personnel was certainly one of the most specific ways through which the UWA was able to influence the direction of local United Ways. The United Way Personnel Development Program (PDP) kept personnel files for most professional staff in the major local United Ways, and provided them with advice, in effect "steering" their careers. The personnel role was even more direct in regard to top executive positions. The UWA was often consulted by local United Ways looking for new chief professional officers (executive directors, presidents), and invited to send files of a few potential candidates. Forwarding these recommended "files" for interviewing could not force the selections, but would narrow the field, and rotation of United Way staff from one community to another helped propagate the United Way culture.

UWA personnel staff would even go to local United Ways to meet with community volunteers and discuss the nature of the executive's job. It could not be said that the UWA selected the local executives for any community, but they were able to influence the process. Some communities were more receptive to United Way suggestions, while others evidently remained more independent, totally rejecting UWA recommended candidates. In some cases Aramony seems to have intervened directly, asking an executive to take a particular job, as was the situation apparently in Tri-State with Alan Cooper and in Phoenix with Mark O'Connell.

In any case, by 1986 the United Way had paid considerable attention to the words of the futurists as well as the lessons of its own environmental scans. It was attempting to bring the United Way back to the community, and to bring a people-oriented, personal approach back to the United Way model.[24] Even Bill Aramony was once again reminding people that the United Way was connected to social work traditions, and the same idea was beginning to emerge in speeches of some UWA corporate volunteers. It may have been basically done for marketing purposes, but it made good sense for an organization funding the human services to connect itself to the service end of the business.

Epilogue: Change, Challenge, and Charity

> Corporate America is gearing up to face its challenges. Can volunteer America do any less? Are we flexible and creative enough to respond to change in the world around us?
>
> James D. Robinson III
> 1987 Volunteer Leaders Conference

> Lowering the drawbridge of opportunity is what the Second Century Iniative is all about.
>
> Richard J. Ferris
> Chairman-Elect, United Way of America, 1987

IN the mid-1980s the United Way prepared to celebrate its one hundredth anniversary, with a spirit of renewal and anticipation. In United Way fashion, the national organization appointed a Second Century Initiative Committee which drew up a plan for the future development and growth of the United Way system. As volunteer chair of that committee, and president-elect of the UWA, Richard J. Ferris, chairman and CEO of United Airlines set the mood for the next year of celebration in an address at the 1986 Volunteer Leader's Conference in Cinncinnati, stating that "our centennial is a perfect time to do what we're always asking others to do —to unite—and achieve together what is impossible to achieve alone." In effect, it was time for the United Way to renew its effort at consensus building among its various constituencies, public and private.

The Second Century Initiative included a five-point strategy: first, United Ways were to be catalysts in solving community problems; second, they were to involve more people, and particularly more volunteers; third, they were to communicate more effectively; fourth, funds were to be distributed more creatively; and fifth, more money was to be raised more dynamically. The goals were clear: the United Way was to raise twice as much money by 1992, and it was to work even harder at running one more inclusive United Way community-wide campaign. In many respects the Second Century Initiative seemed like new wine in old bottles, or a rewriting of many of the key elements in the UWA 1978 long-range planning document, echoed again in the *Three Critical Issue Reports*. Thus, it appeared that United Way was using the centennial as a time to renew its goals, and to gather enthusiasm for accomplishing efforts in which it had made only slight progress in the preceding decade. As always, it was understood that the two key elements were United Way control of one workplace campaign and increased money raised in that campaign, but they were accompanied by the idea of the community problem-solving mission which was in effect the "soul" of the United Way.

Under the brave words and the joyous appearances at the centennial celebration in 1987, there were, however, signs of worry about the future. At the centennial, corporate volunteers and United Way staff wondered about whether the United Way could change enough to master the new environment in which local United Ways were operating, in the corporate world, in the community, and in the country. Indeed, by 1987, the world in which United Ways were operating had changed dramatically. Large corporations were expanding more by merger than by new products; corporate employees had developed awareness of their own entitlements and rights, and productivity and real wages were both decreasing. Industrial America was turning into an information and service economy, with new small businesses providing the major source of growth; internationalism was a fact of life as corporations were increasingly involved in a worldwide economy.

There were other trends which made the climate difficult for traditionally oriented large organizations at the end of the 1980s. The "me" generation wanted representation in decision making, and decentralization was in the air. Big was not beautiful; and the notion of one community consensus, dominated by a middle-class, Judeo-Christian value system had lost credibility as new subgroups gained recognition for their particular issues or needs. These needs were as varied as day care for working women or recognition of the rights of gays and lesbians to their own life-style, and they were based on a sense of empowerment, which had shaken the idea that there could be one communitywide view of the public interest.

The issues of monopoly and bigness had already caused a trauma in the corporate world and in American life generally. AT&T had been in effect forced to trade its virtual monopoly of the telephone system for an opportunity to compete in the broader marketplace of communications systems, which resulted in what many considered a subsequent decrease in the quality of telephone service. Indeed, comparisons to United Way were obvious to people in both systems, and the lesson of the breakup was not lost on the United Way or its competitors. In this changing work environment, the single charitable campaign in the workplace continued to be under attack for monopolistic practices. At the same time, questions about inequity in access to resources in the workplace were leading to a new kind of United Way, struggling with competitiveness in the marketplace, and an intensified urgency to raise more money for diversified agencies and services.

By the time of the United Way centennial celebration, competition in the workplace had become a fact of organized fund raising, with the existence of over eighty-five local aternative funds with their own member agencies and constituency groups. Many of these local funds in turn were connected with some national organizations, like CHADs and BUFs, and, in addition, efforts were being made to establish a national organization of social action funds as part of a strategy for dealing with big national corporations.

Looked at globally, this competition in the workplace was still limited and on the margins. In some respects it seemed like echoes of the past in regard to the popular health agencies, Cancer and Heart. But the extensiveness of competition in the workplace was new, and increasing amounts of money were in fact now going out of the United Way system, through donor designation to special causes or to combined alternative funds like Women's Way locally or the BUFs nationally. Both the growth of the alternative fund movement and the heightened visibility of popular causes were likely to cause concern for the United Way and its corporate supporters. The consensus view of organized charity was seriously threatened by the emergence of these competing groups, while the declining percentage that United Way dollars represented of agency budgets weakened the federation idea.

If the old view was that a single public interest could be served through the traditional United Way package of funded agencies, this could not be possible in the future. The existence of new social action causes, the women's groups, and the Black United Fund continues to suggest that exclusion of any of these groups can be challenged. Indeed, despite the cautious decision of the Supreme Court in 1985, there still remained the possibility that some of the same legal pressures that had contributed to opening up the public workplace could spread to the private sector, and issues of employee rights or questions about the exclusion of particular charities could lead to successful challenges against the one United Way workplace drive. The question of viewpoint neutrality had been clearly signaled in the CFC Supreme Court decision of 1985, and while congressional action has replaced final court determination of the facts of this issue, it was still a spectre that could haunt the private sector.

At the end of the 1980s an unanswered question remains about who owns funds raised in the workplace campaign, and whether the corporate campaign is in any fundamental way different from the proprietary interest of the federal government in the combined campaign. The line between public and private is not so clear when the NLRB has public oversight of what is permitted in the workplace, and the federal campaign has not been defined as a public forum. Consequently, the necessity of insuring choice through one campaign remains constantly before the United Way and its corporate allies.

The result is that organized charity enters the future with a new twist to an old dilemma and increased tension around the workplace campaign. Most corporate leaders do in fact want one workplace drive, and they retain a strong allegiance to the United Way. But at the same time, corporations are concerned that the United Way be responsive to new causes, and therefore that it include an increasingly large array of services under its umbrella. Previous court decisions and congressional action plainly suggested that employees' rights have to be protected and that there are constitutional issues affecting charitable giving. Corporations are sensitive to these issues, but they appear to be less willing to pay the bill that an adequate response would involve.

In fact, it is not at all certain how the bill can be paid for the expanded number of agencies and services that will be included in future workplace drives. In effect, more money will need to be raised in the workplace, in order to spread the funds around to more organizations and services. This need for increased funds will take place in the context of a changing social and economic scene in our country, which is likely to make fund raising more difficult, and in a climate of recognition of workers' rights, which makes it more difficult to put pressure on employees to give. And even more significantly, at least through the end of the 1980s, it would occur within the framework of a tax policy which could not be considered beneficial for charitable giving.

The new tax legislation passed by the Reagan administration (the Tax Reform Act of 1986) phased down, and eventually would eliminate, the federal income tax deduction for non-itemizers, a group considered conservatively to be at least 65 percent of the filers of income tax returns. As indicated in appendix J.2, United Way of America figures suggested that the amount of loss under the new plan could lead to reductions of over 16 percent from 1984 levels of giving. While in the end the loss might actually be much less, given the commitment of companies to United Way giving, nevertheless there was cause for concern.

Therefore, as the United Way movement celebrated its one hundredth anniversary, there really did not seem to be a great deal to cheer about. As one United Way executive expressed it, "This business isn't fun any more." United Way had raised more money in the preceding years, but the campaign had not yet come close to raising the three billion dollars which the UWA *Program for the Future* (1976,1977) had established as the goal to be achieved by 1987 (or "in ten years"). Thus the suggestion that the United Way would double its fund raising by 1992 was a source of skepticism. United Way staff were already working harder to raise their money, while they were also trying to develop a "multi-service" vision of the United Way. United Way retained its bifurcated mission of community leadership broadly defined, and at the same time faced a new intensity in the business of fund raising for the human services.

Meanwhile the alternative fund movement was gaining strength, if slowly. Choice was firmly established in the Combined Federal Campaign, and was increasingly a factor in state and municipal campaigns as well. New corporate managers, and in particular the managerial group connected with corporate contributions, were less susceptible to the United Way idea, and could argue the legally sensitive issues as well. A new generation of Americans, committed to empowerment, sensitive to individual concerns, and skeptical about the virtues of bigness ("small is beautiful"), will have to be convinced that the causes to which they contribute serve their interests, and their interests will be defined in increasingly varied ways.

The United Way, however, is a resilient organization with powerful friends. Thus, as the 1990s approach, corporations continue to "buy into" the National Corporate Leadership program, and to show their support for the continuation of United Way negemony of the workplace. United Ways are also going to market with a vengeance: they have to increase their access to smaller businesses and are seeking to control all monies raised in the workplace through donor option plans and by contractual relationships with competing charities. Overall, the United Way is focusing on developing a marketing capacity which will prepare it for the reality of a new world in which other charities will continue to challenge United Way fund raising in the workplace, and there will be fewer workers in smokestack industries subject to management and union influence. United Way will have to try new methods for reaching the next generation, as it did in the youth convocation held in connection with its centennial celebration. In this regard, therefore, once again, it seems that the community problem-solving role gives the United Way a unique place in the community, and the continued deep involvement of volunteers helps to protect its fund-raising capacity at the same time.

In conclusion, the lessons of history may serve to set the context for interpreting the future for organized charity in our country. Organized charity has survived continued environmental turbulence and constant challenge evidently because it is adaptable to changing circumstances and because it does in the end touch some fundamental core in the American life and value system. Federated fund raising has proven to be remarkably durable, perhaps because the intertwining interests of its many constituents—the corporations, the unions, the agencies they fund, and the volunteers and professionals involved, as well as the government—give them too strong a stake in the organization's existence for them to allow it to be seriously undermined. But the United Way will have to adapt once again, and it is now facing pragmatic and philosophical strains which are deeper and broader perhaps than any it has faced in recent years. It is being forced to respond in many directions at once: to be a universal collection agency, to provide extensive donor designation opportunites, to develop public-private partnerships with government, and to market its own services, as well as to help communities solve problems—but not to give up its hegemony of the one workplace campaign.

In the final analysis, however, it can be argued that the ultimate dilemma of organized charity is probably not being faced at all. It may well be in fact that the remarkable protection afforded organized charity actually results in a kind of issue suppression. Thus, no one seems to ask out loud the fundamental question of whether it is right to ask workers for money in the workplace at all. The question was not addressed even when the Combined Federal Campaign almost collapsed in its constant adjustment to new rules for donor choice. The courts eschew consideration of this issue, possibly because it would undermine the whole establishment of organized charity in our country today, which even the judiciary is not willing to do. Indeed, the social action and advocacy groups connected with the alternative-fund movement also do not want this question asked— they appear to want to come into the system, not to destroy it.

In voting with their purses in workplace fund-raising drives every year, Americans seem to reaffirm their belief in the voluntary sector, and with it the deeply ingrained connection of the sector to corporation and community. Americans clearly believe that some part of our life, some of our major institutions, must not be government run (even if in fact they are often government funded). Human services of a variety of sorts must be available locally, through non-governmental auspices. In this sense, federated fund raising can be considered a kind of secular tithing, representing a form of community charity which may be in a state of transition but to which nevertheless a certain portion of one's weekly earnings should be given. People grumble about it, and object to it, and some may even feel strongly about the kind of choices they are offered. But workplace charity has become part of the mythology of America, embedded in the community, in the public and private workplace, and in the national voice of the president of our country. Powerful interests want it to improve, but they want it to continue.

Appendixes

Appendixes

A	Fund-Raising Record of United Way Campaigns, 1919–1976	271
B	Organizational Chart, United Way of America	272
C.1	Annual Percent Change in National Amounts Raised vs. Inflation, 1955–1986	273
C.2	National Amounts Raised and Economic Indicators, Thirty Years	274
C.3	United Way Campaigns: Corporate Gifts and Corporate Profits	276
C.4	Mean Corporate Contributions to 131 United Ways by Corporation Type, 1983	277
C.5	Mile High United Way Comparison with Other United Way Cities, 1981	278
C.6	Donor Option Summary Report: AT&T/New York Telephone	280
D.1a	Sources of United Way Support, 1983	282
D.1b	Where the Money Comes From	283
D.2a	Services Supported with United Way Contributions	284
D.2b	Where the Money Goes	285
E.1	Partial Listing, Local United Way Allocations to Selected National Health Agencies	286
E.2	Allocations to Seventeen Selected National Agency Groupings, 1981–1983 (Metro I–VIII)	287
E.3a	Allocations to Selected Agencies, 1983–1985 (Aging–Heart)	288
E.3b	Allocations to Selected Agencies, 1983–1985 (Home Health–YWCA)	290
F.1	Total Designations as Percentage of Total Amount Raised, 1981	292
F.2a	Metro I Donor Option Trends, 1984–1986	293
F.2b	Donor Option Trends—Metro I Communities, 1982–1984	294
F.3	Industry/Trade Groups Contributing Largest Dollar Amounts of Positive Designations (August 1985 Figures)	296
F.4	Unaffiliated Agencies Receiving the Largest Dollar Amounts of Positive Designations (August 1985 Figures)	298
F.5	Unaffiliated Agencies Receiving the Largest Dollar Amounts of Positive Designations (October 1987 Figures)	300
F.6	Summary of 1984 Donor Option Dollars by Agency Affiliation	302
G.1	Combined Federal Campaign: Percentage Share of Total Receipts	303

APPENDIXES

G.2	Combined Federal Campaign: Historical Statistics	304
G.3	Combined Federal Campaign: Percentage Distribution of Designated and Deemed-Designated Contributions	306
G.4	Combined Federal Campaign: Miscellaneous	308
H.1	Occupations of Ten Top Planning Council Volunteers in 54 Local Planning Councils	310
H.2	Occupations of Ten Top United Way Volunteers in 131 Local United Ways	311
I	Individual Alternative Funds, 1985: Top Performers by Type	312
J.1	Impact of President Reagan's Tax Plan on Local United Way Contributors (Projected)	314
J.2	UW New Agency Admissions, 1980–1983	316

Appendix A. Fund-Raising Record of United Way Campaigns United States and Canada, 1919–1976

Year[a]	Number of Campaigns	Amount	Percent of Previous Year	Year[a]	Number of Campaigns	Amount	Percent of Previous Year
1919	39	$ 19,651,334		1948	1,153	193,307,693	106.4
1920	61	22,781,834	115.9%	1949	1,319	198,120,167	102.5
1921	96	28,568,453	125.4	1950	1,499	218,421,521	110.2
1922	147	40,280,649	140.1	1951	1,501	246,813,142	113.0
1923	203	50,351,190	125.0	1952	1,561	272,257,433	110.3
1924	240	58,003,965	115.2	1953	1,691	293,898,475	107.9
1925	285	63,677,235	109.8	1954	1,859	308,303,285	104.9
1926	308	66,432,072	104.3	1955	1,940	346,270,606	112.3
1927	314	68,664,042	103.4	1956	1,962	385,240,407	111.3
1928	331	73,276,688	106.7	1957	2,042	421,683,494	109.6
1929	353	75,972,555	103.7	1958	2,105	434,567,603	103.1
1930	386	84,796,505	111.6	1959	2,148	465,801,286	107.2
1931	397	101,377,537	119.6	1960	2,187	486,114,951	104.4
1932	401	77,752,954	76.7	1961	2,190	510,181,047	104.9
1933	399	70,609,078	90.8	1962	2,205	533,904,233	104.7
1934	406	69,781,478	98.8	1963	2,208	556,004,671	104.1
1935	429	77,367,634	110.9	1964	2,232	594,135,545	106.8
1936	452	81,707,787	105.6	1965	2,217	635,570,048	107.0
1937	475	83,898,234	102.7	1966	2,250	680,145,832	107.0
1938	524	86,561,920	103.2	1967	2,272	719,639,697	105.8
1939	562	89,751,702	103.7	1968	2,268	766,870,879	106.6
1940	599	94,161,098	104.9	1969	2,255	816,576,160	106.5
1941	633	108,812,899	115.6	1970	2,241	839,990,142	102.9
1942	650	166,538,363	153.1	1971	2,236	865,300,000	103.0
1943	704	214,757,782	120.0	1972	2,224	914,622,000	105.7
1944	773	225,934,893	105.2	1973	2,192	975,158,000	106.6
1945	799	201,859,357	89.3	1974	2,353	1,038,995,000	106.6
1946	842	173,512,638	86.0	1975	2,354	1,086,605,117	104.5
1947	1,011	181,716,355	104.7	1976[b]	2,350	1,171,410,138	107.8

Source: UWA, *People and Events*, 1977, p. 8.
[a] Campaigns conducted in indicated year for allocations the following year.
[b] Projection based upon 75% of campaigns reported through January, 1977.

Appendix B. Organizational Chart, United Way of America[a]

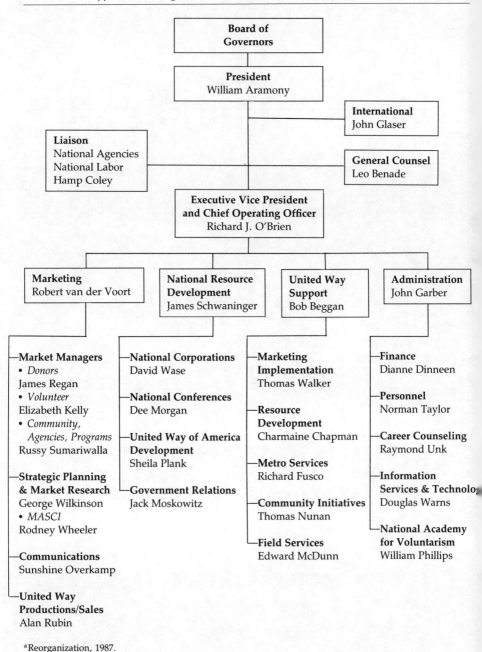

[a] Reorganization, 1987.

Appendix C.1. Annual Percentage Change in National Amounts Raised vs. Inflation (CPI), 1955–1986

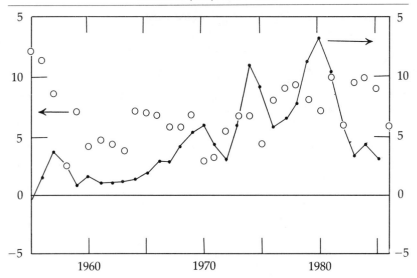

Source: Data from United Way of America and U.S. Dept. of Labor Statistics. Graph designed by John N. Pike.

Note: The small circles represent percentage change in actual dollar amounts raised from previous year. The points connected by a solid line represent the annual inflation rate as measured by changes in the CPI.

Appendix C.2. National Amounts Raised and Economic Indicators
Thirty Year Summary, United Way

		Amount Raised		
Year	Current $	% Change	Constant (1967) $	% Change
1955	$ 329,990,528	12.1%	$411,459,511	12.6%
1956	367,720,884	11.4	451,745,557	10.0
1957	398,967,291	8.5	473,270,808	4.8
1958	409,446,729	2.6	472,802,227	−0.1
1959	438,675,048	7.1	502,491,464	6.3
1960	456,983,942	4.2	515,201,738	2.5
1961	479,086,478	4.8	534,694,730	3.8
1962	501,437,619	4.7	553,463,156	3.5
1963	520,325,952	3.8	567,421,976	2.5
1964	558,559,954	7.3	601,248,605	6.0
1965	597,738,826	7.0	632,527,858	5.2
1966	639,085,139	6.9	657,494,999	3.9
1967	676,729,723	5.9	676,729,723	2.9
1968	716,422,803	5.9	687,545,876	1.6
1969	764,327,412	6.7	696,108,754	1.2
1970	786,985,155	3.0	676,685,430	−2.8
1971	812,924,645	3.3	670,176,954	−1.0
1972	858,122,000	5.6	684,853,951	2.2
1973	916,400,000	6.8	688,504,884	0.5
1974	978,764,132	6.8	662,670,367	−3.8
1975	1,022,906,395	4.5	634,557,317	−4.2
1976	1,104,329,744	8.0	647,700,730	2.1
1977	1,204,825,000	9.1	663,815,427	2.5
1978	1,317,745,690	9.4	674,383,669	1.6
1979	1,423,461,336	8.0	654,766,024	−2.9
1980	1,526,000,000	7.2	619,935,170	−5.3
1981	1,680,000,000	10.1	617,217,327	−0.4
1982	1,780,000,000	6.0	615,703,909	−0.2
1983	1,950,000,000	9.5	653,485,255	6.1
1984	2,145,000,000	10.0	689,488,910	5.5
1985	2,330,000,000[c]	9.0	724,953,329[e]	5.1[e]
1986	2,440,000,000[d]	5.7	NA	NA

Source: CPI and unemployment data: U.S. Dept. of Labor, Bureau of Labor Statistics. All other data for this table from United Way of America.

[a] Defined as the percent change in the annual average Consumer Price Index for all urban consumers (CPI-U).
[b] Based on civilian labor force.
[c] 1985 $2.310,000 (actual), table figures estimated by UWA when table was developed.
[d] 1986 $2.444,000 (est.).
[e] Estimate based on a 3.3% increase in the annual average CPI in the first ten months of 1985.

"Real" New UW Dollars	Inflation Rate[a]	Unemployment Rate[b]
$46.0	−0.4%	4.4%
40.2	1.5	4.1
21.6	3.6	4.3
−0.5	2.7	6.8
29.7	0.8	5.5
12.7	1.6	5.5
19.5	1.0	6.7
18.8	1.1	5.5
13.9	1.2	5.7
33.8	1.3	5.2
31.3	1.7	4.5
25.0	2.9	3.8
19.2	2.9	3.8
10.8	4.2	3.6
8.6	5.4	3.5
−19.4	5.9	4.9
−6.5	4.3	5.9
14.7	3.3	5.6
3.6	6.2	4.9
−25.8	11.0	5.6
−28.2	9.1	8.5
13.1	5.8	7.7
16.1	6.5	6.1
10.6	7.7	6.1
−19.6	11.3	5.8
−34.9	13.5	7.1
−2.7	10.4	7.6
−1.5	6.1	9.7
37.8	3.2	9.6
36.0	4.3	7.5
35.5	3.3[e]	NA
NA	NA	NA

Appendix C.3. United Way Campaigns: Corporate Gifts and Corporate Profits

Corporate Gifts to United Way Campaigns and Corporate Profits Before Taxes

Year[a]	Estimated Total Corporate Gifts to United Way Campaign (in millions)	Total Corporate Profits Before Taxes (in billions)	Gifts as a Percent of Profits
1960	$161.8	$ 49.8	.33
1961	165.3	49.7	.33
1962	170.5	55.0	.31
1963	176.4	59.6	.30
1964	184.9	66.5	.28
1965	190.1	77.2	.25
1966	200.0	83.0	.24
1967	205.0	79.7	.26
1968	218.0	88.5	.25
1969	236.0	86.7	.27
1970	234.0	75.4	.31
1971	238.0	86.6	.27
1972	248.0	100.6	.25
1973	260.0	125.6	.21
1974	271.3	136.7	.20
1975	281.3	132.1	.21
1976	292.8	166.3	.18
1977	308.4	194.7	.16
1978	332.1	229.1	.14
1979	355.9	252.7	.14
1980	387.1	234.6	.17
1981	410.2	227.0	.18
1982	448.6	169.6	.26
1983	481.7	207.6	.23
1984	512.7	235.7	.22
1985	554.5	223.2	.25

Sources: United Way of America's *Survey of Giving by Major Contributor Categories, Campaign Summary Survey, Data Base Report No. 2* and the U.S. Department of Commerce, Bureau of Economic Analysis (BEA). (Note: the United Way of America states that these figures represent the most recent update by the BEA and, thus, may differ somewhat from BEA figures published in earlier volumes.)

[a] Refers to the year in which the campaign was conducted, as well as to the corporate fiscal year.

Appendix C.4. Mean Corporate Contribution to 131 United Ways by Corporation Type, 1983

		Contribution		
Corporation Type	N[a]	Mean	Low	High
MANUFACTURING				
Primary metal industries	12	$139,566	$2,500	$1,000,000
Petroleum and gas	21	122,207	2,500	1,000,000
Chemicals	23	93,193	5,591	921,272
Machinery, electrical	44	92,816	3,500	661,400
Rubber and plastic products	7	89,040	7,500	420,000
Food, beverage, and tobacco	23	63,219	1,216	500,000
Transportation equipment	26	61,753	4,300	125,000
Machinery, nonelectrical	17	47,271	3,000	65,000
Other manufacturing	26	46,879	3,500	410,000
Paper and like products	14	35,473	6,000	103,250
Printing and publishing	10	35,373	4,700	125,000
Textiles	13	32,387	6,500	80,000
Stone, clay, and glass products	8	22,762	5,000	65,000
Fabricated metal products	9	13,666	2,625	35,000
Wood products	8	11,175	1,800	28,000
NONMANUFACTURING				
Insurance	12	110,183	10,000	449,454
Personal services	3	90,333	45,000	178,000
Banking	70	88,927	2,600	1,100,000
Utilities	27	85,085	2,550	935,000
Engineering and construction	5	83,654	3,500	400,000
Business services	3	54,368	3,500	154,000
Transportation	5	53,240	4,200	200,000
Telecommunications	33	49,277	2,250	358,000
Retail and wholesale trade	14	24,288	1,400	125,000
Angricultural products	2	9,250	6,500	12,000

Source: Survey of local United Way organizations, in connection with United Way Study Project, 1984.
Note: The data were examined for differences between the manufacturing and nonmanufacturing groups, and none were found.
[a] Each United Way was asked to list its 5 largest contributors; the data in this table are based on all corporations listed by each United Way. "N" therefore refers to the total number of corporations of a given type in our sample of 131 United Way organizations.

Appendix C.5. Mile High United Way Comparison with Other United Way Cities with Population of 1–3 Million, 1981

City	Population	Percent of Increase Over 1980	Total Amount Raised in 1981
1. Dallas	3,023,500	15.0% (7)	$21,250,714 (9)
2. Houston	2,977,300	20.9% (1)	32,930,120 (2)
3. St. Louis	2,358,100	9.3% (19)	25,226,606 (4)
4. Pittsburgh	2,253,500	9.0% (21)	29,599,090 (3)
5. Baltimore	2,180,600	10.3% (16)	21,902,182 (6)
6. St. Paul	2,127,600	9.1% (20)	11,010,559 (22)
7. Atlanta	2,064,200	12.1% (11)	21,308,065 (8)
8. San Diego	1,904,900	12.8% (9)	13,490,028 (16)
9. Cleveland	1,888,700	10.1% (17)	40,804,797 (1)
10. Miami	1,719,200	5.4% (23)	13,482,934 (17)
11. Denver	1,648,600	17.4% (2)	16,032,000 (12)
12. Seattle	1,621,600	11.7% (12)	20,805,807 (10)
13. Orange, Calif.	1,600,000	16.4% (4)	12,019,785 (21)
14. Cincinnati	1,403,300	11.0% (14)	24,616,615 (5)
15. Milwaukee	1,399,400	5.1% (24)	16,629,513 (11)
16. Kansas City	1,332,500	10.9% (15)	15,676,564 (13)
17. Santa Clara, Calif.	1,295,710	17.0% (3)	12,053,426 (20)
18. Portland	1,262,800	11.3% (13)	13,605,184 (15)
19. Buffalo	1,233,300	7.2% (22)	12,607,737 (18)
20. New Orleans	1,199,000	12.7% (10)	10,474,763 (24)
21. Minneapolis	1,197,945	15.1% (6)	21,624,606 (7)
22. Indianapolis	1,171,400	9.6% (18)	14,001,414 (14)
23. Columbus	1,099,300	14.2% (8)	12,159,552 (19)
24. Hartford	1,051,100	15.5% (5)	10,514,210 (23)

Source: *Strategic Planning Report,* Mile High United Way, 1982.

Household Buying Income and Ranking	Employee Per Capita Gift and Ranking	Total Per Capita Gift and Ranking
$22,409 (5)	$25.77 (15)	$ 7.02 (23)
23,988 (1)	31.56 (5)	15.78 (5)
21,222 (11)	22.96 (17)	10.69 (12)
19,805 (19)	27.55 (13)	13.13 (6)
19,388 (20)	28.86 (9)	10.04 (15)
22,788 (3)	28.46 (10)	5.17 (24)
20,617 (15)	17.52 (21)	10.32 (13)
18,858 (22)	19.19 (20)	7.08 (22)
22,303 (6)	49.41 (1)	21.60 (1)
17,573 (23)	27.62 (11)	7.84 (20)
21,800 (9)	22.69 (18)	9.72 (17)
21,807 (8)	16.39 (22)	12.83 (7)
21,793 (10)	14.79 (23)	7.51 (21)
20,656 (13)	42.50 (2)	17.54 (3)
22,204 (7)	30.13 (7)	16.25 (4)
22,530 (4)	31.27 (6)	11.76 (9)
20,646 (14)	23.01 (16)	9.30 (18)
20,391 (16)	27.03 (14)	10.77 (11)
19,118 (21)	29.77 (8)	10.22 (14)
19,907 (18)	21.16 (19)	8.73 (19)
22,788 (3)	35.54 (3)	18.05 (2)
21,014 (12)	27.59 (12)	11.95 (8)
20,087 (17)	35.54 (3)	11.06 (10)
23,792 (2)	31.67 (4)	10.00 (16)

Table C.6. Donor Option Summary Report
AT&T/New York Telephone (as of June 30, 1984)

	Designations			Total Employment
	Number	Amount	Average	
AT&T-Int'l (018711)	266	$ 40,767	$153	860
AT&T-Central[a] Services (018712)	461	71,797	156	3,000
ATTIS[b] (023775)	1,641	151,529	92	2,577
AT&T Corp Hdqts (032700)	628	102,909	164	2,664
ATTCOM (033750)	5,033	616,092	122	15,045
Sub-Total	8,029	983,094	122	24,086
New York Tel (033400)	27,593	2,139,967	78	51,284
Grand total	35,622	$3,123,061	$ 88	75,370

Source: United Way of Tri-State.

[a] Estimated employment and giving of CSO employees offered Donor Option (excludes personnel transferred from Bell Labs).

[b] Reflects only ATTIS employees transferred from New York Tel. Other ATTIS employees were not offered Donor Option. ATTIS stands for AT&T Information Systems. ATTCOM stands for AT&T Communications—long distance lines.

Total Pledged	Per Capita Gift	Designations as Percent of Total
$ 134,593	$168.24	30.2%
570,000	190.00	12.5%
325,423	126.28	46.5%
558,629	209.70	18.4%
2,628,028	174.68	23.4%
4,216,673	175.07	23.3%
5,658,674	110.34	37.8%
$9,875,347	$131.02	31.6%

Appendix D.1a. Sources of United Way Support, 1983

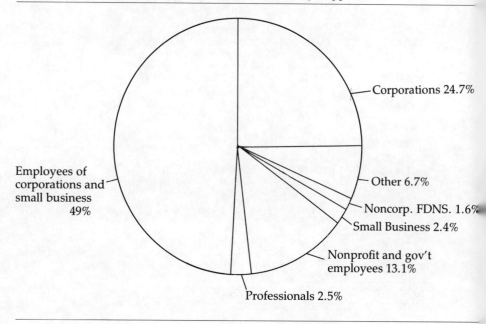

Source: United Way of America. Based on 1983 data.

Appendix D.1b. Where the Money Comes From

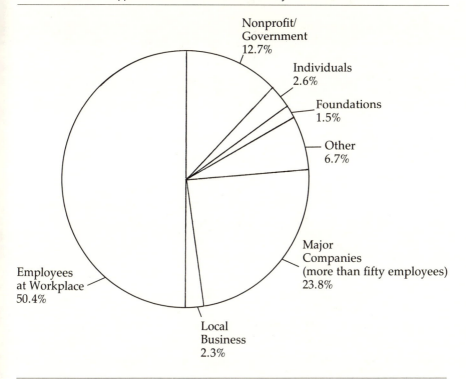

Source: United Way of America. Based on 1986 data (reflects the 1985 campaign).

Appendix D.2a. Services Supported with United Way Contributions

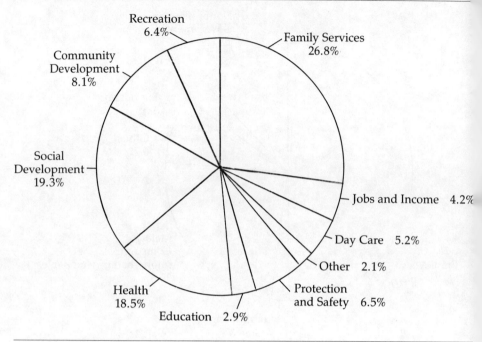

Source: United Way of America. Based on 1983 data.
Note: Two percent of all services are food related.

Appendix D.2b. Where the Money Goes

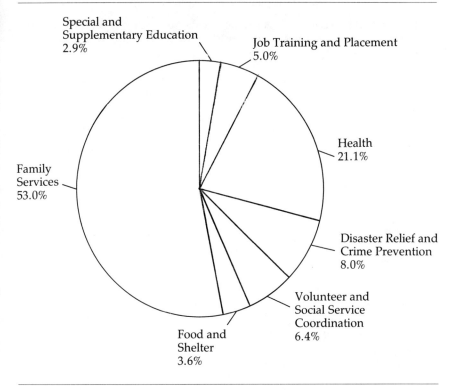

Source: United Way of America. Based on 1986 data.

Appendix E.1. Partial Listing, Local United Way Allocations to Selected National Health Agencies

The overall field of health is a major priority within the United Way system representing 18.5% of local allocations. In the 1983 Fall campaign, United Ways collectively raised $1,950,000,000.[b]

	Number of United Ways	Dollars Allocated to NHAs
American Cancer Society	110	$22,500,000
National Association of Retarded Citizens	400	$17,364,571
National Mental Health	395	$12,306,043
American Heart Association	81	$10,500,000
United Cerebral Palsy	195	$10,158,984
Society for the Blind[a]	100	$ 7,435,336
Arthritis Foundation	132	$ 3,622,924
Easter Seals/Society for Crippled Children	80	$ 3,395,153
National Council on Alcoholism	51	$ 1,436,429
Epilepsy Foundation	56	$ 1,388,274
American Diabetes Association	30	$ 1,196,187
Multiple Sclerosis Society	35	$ 1,071,091
National Kidney Foundation	40	$ 1,069,700
Cystic Fibrosis	20	$ 902,421
American Lung Association	9	$ 700,480
American Social Health Association	110	$ 547,156
Hemophilia Foundation	25	$ 338,353
Autistic Children's Foundation	30	$ 117,708
Muscular Dystrophy	1	$ 73,176

Source: United Way of America
Note: The March of Dimes/National Foundation is one of the few major national health agencies which does not participate with any United Way. The reader is cautioned that these data are partial reports and subject to change.
[a] May be more than one organization.
[b] According to United Way, this is a partial listing and represents a conservative statement of dollars allocated.

Appendix E.2. Allocations to Seventeen Selected National Agency Groupings, 1981–1983 (Metro I–VIII)

	Percentage of Total Allocations for UWs Reporting		
Agency Groupings	1981	1982	1983
American Red Cross chapters	13.2% (n = 506)[a]	12.8% (n = 500)	12.1% (n = 499)
Big Brothers, Big Sisters	1 (n = 214)	1.1 (n = 228)	1.1 (n = 231)
Boy Scout councils	5 (n = 486)	4.7 (n = 485)	4.5 (n = 483)
Boys Clubs, Boys and Girls Clubs	3.6 (n = 324)	3.6 (n = 324)	3.8 (n = 327)
Camp Fire	0.9 (n = 163)	0.8 (n = 162)	0.8 (n = 161)
Catholic Charities, Catholic Family Services	4.1 (n = 247)	4.1 (n = 251)	4.1 (n = 264)
Cerebral palsy agencies	1.1 (n = 157)	1.1 (n = 149)	1.1 (n = 150)
Family Service—nonsectarian	7.2 (n = 487)	7.2 (n = 503)	7.0 (n = 512)
Girl Scout councils	3.3 (n = 475)	3.0 (n = 470)	2.9 (n = 468)
Goodwill Industries	0.8 (n = 106)	0.8 (n = 107)	0.7 (n = 109)
Home Health Agencies/VNA	2.8 (n = 368)	2.7 (n = 373)	2.6 (n = 375)
Jewish Community Centers	1.1 (n = 98)	1.0 (n = 99)	1.0 (n = 100)
Retarded citizens' agencies	1.8 (n = 421)	1.9 (n = 452)	2.0 (n = 462)
Salvation Army	4.7 (n = 525)	4.6 (n = 521)	4.8 (n = 526)
Urban League affiliates	1.7 (n = 108)	1.7 (n = 105)	1.7 (n = 105)
YMCA, YMCA-YWCA	5.9 (n = 537)	5.7 (n = 521)	5.6 (n = 519)
YWCA	3.5 (n = 269)	3.4 (n = 262)	3.2 (n = 257)

Source: United Way of America.
[a] Number of agencies in category receiving UW Supports, as reported by local UWs.

Appendix E.3a. Allocations to Selected Agencies, 1983–1985
(Aging-Heart)

Metro I–VIII 446 United Ways Reporting for 1983, 1984, and 1985	Number of Agencies Reported Receiving Support for			Allocations to Agencies by United Ways Reporting Allocations in 1983, 1984, and 1985[a]
Agency	1983	1984	1985	1983
Agencies for the aging	490	570	663	$ 17,189,472
Alcoholism agencies	245	283	317	7,085,634
American Red Cross chapters	491	529	539	133,166,160
Arthritis agencies	105	114	106	
Big Brothers, Big Sisters	220	235	264	11,177,453
Boy Scout councils	468	508	515	49,639,002
Boys Clubs, Boys and Girls Clubs	300	315	333	37,492,546
Camp Fire	148	161	162	8,799,497
Camping agencies	94	91	82	3,082,343
Cancer agencies	86	114	151	15,370,678
Catholic Charities/Family Services	241	267	268	41,571,856
Catholic Youth Organizations	38	39	37	3,035,751
Cerebral palsy agencies	150	160	168	11,730,325
Child welfare agency	192	234	291	12,697,438
Children's Home societies	218	235	237	17,637,642
Community/neighborhood development	150	165	206	9,889,336
Crippled children and adults agencies	80	79	90	4,580,389
Cystic fibrosis agencies	19	23	22	708,886
Day care centers	561	612	689	26,172,692
Drug abuse agencies	90	105	133	3,185,265
Epilepsy agencies	76	86	90	1,636,088
Family Service—nondenominational	487	521	571	74,157,984
Florence Crittenton agencies	42	39	41	1,534,120
Girl Scout councils	454	490	494	31,839,947
Girls' Clubs	79	90	93	5,639,223
Goodwill Industries	101	107	107	8,207,008
Health planning agencies	16	14	17	1,012,720
Health, not elsewhere classified	359	402	393	13,640,155
Hearing and speech agencies	144	156	183	8,525,329
Heart agencies	53	55	58	7,334,466

Source: UWA Research Division, *1985 Local United Way Allocations*, table 1.
[a] Dollar amounts for 1983, 1984, and 1985 represent total dollars allocated in the communities submitting an allocations survey in each of these three years. For total dollars allocated to these agencies from all allocation survey respondents, see the companion publication, *Allocations to agencies, detail listing 1983–1985*.

Allocations to Agencies by United Ways Reporting Allocations in 1983, 1984, and 1985[a]		Agency Allocations as a Percent of Reporting U.W.'s Total Aggregate Annual Allocations		
1984	1985	1983	1984	1985
$ 19,983,853	$ 26,878,400	1.50%	1.60%	2.00%
8,302,493	11,180,160	.60	.70	.80
139,060,061	158,475,447	11.60	11.20	11.90
3,394,083	4,043,823	.30	.30	.30
12,256,293	15,594,065	1.00	1.00	1.20
52,816,152	57,418,985	4.30	4.30	4.30
44,186,238	48,214,830	3.30	3.60	3.60
9,633,774	10,486,942	.80	.80	.80
2,743,752	2,615,813	.30	.20	.20
20,390,587	26,994,570	1.30	1.60	2.00
45,479,958	52,052,476	3.60	3.70	3.90
3,180,338	3,698,800	.30	.30	.30
13,074,100	15,542,216	1.00	1.10	1.20
16,532,262	22,022,094	1.10	1.30	1.70
18,686,697	27,588,293	1.50	1.50	2.10
10,782,466	13,466,433	.90	.90	1.00
4,153,914	5,562,631	.40	.30	.40
945,166	950,831	.10	.10	.10
29,612,038	36,862,893	2.30	2.40	2.80
3,859,769	5,090,899	.30	.30	.40
1,893,362	2,232,999	.10	.20	.20
79,546,015	91,598,458	6.50	6.40	6.90
1,155,806	1,428,321	.10	.10	.10
33,721,629	36,664,312	2.80	2.70	2.80
6,549,610	7,903,617	.50	.50	.60
8,412,949	9,360,348	.70	.70	.70
1,092,009	713,369	.10	.10	.10
16,805,883	17,742,439	1.20	1.40	1.30
9,462,928	10,958,311	.70	.80	.80
8,412,550	11,448,018	.60	.70	.90

Appendix E.3b. Allocations to Selected Agencies, 1983–1985
(Home Health—YWCA)

Metro I–VIII 446 United Ways Reporting for 1983, 1984, and 1985	Number of Agencies Reported Receiving Support for			Allocations to Agencies by United Ways Reporting Allocations in 1983, 1984, and 1985[a]
Agency	1983	1984	1985	1983
Home Health agencies/visiting nurse	360	389	382	$28,207,008
Hospitals	109	126	110	9,249,853
Information and referral agencies	127	146	157	3,885,966
Jewish Community Centers	100	104	102	10,422,796
Labor agencies	26	25	26	1,470,171
Legal Aid agencies	166	187	213	8,558,138
Lung and Tuberculosis agencies	13	17	18	688,243
Mental health agencies	564	619	677	25,048,095
Military base recreation programs	72	78	78	1,438,116
Muscular dystrophy agencies	4	4	4	223,403
Planned Parenthood	33	36	35	1,720,739
Planning Organizations (social welfare)	128	138	131	11,178,035
Rehabilitation centers	120	156	171	7,549,362
Retarded Citizens' agencies	433	471	494	19,499,184
Salvation Army	497	538	526	48,563,287
Settlement House/neighborhood centers	449	458	488	50,441,087
Travelers' Aid	62	65	66	6,029,328
Urban League affiliates	105	113	112	18,044,048
USO-local	44	51	46	1,847,575
Vocational services	135	156	214	6,419,290
Volunteer centers, VACs	126	132	148	4,696,995
Volunteers of America affiliates	20	23	21	2,357,896
Women's crisis agencies	197	286	389	4,934,825
YMCA, YMCA-YWCA	510	548	551	58,683,167
YWCA	259	274	268	34,892,247

Source: UWA Research Division, *1985 Local United Way Allocations,* table 1.

[a] Dollar amounts for 1983, 1984, and 1985 represent total dollars allocated in the communities submitting an allocations survey in each of these three years. For total dollars allocated to these agencies from all allocation survey respondents, see the companion publication, *Allocations to Agencies, Detail Listing 1983–1985.*

Allocations to Agencies by United Ways Reporting Allocations in 1983, 1984, and 1985[a]		Agency Allocations as a Percent of Reporting U.W.'s Total Aggregate Annual Allocations		
1984	1985	1983	1984	1985
$30,161,499	$32,833,135	2.50%	2.40%	2.50%
9,723,221	11,688,112	.80	.80	.90
5,036,193	6,820,032	.30	.40	.50
11,075,703	12,351,038	.90	.90	.90
1,389,074	1,517,918	.10	.10	.10
10,050,752	12,130,639	.70	.80	.90
786,407	1,026,841	.10	.10	.10
28,175,639	33,841,761	2.20	2.30	2.50
1,541,748	1,739,181	.10	.10	.10
206,021	207,954	.00	.00	.00
1,876,422	2,052,988	.20	.20	.20
11,728,104	11,575,867	1.00	.90	.90
8,906,252	10,801,142	.70	.70	.80
22,333,881	26,001,964	1.70	1.80	2.00
56,591,370	62,979,490	4.20	4.60	4.70
52,587,174	62,190,775	4.40	4.20	4.70
6,747,713	7,710,141	.50	.50	.60
20,164,041	23,603,689	1.60	1.60	1.80
1,816,226	1,953,799	.20	.10	.10
8,296,105	11,744,902	.60	.70	.90
5,087,572	6,230,529	.40	.40	.50
2,497,133	2,684,748	.20	.20	.20
7,622,852	12,992,074	.40	.60	1.00
64,685,021	70,422,224	5.10	5.20	5.30
37,629,536	40,375,799	3.00	3.00	3.00

Appendix F.1. Total Designations as a Percentage of Total Amount Raised
Fall 1981 Campaign

Total Amount Raised	Total Amount Designated	Percentage	Metro	United Way
$ 21,902,182	$ 4,528,418	20.68	1	Baltimore
31,951,000	4,067,920	12.73	1	Philadelphia
29,350,026	3,273,219	11.15	1	San Francisco
6,027,000	592,606	9.83	2	Sacramento
13,490,028	1,221,913	9.06	1	San Diego
47,128,411	4,259,614	9.04	1	Los Angeles[a]
820,024	63,322	7.72	5	Ashtabula, Ohio
1,289,931	95,712	7.42	4	Downingtown, Pa.
855,000	52,628	6.16	5	St. Cloud, Minn.
22,617,721	1,350,000	5.97	1	Rochester[b]
730,000	41,264	5.65	6	Modesto, Calif.
1,228,386	66,733	5.43	4	Stockton, Calif.
12,019,705	526,837	4.38	1	Orange, Calif.
1,120,458	48,387	4.32	4	Santa Barbara
1,415,070	59,456	4.20	4	Santa Rosa, Calif.
12,053,426	500,360	4.15	1	Santa Clara, Calif.
810,000	32,962	4.07	5	Bangor, Maine
1,802,204	71,851	3.99	4	Fairless Hills, Pa.
7,564,062	297,188	3.93	2	Omaha
2,030,000	75,234	3.71	4	Springfield, Ill.
961,824	35,072	3.65	5	Vallejo, Calif.
1,175,000	42,720	3.64	5	Garden Grove, Calif.
14,001,414	502,839	3.59	1	Indianapolis
1,650,000	59,022	3.58	4	San Bernardino, Calif.
735,000	25,102	3.42	5	Owensboro, Ky.
881,691	29,807	3.38	5	Terre Haute, Ind.
6,353,008	135,255	2.13	2	Syracuse, NY
1,082,200	14,764	1.36	5	Bakersfield, Calif.
16,629,513	218,478	1.31	1	Milwaukee
1,487,397	18,563	1.25	4	Augusta
1,007,678	12,087	1.20	5	Bellingham, Wash.
580,200	3,563	0.61	6	Provo, Utah
$262,749,559	$22,322,896			

Source: "Donor Option—Future Modeling," Internal Report for the United Way of America, prepared by Russy D. Sumariwalla, March 1983.
[a] 1979–80 campaign.
[b] Spring 1982 campaign.

Appendix F.2a. Metro I Donor Option Trends, 1984–1986: Communities reporting for 1986

United Way	1984 Percent of Employee $ Designated[a]	1986 Percent of Employee $ Designated[a]	1986 Employee Dollars	1984 Percent of Designated $ to Other Agencies[b]	1986 Percent of Designated $ to Other Agencies[b]
Buffalo	3.6	5.1	$10,392,176	23.4	23.2
Columbus	9.4	11.0	16,169,855	17.9	23.2
Dayton	21.9	18.9	11,402,068	31.2	35.6
Indianapolis	8.8	7.7	13,118,547	9.2	10.9
Kansas City	10.8	11.3	20,179,302	8.3	17.9
Miami	4.8	4.9	13,178,573	48.3	51.5
Milwaukee	6.6	8.8	14,749,900	18.2	27.0
New Orleans	12.4	13.5	8,941,573	7.5	10.0
Omaha	5.8	7.5	7,255,330	14.6	20.5
Orange, Calif.	7.5	NC[c]	NC[c]	30.3	26.9
Philadelphia	24.4	30.8	33,150,178	64.8	63.6
Pittsburgh	11.8	14.1	19,249,164	50.7	49.1
Providence, R.I.	4.1	5.2	7,874,651	32.8	36.5
Rochester, N.Y.	10.8	15.2	21,500,733	36.2	48.9
Sacramento	NR[d]	20.6	5,992,509	NR	52.7
San Diego	13.7	15.2	14,155,779	22.4	25.1
San Francisco	18.5	21.8	27,671,368	37.5	39.1
Santa Ciara, Calif.	7.6	8.2	13,628,316	15.6	21.9

Source: UWA Strategic Planning and Market Research Division, October 1987.
Note: Cities are grouped according to their current Metro size.
[a] This percentage is calculated by dividing the dollar amount of positive designations, net of unprocessible designations, by the total employee dollars raised in the campaign. Therefore, corporation, small business and noncorporate foundation gifts, as well as the entire CFC campaign, are excluded.
[b] This percentage is calculated by dividing the dollar amount designated to other agencies by the amount of positive designations, net of unprocessible designations. Other agencies include agencies unaffiliated with United Way and those agencies affiliated for the donor option program only.
[c] NC = No Data Base II was received from these communities; therefore, these figures cannot be calculated.
[d] NR = No Donor Option Survey was received from these communities for 1984.

Appendex F.2b. Donor Option Trends—Metro I Communities, 1982–1984

United Way	1982 Percent of Campaign Designated[a]	1982 Percent of Designated Dollars to Other Agencies[b]	1983 Percent of Campaign Designated[a]
Baltimore	29.1	6.9	40.0
Buffalo	NR	NR	NR
Columbus	NR	NR	7.6
Dayton	NR	NR	14.0
Denver	NR	NR	2.2
Indianapolis	6.5	3.7	9.5
Kansas City	NR	NR	NR
Los Angeles	14.6	40.5	12.8
Miami	1.9	39.0	3.8
Milwaukee	NC	14.2	5.4
New Orleans	NR	NR	NR
Omaha	5.6	8.4	5.7
Orange, Calif.	10.0	31.0	8.1
Philadelphia	[c]	[c]	25.9
Pittsburgh	7.0	48.2	9.9
Providence, R.I.	1.8	0.0	3.5
Rochester, N.Y.	NR	NR	9.6
San Diego	12.2	42.5	13.5
San Francisco	21.9	43.0	17.7
Santa Clara, Calif.	4.8	18.9	7.3
Tri-State, N.Y.	NR	NR	NC

Source: UWA Research Division, October 1985.
Note: Cities are grouped according to their current Metro size.
[a] This percentage is calculated by dividing the dollar amount of positive designations, net of unprocessable designations, by the designatable portion of the campaign. The designatable portion of the campaign excludes corporation, small business and noncorporate foundation gifts, as well as the entire CFC campaign.
[b] This percentage is calculated by dividing the dollar amount designated to other agencies by the amount of positive designations, net of unprocessable designations. Other agencies include agencies unaffiliated with United Way and those agencies affiliated for the donor option program only.
[c] Figures for Philadelphia have not been calculated due to inconsistencies in the 1982 data.

1983 Percent of Designated Dollars to Other Agencies[b]	1984 Percent of Campaign Designated[a]	1984 Percent of Designated Dollars to Other Agencies[b]
9.3	37.9	12.3
NR	3.6	23.4
12.7	9.4	17.9
17.8	21.9	31.2
1.9	0.9	0.8
5.0	8.8	9.2
NR	10.8	8.3
37.9	11.3	37.6
43.7	4.8	48.3
16.1	6.6	18.2
NR	12.4	7.5
8.6	5.8	14.6
29.7	7.5	30.3
59.2	24.4	64.8
52.7	11.8	50.7
28.3	4.1	32.8
29.6	10.8	36.2
18.7	13.7	22.4
34.1	18.5	37.5
16.7	7.6	15.6
44.7	NR	NR

Appendix F.3. Industry/Trade Groups Contributing Largest
Dollar Amounts of Positive Designations
(August 1985 Figures)

Trade Group	Number of Designations	Dollars Designated
Communications	30,734	$ 4,080,556
Electrical equipment	6,827	1,851,018
Chemical products	10,995	1,698,360
Utilities	11,654	1,561,683
Instruments and special manufacturing	11,433	1,097,294
Banking/finance	5,477	963,288
State/local government	12,047	867,019
Transportation	5,925	662,324
Paper products	3,842	635,888
Retail hardware/building materials trade	4,812	598,520
Subtotal	103,746	$14,015,950
All other trade groups reported	28,532	$ 2,957,830
Total	132,278	$16,973,780

Source: UWA Research Division, August 1985.

Note: The data shown in this table are based on the following question: List the five companies whose employees contributed the largest dollar amounts of *positive designations*. The data shown here for these industries are drawn from responses to this question only and thus do *not* represent total dollars or designations by these industries. The designations by these industries accounted for here ($16,973,780) is 35% of all dollars positively designated to *all* agencies as reported by survey respondents.

[a] Average designation based on matched data only.

Average Designation[a]	Percent of Total Dollars	Number of United Ways Represented
$131.89	24.0%	26
221.71	10.9	13
152.01	10.0	15
134.00	9.2	6
94.14	6.5	6
173.98	5.7	10
71.97	5.1	6
111.78	3.9	5
165.51	3.8	8
124.38	3.5	2
$131.02	82.6%	47
$100.02	17.4%	38
$124.34	100.0%	47

Appendix F.4. Unaffiliated Agencies Receiving the Largest
Dollar Amounts of Positive Designations
(August 1985 Figures)

Agency	Number of Designations	Dollars Designated
Catholic Family Services	3,815	$514,668
Hospitals	5,452	412,338
Short-term tangible aid	4,826	338,924
Health—general	3,367	292,464
Cancer, all other	2,074	209,700
Women's Way	1,415	178,628
Catholic Charities	1,127	170,930
Lutheran Family Services	1,035	136,748
American Cancer Society	1,369	135,634
Sickle cell disease agencies	1,454	112,870
Subtotal	25,934	$2,502,904
All other agencies reported	12,444	$1,346,264
Total	38,378	$3,849,168

Source: UWA Research Division, August 1985.

Note: The data shown in this table are based on the following question: List the five *unaffiliated* agencies who received the largest dollar amounts of *positive designations*. The data shown here for these agencies are drawn from responses to this question only and thus do *not* represent total dollars or designation to these agencies. The designation to these agencies accounted for here ($3,489,168) is 25% of all dollars positively designated to *all* agencies either unaffiliated with United Way or affiliated for the donor option program only, as reported by survey respondents.

[a] Average designation based on matched data only.

Average Designation[a]	Percent of Total Dollars	Number of United Ways Represented
134.91	13.4%	2
74.47	10.7	34
70.15	8.8	6
86.86	7.6	6
101.11	5.5	3
126.24	4.6	1
151.44	4.4	8
132.12	3.6	7
99.08	3.5	18
77.63	2.9	2
96.20	65.0	45
106.12	35.0	55
99.41	100.0	56

Appendix F.5. Unaffiliated Agencies Receiving the Largest
Dollar Amounts of Positive Designations
(October 1987 Figures)

Agency	Number of Designations	Dollars Designated
Hospitals	9,133	$ 908,123
Local Catholic Charities Federation	5,426	832,904
General health agencies	3,982	484,207
Planned Parenthood	3,000	401,723
Cancer agencies	3,806	355,956
Women's Way	1,321	211,658
American Cancer Society	3,017	205,590
Education agencies	2,432	204,519
Retarded citizen's agencies	1,438	177,604
Sunshine Foundation (Child Welfare Agency)	1,953	161,902
Subtotal	35,508	$3,944,186
All other agencies reported	21,376	$2,201,545
Total	56,884	$6,145,731

Source: UWA Strategic Planning and Market Research Division, October 1987.

Note: The data shown in this table are based on the following: "List the ten unaffiliated agencies who received the largest dollar amounts of *positive designations*." The data shown here for these agencies are drawn from those responses only and thus do *not* represent total dollars or designations to these agencies. The designations to the agencies accounted for here ($6,145,731) are 33.3% of all dollars positively designated to *all* unaffiliated agencies as reported by survey respondents.

[a] Average designation based on communities reporting both number of designations and total dollars designated.

Average Designation[a]	Percent of Total Dollars	Number of UWs
$ 98.75	14.8%	53
151.71	13.6	12
121.39	7.9	33
133.06	6.5	31
93.52	5.8	11
160.23	3.4	1
66.00	3.3	30
84.09	3.3	13
123.51	2.9	6
82.90	2.6	1
$110.35	64.2%	—
$101.88	35.8%	—
$107.17	100.0%	—

Appendix F.6. Summary of 1984 Donor Option
Dollars by Agency Affiliation

	1984 Dollars Designated
United Ways and member agencies[a]	$32,941,417
Other agencies[b]	$15,285,965
Total designations (net of unprocessable)	$48,227,382

Source: UWA Research Division, August 1985.
Note: Positive designations only.
[a] Includes United Way agencies, other United Ways, and the United Way System.
[b] Includes unaffiliated agencies, and those agencies affiliated for the donor option program only.

Appendix G.1. Combined Federal Campaign: Percentage Share of Total Receipts

	UW	NVHA	ISA	ARC	NSA	LNA	W-I	Total
1985[a]	49.4%	19.6%	7.8%	0.2%	7.3%	6.8%	9.0%	100.0%
1984	54.4%	22.4%	9.1%	0.2%	8.1%	2.6%	3.0%	100.0%
1983	59.6%	22.5%	8.3%	0.3%	7.6%	1.7%		100.0%
1982	61.8%	22.2%	7.3%	0.4%	7.0%	1.3%		100.0%
1981	68.8%	20.2%	7.7%	0.5%	1.8%	1.0%		100.0%
1980	67.8%	19.5%	6.9%	0.7%	0.7%	0.6%		96.2%
1979	72.8%	19.6%	6.8%	0.8%				100.0%
1978	71.2%	21.3%	6.7%	0.8%				100.0%
1977	70.6%	21.6%	6.7%	0.7%				99.6%
1976	70.9%	21.3%	6.8%	0.7%				99.7%
1975	70.8%	20.3%	6.7%	0.6%				98.5%
1974	72.1%	20.0%	6.9%	0.8%				99.8%
1973	72.0%	19.1%	6.8%	0.7%				98.6%
1972	72.0%	19.0%	6.9%	0.8%				98.7%
1971	71.4%	17.4%	6.8%	0.5%				96.1%
1970	74.3%	17.9%	7.2%	0.2%				99.6%
1969	74.0%	17.9%	7.2%	0.2%				99.3%
1968	74.1%	17.9%	7.2%	0.5%				99.7%
1967	74.3%	18.1%	7.1%	0.5%				100.0%
1966	73.0%	19.1%	7.4%	0.4%				99.8%
1965								

Source: United States Office of Personnel Management, March 1986.

Note: Abbreviations as follows: UW = United Way; NVHA = National Voluntary Health Agencies; ISA = International Service Agencies; ARC = American Red Cross; NSA = National Service Agencies; LNA = Local Non-affiliated Agencies; W-I = Write-ins.

[a] Projected

Appendix G.2. Combined Federal Campaign: Historical Statistics

	United Way		National Voluntary Health Agencies		International Service Agencies		American Red Cross	
1985[a]	$64,207,000	−3.9%	$25,441,000	−7.6%	$10,127,000	−9.6%	$221,000	−27.7%
1984	66,790,728	1.7%	27,532,234	10.7%	11,206,791	22.8%	305,502	−11.5%
1983	65,681,437	5.1%	24,864,489	10.4%	9,129,179	22.9%	345,016	−11.8%
1982	62,500,491	−4.3%	22,514,014	17.4%	7,430,822	1.7%	391,170	−17.9%
1981	65,297,189	9.8%	19,184,125	12.4%	7,306,957	20.5%	476,322	−24.5%
1980	59,480,299	−1.4%	17,074,904	5.2%	6,063,373	7.6%	631,260	0.9%
1979	60,306,856	2.1%	16,231,136	−8.1%	5,636,104	1.2%	625,741	−6.2%
1978	59,074,434	5.2%	17,660,107	2.7%	5,571,631	4.5%	666,887	26.7%
1977	56,140,434	11.3%	17,194,810	13.3%	5,332,629	10.2%	526,263	3.4%
1976	50,451,887	8.1%	15,177,010	13.3%	4,837,847	9.1%	509,064	30.0%
1975	46,650,439	6.2%	13,391,406	10.2%	4,436,185	6.1%	391,508	−20.0%
1974	43,921,499	10.7%	12,147,906	15.7%	4,180,833	12.4%	489,168	22.8%
1973	39,673,640	7.6%	10,501,025	8.0%	3,719,853	4.9%	398,285	−7.4%
1972	36,887,261	12.5%	9,722,148	21.9%	3,546,334	13.5%	430,154	89.0%
1971	32,801,979	23.0%	7,975,167	24.0%	3,123,336	21.5%	227,628	209.2%
1970	26,672,476	8.5%	6,431,053	8.4%	2,570,808	8.2%	73,617	−3.2%
1969	24,582,965	12.9%	5,930,442	12.7%	2,376,374	13.1%	76,034	−51.4%
1968	21,769,108	19.4%	5,261,087	18.8%	2,101,773	19.9%	156,494	27.8%
1967	18,224,885	13.8%	4,427,990	5.7%	1,752,588	8.6%	122,481	27.8%
1966	16,018,210		4,190,790		1,613,714		95,830	
1965								
1964								

Source: United States Office of Personnel Management, March 1986.

National Service Agencies		Local Nonaffiliated Agencies		Write-Ins		Total	
$9,425,000	−5.6%	$8,853,000	173.8%	$11,739,000	224.2%	$130,000,000	5.98%
9,980,921	19.9%	3,233,524	68.4%	3,620,376		122,670,076	11.25%
8,327,834	18.2%	1,920,681	46.0%			110,268,636	8.97%
7,043,622	305.8%	1,315,199	37.4%			101,195,318	6.57%
1,735,556	199.1%	956,871	72.4%			94,957,020	8.26%
580,336	0.0%	554,895	0.0%			87,712,716	5.89%
						82,833,617	−0.21%
						83,006,726	4.39%
						79,516,049	11.69%
						71,192,475	8.11%
						65,851,564	8.17%
						60,878,006	10.53%
						55,077,890	7.50%
						51,234,426	11.60%
						45,909,421	27.87%
						35,903,959	8.11%
						33,210,610	13.02%
						29,385,213	19.80%
						24,527,944	11.73%
						21,953,452	21.63%
						18,049,436	40.16%
						12,877,942	
					Grand Total	1,165,542,420	

Source: United States Office of Personnel Management, March 1986.
[a] Projected.

Appendix G.3. Combined Federal Campaign: Percentage Distribution of Designated and Deemed-Designated Contributions

	UW		NVHA		ISA		ARC	
	Des	Undes	Des	Undes	Des	Undes	Des	Undes
1985[a]	37.3	91.0	24.3	3.3	8.6	5.0	0.2	0.1
1984	42.0	90.7	29.1	3.2	10.6	5.0	0.2	0.3
1983	44.3	90.5	32.3	2.9	9.6	5.5	0.3	0.3
1982	46.5	89.9	32.6	3.1	7.9	6.3	0.3	0.5
1981	48.4	88.9	36.9	3.8	8.9	6.5	0.5	0.4
1980	49.4	88.6	47.3	4.0	13.3	6.5	0.9	0.6
1979	48.2	89.4	43.2	3.8	8.0	6.0	0.7	0.8
1978	42.7	88.9	50.0	3.4	6.8	6.7	0.5	1.0
1977	41.6	88.6	51.3	3.9	6.8	6.7	0.4	0.7
1976	44.0	86.9	49.0	5.2	6.7	6.9	0.3	1.0
1975	43.8	87.5	48.3	5.0	7.2	6.6	0.0	0.9
1974	45.6	86.5	47.6	5.3	6.3	7.2	0.5	1.0
1973	48.7	85.8	44.9	6.1	6.1	7.2	0.4	0.9
1972	48.8		44.9		5.8		0.4	
1971	50.4		42.1		6.2		0.3	
1970	56.5		37.6		5.8		0.1	
1969	57.0		37.0		5.9		0.1	
1968	57.0		36.9		6.0		0.1	
1967	61.9		33.4		4.5		0.2	
1966								
1965								

Source: United States Office of Personnel Management, March 1986.
Note: Abbreviations as follows: UW = United Way; NVHA = National Voluntary Health Agencies; ISA = International Service Agencies; ARC = American Red Cross; NSA = National Service Agencies; LNA = Local Non-affiliated Agencies; W-I = Write-ins; Des = Designated; Undes = Undesignated.
[a] Projected.

NSA		LNA		W-I	
Des	Undes	Des	Undes	Des	Undes
9.3	0.3	8.7	0.4	11.6	0.0
10.8	0.4	3.4	0.5	4.0	0.0
11.1	0.3	2.4	0.5		
10.6	0.2	2.0	0.1		
3.3	0.4	2.0	0		
1.2	0.3	1.4	0		

Appendix G.4. Combined Federal Campaign: Miscellaneous

	Number of Campaigns	Number Solicited	Number of Contributors	Participation Rate	Percent Designated	Percent Undes
1985[b]	514			59.35%	77.5	22.5
1984	513	4,158,229	2,414,254	58.06%	74.4	25.6
1983	519	4,050,933	2,337,223	57.70%	67.0	33.0
1982	511	3,934,499	2,280,436	57.96%	64.8	35.2
1981	532	3,910,915	2,346,549	60.00%	49.5	50.5
1980	532	3,777,464	2,243,814	59.40%	45.9	54.1
1979	534	3,785,814	2,756,073	72.80%	40.1	59.9
1978	538	3,832,259	2,705,575	70.60%	38.4	61.6
1977	535	3,848,792	2,763,433	71.80%	37.5	62.5
1976	526	3,819,339	2,727,008	71.40%	36.8	63.2
1975	526	3,620,207	2,787,559	77.00%	35.6	64.4
1974	519	3,496,726	2,702,969	77.30%	34.7	65.3
1973	506	3,767,298	2,704,920	71.80%	33.7	66.3
1972	493	3,849,318	2,798,454	72.70%	31.3	68.7
1971	462	3,835,374	2,822,835	73.60%	29.9	70.1
1970	226	3,516,548	2,662,027	75.70%	29.8	70.2
1969	196	2,920,898	2,316,272	79.30%	30.1	69.9
1968	174	2,720,853	2,198,449	80.80%	28.3	71.7
1967	144	2,541,756	2,038,488	80.20%	28.1	71.9
1966	101	2,308,460	1,876,778	81.30%	29.6	70.4
1965	33	1,560,020	1,258,629	80.68%	28.8	71.2

Source: United States Office of Personnel Management, March 1986.
[a] PRD = Payroll Deduction.
[b] Projected.

Per Capita Gift	Average Gift	% Receipts Thru PRD[a]	% Employees Using PRD[a]	Average PRD[a] Gift	Average All Other	Campaign Cost	Campaign Cost (%)
$31.49	$53.05	89.3	71.6	$67.11	$20.24	$6,188,000	4.76
29.50	50.81	88.5	68.9	65.24	18.79	5,393,391	4.40%
27.22	47.18	88.8	77.8	53.85	23.69	4,525,914	4.10%
25.72	44.37	88.4	67.9	57.77	16.04	3,990,925	3.94%
24.28	40.32	86.6	67.0	52.19	16.39	3,105,046	3.27%
23.22	39.09	86.4	66.0	50.77	15.93	2,710,776	3.09%
21.88	30.05	85.5	54.6	47.00	9.60	2,314,332	2.79%
21.66	30.68	84.9	61.6	42.30	12.10	2,186,111	2.63%
20.66	28.77	84.0	61.4	39.36	11.97	1,987,901	2.50%
18.64	26.11	82.1	57.5	37.28	11.09	1,851,004	2.60%
18.19	23.62	77.6	51.0	35.94	11.19	1,712,141	2.60%
17.41	22.52	78.5	52.5	33.68	10.10	1,948,096	3.20
14.62	20.36	75.4	48.5	31.69	12.76	1,487,103	2.70
13.31	18.31	72.0	44.1	29.87	9.19	1,332,095	2.60
11.97	16.26	71.9	39.3	28.28	8.57	1,331,373	2.90
10.21	13.49	69.1	38.8	25.44	8.04	1,041,215	2.90
11.37	14.34	67.0	37.5				
10.80	13.37	63.2	36.2				
9.65	12.03	59.3	32.4				
9.51	11.70	57.6	29.3				
11.57	14.34	55.0	29.0				

Appendix H.1. Occupations of Ten Top Planning Council Volunteers in 54 Local Planning Councils

Occupation	Number	Percent
Professional (e.g., doctor, lawyer)	98	20.5
Homemaker	57	11.9
Vice-president/branch manager	50	10.5
Corporate chief executive officer	49	10.2
Retiree—full time	48	10.0
Other	39	8.1
Middle manager/supervisory	37	7.7
Government employee	36	7.5
Small business owner	23	4.8
Specialist in large firm (e.g., sales)	20	4.2
Public official	15	3.1
Union/labor	7	1.5
Total	479[a]	100.0

Source: Survey of local Planning Councils, in connection with United Way Study Project, 1984.

[a] The total number here refers to the total number of (top ten) volunteers described by each of the fifty-four planning councils in the study. Some planning councils did not list ten volunteers, and that is why the total number is less than 540.

Appendix H.2. Occupations of Ten Top United Way Volunteers in 131 Local United Ways

Occupation	Number	Percent
Corporated chief executive officer	246	21.2
Vice-president/branch manager	232	20.0
Professional (e.g., doctor, lawyer)	232	11.8
Middle manager/supervisory	117	10.1
Specialist in large firm (e.g., sales)	83	7.2
Small business owner	67	5.8
Homemaker	62	5.3
Retiree—full time	52	4.5
Union/labor	50	4.3
Government employee	47	4.1
Other	46	4.0
Public official	22	1.9
Total	1,161[a]	100.0

Source: Survey of local United Way organizations, in connection with United Way Study Project, 1984.

[a] The total number here refers to the total number of (top 10) volunteers described by each of the 131 United Way organizations in the study. Some United Way organizations did not list 10 volunteers, and that is why the total number is less than 1,310.

Appendix I. Individual Alternative Funds, 1985: Five Top Performers in Each Type of Fund

	Total Revenues		Employee Contributions Only	
	1985	Increase (Decrease) '85/'84	1985	% of Total Revenues
Social Action Funds				
1. Womens Way —Philadelphia	$ 594,281	15%	$ 255,827	43%
2. Cooperating Fund Drive —Minneapolis-St. Paul	421,730	40%	312,000	74%
3. Bread & Roses Community Fund —Philadelphia	265,000	(2%)	32,000	12%
4. Fund for Community Progress —Providence, RI	133,146	54%	101,778	76%
5. Aid to Wisconsin Organizations —Madison	131,438	12%	106,020	81%
Black United Funds				
1. Los Angeles	$ 1,983,324	17%	845,455	43%
2. New York City	575,000 *est.*	13%	400,000 *est.*	70%
3. Detroit	551,165	23%	483,125	88%
4. San Francisco Bay Area	497,741	(21%)	200,000	40%
5. New Jersey	285,000	13%	230,000	81%
United Arts Funds				
1. Cincinnati			$ 592,942 (+15%)	16%
2. Louisville			275,000	na
3. Charlotte, NC			183,000 (+5%)	13%
4. St. Paul, MN			158,496 (+31%)	10%
5. Milwaukee			156,000 (+74%)	3%

Combined Health Appeals			
1. Hartford, CT	$ 3,400,000	10%	$2,227,000 est.
2. Illinois	1,725,000	15%	na
3. Maryland	1,700,000	4%	1,113,500 est.
4. San Diego	1,200,000	20%	786,000 est.
5. (Northern) California	630,000	13%	na
National Health Agencies			
1. National—CFC	$27,430,000	(0.4%)	Same as Col. 1	66%
2. Pennsylvania	426,000	20%	Same as Col. 1	100%
3. New York	250,000 est.	0%	Same as Col. 1	100%
4. Florida	199,000 est.	20%	Same as Col. 1	100%
5. North Carolina	150,000	0%	Same as Col. 1	100%
International Service Agencies[a]				
1. National—CFC	$ 9,997,000	(11%)	Same as Col. 1	100%
2. Pennsylvania	157,998	27%	Same as Col. 1	100%
3. New York	150,000	0%	Same as Col. 1	100%
4. Wisconsin	118,995	17%	Same as Col. 1	100%
5. Washington State	85,394	[b]	Same as Col. 1	100%
National Service Agencies				
1. National—CFC	$ 8,696,000	0%	Same as Col. 1	100%
a. Social Justice Org's	1,018,000	(3%)	Same as Col. 1	100%
b. Environmental Org's				
Local Environmental Fund				
1. Environmental Fed. of CA—San Francisco Bay Area	153,600	69%	91,000	59%

Source: National Committee for Responsive Philanthropy (NCRP), *The Workplace Giving Revolution: A Special Report*, Spring 1987.

Note: Some of these organizations are "partners" with United Way.

[a] ISA has three national organizations, each of which solicits separate employee groups: (1) Combined Federal Campaign (CFC), (2) state and local governments, and (3) corporate. Above are presented the top 1985 results from (1) and (2) only.

[b] New campaign in 1985.

Appendix J.1. Impact of President Reagan's Tax Plan on Local United Way Contributors (Projected)

Metro One Cities	Amount Raised '84	At Risk	Non-Itemized 8.0% Reduction	Tax Changes 8.4% Reduction	Total 16.4% Reduction
Atlanta	$ 30,005,190	$ 21,033,638	$ 1,682,691	$ 1,766,826	$ 3,449,517
Baltimore	28,080,775	19,684,623	1,574,770	1,653,508	3,228,278
Birmingham, Ala.	11,502,616	8,063,334	645,067	677,320	1,322,387
Boston	35,236,864	24,701,042	1,976,083	2,074,887	4,050,971
Buffalo	13,051,109	9,148,827	731,906	768,502	1,500,408
Chicago	82,250,000	57,657,250	4,612,580	4,843,209	9,455,789
Cincinnati	30,242,400	21,199,922	1,695,994	1,780,793	3,476,787
Cleveland	44,595,896	31,261,723	2,500,938	2,625,985	5,126,923
Columbus	18,014,097	12,627,882	1,010,231	1,060,742	2,070,973
Dallas	29,007,705	20,334,401	1,626,752	1,708,090	3,334,842
Dayton	14,728,579	10,324,734	825,979	867,278	1,693,256
Denver	23,256,000	16,302,456	1,304,196	1,369,406	2,673,603
Detroit	50,860,966	35,653,537	2,852,283	2,994,897	5,847,180
Fort Worth	15,641,784	10,964,891	877,191	921,051	1,798,242
Hartford	16,960,228	11,889,120	951,130	998,686	1,949,816
Honolulu	11,258,192	7,891,993	631,359	662,927	1,294,287
Houston	39,509,023	27,695,825	2,215,666	2,326,449	4,542,115
Indianapolis	17,355,535	12,166,230	973,298	1,021,963	1,995,262
Kansas City, Mo.	22,842,841	16,012,832	1,281,027	1,345,078	2,626,104
Los Angeles	72,624,189	50,909,556	4,072,765	4,276,403	8,349,167
Louisville	11,189,804	7,844,053	627,524	658,900	1,286,425
Memphis	11,242,419	7,880,936	630,475	661,999	1,292,473
Miami	15,523,084	10,881,682	870,535	914,061	1,784,596
Milwaukee	18,977,475	13,303,210	1,064,257	1,117,470	2,181,726
Minneapolis	28,875,830	20,241,957	1,619,357	1,700,324	3,319,681
New Orleans	12,855,000	9,011,355	720,908	756,954	1,477,862

New York	59,700,000	41,849,700	3,347,976	3,515,375	6,863,351
Norfolk	11,940,800	8,370,501	669,640	703,122	1,372,762
Omaha	10,134,710	7,104,432	568,355	596,772	1,165,127
Orange, Calif.	16,426,915	11,515,267	921,221	967,282	1,888,504
Philadelphia	44,011,909	30,852,348	2,468,188	2,591,597	5,059,785
Pittsburgh	28,207,525	19,773,475	1,581,878	1,660,972	3,242,850
Portland	16,303,546	11,428,786	914,303	960,018	1,874,321
Providence	12,539,093	8,789,904	703,192	738,352	1,441,544
Richmond	10,434,117	7,314,316	585,145	614,403	1,199,548
Rochester	26,007,721	18,231,412	1,458,513	1,531,439	2,989,952
Saint Louis	32,515,430	22,793,316	1,823,465	1,914,639	3,738,104
San Antonio	14,610,220	10,241,764	819,341	860,308	1,679,649
San Diego	20,073,817	14,071,746	1,125,740	1,182,027	2,307,766
San Francisco	41,853,420	29,339,247	2,347,140	2,464,497	4,811,637
Santa Clara, Calif.	20,012,272	14,028,603	1,122,288	1,178,403	2,300,691
Seattle	25,461,800	17,848,722	1,427,898	1,499,293	2,927,190
St. Paul	13,870,207	9,723,015	777,841	816,733	1,594,574
Toledo	10,620,442	7,444,930	595,594	625,374	1,220,968
Washington, D.C.	43,523,954	30,510,292	2,440,823	2,562,865	5,003,688
White Plains, N.Y.	11,524,410	8,078,611	646,289	678,603	1,324,892
Wilmington	12,480,000	8,748,480	699,878	734,872	1,434,751
	$1,187,939,909	$832,745,876	$66,619,670	$69,950,654	$136,570,324

Source: *Today, Tomorrow and Beyond: Environmental Scan Report II* (Detroit, Michigan: United Foundation, Strategic Planning Committee, 1986). p. 43, based on material from the United Way of America.

Appendix J.2. UW New Agency Admissions, 1980–1983: Numbers of Non-Traditional Advocacy Oriented Agencies by Subcategory and Metro

Subcategory	Number of Metro I New Admissions (N=12) (excludes San Francisco)	Number of Metro II New Admissions (N=4)	Number of Metro III New Admissions (N=14)	Number of Total New Admissions (N=30)
Women's issues	21	3	12	36
Black	10	1	3	14
Hispanic	5	1	3	9
Other minority groups	4	2	1	7
Minority groups—Mixed or unspecified	1	0	0	1
Social action	1	1	0	2
Legal Aid	2	0	1	3
Offender and ex-offender programs	0	0	0	0
Category totals	44	8	20	72

Note: This table includes 30 out of 32 Metro I–III local United Ways, out of 83 local United Ways originally included in our sample of local United Ways in Metros I–III. In our initial survey 32 local United Ways in these Metro groups had answered positively to questions concerning new admissions and special funding for agencies in the years 1980–1983. In follow-up phone calls, 31, or all but one, of these 32 United Ways supplied additional data about non-traditional advocacy oriented agency admissions, and together they had admitted 247 new agencies in this period. This table excludes one of these United Ways which had a total of 31 new admissions and 24 in the category of this table. Inclusion of this one United Way consequently would have skewed the data.

Notes

Introduction

1. For estimated figures of giving in 1985, see *Giving USA: Estimates of Philanthropic Giving in 1985 and the Trends They Show* (New York: AAFRC Trust for Philanthropy, 1986), p. 7. Estimates of the worth of volunteer time come from *Americans Volunteer 1985: An Independent Sector Summary Report* (Washington, D.C.: April 1986), pp. 4–5.

2. The Internal Revenue Service (IRS) reported 352,884 organizations with 501(c)(3) tax-exempt status in 1984. These organizations have educational, research, scientific, philanthropic, religious, and other functions that are defined as charitable under the United States Tax Code, and therefore are eligible to receive tax deductible contributions. See Virginia Ann Hodgkinson and Murray S. Weitzman, *Dimensions of the Independent Sector: A Statistical Profile*, 2d ed. (Washington, D.C.: Independent Sector, 1986), pp. 9–11.

3. *Dimensions of the Independent Sector*, pp. 9–13. See also Joseph J. DioGuardi, "Tax-Exempt Organizations in a Technical Perspective," in Tracy Daniel Connors, ed., *The Nonprofit Handbook* (New York: McGraw-Hill, 1980), section 1, pp. 65–75; and Burton S. Weisbrod, *The Voluntary Sector* (Lexington, Mass: D.C. Heath, 1977).

4. A brief discussion of the history of the Commission on Private Philanthropy and Public Needs is given in *Giving in America: Toward a Stronger Voluntary Sector* (Report of the Commission on Private Philanthropy, 1975). This report and all the voluminous research papers of the Commission (vols. 1–5) will hereafter be cited as the Filer Commission Reports, or *Research Papers*.

5. See David Horton Smith, "The Role of the United Way in Philanthropy," and also Geno Baroni et al., "Patterns of Class and Ethnic Discrimination by Private Philanthropy," among the papers submitted in opposition to the earlier mainstream direction of the Commission; in *Research Papers* of the Filer Commission, vol. 2, part 2, "Additional Perspectives" (1977). Comments by members of the dissenting group in the Filer Commission are also found in *Giving in America*, pp. 197–222.

6. For a classic discussion of some of the early controversies faced by federated fund raising and charity organization, see William J. Norton, *The Cooperative Movement in Social Work* (New York: Macmillan, 1927). See also the historical perspective of the United Way itself concerning criticism presented in *People and Events: A History of the United Way* (Alexandria, Va.: UWA, 1977). For an earlier seminal discussion of federated fund raising, see John Seeley et al., *Community Chest: A Case Study in Philanthropy* (Toronto: University of Toronto Press, 1957).

7. Both Family Service of America and the United Way of America acknowledge the Charity Organization Society as their predecessor organization, and since early local coordinating organizations took a variety of forms, and names, this is understandable.

8. United Way sources usually report there are somewhere between 2,100 and 2,200 local United Way organizations, but, according to their own count, in the mid-

1980s only about 1,200 of these local organizations were official, dues-paying members of the national organization, and many of the others are very small. However, numbers change slightly from year to year and vary somewhat in different United Way materials.

9. Our study included a survey of 79 independent local planning organizations listed in the *1981–1982 International Directory* of the United Way of America or on other United Way lists. Several of these planning councils were facing serious difficulties at that time, and some have since gone out of existence. The concept of planning councils as a sub-system of the United Way was utilized by Ruth Brandwein in "A Working Framework for Approaching Organizational Change: The Community Chest-Council System" (Ph.D. dissertation, Florence Heller Graduate School, Brandeis University, 1977), p. 247.

10. Local United Ways now generally allocate funds as well as raise them; planning, however, tends to be more ambiguous. In the United Way *Directory*, prior to 1984 the functions performed by local United Ways were indicated by letters next to the name of the organization, "p" for planning; "f" for fund raising; and "a" for allocations. See, for example, the *1982–1983 International Directory* (Washington, D.C.: UWA, 1982). This practice has since been discontinued.

11. Unless stated otherwise specifically, figures about United Way dollars and services come from the United Way Public Relations office, or the Research Division of the United Way of America.

12. For example, arts organizations or educational programs. For a technical discussion of the 501(c)(3) code and eligibility, see also Joseph J. DioGuardi, "Tax-Exempt Organizations in a Technical Perspective," In Tracy Daniel Connors, ed., *The Nonprofit Handbook*, section 1, pp. 65–75.

13. This figure is an estimate, based on discussions with United Way staff in the spring of 1984. In any case, there is a great range in the amount of support which agencies receive from the United Way, from those that receive less than 1 percent to those that receive over 90 percent of their revenues from the United Way.

14. United Way of America data chart, "Source of Campaign Giving, 1983," in *Measurements of Campaign Performance* (Alexandria, Virginia: UWA, 1984). Throughout this book references to the United Way of America will be cited in the short form, as UWA.

15. An impressive gain in workplace fund raising was, however, being reported by alternative funds in the 1980s. See *The Workplace Giving Revolution: A Special Report* (Washington, D.C.: National Committee on Responsive Philanthropy, 1987). This issue is also discussed extensively below in chapters 7 and 10. See also Stanley Wenocur, Richard V. Cook, and Nancy L. Steketee, "Fund Raising at the Workplace," *Social Policy* (Spring 1984), 14(4):55–60.

16. See Eleanor L. Brilliant, "Private or Public: A Model of Ambiguities," *Social Service Review* (September 1973), 47(3):384–96. An earlier seminal discussion of this issue is to be found in Robin Marris and Adrian Wood, *The Corporate Economy: Growth, Competition, and Innovative Potential* (London: Macmillan, 1971).

17. For examples see, Eleanor L. Brilliant, "United Way at the Crossroads," in *Social Welfare Forum 1982/83* (Washington, D.C.: National Conference on Social Welfare), pp. 251–262; Richard Bartlett, "United Charities and the Sherman Act," *Yale Law Journal* (July 1982), 91(8):1593–1613; and the earlier work by John Seeley on one case example, John R. Seeley et al., *Community Chest, A Case Study in Philanthropy* (Toronto: University of Toronto Press, 1957). The connection was also discussed in relation to early social welfare history in Roy Lubove, *The Professional Altruist: The Emergence of Social Work as a Career, 1880–1930* (New York: Atheneum, 1969).

18. An excellent discussion of the problematic notion of goals in human service

organizations is given in Yeheskel Hasenfeld, *Human Service Organizations* (Englewood Cliffs, N.J.: Prentice-Hall, 1983), pp. 84–109. For a clear exposition of the importance of goal congruence, see Edgar H. Schein, *Organizational Culture and Leadership: A Dynamic View* (San Francisco: Jossey-Bass, 1985), pp. 49–64.

19. For a thought-provoking analysis of federated organizations see Martin Rein, "Goals, Structures, and Strategies for Community Change," in Rein, *Social Policy: Issues of Choice and Change*, pp. 178–192 (New York: Random House, 1970). For a somewhat different approach, see also Eugene Litwak and Lydia F. Hylton, "Interorganizational Analysis: A Hypothesis on Coordinating Agencies," in Yeheskel Hasenfeld and Richard A. English, eds., *Human Service Organizations: A Book of Readings* (Ann Arbor: University of Michigan Press, 1978), pp. 561–583. The issue of federation and consensus was also discussed in Seeley, *Community Chest*, pp. 153–157, and extensively by Stanley Wenocur, in "The Adaptability of Voluntary Organizations: External Pressures and United Way Organizations," in *Policy and Politics* (June 1975), 3(4):3–23.

20. For a seminal discussion of a related concept, see Joanne Martin et al., "The Uniqueness Paradox in Organizational Stories," *Administrative Science Quarterly* (September 1983), 28(3):438–53. The concept of organizational "myth" is increasingly becoming a part of organizational theory. See Edgar H. Schein, *Organizational Culture and Leadership: A Dynamic View* (San Francisco: Jossey-Bass, 1985), and John W. Meyer and Rowan Brian, "Institutionalized Organizations: Formal Structure as Myth and Ceremony," *American Journal of Sociology* (September 1977), 83(2):211–228. See also the United Way story as told by William Aramony, in *The United Way: The Next Hundred Years* (New York: Donald I. Fine, 1987).

21. The influential concept of "cognitive dissonance" was first formulated by Leon Festinger, *A Theory of Cognitive Dissonance* (Evanston, Ill.: Row-Peterson, 1957).

22. See Stanley Wenocur, "The Structure and Politics of Local United Way Organizations," *Grantsmanship Center News*, September–December 1978, pp. 24–43.

1. *Historical Themes: Origins of American Charity Organization*

1. June Axinn and Herman Levine, *Social Welfare: A History of the American Response to Need*, 2d ed. (New York: Longman, 1982), pp. 92–95. See also King E. Davis, *Fund Raising in the Black Community: History, Feasibility and Conflict* (Metuchen, N.J.: Scarecrow, 1975), pp. 1–17.

2. Ralph E. Pumphrey and Muriel W. Pumphrey, eds., *The Heritage of American Social Work* (New York, Columbia University Press, 1961), pp. 141–167; James Leiby, *A History of Social Welfare and Social Work in the United States* (New York: Columbia University Press, 1978), pp. 90–110; and Axinn and Levine, *Social Welfare*, pp. 95–99.

3. There is an extensive literature on this issue. See, for example, Robert H. Bremner, *American Philanthropy* (Chicago: University of Chicago Press, 1960); and Ben B. Seligman, *The Potentates: Business and Businessmen in American History* (New York: Dial Press, 1971).

4. For discussion of Sumner and Spencer and the connection between Social Darwinism and scientific charity, see Richard Hofstadter, *Social Darwinism in American Thought* (Boston: Beacon Press, 1967); also discussed in Leiby, *History of Social Welfare*, pp. 111–18.

5. See Edward C. Jenkins, *Philanthropy in America: An Introduction to the Practices and Prospects of Organizations Surrounded by Gifts and Endowments, 1924–1948* (New York: Association, 1950), pp. 82–85.

6. Roy Lubove, *The Professional Altruist: The Emergence of Social Work as a Career, 1880–1930* (New York: Atheneum), pp. 1–8; Pumphrey and Pumphrey, *The Heritage of American Social Work*, pp. 168–191. There are various points of view about the nature

1. ORIGINS OF AMERICAN CHARITY ORGANIZATION

of the early COS's, and their relationship to later councils of social agencies, direct service agencies, and federated fund raising. Sources for the connection between federations and COS's, are to be found in Edward C. Jenkins, *Philanthropy in America*, (New York: Association, 1950); William S. Norton, *The Cooperative Movement in Social Work* (New York: MacMillan, 1927), pp. 51–54, 135–137; UWA, *People and Events: A History of the United Way* (Alexandria, Va.: UWA, 1977), pp. 21–24, 28–32. See also Walter S. Ufford, "Methods of Raising Funds for a Charitable Society," in *Proceedings of the National Conference of Charities and Correction*, 33d annual session, Philadelphia, Pa., May 9–16, 1906, pp. 213–222.

7. This version of the Denver history comes primarily from archival material supplied by the Mile High United Way in Denver, including parts of the "First Annual Report of the Charity Organization Society of Denver, Colorado," presented November 24, 1889 (C. J. Kelly's Book Rooms); the report of "the Second Annual Mass Meeting of the Associated Charities of Denver at the Tabor Grand Opera House, November 24, 1889 in Denver's *Rocky Mountain News Print*; and John C. Fleming, "Charity in Denver" (Program of the Golden Anniversary of the Denver Community Chest, 1887–1927). From these records, it seems that by 1889 for a brief period there may have been two closely interrelated, overlapping, but separately defined organizations, The Associated Charities of Denver, and the Charity Organization Society, the latter with responsibility for raising the money, while the former was primarily concerned with coordinating services. For many years, however, United Way mythology had held that the Denver organization was started by a rabbi, a priest, and two ministers. Material unearthed by Denver's Jewish community for the centennial of the United Way movement (1987) revealed that Mrs. Jacobs, rather than the rabbi, had been one of the initial organizers, with Rabbi Friedman (and another Catholic priest) also involved later.

8. See Lubove, *The Professional Altruist*, p. 186–188; and Norton, *The Cooperative Movement in Social Work*, pp. 68–72, 89–92.

9. Martin A. Marks, "The Cleveland Federation of Charity and Philanthropy," comments on the Report of the Cleveland Chamber of Commerce, presented at a membership meeting, January 7, 1913; cited in Elwood Street, *History of Federation*, p. 23, n. 22 (unpublished manuscript from the United Way archives, which is the basis for the book, *People and Events*).

10. Although there have been disputes about which came first, the first Council of Social Agencies is generally considered to be the one started in Pittsburgh in 1908. See Pumphrey and Pumphrey, p. 372, and Street, pp. 18–19.

11. Jenkins, *Philanthropy in America*, p. 106.

12. Leiby, *History of Social Welfare*, pp. 110–135; Lubove, pp. 1–21, 157–182.

13. Lubove, *The Professional Altruist*, pp. 157–159.

14. The term "community organization" seems to have been first used publicly by Allen T. Burns (a federation professional) at a meeting of the National Conference on Charities and Corrections, in a talk on "Community Organization of Promotion of Social Programs." The term was later incorporated in the title of the new organization of federations and councils in 1918, as the American Association for Community Organization. For a comprehensive discussion of the two organizations, the American Association for Community Organization and the American Association for Organizing Charity, see below, particularly chap. 4; and Street, *History of Federation*, pp. 31–32.

15. For a discussion of the issues of tax exemption see Henry Hansmann, "The Rationale for Exempting Nonprofits from Corporate Income Taxation" (New Haven, Conn.: PONPO Working Paper 23, February 1981).

16. Bremner, *American Philanthropy*, p. 122–142; Jenkins, *Philanthropy in America*,

1. ORIGINS OF AMERICAN CHARITY ORGANIZATION 321

pp. 107–108; Norton, *The Cooperative Movement in Social Work*, pp. 112–130. An in-depth discussion from the federation point of view is also given in Street, *History of Federation*, pp. 30–37. (By and large *People and Events* incorporates the entire unpublished work by Street, but I have generally used the earlier Street version when referring to the earlier days of federation.)

17. Jenkins; *Philanthropy in America*, p. 107, quotes a contemporary authority, Sherman C. Kingsley, as saying that "not a single war chest failed to meet its quota." Street also suggests that in 1919 there was money left over from the war chest campaign; Street, "History of Federation," p. 38.

18. The report is quoted at length in Norton, *The Cooperative Movement in Social Work*, pp. 102–109.

19. This issue is discussed in Bremner, *American Philanthropy*, pp. 122–142.

20. Norton, *The Cooperative Movement in Social Work*, pp. 202–204.

21. According to Norton, "no one ever knew how many of the war chests there were or how much they produced, although at the close of the war, it was said there were close to four hundred of them, and they were supposed to have raised far over $100,000,000." (*The Cooperative Movement in Social Work*, p. 113).

22. United Way sources in the past generally included funds raised in Canada in their official list of funds raised in their campaigns. See "Fund Raising Record of United Way Campaigns, United States and Canada, 1919–1976," in UWA, *People and Events*, p. 8. See also "Fund Raising Record of United Way Campaigns," below, appendix A.

23. UWA, *People and Events*, p. 40.

24. Corning Glass Works v. Lucas, Commissioner of Internal Revenue, 37F2d798 (citation at 800). According to UWA, *People and Events*, "by 1929 . . . 34,000 incorporated businesses were already giving about 22 percent of the total raised for chests included in one study, and they had been giving about that proportion for years" (p. 63). The study cited is Pierce Williams and Frederick E. Croxton, *Corporation Contributions to Organized Community Welfare Services* (New York: National Bureau of Economic Research, 1930).

25. See for example, Lubove, *The Professional Altruist*, pp. 188–219; and Norton, *The Cooperative Movement in Social Work*, throughout.

26. Lubove, *The Professional Altruist*, pp. 55–156; Leiby, *History of Social Welfare*, pp. 163–190, has a slightly different version; and see also Walter I. Trattner, *From Poor Law to Welfare State: A History of Social Welfare in America*, 3d ed. (New York: Free, 1984), pp. 239–262.

27. This period is well covered in many texts dealing with the history of social welfare. A particularly good discussion is that by Arthur M. Schlesinger, Jr., *The Age of Roosevelt: The Crisis of the Old Order, 1919–1933* (Boston: Houghton Mifflin, 1957). See also, for one recent discussion by an historian, James T. Patterson, *America's Struggle Against Poverty, 1900–1985* (Cambridge, Mass.: Harvard University Press, 1986), pp. 56–77; for analysis from social work point of view see Leiby, *History of Social Welfare*, pp. 217–244.

28. For discussion of the rise of the medical profession and voluntary hospitals, see Paul Starr, *The Social Transformation of American Medicine* (New York: Basic Books, 1982).

29. The amounts raised in the campaigns of 1933 and 1934 were below the $77,752,954 raised in 1932 (401 campaigns). However, despite the problems of the time, the 1935 amounts went back to $77,367,634 (429 campaigns), and in the 1936 campaign, with 452 communities, $81,707,789 was reported as raised; but the growth seems more due to an increase in the *number of campaigns* than to increased amounts raised in each individual campaign.

30. United States Internal Revenue Act of 1935, 49 Stat. 1016 (r). For a discussion of the national Community Chests and Councils (CCC) role in lobbying for this legislation from the United Way point of view, see UWA, *People and Events*, p. 63. See also discussion below chapter 7. For figures on corporate giving between 1930 and 1950, see F. Emerson Andrews, *Corporation Giving* (New York: Russell Sage Foundation, 1952), pp. 156–163.

31. UWA, *People and Events*, p. 8.

32. USO stands for the United Service Organizations, formed in February 1941 out of six separate agencies: YMCA, YWCA, National Catholic Community Service, Salvation Army, Jewish Welfare Board, and the National Travelers Aid Association.

33. For an early mention of the checkoff in relation to voluntary agency contributions (in this case to the Red Cross) see Herbert Harris, *American Labor* (New Haven: Yale University Press, 1939), p. 138. Discussion of the initiation of checkoffs and union contracts in the automobile industry is to be found in Richard C. Wilcock, "Industrial Management's Policies Toward Unionism," in Milton Derber and Edwin Young, eds., *Labor and the New Deal* (Madison, Wisconsin: The University of Wisconsin Press, 1957), p. 300. For later developments concerning checkoffs and collective bargaining, see Arthur A. Sloane and Fred Witney, *Labor Relations*, 4th ed. (Englewood Cliffs, N.J.: Prentice-Hall, 1981), pp. 379–381.

2. From Community Chest to United Way

1. See papers by Abraham Bluestein, "American Federation of Labor Participation in Health and Welfare Planning" (pp. 220–227), Robert L. Kinney, "Should Unions Organize Their own Social Services?" (pp. 234–241), and Leo Perlis, "CIO Participation in Health and Welfare Planning" (pp. 228–233), in *Proceedings of the National Conference of Social Work, 1945* (New York: Columbia University Press, 1945); and for the year before, Irving Abramson, "The Social Responsibility of Labor in the Post War World" (pp. 67–73), and Robert H. MacRae, "Organized Labor in Social Planning" (pp. 219–227), in *Proceedings, 1944*. Labor's new involvement with health and welfare activities is also noted in the study carried out of voluntary health agencies at that time; see Selskar M. Gunn and Philip S. Platt, *Voluntary Health Agencies: An Interpretive Study* (New York: Ronald Press, 1945), pp. 80–83. (The study also recommended the formation of one coordinated National Health Campaign, which had implications for the community chest movement.) One of the underlying issues of the Gunn and Platt report clearly was the nature of labor's role, i.e., whether labor would deliver its own social services to workers, or would use the existing service system for which community chests were the intermediaries, and how labor would be involved in organized charity.

2. "Thunder Over Michigan: The United Health and Welfare Fund of Michigan is Born in Detroit," *Community* (September 1947), 23(1):4–6.

3. The theme of "grass roots" is used frequently in the history of federated fund raising, and is part of the myth of Americana expressed in statements of volunteer leaders. See, for example, Bayard Ewing, president of the UWA, "Excerpts from Address," *Rebirth and Renewal* (Proceedings of the Annual Meeting of the Trustees, United Way of America, Dallas, Texas, December 3, 1970), p. 14: "The National Association of United Way evolved gradually from the grass roots." A similar theme was used by Robert Cutler, president of Old Colony Trust, and National Chest president, 1939–42, in 1947 when he wrote, "In America we decide things in a town meeting . . ." Cutler, "An Open Letter to Mr. Basil O'Connor, Chairman, General Committee, American Red Cross, Washington, D.C.," *Atlantic Monthly*, October 1947, pp. 48–50.

2. COMMUNITY CHEST TO UNITED WAY

4. An early reference to payroll deduction suggests that it was working successfully among city employees in Newton, Mass., as early as 1935 ("Community Chests and Councils," *News Bulletin*, November 1936). According to one author, the payroll deduction, or more specifically the check off, originated earlier in the miners' unions, and was used for donations to the Red Cross. Herbert Harris claims that the best explanation of the origin of the check off is given by the former head of the miners' union, John L. Lewis. Lewis states that "the system (the check-off) is the traditional way for the miner to pay any debt he owes. It started with the operators who checked off money for rent, insurance ... taxes ... and even Red Cross contributions." Lewis puts this in a positive context, saying, "United Mine Workers of America ... pioneered the eight hour day, the sliding wage scale, the 'check-off' "; John L. Lewis, *The Miners Fight For American Standards*, cited in Herbert Harris, *American Labor* (New Haven: Yale University Press, 1938), p. 138.

5. Several respondents suggested that Laidlaw was instrumental in the events that took place in Detroit. For a discussion of these events in some detail, see UWA, *People and Events*, pp. 108–116; and Scott M. Cutlip, *Fund Raising in the United States: Its Role in American Philanthropy* (New Brunswick, N.J.: Rutgers University Press, 1965), pp. 495–500. It was also the subject of a considerable number of articles in *Community* (the community chest journal) during the years 1947–1950.

6. Richard Carter, *The Gentle Legions* (Garden City, N.Y.: Doubleday, 1961), p. 262. Even community chest professionals openly recognized the conflictual nature of the event, and referred to it as a "Bombshell from Detroit." See Barbara Abel, "The Cincinnati Story: Eyewitness Account of CCC's Biennial Conference and Annual Meeting, Cincinnati," *Community* (February 1950), 25(6):125–128.

7. The idea of a state chest had its origins fundamentally in the forty-eight state war chests organized to deal with fund raising for national agencies without widespread local units in the community. Despite great hopes for this idea, state fundraising organizations were never successful in peacetime. In the October 1949 issue of *Community* (vol. 25, no. 2) the "Michigan Roundup" was reported with some interest, and it was noted that "other state organizations were going ahead with their own plans," but by the issue of *Community* in February 1950, in Abel's article on "The Cincinnati Story" the role of the state organization was already being played down.

8. Leo Perlis, quoted in Carter, *The Gentle Legions*, p. 267.

9. Most studies of corporate giving show a definite positive relationship between high taxes and corporate giving, and in particular show that giving goes up in the years of high excess-profits taxes (often connected with wartime). For a brief discussion of the impact of the repeal of the excess-profits tax in 1946, see F. Emerson Andrews, *Philanthropic Giving* (New York: Russell Sage Foundation, 1950), pp. 64–66. Source for the figures cited is the Internal Revenue Service Statistics of Corporation Income, given in Marion R. Fremont-Smith, *Philanthropy and the Business Corporation* (New York: Russell Sage Foundation, 1972), table 1, "Fiscal Contributions by Corporations," p. 34. Fremont-Smith also refers to an authoritative earlier study by Ralph L. Nelson, which demonstrates the influence of taxes on corporate contributions. See Nelson, *Economic Factors in the Growth of Corporation Giving* (New York: Russell Sage Foundation, National Bureau of Economic Research, 1970), pp. 2–5; also discussed in Andrews, *Corporations Giving* (New York: Russell Sage, 1952) and in the *Research Papers* of the Filer Commission, (Thomas Vasquez, "Corporate Giving Measures," vol. 3, pp. 1839–1852).

10. See chapter 1. This concern is also discussed in Fremont-Smith, *Philanthropy and the Business Corporation*, p. 53, with reference to a Cleveland Survey of Contributors (1952), which suggests that corporate interests were turning toward education. Andrews notes that community chests in the late 1940s were usually "favored beneficiar-

ies" of corporations, but it should be noted that by 1956, for the first time, gifts by individuals surpassed gifts by corporations; see Eleanor L. Brilliant, "Corporate Giving Patterns to United Ways," in *Giving and Volunteering: New Frontiers of Knowledge* (Working Papers of the Spring Research Forum of the Independent Sector and the United Way Institute, March 15, 1985), "Table 1, Summary of Corporate, Employee and Executive Gifts, as a Percent of Total Gifts to the United Way, 1954–1970," p. 279.

11. For a discussion of this period from a left-of-center labor viewpoint, see Richard O. Boyer and Herbert M. Morais, *Labor's Untold Story* (New York: United Electrical, Radio, and Machine Workers of America, 1955), pp. 290–370. The role of labor in relationship with community chests is also noted by Gunn and Platt, *Voluntary Health Agencies*, pp. 80–83, and was the subject of the Ph.D. dissertation by Arthur Katz, "A Study of Conflict and Cooperation in the Relationship Between Organized Labor and Voluntary Social Welfare During the Years 1905–1955" (New York University, School of Education, 1968). See also Walter Reuther, "Industry and Social Work from the View Point of Labor CIO," *Proceedings of the National Conference of Social Work, 1949*, pp. 113–124, and from the AFL point of view, see Harry E. O'Reilly, "From the Viewpoint of Labor AFL," *Proceedings, 1949*, pp. 109–113.

12. This became a kind of "Chapter Plan." Cutlip, *Fund Raising*, pp. 497–498; UWA, *People and Events*, p. 113; and the earlier article, "The Fund Raising Muddle," Special Nationwide Report, in *Newsweek*, June 15, 1959, p. 32, all note the accommodation with the Red Cross.

13. Interviews with United Way staff members and with staff of the American Cancer Society. Reasons for the development of consolidated health organizations, and other community health programs, are openly discussed in "The Second United Way Health Conference," *Community* (March–April 1968), 43(3):9–1.

14. See Carter, *The Gentle Legions*, p. 269. See also UWA, *People and Events*, which gives dollar amounts raised by community chests in 1945 to be $201,859,351, and indicates that in 1948 only $193,307,693 was raised despite increased numbers of campaigns.

15. Mary Fry, "The Fire Gong Clangs! Let's Drop the Chest-Agency Checkers Game and Get Going," *Community* (September 1949), 25(1):8–9.

16. See F. Emerson Andrews, *Corporate Giving* (New York: Russell Sage Foundation, 1952), p. 166. The argument in this section also relies on interviews with United Way staff who were in the field at that time.

17. *Community* (October 1949), 25(2):24.

18. Basil O'Connor was at that time both the president of the National Foundation for Infantile Paralysis and the head of the American Red Cross, in his capacity as chairman of its general committee.

19. Carter, *The Gentle Legions*, pp. 266–267. For the Pittsburgh connection, see also Carter, ibid., p. 263. The original study of the United Fund by the Pennsylvania Economy League (1955) is reported by Donald S. Connery, in "Business and Charity: The Pittsburgh Skirmish," *Fortune*, April 1957, p. 144.

20. Gunn and Platt, *Voluntary Health Agencies*, p. 9. Including the Red Cross, these authors considered that number to be conservative.

21. Gunn and Platt, *Voluntary Health Agencies*, p. 177.

22. At least for the community chests and burgeoning funds in the larger communities. In "More, Not Less Federation" in *Community* (June 1950), 25(10):187–188, a citizen's committee recommended that a new organization be formed, "which would cover solicitation at the place of business for the major appeal; with the Community Chest covering its residential and individual gift solicitation at the same time." Andrews, in *Philanthropic Giving* (1950), p. 63, already notes "the increased willingness of

employers in recent years to make payroll deductions for welfare contributions" which "has facilitated larger gifts from employee groups."

23. The first study was proposed by the National Information Bureau (1924) at the suggestion of the national AACO leadership, and was financed by the Rockefeller Foundation. Mark M. Jones of the Rockefeller Foundation was the principal investigator. According to Cutlip, when it reported finding high fund-raising expenses (25 percent) for the National Tuberculosis Association, that organization effectively blocked its publication (Cutlip, *Fund Raising*, pp. 218–219). The second report was the Gunn and Platt study, *Voluntary Health Agencies* (1945), already cited; and the third was the study conducted by Robert Hamlin, *Voluntary Health and Welfare Agencies in the United States* (May 1960).

24. In the Gunn and Platt study, thirteen agencies were asked questions about unification of national health agencies; five answered that they could see no advantage to unification; eight gave qualified "yes" responses (Gunn and Platt, *Voluntary Health Agencies*, pp. 194–200). See also letter from Louis I. Dublin, chairman of the executive committee for the Gunn and Platt study, to Elwood Street, cited in *People and Events*, p. 106.

25. Interview with Dr. Robert Hamlin, director of the study.

26. The principal authorities on the "health wars" have already been cited: Carter, *The Gentle Legions*; Cutlip, *Fund Raising*, pp. 488–500; Donald S. Connery, "Business and Charity: The Pittsburgh Skirmish" (1957); UWA, *People and Events*, pp. 105–116, 130–156. It was also reported in articles of *The New York Times* during that period and in local newspapers referring to particular community funds; see, for example, "Red Cross in Legal Test," *New York Times*, October 17, 1951, p. 34; "Polio Group Spurns Jersey Chest Cash," ibid., February 13, 1954, p. 19; "Two Assail Tactics of United Funds", ibid., June 22, 1959, p. 1; and "Charity Drive Curb Upset by U.S. Court," ibid., August 23, 1961, p. 33.

27. Cutlip, *Fund Raising*, p. 422. See also Foster Rhea Dulles, *The American Red Cross: A History* (New York: Harper, 1950).

28. Dulles, *The American Red Cross*, pp. 303–304. Dulles discusses labor problems with the Red Cross, and notes that labor criticism came to a head at the CIO convention in 1939, when John L. Lewis "took up the attack," saying that " 'the American Red Cross needs to be democratized.' " See also Cutlip, *Fund Raising*, p. 417.

29. See UWA, *People and Events*, p. 130. For more discussion of the influential people who made this happen, see Cutlip, *Fund Raising*, p. 498. The idea that "equal billing" was essential for Red Cross was even reported in the newspapers; see, for example, "Red Cross in Legal Test," *New York Times*, October 17, 1951, p. 34.

30. Gunn and Platt, *Voluntary Health Agencies*, p. 5. The authors explain what makes the organization unique: "The American National Red Cross is in many ways the largest voluntary welfare organization in the world. Because of its origins and its charter, its greatest opportunity to serve comes in wartime. Yet it has been a potent force . . . in . . . peace." "The Red Cross has long been known as the 'Greatest Mother.' . . . "The American National Red Cross is distinctive in being one of the very few organizations with a quasi-governmental status, having been incorporated under a charter by Congress. Its President is the President of the United States" (p. 245).

31. In 1959, writing in *The Social Work Yearbook*, Wayne McMillen identified the "spearhead of resistance to united funds as a group of national agencies, sometimes called the big six: The American Cancer Society, the American Heart Association, The American National Red Cross, the National Foundation for Infantile Paralysis, the National Society for Crippled Children and Adults, and the National Tuberculosis Association." But the Red Cross had already modified its firm stand against united

326   2. COMMUNITY CHEST TO UNITED WAY

funds (McMillen, "Financing Social Welfare Services," in *Social Work Yearbook, 1957* (New York: National Association of Social Workers, 1957), pp. 260–267). The situation appears to have been somewhat more accurately reported by *Newsweek*, June 15, 1959, pp. 31–32, in "The Fund Raising Muddle," where it indicates "there are four major holdouts against the United Fund philosophy: They are the Tuberculosis Association, the National Foundation (formerly the National Foundation for Infantile Paralysis), and the heart and cancer groups."

32. For a discussion of this issue in relation to the Combined Federal Campaign, see below, chapters 5 and 6. A related issue is also discussed in regard to "the Philadelphia story," concerning women's organizations; and there were many times that the relationship between local United Ways and Planned Parenthood have been explosive, including incidents in Amarillo, Texas (1981) and Corpus Christi, in 1982.

33. In the 1970s, the relationship with these agencies begins to change again. See below, chapters 3, 4, and 8.

34. See Carter, *The Gentle Legions*, p. 252, where the American Cancer Society document explaining this policy is quoted, noting that only 15 percent of local units were member agencies of federated funds at that time. In the years 1950–1957 the ACS modified its non-participation policy to enable units of the Society to participate in (in-plant) solicitations under certain specified conditions. "These conditions related to pressures in the local community, presumably from business and labor." See Robert Cutler, "Open Letter to Basil O'Connor" (1947), which states *"Leave it to the 'little people' back home in each community to settle. . . . After all, they are America"* (italics his). The reference in the text (below) to door-to-door visiting on Heart Sunday comes from Betts, "Free Choice in Giving" in Ernest B. Harper and Arthur Dunham, eds., *Community Organization in Action*, (New York: Association, 1959), p. 424.

35. In 1960 the Red Cross also reported to its Annual Convention that it fell $12 million short of its goals in the two preceeding campaigns, fall 1958 and March 1959 ("The Fund Raising Muddle," *Newsweek*, June 15, 1959, pp. 31–33).

36. Charles Livermore, then assistant director of the national CIO War Relief Committee, "Labor and Social Agencies," *Survey Midmonthly*, September 1943, p. 14; cited in Gunn and Platt, *Voluntary Health Agencies*, pp. 80–81.

37. The question of top-down, and strongly centralized agencies, versus local bottoms-up organization, is a constant issue for federated fund-raising organizations and will be discussed further below.

38. One supposedly "official" definition of the time is given in Connery, "Business and Charity," *Fortune*, April 1957, p. 145. He cites the definition as being "any community-wide federated fund-raising effort that includes one or more of the big national agencies." However, a staff member involved in definitional discussions in those years informed the author that practically speaking this meant that a united fund was really defined as consisting of the local community chest agencies plus the Red Cross, and *"other* federations" was used to refer to funds which included other health agencies, such as the Heart Association or the Cancer Society.

39. *The United Way: Backdrop and Breakthrough* (New York: UCFCA, 1967) indicates the number of local health foundations grew during the year to thirty eight. Also discussed in *People and Events*, pp. 130, 140–141, and 153–154.

40. Among others, John C. Donovan holds that "the Eisenhower decade of the fifties . . . was not quite . . . [a] total loss"; *The Politics of Poverty*, 2d ed. (Indianapolis: Bobbs-Merrill, 1973), p. 19. The term "Seedtime of Reform," as used to describe the 1920s, has been made famous by a book of that title by Clarke A. Chambers.

41. *The Other America* was published in 1962 but did not really have widespread attention or influence until 1963. See Sar A. Levitan, *The Great Society's Poor Law: A*

New Approach to Poverty (Baltimore: Johns Hopkins Press, 1969), pp. 12–15. The social legislation of the Johnson-Kennedy years was, moreover, apparently greatly influenced by the work of the economist Robert Lampton, who had completed studies on poverty in America in the late 1950s. There is considerable literature on the period of the early sixties, including Frances Fox Piven and Richard A. Cloward, *Regulating the Poor: The Functions of Public Welfare* (New York: Pantheon Books, 1971), pp. 183–338; John C. Donovan, *The Politics of Poverty;* Sar A. Levitan, *The Great Society's Poor Law;* Peter Marris and Martin Rein, *Dilemmas of Social Reform: Poverty and Community Action in the United States* (New York: Atherton, 1967); Daniel P. Moynihan, *Maximum Feasible Misunderstanding: Community Action in the War on Poverty* (New York: Free Press, 1969); Gilbert Steiner, *The State of Welfare* (Washington, D.C.: The Brookings Institution, 1971); and James L. Sundquist, *On Fighting Poverty* (New York: Basic Books, 1969).

42. Seminal discussion of the 1962 and 1967 amendments to the Social Security Act is found in Martha Derthick, *Uncontrollable Spending for Social Service Grants* (Washington, D.C.: The Brookings Institution, 1975), and in Steiner, *The State of Welfare*, pp. 31–121. The classic discussion of the political reasons for rising welfare rolls generally is found in Piven and Cloward, *Regulating the Poor*.

43. The passage of the Model Cities Legislation was not as threatening to many groups, including the United Funds and Councils, as the earlier legislation of the War on Poverty, at least partly because city hall was involved.

44. The influence of the "gray area" projects and the President's Committee on Juvenile Delinquency is discussed in Marris and Rein, *Dilemmas of Social Reform*, and is incorporated also in the analysis of other sources; see particularly Donovan, *The Politics of Poverty*, pp. 31–41.

45. This feature, embedded in Title II ("Urban and Rural Community Action Programs") of the Economic Opportunity Act, became the keystone of the War on Poverty. Although its meaning was not precise, and was subsequently subject to a variety of interpretations, it ultimately resulted in new groups, particularly urban blacks, entering into decision-making structures of the local community. For a critique of the politics involved, see Moynihan, *Maximum Feasible Misunderstanding*. The impact of maximum feasible participation is also viewed somewhat cynically by Neil Gilbert, in his case study of the War on Poverty in Pittsburgh, *Clients or Constituents: Community Action in the War on Poverty* (San Francisco: Jossey-Bass, 1969). Somewhat more mixed conclusions are reached in the analyses by other authors; see, for example, Ralph M. Kramer, *Participation of the Poor: Comparative Case Studies in the War on Poverty* (Englewood Cliffs, N.J.: Prentice-Hall, 1969); Levitan, *The Great Society's Poor Law;* and Marris and Rein, *The Dilemmas of Social Reform*, as well as in Donovan, *The Politics of Poverty*.

46. Jack A. Meyer, "Budget Cuts in the Reagan Administration: A Question of Fairness," in D. Lee Bawden, ed., *The Social Contract Revisited: Aims and Outcomes of President Reagan's Social Welfare Policy*, p. 35 (Washington, D.C.: The Urban Institute, 1984). See also Martha Derthick, *Uncontrollable Spending*.

47. See Steiner, *The State of Welfare*, pp. 40–41. The impact of the climate of the times, and the War on Poverty, specifically on rising relief rolls is analyzed in Piven and Cloward, *Regulating the poor*, particularly pp. 330–348. For comparison of costs of income transfers in relation to other health and welfare expenditures, see John L. Palmer and Gregory B. Mills, "Budget Policy," in John L. Palmer and Isabel V. Sawhill, eds., *The Reagan Experiment: An Examination of Economic and Social Policies Under the Reagan Administration* (Washington, D.C.: The Urban Institute, 1982). See also ibid., appendix, table A.2, "Federal Outlays by Domestic Program Area (FY 1966-FY 1981)," p. 486.

48. Amounts for social services and health expenditures are given in Palmer and Sawhill, *The Reagan Experiment*, appendix, table A.2, p. 486.

2. COMMUNITY CHEST TO UNITED WAY

49. See Michael F. Gutowski and Jeffrey J. Koshel, "Social Services," in Palmer and Sawhill, *The Reagan Experiment*, pp. 307–328. According to these authors, although the federal share of total public expenditures grew (from 41 percent in 1955 to over 60 percent in 1979), nevertheless, there was also steady, if less spectacular, growth in social service spending by state and local levels of government "beyond that required to meet matching requirements for . . . federal funds."

50. The phrase was used in the opening paragraphs of the report written on the riots, which was widely read and disseminated. See *Report of the National Advisory Commission on Civil Disorders* (New York: Bantam Books, 1968), also known as the Kerner Commission Report.

51. For discussion of these changes particularly, see Kramer, *Participation of the Poor;* and Donovan, *The Politics of Poverty*. The classic earlier studies of elite community leadership are well known and include: Robert A. Dahl, *Who Governs? Democracy and Power in an American City* (New Haven: Yale University Press, 1961); R. Hunter et al., *Community Power Structure* (Chapel Hill: University of North Carolina Press, 1956); Robert S. Lynd and Helen M. Lynd, *Middletown* and *Middletown in Transition* (New York: Harcourt, Brace, 1929 and 1937, respectively); and in a somewhat different vein, W. Lloyd Warner and Paul S. Lunt, *The Status System of a Modern Community* (New Haven: Yale University Press, 1945). The notion of an elite business leadership with influence on organized charity is one of *the* major themes of the seminal work on the community chest in Indianapolis; see John Seeley et al., *Community Chest*.

52. For examples of the older view of community organization, which was tied to formal community structures and often specifically to the health and welfare movement, see Ernest B. Harper and Arthur Dunham, eds., *Community Organization in Action* (New York: Association, 1959); C. F. McNeil, "Community Organization for Social Welfare" in *Social Work Yearbook* (New York: American Association of Social Workers, 1954); Wayne McMillen, *Community Organization for Social Welfare* (Chicago: University of Chicago Press, 1945); and Herbert Hewitt Stroup, *Community Welfare Organization* (New York: Harper, 1952). A view of organizing more akin to community development is presented in the classic by Murray G. Ross, *Community Organization: Theory and Principles* (New York: Harper, 1955). By the 1970s there was no doubt about the change to community organizing practice as meaning social change, and defining this in terms of advocacy for the disadvantaged was widely accepted. See the seminal work by George Brager and Harry Specht, *Community Organizing* (New York: Columbia University Press, 1973). A discussion of the various points of view arising after the 1960s and their implications for social work education is given in Robert Perlman and Arnold Gurin, *Community Organization and Social Planning* (New York: John Wiley and Sons and The Council for Social Work Education, 1972).

53. Local controversies were not only reported in local newspapers, but in the *New York Times*. See, for example, "Negro-Aid Group will Lose Funds: Action by Community Chest in Jacksonville, Florida is Blamed on Racists," *New York Times*, September 15, 1956, p. 6; "Fund Aides Criticized: Urban League's Withdrawal in Little Rock Scored," ibid., October 10, 1957, p. 29; and "South Cuts Funds of Urban League: Hate Groups Forcing Ouster of Interracial Body from Community Chests," November 18, 1957, p. 20.

In an interview with the author, Leo Perlis, director of the Community Service Committee of the AFL and CIO, cited difficulty in getting the UCFCA to take a pro-League support stand, and this is also documented in the Minutes of the Board of Directors of the UCFCA, September 21, 1956. Not only was Perlis' motion for a resolution about the Urban League situation defeated, but the board also turned down his request for a study of the situation, along with that of other national organizations such as the YWCA. On August 7, 1964, the UCFCA issued the cautious memorandum stating that each "United Fund should do what it thinks is right and move in the direction of what it considers to be the long-term trend" (*People and Events*, p. 166).

54. Minutes of the meeting of the UCFCA board of directors, May 24, 1963, Chicago, Illinois. On September 20, 1963 the UCFCA executive committee voted unanimously to recommend a statement reaffirming UCFCA's long-standing policy on non-discrimination ". . . in anticipation of the announcement by the Chairman of the Civil Service Commission of a policy that would require such a formal statement of all organizations whose members wish to solicit federal employees at their place of employment."

55. "Summary of 1963 Progress/Challenges in Community Planning," *Community* (March–April 1965), 40(3):9.

56. UCFCA became deeply involved in a joint UCFCA-OEO leadership training project nationally. See *Report of UCFCA-OEO Leadership Training Project* (UCFCA, September 1968): "The Voluntarism Project: An Interim Report," *Community* (March–April 1968), pp. 13–15. Labor might have had equally strong reservations about the poverty program, but while business was specifically concerned about some aspects of the program, it also benefited from a variety of contractual opportunities, most notably with the Job Corps. See Sar A. Levitan, *The Great Society's Poor Law: A New Approach to Poverty* (Baltimore, Maryland: Johns Hopkins University Press, 1969), pp. 83–85. Sargeant Shriver's interest in involving local United Fund leadership and in financial support from local United Funds, is noted in the Minutes of the Executive Committee of the UCFCA, February 10, 1967. (This was also a period in which OEO was facing difficulties with Congress in relation to its funding.) Remarks about business bias against the federal government also were made during that meeting of February 10th.

57. Many of the organizations, such as Head Start, or the Community Action Agencies themselves, which were created under the anti-poverty program, had a new status as quasi-public organizations, since they were almost entirely funded by government, were defined in purpose and activities largely by government policies, and included on their boards representatives of the government sector, by mandate.

A Time of Transition

1. "Organization and Management Study," report of the study committee as approved by the board of directors of the UCFCA, January 30, 1970, p. 1.

2. "Organization and Management Study," p. 3.

3. See Chester H. Jones, "A Challenge to Business," *Community*, (September-October 1968), 43(6):7–9.

4. See *Rebirth and Renewal: United Way of America*, Proceedings of the Annual Meeting of the Trustees, Dallas, Texas, December 3, 1970. Also in the Minutes of the Board of Directors of the United Way of America, September 18, 1970 and the Minutes of the Executive Committee of the UWA, December 2, 1970. For a later review of this period by the UWA, see also *People and Events*, pp. 203–216.

5. The increase for annual membership dues was to be "from $\frac{3}{16}$ of 1% (approximately) to $\frac{3}{16}$ of 1% of the amount raised in the previous year's campaign" (*Rebirth and Renewal*, p. 3).

6. Excerpts from address of Bayard Ewing, president of the UWA, at the annual meeting of the trustees (*Rebirth and Renewal*, p. 14).

3. Community Planning in the United Way

1. "Organization and Management Study," report of the study committee as approved by the board of directors of the UCFCA, January 30, 1970, p. 3.

2. In the early 1950s, the CCCA actually gave a grant for salary of the director of the School of Social Administration of Ohio State University, in a period that one respondent called dominated by "Charlie Stillman's Boys"—Stillman was director of the Ohio State School. The relationship between the CCCA and the School cooled, however, and in October 1954, the dean of the College of Commerce and Administration, Ohio State University, informed the executive director of the CCCA of the decision to handle the salary of the director of the School of Social Administration directly out of their own resources (Minutes of the Executive Committee of the CCCA, New York City, November 5, 1954). By February 24, 1955, criteria were discussed for utilization of schools of social work for training of "Chest, Fund and Council personnel" (CCCA, *Report of Committee on Recruitment and Training*, [New York, N.Y., February 24, 1955]). In the next ten years, the CCCA/UCFCA was instrumental in obtaining grants from foundations and businesses for schools of social work to train professionals in the federation field. By the 1960s the idea of a "National Training Center" of the UCFCA had already emerged, targeted for executive personnel of smaller communities, and by 1963 recruitment and training in fields other than social work was already being given serious consideration (Minutes of the Board of Directors, UCFCA, Chicago, May 24, 1963).

3. The original plan for the National Academy of Voluntarism called for it to be based at the University of Miami, but the NAV opened in the United Way building in Alexandria, in January 1973. During a discussion of the plan in February 1972, George Shea, Labor staff member of the United Way of America, noted that recruitment sources for the field have been "broadened considerably beyond the graduate schools of social work, to business schools, schools of government, and other sources" (Minutes of the Meeting of the Executive Committee, United Way of America, Alexandria, February 24, 1972).

4. Clearly, small communities have more difficulty carrying out all these varied activities, but nevertheless many apparently do so to some extent. The author observed this firsthand in her own community, Scarsdale, New York, where fund volunteers attempted to fulfill all the basic functions of council-funds through the mid-1970s.

5. Frederick J. Ferris, "The First Councils of Social Agencies" (Ph.D. diss., Columbia University School of Social Work, 1968), vol. 2. Early history of the councils, and their complicated and changing relationships with the Charity Organization Movement (COS) and Associated Charities, is discussed extensively in Frank Dekker Watson, *The Charity Organization Movement in the United States: A Study in American Philanthropy* (New York: Macmillan, 1922); and also is discussed briefly in Roy Lubove, *The Professional Altruist* (New York: Macmillan, 1969), pp. 181–182.

6. Ferris, "The First Councils of Social Agencies."

7. Ferris, "The First Councils of Social Agencies"; Watson, *The Charity Organization Movement*, particularly pp. 337–365, 422–428. For an early discussion of this issue, see also J. J. O'Connor, "Cooperation Between Agencies," in *Proceedings of the National Conference of Charities and Corrections, 1913*, pp. 340–344. In their eighty-year history, councils have also held a variety of names, including, but not limited to, the following: Central Council of Social Agencies, Councils of Social Agencies, Health and Welfare Councils, and Community Service Councils.

8. For the Lane Report and other definitions, see Ernest B. Harper and Arthur Dunham, eds., *Community Organization in Action: Basic Literature and Critical Comment* (New York: Association, 1959), pp. 51–70. The Lane Committee Report can be found in its entirety in "The Field of Community Organization," *Proceedings of the National Conference of Social Work* (New York, 1939), pp. 495–511.

9. John E. Tropman, "A Comparative Analysis of Welfare Councils" (Ph.D. diss.,

3. COMMUNITY PLANNING IN THE UNITED WAY   331

University of Michigan, 1967). Figures for the war years also appear in Selskar M. Gunn and Philip S. Platt, *Voluntary Health Agencies: An Interpretive Study*, (New York: Ronald, 1945), p. 123. Councils apparently continued their growth. According to the *1965 Directory* of the UCFCA, there were 460 councils that year, of which 426 were in the United States (with the remaining 34 in Canada), and 2,120 campaigns in the United States (with another 111 in Canada). However, in an attachment to a somewhat later paper from the United Way files, "Some Comments on Council Structure" (UCFCA, 1968), a description of community planning councils by types of organization and population size indicated that 182 out of 376 identified councils were totally separate; another 90 had separate boards from the United Fund/Chest, but shared a "Joint Executive".

10. For a discussion of neighborhood organization and district councils generally, see Harper and Dunham, *Community Organization in Action*, pp. 327–340, 350; for the connection with civil defense, see UWA, *People and Events*, pp. 90–91.

11. See, for example, Frank J. Bruno, *Trends in Social Work* (New York: Columbia University Press, 1948), p. 198; for the emphasis on community organization also as democratic process, see Kenneth L. M. Pray, "Community Organization as Social Work Practice," in *Proceedings of the National Conference of Social Work, 1947* (New York: Columbia University Press, 1948), pp. 194–204; Harper and Dunham, *Community Organization in Action*, pp. 106–111; and Herbert Hewitt Stroup, *Community Welfare Organization*, (New York: Harper, 1952), p. 108.

12. See above, note 9. See also debate on this issue by various authors connected with the chest/council movement in the 1950s, in Harper and Dunham, *Community Organization in Action*, pp, 369–407.

13. Author's interview with Violet Sieder and others, 1985; see also C. Whit Pfeiffer, "Chest Council Relations—the Case for Separate Councils," in Harper and Dunham, *Community Organization in Action*, pp. 402–407.

14. Leo Perlis, "Congress of Industrial Organizations Participation in Health and Welfare Planning," in *Proceedings of the National Conference of Social Work* (New York: Columbia University Press, 1945), pp. 228–241.

15. See above, chapter 2. Note also that the constitution of the AFL-CIO, article 13, Section 1, adopted September 2, 1955, gives authority to organized labor to participate formally in cooperative activities with community social welfare organizations. This issue is discussed in Arthur Katz, "A Study of Conflict and Cooperation in the Relationship Between Organized Labor and Voluntary Social Welfare in America— During the Years 1905–1955," (Ph.D. diss., New York University, School of Education, 1968.)

16. See Bell, *The End of Ideology: On the Exhaustion of Political Ideas in the Late Fifties* (New York: Free, 1960).

17. The beginning of the real turn-around in civil rights, with court decisions, and actions, was marked by the decision of the Supreme Court in *Brown v. Board of Education in Topeka* (1954), concerning the unconstitutionality of the separate but equal doctrines, and segregation, in public school. Also, see above, chapter 2.

18. See Ralph Kramer, *Participation of the Poor* (Englewood Cliffs, N.J.: Prentice-Hall, 1969); Peter Marris and Martin Rein, *Dilemmas of Social Reform* (New York: Atherton Press, 1967); Daniel Moynihan, *Maximum Feasible Misunderstanding* (New York: Free Press, 1969).

19. This was recognized by UCFCA leaders; for an example, see the "Report of the Chairman, Community Planning Advisory Council to the Annual UCFCA Trustee Meeting," November 30, 1967, pp. 1–2 (from UWA files), which states that "local Health and Welfare Councils . . . have been confronted by the appearance of multiple planning organization . . . [with] . . . new approaches to planning," and therefore

332   **3. COMMUNITY PLANNING IN THE UNITED WAY**

councils have had "to reassess their role in relation to many new separate mechanisms." The issue was discussed earlier in the 1960s in a seminal staff paper, "An Hour of Decision: An Assessment of Fundamental Issues Confronting the Council Movement Today and an Outline of UCFCA's Plan of Action to Facilitate Their Resolution," September 11, 1963.

20. This was one of the issues most argued over in questioning the council role in the fund system. For a factual consideration of this role, see *Council Facts 1965*, pp. 33–34. Table 29 suggests that the majority of councils (84 out of 130 respondents) were involved in fund budgeting efforts, but the level of their involvement was clearly circumscribed. Further analysis of the responses indicated that few councils had "Budget Direction" responsibility (only 18 out of 130) and even fewer (11) had complete responsibility for the process (table 30). An even earlier statement to this effect is found in "What Councils of Social Agencies Do" (C.C.C. 1939), p. 27.

21. Comparison of the status of planning council and United Way leadership is shown in tables in appendix H.1 and 2, based on a later survey.

22. Figures from *People and Events*, p. 164.

23. See George A. Brager and Francis P. Purcell, *Community Action Against Poverty: Readings from the Mobilization Experience* (New Haven, Conn.: College and University Press, 1967); and Ralph M. Kramer, *Participation of the Poor: Comparative Community Case Studies in the War on Poverty* (Englewood Cliffs, N.J.: Prentice-Hall, 1969.) In his case study of one city, Gilbert takes a somewhat less optimistic view of the successful participation of new leaders; see Neil Gilbert, *Clients or Constituents* (San Francisco: Jossey-Bass, 1970.)

24. *The United Way: Backdrop and Breakthrough* (New York: UCFCA, 1967), p. 6. Contrast this 61 percent (1965) with the percentage of support councils received in 1960, when United Way funds averaged out to 78.4 percent of all council income. In 1960 less than 5 percent of Council income came from public funds, and in 1965 (only five years later!) the share had risen to 28.6 percent from public funds.

25. Joseph A. Beirne "The State of the United Way," *Community* (January–February 1968), 43(1):3–6.

26. This issue was certainly recognized by the UCFCA. See "The Role of Health and Welfare Councils in Comprehensive Community Health Planning," A Report on Fulfillment of a Contract Between United States Public Health Services and the United Funds and Councils of America, February 28, 1966 (unpublished). Thus, even though the actual dollar amounts that councils received from united funds increased during this period, they declined as a percentage of total income, concomitantly with the increase in funding from the public sector.

27. See Martha Derthick, *Uncontrollable Spending for Social Service Grants* (Washington, D.C.: The Brookings Institution, 1975). Spending grew more slowly after the loophole was closed in 1972, but it was not really until the enactment of P.L. 93–637, the Social Security amendments of 1974, that Title XX effectively put a cap on much of this service spending.

28. *Backdrop and Breakthrough*, (1967), p. 4. For example, by 1967 Combined Federal Campaigns (CFCs) were being held in 135 communities. CFCs are discussed below in chapters 6 and 7.

29. Priority studies conducted during the 1970s caused problems in many local communities. The Toledo story is discussed below as the case study of councils. In Westchester a priority study conducted in 1972 (which remained controversial for many years) gave low priority ranking to the fundamental service areas of youth and children.

30. In at least two communities, our survey found that the LUW allocation was over $500,000 (Philadelphia, Boston). For further discussion, see Eleanor L. Brilliant,

3. COMMUNITY PLANNING IN THE UNITED WAY   333

"Community Planning and Community Problem Solving: Past, Present, and Future," *Social Service Review* (December 1986), 37(4): 566–589.

31. See Brilliant, "Community Planning and Community Problem Solving," p. 576. See "Meeting the Planning Needs of United Way of Massachusetts Bay," A Report of the Study Committee, April 1985, Management and Community Studies Institute (MACSI), (UWA), pp. 28–29.

32. For one example of this kind of consideration, see "Meeting the Planning Needs of Massachusetts Bay," also discussed in relation to Boston, specifically in Ruth Brandwein, "A Working Framework for Approaching Organizational Change: The Community Chest–Council System from 1946 to 1971" (Ph.D. diss., Florence Heller Graduate School for Advanced Studies in Social Welfare, 1977).

33. *Standards of Excellence for Local United Ways* (UWA, 1973). This document seemed to have been taken very seriously by local United Way professionals in the 1970s.

34. *People and Events* (UWA), p. 204.

35. Donald S. McHaughton, as quoted in *People and Events*, p. 204. There was also a conference held in Detroit, April 6–7, 1972, on the future of independent planning councils.

36. "Plan X" was presented at the United Way of America Biennial Staff Conference in Hollywood Beach, Florida, in March 1970 and by Don McHaughton at a volunteer leaders conference (ULC) in May 1971. It is discussed in Paul Akana, "Some Thoughts on Planning" (UWA, Research, Development & Program Evaluation Division, 1977), pp. 6–8. Plan X and Y are also mentioned in *Proceedings: Planning and Allocations Sessions*, ULC, Chicago, Ill., May 6, 1974 (UWA, July 1974), pp. 1–8.

37. "United Way—1996," Address by Paul Akana at the United Way staff conference, Boston, Mass., March 9, 1976. See also Akana, "Planning," pp. 2, 7.

38. Akana, "Planning," pp. 7–8.

39. See Memo to Planning Advisory Committee, from Dick Huegli, Chairman, Re: PAC Retreat in Scottsdale, June 22–25, 1977, with early Akana paper attached; see later "Planning," p. 3.

40. Harold C. Edelston, "Fund-Council Relationships: A Proposed Division of Responsibility," (paper presented to the UWA, March 22, 1972), p. 1.

41. Edelston, "Fund-Council Relationships," chart I, pp. 8–13.

42. *UWASIS, United Way of America Services Identification System* (UWA, January 1972); *UWASIS II, A Taxonomy of Social Goals and Human Service Programs* (UWA, November 1976); *Needs Assessment: The State of the Art* (UWA Planning and Allocations Division and United Way Institute, November 1982).

43. Russy D. Sumariwalla, "Planning and Managing Human Services in Local Communities Under Non-Governmental Auspices: An Outline of an Organizational Model for Pure Planning Based on a Strategy of Disjointed Incrementalism: An Ideal Type" (paper presented to the UWA, March 1973).

44. This point is made explicitly by two Council executives, Jerry A. Shroder and Bernard M. Shiffman, "A Metropolitan City Council Model for the Planning and Managing of Human Services in Local Communities Under Voluntary Auspices" (New York: Community Council of Greater New York, May 1974).

45. Akana, "Planning," p. 4.

46. Akana, "Planning," p. 3. However, some strong local councils were still operating in 1986, including the powerful Federation for Community Planning in Cleveland and the much smaller Yonkers Community Planning Council in New York State (Westchester county).

47. This was done partly in the process of carrying out studies of managerial/planning functions of local United Ways or of United Ways and planning councils, by

the United Way of America Management and Community Studies Institute, known as MACSI (1972), originally called the Institute of Community Studies. Staff for this "institute" included Edelston until he died in 1979, Sumariwalla, and occasionally other staff including Dick O'Brien. Many United Ways undertook some form of strategic planning during the late 1970s and early 1980s, and this was frequently done with assistance from other national United Way staff. The national organization took a leadership role in encouraging strategic planning efforts. A brief written history of MACSI was given in a report to the board, January 1983, *"United Way of America: Management and Community Studies Institute (MACSI),"* in the 1983 Minutes Book.

48. Data sources for this section include U.S. Bureau of the Census, *County and City Data Book, 1983* (Washington, D.C.: Government Printing Office, 1983), table B, "Counties-Area and Population," p. 424; and *A Look at the Numbers that Make the Toledo Area, 1982 Edition* (Toledo Area Chamber of Commerce).

49. Site visit and personal interviews. Among the prestigious names are the Stranahans (Champion Spark Plug Company), Thomas H. Anderson (the Andersons), George W. Haigh (chairman of the board and CEO of the Toledo Trust Company), and Charles L. McKelvey (president of the First National Bank of Toledo). Paul Bloch, editor of the *Toledo Blade*, was also mentioned as a community influential, although he is not one of the "old-line" crowd.

50. "Ohio Labor Market, October 1982," mimeographed fact sheet supplied by local business leader.

51. Crossing of state lines for service areas of agencies is a not-uncommon feature of United Ways. The Toledo Standard Metropolitan Statistical Area (SMSA) includes Monroe County, Michigan, and, for example, the Salvation Army funded by the Toledo United Way has units in Grand Rapids and Wayne, Michigan.

52. "United Way Campaign Gets $9.6 Million, Up $200,000," *The Toledo Blade*, October 29, 1982. Personal interviews, fall 1982.

53. "We propose that the current Red Cross share of the Campaign (12.29%) be built into the 5 year agreement" ("Chest Perspective on Future Relations with American Red Cross," United Way of Greater Toledo, file document, October 19, 1982, point no. 4).

54. Allocations "package" approved at the meeting of the board of directors of the Greater Toledo Community Chest, December 15, 1981, p. 5 and p. 24 of the Minutes of the Board of Directors.

55. "Report of the Joint Committee on Chest/Community Planning Council Relations," Revised Draft, October 22, 1982.

56. Interviews with staff and volunteers of the council and of the United Way, fall 1982 and spring 1986.

57. This history is described in "Position Paper, Community Planning Council of Northwestern Ohio, Inc.," prepared for the Joint Chest-Council Task Force by the Community Planning Council of Northwestern Ohio, Inc., September 1982.

58. "Priority Determination Plans—Past, Present and Future," report in the United Way of America files, n.d. See also UWA, *The Painful Necessity of Choice: An Analysis of Priorities Plans and Policies in the United Way Movement* (May 1974).

59. "Priority Determination Project," sponsored by the Community Planning Council of Northwestern Ohio, Inc. in cooperation with the City of Toledo, the Community Chest of Greater Toledo, the Economic Opportunity Planning Association of Greater Toledo, and Lucas County, July 1973.

60. Both studies were mentioned by respondents at the time of the site visit.

61. For an earlier expression of this problem by a planning council executive, see Harold W. Demone and Herbert C. Schulberg, "Planning for Human Services: The Role of the Community Council," in Harold Demone and Dwight Harshbarger, *A*

4. ALLOCATIONS TO ALTERNATIVE FUNDS   335

Handbook of Human Service Organizations (New York: Behavioral Publications, 1974), pp. 546–558. Demone was the executive of the United Community Services in Boston at the time it was reorganized as the United Community Planning Corporation (1973).

62. Given the close interrelationships of much of Toledo's leadership, it is not surprising to find wives on boards of local agencies funded by the United Way, and the same family, such as the Stranahans, represented in opposing camps; for example, at one time Robert Stranahan had a leadership position in the United Way/Chest, while Duane ("Pat") Stranahan (his cousin) had a significant volunteer role in the planning council.

63. "1982 United Way Community Chest and Red Cross Service Allocations—Your Money at Work," United Way of Greater Toledo (information sheet).

64. See "Report of Special Study Committee in [sic] the Role of United Way in Community Problem Solving" adopted by the Strategic Planning Committee of the United Way of America as one of *Three Critical Reports*, (UWA, October 1985). Brought to the UWA Board for action on May 25, 1983.

65. Discussed in Minutes of the Board of Directors of the Greater Toledo Community Chest, December 15, 1981, p. 2.

66. "Statement of Agreement for Participation as Associates Between the Lucas, Wood, Ottawa, and Fulton County Units of the American Cancer Society (ACS) and the Greater Toledo Community Chest."

67. The intention of developing "its own corporate planning capability" was spelled out in the "Report of the Joint Committee on Chest/CPC Relations," October 1982, and goals for this unit were specifically outlined in a printed booklet, "Operational Goals for the Greater Toledo United Way."

68. Telephone interviews in winter-spring 1986. Several respondents indicated that Shaffer had been successful in negotiating extra time for United Way support, and additional funds ($75,000 in 1985–86), but that this was likely to be the last year of guaranteed United Way funding for the council.

4. From Allocations to Alternative Funds

1. Leonard L. Silverstein, Preface to the *Research Papers Sponsored by the Commission on Private Philanthropy and Public Needs*, vol. 1: *History, Trends, and Current Magnitude* (U.S. Dept. of Treasury, 1977), p. v.

2. Silverstein, "Preface," pp. vi. Also it should be noted that the research director for the commission, Gabriel Rudney, was given leave from the Treasury Department in order to carry out this work. Silverstein was executive director of the Commission.

3. See for example, Martin S. Feldstein and Charles Clotfelter, "Tax Incentives and Charitable Contributions in the United States: A Microeconometric Analysis," in *Research Papers*, vol. 3: *Special Behavioral Studies, Foundations and Corporations*, pp. 1393–1439; Michael J. Boskin and Martin S. Feldstein, "Effects of the Charitable Deduction on Contributions by Low-Income and Middle-Income Households: Evidence from the National Survey of Philanthropy," *Research Papers*, vol. 3, pp. 1441–1451; George F. Break, "Charitable Contributions Under the Federal Individual Income Tax: Alternative Policy Options," in *Research Papers*, vol. 3, pp. 1521–1555; and David A. Good and Aaron Wildavsky, "A Tax by Any Other Name: The Donor-Directed Automatic Percentage Contribution Bonus, a Budget Alternative for Financing Governmental Support of Charity," in *Research Papers*, vol. 4, pp. 2389–2416; tax issues were clearly the basic theme of volumes 3 and 4 of the published *Research Papers*. See also *Giving in America: Toward a Stronger Voluntary Sector* (Report of the Commission on Private Philanthropy and Public Needs, The File Commission, 1975), pp. 1–3.

4. Based on interviews with key respondents. Criticism was also expressed openly

4. ALLOCATIONS TO ALTERNATIVE FUNDS

at the time the report was published, and Leo Perlis (director of the Department of Community Services of the AFL-CIO) even resigned from the commission. For two newspaper accounts of the dissension, see Mary Jean Tully, "Commission Pluralism," *New York Times*, December 15, 1975, p. 31; also, Eileen Shanahan, "Report by Philanthropic Group: Proposed Ways to Spur Giving," ibid., December 3, 1975, p. 16. See also Pablo Eisenberg, "Private Philanthropy: Vital and Innovative or Passive and Irrelevant," *The Grantsmanship Center News* (January 1975), p. 50.

5. Mary Jean Tully, "Commission Pluralism."

6. These groups were described by David Horton Smith as having characteristics which included the following: "smaller, newer, poorer, local, 'grassroots,' unaffiliated, self-help, technical assistance oriented, minority, disadvantaged, social action, advocacy, experimental, social change oriented . . . corporate/governmental monitoring." See, "Donee Group Report," Filer Commission, *Research Papers*, vol. 1, p. 85, n. 1. The Donee Group staff included James W. Abernathy, Jr., and Theodore J. Jacobs, and the report was apparently written primarily by Abernathy.

7. The Donee Group is formally described as "a coalition of public interest, social action, and volunteer groups acting as advisors to the Commission on Private Philanthropy and Public needs," and it was noted that it had disbanded by the time of publication; see Filer Commission, *Research Papers*, vol. 1, p. 49 (note). For the complete list of members of the Donee group, see "Private Philanthropy: Vital and Innovative or Passive and Irrelevant: The Donee Group Report and Recommendations" in Filer Commission, *Research Papers*, vol. 1. pp. 84–85.

8. David Horton Smith, "The Role of the United Way in Philanthropy," in Filer Commission, *Research Papers*, vol. 2, part 2, pp. 1353–1382.

9. An explanatory note to the Donee Group Report stated that "Inquiries about this report should be made to the National Committee for Responsible Philanthropy, Washington, DC organized in 1976 to follow up on many of the Donee Group concerns," in Filer Commission, *Research Papers*, vol. 1, p. 49.

10. According to one critic, "For twenty years, nearly half of the United Way's support has gone to eight tried and true favorites." See "The Charity Battle," *Newsweek*, May 7, 1979, pp. 33 ff. One of Smith's basic criticisms earlier had been that United Ways tended to give the bulk of their funds to a group of organizations which were "quite well established, well known locally and nationally" and were "almost always noncontroversial." See Smith, "The Role of the United Way," *Research Papers*, vol. 2, part 2, p. 1373–74. This issue is also discussed above, chapter 3.

11. Association of Community Chests and Councils (ACCC) *News Bulletin*, June 1, 1932 (New York: ACCC), p. 7.

12. Indeed, Alvin W. Gouldner has suggested that some secrets are essential to organizational functioning; see Gouldner, "The Secrets of Organizations," in *Social Welfare Forum* (New York: Columbia University Press, 1963), pp. 161–177.

13. Seeley et al., *Community Chest*, p. 367.

14. Seeley et al., *Community Chest*, p. 367, footnote 46.

15. The issue of change is also one of the underlying themes of this book, as outlined above in the introduction. For the Dinerman article, see Beatrice Dinerman, "Community Chests: The Ignorant Philanthropists," *The Nation*, March 30, 1970, pp. 369–72.

16. The author visited Corpus Christi in January 1983. At the time of the site visit, Corpus was a Metro III United Way, and raised $2,806,400 in the previous campaign (1982), or $7.42 per capita (which placed it in the lower third of United Ways in the Metro III category for fund raising per capita). Descriptive background in this section comes from "United Way of the Coastal Bend Long Range Plan" (Draft), January 10, 1983, n.p.

4. ALLOCATIONS TO ALTERNATIVE FUNDS 337

17. Personal observation at site visits and as a staff member of United Way; also by attending staff conferences. Increasingly in the 1980s, large United Ways began to implement a multi-year funding cycle for at least their larger, core agencies, but this was not yet routine.

18. "Issues and Answers, 1983," United Way of Massachusetts Bay (Boston, Mass.), p. 22, unpublished compilation of questions and answers for volunteer and staff use. United Way of America literature after 1985, however, seems to make less of "the citizen review process." For example, the expression is not used in the widely disseminated *Rethinking Tomorrow and Beyond* (UWA, May 1985) where in reference to fund distribution as one of the five core strategies, the expressions used are "a community allocations system" and a "donor allocations program," p. 23.

19. This complaint was heard in interviews and discussions with staff of alternative funds, which also considered the matter at their annual conferences. See also "Testimony of Robert Bothwell, Executive Director of the NCRP," United States House of Representatives, 96th Congress, First Session (October 11, 12, 18, 19, 1979), *Combined Federal Campaign*, (Hearings at the Subcommittee of the Committee on Post Office and Civil Service), p. 66.

20. "United Way of the Coastal Bend Long Range Plan" (Draft), 1983.

21. Based on interviews and observations in Corpus Christi, Texas. The leading Catholic prelate, the Bishop of the community had, in fact, a few years before, withdrawn his support for the United Way in an open controversy about the funding of Planned Parenthood, and funding in that campaign (1980) had accordingly declined; but good will was later restored.

22. This is a reference to the publication of that name put out by the UWA in 1973, which considered the necessities of priority-setting as well as the difficulties it entailed. See above, chapter 3.

23. Susan-Rose Ackerman, "United Charities: Economic Analysis," *Public Policy* (Summer 1980), 28(3): 336. Also based on observation of local United Way reports at staff conferences (1975–1982).

24. San Diego site visit, June 1982; the year before the Planning-Allocations-Research Council (PAR) of the United Way had made the recommendation for a decrease in Red Cross funding and apparently it was modified by the United Way board, after considerable pressure and controversy.

25. A seminal discussion of the nature of federated organizations with reference to the problem of change is found in Martin Rein and Robert N. Morris, *Social Work Practice* (New York: Columbia University Press, 1962), pp. 127–145. Wenocur has considered the problem in depth in relation to the United Way system; see Stanley Wenocur, "Confederation Adaptability to External Change Pressures" (D.S.W. diss., University of California, 1974). Also see above, chapter 1, n. 27.

26. Gabriel Rudney, *A Quantitative Profile of the Non-Profit Sector*, Working Paper #40, Program on Non-Profit Organizations, (New Haven: Yale University, Institution for Social and Policy Studies, 1981), p. 15.

27. Rudney, *"A Quantitative Profile of the Non-Profit Sector,"* p. 16.

28. The Nonprofit Sector Project, Progress Report No. 3, "Serving Community Needs: The Nonprofit Sector in an Era of Governmental Retrenchment" (Washington, D.C.: The Urban Institute, 1983), p. 3.

29. It was also evident in the recommendations of the commission "Broadening the Base of Philanthropy," beginning with recommendation 1, "That to increase inducements for charitable giving all taxpayers who take the standard deduction should also be permitted to deduct charitable contributions as an additional, itemized deduction." See "Commentary on Commission Recommendations," prepared by the

staff of the Commission, in Filer Commission, *Research Papers*, vol. 1, pp. 3–11. For an example of the studies in this connection, see above, n. 6.

30. Examples of each group will be discussed in the text below. See also the discussion of the growth of the Black United Fund movement in King E. Davis, *Fund Raising in the Black Community: History, Feasibility and Conflict* (Metuchen, N.J.: Scarecrow, 1975).

31. The tensions and stresses of this period are encapsulated in a volume of papers compiled by an activist group in San Francisco, the Concerned Citizens for Charity. See Concerned Citizens for Charity (CCC), "The Charity War Papers" (San Francisco, June 1978), unpublished document in the files of the United Way of America, hereafter referred to as "Charity Wars." This organization, which described itself as "a non-profit voluntary association of and for charitable contributors," has since gone out of business.

32. Deborah Kaplan Polivy, *A Study of the Admissions Policies and Practices of Eight Local United Way Organizations* (New Haven: Program on Non-Profit Organizations, Working Paper #49, May 1982), table 1, p. 13, gives seventy-one as the total number of agencies admitted by the San Francisco United Way, and on p. 14 the text states that forty-six of these new agencies were admitted prior to 1975, apparently in response to the New Directions thrust and community pressure.

33. *Changing Times* (Kiplinger Magazine, 1977) reported that "on the average, individual agencies within local United Ways get about 25 percent of their funds from the annual UW Campaign." A slightly smaller figure is indicated for 1974 (22 percent of the year's total budget) according to Herman Levin, who states that the figure came from a senior consultant to the United Way of America; see Levin, "Voluntary Organizations in Social Welfare," *Encyclopedia of Social Work*, 17th ed. (Washington, D.C.: National Association of Social Workers, 1977), vol. 2, p. 1575. According to Joseph McGavrick, a leading United Way volunteer, in 1981–82 only 17 percent of agency budgets came from United Way funding. He made this statement in his remarks to the Volunteer Leaders Conference, Miami, Florida, April 21, 1982 (personal notes of the author). According to the UWA, *1985 Local United Way Allocations to Agencies and Program Services, Metros I–VIII* (Allocation Profiles), the percent averaged around 11 percent.

34. Peter Whitaker, "King Kong Ain't No Ordinary Monkey," *Perspective* (the YMCA journal for professional directors), September 1977; cited in CCC, "The Charity Wars," p. 90. The "no ordinary monkey" is the monkey on one's back, that is, a nuisance or bother.

35. Discussions with local United Way executives; also interviews with staff and volunteers of Jewish agencies.

36. Examples of cross-cutting local funds organized on an industrywide basis existed in both Baltimore and Los Angeles by the early 1960s.

37. See John Naisbitt, *Megatrends: Ten New Directions Transforming Our Lives* (New York: Warner Books, 1984).

38. Disruptions had occurred in San Francisco around the issue of minority funding, and also in connection with the adoption of the New Directions Priority Plan discussed above in chapter 3. For the Los Angeles story, see Davis, *Fund Raising in the Black Community*, pp. 48–62, from which this background material is taken.

39. Davis, *Fund Raising in the Black Community*, pp. 48–49.

40. Davis, ibid., p. 49.

41. Davis, ibid., p. 3.

42. The use of a local citizens group for planning and carrying out of Model Cities Programs was initially a key element of that program in 1969–70.

4. ALLOCATIONS TO ALTERNATIVE FUNDS

43. There are several different versions of the origins of the National Black United Fund (NBUF). See the publication of the New York City Black United Fund, the *BUF Newsline* (Fall 1983) 1(1):1. Also see King E. Davis, "The National Black United Fund: Self-Help for People" (n.d., unpublished manuscript), p. 6. A different date is given for funding of NBUF (1976) with four affiliates (Los Angeles, Detroit, Boston, and Forth Worth) in Patricia Jenkins, "The Black United Fund Movement: An Interview with Walter Bremond and James Joseph," reprint from the *Grantsmanship Center News* (1975), p. 20.

44. Ken Phillips, United Way regional director, March 1977, "The Charity War Papers," p. 49. Much of the background information on the AIDs controversy is to be found in this compilation of documents put together by the Concerned Citizens for Charity, "The Charity Wars Papers."

45. In 1981, an internal United Way document listed AID as one of a few "Isolated and Novel Signals" in a chart analyzing the "Life Cycle of the Donor Designation Issue," but the group in that category also included CFC, and workplace in-plant federations, under the general classification of "Precursor Period: Evidence of Change." Table found in "Donor Designation: An Applications Paper" (Fund Raising and Corporate Relations Division, UWA, June 10, 1981, an internal and confidential draft report), figure 1.

46. Mary Neiswender, "AID Sues United Way in 'Charity Fund' War," *Independent* (Long Beach, California), March 1978, newspaper article reprinted in "The Charity Wars," p. 72.

47. Comment of the editors of "Charity Wars," in relation to "AID vs. United Way: Stipulation and Agreement for Judgment—Excerpts," "Charity Wars," p. 77. However, the newspaper articles and interviews with United Way personnel confirm that this was indeed a "hot" case, and that there was a change of judges.

48. Editors' comments, "Charity Wars," p. 77. Also discussions with United Way staff at the time.

49. "AID vs. United Way: Stipulation and Agreement for Judgement—Excerpts," in "Charity Wars," p. 77.

50. Comprehensive coverage of the AID situation was given by the *Los Angeles Times*. See, for example, John Kendall, "Neither Side Willing to Give in Los Angeles Charity War," *Los Angeles Times*, April 11, 1977. Figures and quote from "AID vs. United Way" (outline of the brief filed March 13, 1978, in Superior Court for Los Angeles County), in "Charity Wars," pp. 67–68.

51. *Donor Option: A Consideration* (UWA, 1982), p. 3.

52. *Donor Option* (UWA, 1982), p. 4.

53. Frequently voiced sentiment by older executives in the larger United Ways, stated in interviews and staff meetings of the time.

54. "Donor Option Resource Packet" (Internal document of the UWA, June 25, 1982), p. 2. Note that the terms "donor designation" and "donor option" are often used interchangeably, although the formal program is generally referred to as a "Donor Option Plan."

55. A commonly asked question in United Way staff circles in the late 1970s.

56. In both of those communities, funding of Planned Parenthood became a lively issue, with the Catholic Church putting a great deal of heat on the United Way *not* to fund the organization, and the newspapers reporting the events in the community.

57. Population and campaign figures from the *1981–1982 International Directory* (UWA, 1981).

58. Amounts of money reported to be available for allocations (1980–1981), given in "The United Way of Southeastern Pennsylvania (A): The Philadelphia Story," case

written by Deborah C. Brown, under the supervision of Professor Thomas J. Raymond of the Harvard Business School, p. 3. It was an attachment to the "Donor Option Resource Packet," June 25, 1982, cited above, n. 54.

59. Brown, "The Philadelphia Story," pp. 4–6.

60. Brown, "The Philadelphia Story," p. 7. The discussion on these pages is based also on extensive interviews in Philadelphia in March 1984.

61. Emma Edmunds, "Faith, Hope and Charity," article about Women's Way, *Philadelphia Inquirer* (Sunday magazine), March 24, 1985.

62. Edmunds, "Faith, Hope and Charity"; Brown, "The United Way of Southeastern Pennsylvania: Post Campaign Review," Part B of the case prepared for Harvard Business School, p. 1, and Part A of the case, "The Philadelphia Story," p. 6–8.

63. Robert W. Reifsnyder, executive director, United Way of Southeastern Pennsylvania, in "The Philadelphia Donor Option Story," address to the 1981 Northeast Regional Staff Conference, March 1981, p. 1, cited in Brown, "The Philadelphia Story," p. 6.

64. A donor option plan was hurriedly installed for the fall 1980 campaign, after it was approved by the United Way Executive Committee on July 23, 1980. Women's Way received $94,000 through the United Way campaign, but the publicity helped it raise money generally. See Edmunds, "Faith, Hope and Charity," and also based on personal interviews.

65. Nan Steketee used her organization to help maintain and support the alternative fund movement in Philadelphia; she was also on the board of the National Committee for Responsive Philanthropy, and has co-authored several articles on the United Way and the alternative fund movement.

66. "Status of Donor Option Programs" (UWA, June 25, 1982; internal United Way document). See also tables in appendixes F.1 and 2a for donor option figures.

5. Donor Option and Controversy in the Combined Federal Campaign

1. "Status of Donor Option Programs," June 1982 (United Way file materials). The forty-five programs included forty-four in communities in the United States, and one pilot program in Canada. The Metro I United Ways communities which had programs in place or about to start in 1982 were Baltimore; Indianapolis; Los Angeles; Miami, Florida; Milwaukee; Orange, California; Philadelphia; Rochester, New York; and Santa Clara, California. By 1985 some form of donor option was also in place in eight more Metro I cities: Buffalo; Columbus, Ohio; Dayton, Ohio; Denver; Kansas City, Missouri; New Orleans; Omaha; Pittsburgh; and Providence, Rhode Island.

2. This will be discussed below in chapter 8. By 1985 both IBM and AT&T had some donor choice for their employees, but the AT&T donor option plan was far more extensive.

3. In earlier programs agencies were not always notified about any specific contribution made to them. Since it did not actually affect agency allocations, there was no incentive for a local United Way to systematize these procedures.

4. Personal observation and discussions with United Way staff for the five-year period 1975–1980. This practice was also part of the history of the early formation of the federated fund-raising movement, and was similar to the methods originally used for fund raising.

5. In these years United Way documents were to some extent equivocating. See, for example, Russy D. Sumariwalla, "Donor Option: Some Thoughts on Future Modeling" (confidential UWA internal document), March 14, 1983; and Russy D. Sumariwalla, "Donor Option Study Committee," confidential document (draft 2), United

5. DONOR OPTION AND CONTROVERSY 341

Way of Massachusetts Bay, July 26, 1983. For later evidence of the effect of a wide-open donor option campaign, see table in Appendix G. According to later studies, the ability to designate does increase employee giving somewhat. See chapters 6 and 9, as well as Karen A. Curtis and Nikomis B. Wood, "Changing Factors in Charitable Campaigns" (report prepared for the Center for Responsible Funding, Philadelphia, The Institute for Public Studies, Temple University, March, 1987), p. 51.

6. See table 5.1. Also discussed in Sumariwalla, "Donor Option," and in the United Way of Massachusetts Bay study, which also points out that all donor option programs have to deal with certain common problems such as eligibility, negative designations, verification processes, limitations on the numbers of options, handling of designated dollars, and administrative procedures and charges.

7. Personal interviews with Steketee and Yeakel. See also "Summary of Donor Option Implementation Committee," Lynn Yeakel, chair, November 13, 1984, United Way of Southeastern Pennsylvania (file notes). In this case, there was also a problem of delays in determining eligibility of one particular agency, Delaware, which according to the summary minutes, might have been postponed for consideration because it was "controversial." See also Violette Phillips, "Divided Way" in *Philadelphia City Paper*, (December 6–13, 1985, issue no. 74). See also discussion of this issue in Richard Cook, Nancy Steketee, and Stanley Wenocur, "Donor Option: A New Strategy to Grassroots Fund Raising," January 1985 (unpublished manuscript).

8. See above, chapter 4. See also for discussion of the United Way allocations process, Susan-Rose Ackerman, "United Charities: An Economic Analysis," *Public Policy*, (Summer 1980), 28(3): 323–350; and the study by David Horton Smith for the Filer Commission, "The Role of the United Way in Philanthropy," in Filer Commission, *Research Papers*, vol. 2, pp. 1353–1382.

9. For an interesting discussion of the earlier stages of the new donor option plans, see Stanley Wenocur, Richard V. Cook, and Nancy L. Steketee, "Fund-Raising at the Workplace," *Social Policy* (spring 1984), 14(4): 55–60. The impact of volunteering on giving is reported in Arthur H. White, Yankelovich, Skelly, and White, *The Charitable Behavior of Americans, Management Summary* (Rockefeller Brothers Fund, 1986).

10. For the discussion of this dilemma, I am indebted to a United Way professional who presented it to me candidly.

11. These groupings of agencies, that is, the National Health Agencies (NHAs), the International Service Agencies (ISAs), the United Way, and the independent American Red Cross, were the historical by-product of the old campaigns run in two world wars, and most particularly in the Second World War.

12. There were at least two major lawsuits filed on this issue; see *National Health Agencies Committee for the Combined Federal Campaign, v. Alan K. Campbell*, (filed December 8, 1979), and *NAACP Legal Defense and Educational Fund v. Donald Devine*, 560 F. Supp. 667 (D.C. 1983).

13. This is evident in all the testimony and from personal interviews, and in fact resulted in the definition of the local management group for the campaign, the PCFO (Principal Combined Fund Organization) being defined in such a way that the only group who could conceivably qualify in most communities would be a local United Way.

14. See, for example, Robert O. Bothwell and Timothy Saasta, "Donor Option: There's Less to It than Meets the Eye." NCRP has continuously monitored donor option, including a series of studies on it. See Dick Cook, "Study of United Way's Donor Option Programs for the National Committee for Responsive Philanthropy," February 4, 1986 (draft).

15. In numerous interviews, corporate executives indicated plainly that they wanted United Way because it represented only *one* campaign, and several executives sug-

gested that while United Way was not perfect, it was the best thing going. Some executives also suggested that any open serious problem in the United Way would be an embarassment for them as well.

16. The White House, Washington, D.C., "Fund-Raising Within the Federal Establishment—Approved Policy and Program," June 27, 1956 (attachment in UCFCA minutes book, 1956–57). See also Executive Order No. 10728, 3 CFR 387 (195401958 Compilations).

17. Foreword by Dwight D. Eisenhower to "Fund-Raising Within the Federal Establishment" (1956).

18. "Fund-Raising Within the Federal Establishment" (1956).

19. This was one of the first shots in a series of continuous battles between the federated fund-raising movement and the federal establishment charged with responsibility for the campaign for federal employees. See "United Fund Advisory Committee Recommendation Concerning Federal Solicitation Plan approved by Board of Directors," December 7, 1956, Attachment C, Minutes of the UCFCA Board of Directors, December 7, 1956.

20. President John F. Kennedy, Executive Order 10927, "Abolishing the President's Committee on Fund Raising Within the Federal Establishment and Providing for the Conduct of Fund Raising Activities," March 18, 1961.

21. Letter from Robert E. Hampton, chairman, U.S. Civil Service Commission to Bayard Ewing, chairman, United Community Funds and Councils of America, May 5, 1970.

22. "Resolution of the Board of Directors, UCFCA, December 6, 1963," UCFCA Minutes Book.

23. "Briefing Paper: Combined Federal Campaign (CPC)," May 6, 1981, United Way of America files.

24. Hampton letter to Ewing, May 5, 1970.

25. Letter from Harry T. Sealy, chairman, executive committee, UCFCA, to Robert F. Hampton, chairman, Civil Service Commission, May 20, 1970, summarizing points made at the meeting of the UCFCA leadership with members of the commission.

26. The question of a nationally dominated campaign versus a locally run campaign was to remain an issue in the CFC. See "Combined Federal Campaign Statement," adopted by participants in Annual Campaign Leaders Conference, New Orleans, La., May 6, 1970.

27. *CFC Manual* (1977), Section 4.2, in *Combined Federal Campaign*, Hearings, (1979), p. 683. The structure was such that these four groups in effect controlled the campaign. See King E. Davis, *Private Charity and the Federal Government: An Analysis and Description of Federal Policy*, January 1, 1976, (unpublished paper), p. 11.

28. *CFC Manual* (1977), sections 5.24 and 5.34, pp. 31–32.

29. *CFC Manual*, (1977), Section 4.7, pp. 17–18. The five years covered in that year would have been 1972–1976.

30. "House Approves a Two-Year Civil Service Authorization: Ends Open-Ended Funding," *Congressional Quarterly Report*, (December 8, 1979), 37(49): 2796.

31. *Combined Federal Campaign*, Hearings (1979), p. 1.

32. See letter from Congresswoman Patricia Schroeder to Alan K. Campbell, director, Office of Personnel Management (OPM), April 11, 1980, in U.S. Congress, House, Committee on Government Operations, Subcommittee on Manpower and Housing, *Executive Orders 12353 and 12404 as They Regulate the Combined Federal Campaign*, Hearing, Part I, 98th Cong., 1st sess., 1983, pp. 17–19.

33. Office of Personnel Management, "Amendment of Manual on Fund Raising Within the Federal Service for Voluntary Health and Welfare Agencies," Notice of

5. DONOR OPTION AND CONTROVERSY   343

Amendments, publication date, April 11, 1980 (Document no 6325–01). Also discussed in Schroeder letter to Alan Campbell, April 11, 1980.

34. In interviews in Denver (1982), local United Way volunteers expressed anger at Congresswoman Schroeder's betrayal of the United Way.

35. *U.S. District Court for the District of Columbia, Benjamin T. Riddles et al. v. Department of the Army*, Civil Action, No. 78-1037, Consent Order, March 16, 1979, in *Combined Federal Campaign* (1979), pp. 736–777.

36. Statement of Benjamin T. Riddles, accompanied by Raymond N. Miller and John C. Sims, in *Combined Federal Campaign*, p. 245.

37. Attachment A to Consent Order, Riddles et al., Department of the Army, March 6, 1979, and Consent Order, section 5, in *Combined Federal Campaign*, Hearings (1979), p. 737.

38. The argument in this paragraph is largely from the discussion in *United Black Fund v. Robert E. Hampton et al.*, 352 F. Supp. 898 (1972).

39. *UBF v. Hampton*, 352 F. Supp. 898.

40. The decision over whether there was discriminatory practice against black groups rested heavily on the finding that there were non-discriminatory *regulations* for membership on the United Fund and Health and Welfare Council boards, but did not even go so far apparently as examining evidence of *actual membership* on those boards, or fund distribution.

41. *UBF v. Hampton*, 352 F. Supp. at 905 (1972). In defining the governmental *function* in the CFC as that of a "proprietor," the court set a significant precedent, by differentiating clearly the CFC as a private charitable drive held in the federal workplace, from the workplace itself, which could be considered a governmental establishment.

42. For a brief recapitulation of this occurrence, see statement of Calvin Rolark, United Black Fund of America, Inc., Attachment B, in *Combined Federal Campaign*, Hearings (1979), pp. 369–370. Eventually there were three different kinds of black fund-raising organizations. There were the Black United Funds (BUFs) which were generally more independent and separatist, and those few (BUFs) that followed the pattern, set by this United Black Fund in Washington, of forming a partnership. (However, at least one BUF, in San Francisco, also became a partner in the United Way campaign, which was a source of some consternation to leadership in the more militant BUF group, according to personal interviews with BUF leaders). There was also (later) Associated Black Charities, which in several cities received funds from the United Way.

43. Discussed in *National Black United Fund v. Donald J. Devine, Director, Office of Personnel Management*, U.S. Court of Appeals for the District of Columbia Circuity No. 80-201, D.C. Civil Action No. 76-01431 (Judgment October 20, 1981).

44. *NBUF v. Devine*, U.S. Court of Appeals (D.C. Circuit, 1981), p. 5.

45. *National Black United Fund v. Alan Campbell*, 494 F. Supp. 748 (D.D.C., 1980), p. 753. In its background discussion the court in this case stated that the chairman suggested that NBUF "negotiate with United Way"; when the case was tried in the Court of Appeals (1981) the court used the phrase "make arrangements to participate in local United Ways."

46. *NBUF v. Campbell*, 494 F. Supp. 748 (D.D.C., 1980).

47. *NBUF v. Devine*, U.S. Court of Appeals (D.C. Circuit, 1981), p. 16.

48. *Village of Schaumburg v. Citizens for a Better Environment*, 444 U.S. 620 (1980). The court argued that limiting charitable appeals to organizations that spent under 25 percent on administrative and fund-raising costs deprived those who spent over 25 percent of rights connected to free speech under the First Amendment to the constitution. The second case was equally significant. According to the United States District

Court Judge Gerhard Gesell, the issue of "vagueness" in standards was defined as critical in *Big Mama Rag v. United States*, 631 F 2d 1030 (D.C. Cir. 1980). See "Memorandum," in *NAACP Legal Defense and Educational Fund and Puerto Rican Legal Defense and Education Fund v. Alan Campbell;* filed by Judge Gerhard Gesell in the United States District Court for the District of Columbia, Civil Actions No. 30-1888 on 30-2070 (January 1981), p. 5.

49. "Key Issues Confronting United Way in the Combined Federal Campaign," May 5, 1981, attachment to "United Way America, Report on Combined Federal Campaign," Paul Miller, chairman of the board of Pacific Lighting Corporation, United Way files, 1981.

50. *NAACP Legal Defense and Educational Fund v. Alan Campbell*, 504 F. Supp. 1365 (D.D.C. 1981). The Puerto Rican Legal Defense and Education Funds and the NAACP Special Contributions Fund were also included as respondents in this case.

51. U.S. Office of Personnel Management, CFC Memorandum, No. 81-1, Subject: 1981–82 Fund Raising Bulletin. The number of twenty new organizations is derived from the author's counting of organizations which were asterisked (*) as being admitted for the first time in the 1981 campaign. This included some direct health services, such as the City of Hope, as well as such advocacy organizations as the NAACP-Legal Defense and Education Fund, the Federally Employed Women Legal Defense and Education Fund, the Native American Rights Fund, and the Puerto Rican Legal Defense and Education Fund, among others, and NBUFs for five cities.

52. Memorandum from Donald J. Devine, director, Office of Personnel Management, to David A. Stockman, director, Office of Management and Budget, "Proposed New Executive Order for the Combined Federal Campaign," October 22, 1981, Attachment A, Section 3(h) in U.S. Congress, House, *Executive Orders 12353 and 12404*, Part I, 1983, pp. 29–32. As of August 1981, United Way was already corresponding with OPM about the content of the president's executive order; see letter from Leo E. Benade, General Council, UWA, to Roger Pilon, Special Assistant to the Director, OPM, August 13, 1981 (UWA files).

53. FR. Doc 82-8279. Executive Order 12353 of March 23, 1982, in the *Federal Register*, vol. 47, 58 (March 25, 1982), pp. 12785–12786.

54. Statement of Rep. Pat Schroeder before Subcommittee on Manpower and Housing of the Committee on Government Operations, on Combined Federal Campaign, March 24, 1983, in U.S. Congress, House, *Executive Orders 12353 and 12404*, Part 1, 1983, p. 11.

55. 5 CRF Part 950 (1982), Sub Part E, Section 501, p. 29506. "Solicitation of Federal Civilian and Uniformed Service Personnel," July 6, 1982. There were also a number of other requirements including, for example, that at least 50 percent of an organization's revenues must have come from other than federal government agencies or that at least 20 percent came from direct or indirect contributions in the year preceding a request for admission. (There was also a year of grace for this requirement) [Section 950.405]).

56. In deciding whether an organization would be the PCFO in the CFC area, the Federal Coordinating Committee for the CFC was to consider: "the number of local charitable voluntary agencies or affiliates that rely on the applicant organization and that meet the prescribed eligibility criteria for . . . the CFC"; "the number of dollars raised by the applicant organization" in its last campaign in the area; "the percentage of dollars dispersed to the charitable voluntary agencies"; "the local capacity . . . to provide the necessary campaign services and administrative support"; and the terms of CFR Part 950 (1982), Section 950.509 (a). This description meant that in most communities only the United Way would qualify. In Baltimore, however, the local form of Combined Health Appeal, the Commerce and Industry Combined Health

6. CHARITABLE CONTROVERSY TO CONGRESSIONAL ACTION 345

Appeal, known as CICHA, threatened to challenge the United Way for PCFO status in the fall campaign of 1985. Although United Ways were selected as the PCFOs in 90.5 percent of all local campaigns in 1983, according to findings reported by the U.S. General Accounting Office, in U.S. Congress, House, Committee on Government Operations, *Fiscal Management of the Combined Federal Campaign,* Report (U.S. GAO, July 29, 1985), challenges to their PCFO status later intensified in major communities and some were successful.

57. 5 CFR Part 950, Section 521.

58. There was a considerable difference of opinion between supporters of the alternative funds, including Congresswoman Schroeder, on the one hand, and the United Way and Dr. Devine on the other, about the significance of these boycotts for the CFC, as distinct from the United Way campaign. See Statement of Schroeder, before Subcommittee on Manpower and Housing, March 24, 1983, in U.S. Congress, House, *Executive Orders 12353 and 12404,* Part 1, 1983, p. 12.

59. "Resolution, Requesting President Reagan to Amend E.O. 12353 Governing Combined Federal Campaign," adopted by the Executive Committee, Board of Governors, United Way of America, September 8, 1982.

60. Letter from Donald V. Seibert, chairman, board of governors, United Way of America, to the president of the United States, September 15, 1982, in U.S. Congress, House, *Executive Orders 12353 and 12044,* Part 1, 1983, p. 248.

61. *NAACP Legal Defense and Educational Fund, Inc., et al., Plaintiffs, v. Honorable Donald J. Devine, Director, U.S. Office of Personnel Management, Defendent,* Civil Action No. 83-0928, Attachment A, Supplemental Affidavit of P. Kent Bailey (program analyst providing staff support to the Deputy Director for Regional Operations, OPM), in U.S. Congress, House, *Executive Orders 12353 and 12044,* Part I, 1983, p. 407. Pat Schroeder cited a figure of 7.5 percent in her statement (*Executive Orders,* Part I, 1983, p. 11), and the "Government Employee Relations Report" used the same figure, citing Robert Bothwell of the NCRP. The most definitive details cited come from the Office of Personnel Management.

62. Delfin figures cited in Karlyn Barker, "Advocacy Groups Protest New Rules Restricting the Federal Charity Drive," *Washington Post,* February 23, 1983.

63. Statement of John Echohawk, executive director, on behalf of the Native American Rights Fund (NARF), in *Executive Orders 12353 and 12044,* Part I, 1983, p. 342. NARF had received 210 rejection letters from local CFCs across the country but many of the others never responded at all, according to Echohawk.

64. 5 CFR Part 950, Section 405(a)(6). A close reading of Section 407(b) suggests that traditional national health agencies which had been previously approved for the campaign historically would also not be held fully accountable for the direct and substantial community presence requirement (that is, the provision of services or benefits to a large number of local federal employees).

65. For the story of these years from the point of view of one of the chief actors, see Donald J. Devine, *Politicizing Charity: A Case Study,* Studies in Philanthropy, no. 2 (Washington, D.C.: Capital Research Center, 1986).

6. From Charitable Controversy to Congressional Action

1. Office of Personnel Management, "Solicitation of Federal Civilian and Uniformed Services Personnel for Contributions to Private Voluntary Organizations" (5 CFR Part 950), Final Rule, *Federal Register,* 47 (July 6, 1982), pp. 29503–29504 (Sect. 405[a] and Sect. 497[d]).

2. "Assault on Charities: Reagan Rules Exclude Organizations from the Combined Federal Campaign," Report by the Alliance for Justice, Washington, D.C., 1984,

346   6. CHARITABLE CONTROVERSY TO CONGRESSIONAL ACTION

pp. 12, 39. Among the "controversial" agencies rejected frequently at the local level were the National Child Labor Committee, the Native American Rights Fund, the National Parks and Conservation Association, and the NAACP-LDF, which reported that it received no notification concerning its admission in 224 of the over 500 campaigns to which it applied.

3. For examples of this extensive correspondance and discussion, see U.S. Congress, House, Committee on Government Operations, Subcommittee on Manpower and Housing, *Executive Orders 12353 and 12404 As They Regulate the Combined Federal Campaign*, Hearing Before the *Committee on Government Operations*, Hearing, Part 1, 98th Cong, 1st. sess., March 24, 1983, pp. 71–171.

4. Letter from Milton J. Socolar, acting comptroller general of the United States, to Honorable Jack Brooks, chairman of the Committee on Governmental Operations of the U.S. House of Representatives, June 24, 1984, in U.S. Congress, House, Committee on Government Operations, *Federal Personnel Should Be Better Informed of How Undesignated Contributions to the CFC Will Be Distributed*, report prepared by the Comptroller General of the United States, U.S. General Accounting Office, June 27, 1984.

5. Personal interviews at San Diego Naval Base with personnel involved in the CFC, June 1982.

6. Office of Management and Budget (OMB), Circular A-122, "Cost Principles for Non-Profit Organizations," Proposed revisions, *Federal Register*, 48 (January 24, 1983) p. 3348.

7. OPM claimed that of the over 48,000 responses and comments received, approximately 31,800 were in support of the proposal, while 16,500 opposed them. See OMB Circular A-122, "Cost Principles for Non-Profit Organizations, Lobbying and Related Matters," *Federal Register* 48 (November 3, 1983), p. 50869. For a discussion of this issue, see also "OMB Backs Off More, Won't Put Revised A-122 Out Now but 'Sometime'," *Association Trends*, March 11, 1983, no. 473.

8. Executive Order 12404, (February 10, 1983), "Charitable Fund Raising," in *Federal Register*, 48, p. 6685. The question raised by Congresswoman Schroeder was part of a series of questions addressed to Devine about the civil service and the CFC. See U.S. Congress, House, Committee on Post Office and Civil Service, Subcommittee on Civil Service, *Civil Service Oversight*, Hearing, 98th Cong., 1st sess., March 9 and 10, 1983, pp. 18–21 and p. 76.

9. Executive Order 10927, issued by President John F. Kennedy, March 18, 1961 stated that "the Chairman of the Civil Service Commission shall make arrangements for such voluntary health and welfare agencies and *such other national voluntary agencies as may be appropriate* to solicit funds from federal employees and members of the armed forces" (emphasis added). Executive Order 10927 cited in "Manual on Fund-Raising Within the Federal Service, for Voluntary Health and Welfare Agencies, CFC," U.S. Civil Service Commission, April 1977.

10. Letter from Donald V. Seibert, chairman, board of governors, United Way of America, to the president of the United States, February 17, 1983. A press release in support of the proposed regulations was also issued on February 10, 1983 by a coalition of twenty-one major "traditional" health and welfare agencies, including American Cancer Society, the American Heart Association, United Way of America, Girl Scouts, the national board of the YWCA and the national YMCA, the National Conference of Catholic Charities, and the Council of Jewish Federations, as well as the March of Dimes Birth Defects Foundation.

11. Also see above, notes 3 and 8. The two hearings of the Subcommittee on Civil Service of the Committee on Post Office and Civil Service, of the U.S. Congress, House, 98th Cong., 1st sess., were held on March 9 and 10, 1983, and were published as *Civil Service Oversight*, serial no. 98-6 (Washington, D.C.: Government Printing

6. CHARITABLE CONTROVERSY TO CONGRESSIONAL ACTION   347

Office, 1983). These hearings dealt with a range of issues related to efforts by the Reagan administration to cut benefits and pay of federal workers. The hearings held by the Subcommittee on Manpower and Housing of the Committee on Government Operations of the U.S. Congress, House, were published as *Executive Orders 12353 and 12404 as They Regulate the Combined Federal Campaign*, 98th Cong., 1st sess., Part 1, March 9 and 10, 1983, and Part 2, June 23 and July 19, 1983.

12. In interviews with key respondents in Washington, it was pointed out that since President Kennedy had started the CFC (1961), Senator Edward Kennedy, the former president's brother, and a colleague of Frank's from Massachusetts, might also have a particular interest in the CFC.

13. Personal interviews in Denver with local businessmen connected with United Way and with congressional staff aides in Washington. With the modifications in the rules of 1980, the American Lung Association became part of the NHA group and was admitted to the CFC. The center of activities for the American Lung Association was Denver. It is important also to note that minority employees were a significant factor in some branches of the civil service, particularly in lower levels of the Postal Field Service, where some of the boycotts of 1981–1983 took place, and of course, Congresswoman Schroeder was chair of the Civil Service Oversight Committee.

14. This point was made by several respondents in personal interviews. In the legislative arena "pro-lifers" could always muster support on a pro-abortion issue, particularly in a conservative climate, while the courts were presumed to be more independent of this pressure. See also U.S. Congress, House, *Civil Service Oversight* (1983).

15. *NAACP Legal Defense and Educational Fund v. Donald Devine*, 567 F. Supp. 401 (D.D.C. 1983).

16. See statement of Donald J. Devine, director, Office of Personnel Management, before the Subcommittee on Manpower and Housing of the Committee on Government Operations, July 19, 1983, in U.S. Congress, House, *Executive Orders 12353 and 12404*, Part 2, 1983, pp. 84–95.

17. *NAACP Legal Defense and Educational Fund v. Alan Campbell*, 504 F. Supp. 1365 (D.D.C. 1981) (NAACP I).

18. 5 CFR Part 950, *Federal Register*, 48 (June 24, 1983), pp. 29458–29462.

19. 5 CFR Part 950, *Federal Register*, 48 (August 1, 1983), p. 34912, sections 950.303 (a) and 950.403 (c) (3)(iv).

20. See preliminary discussion to 5 CFR Part 950, *Federal Register*, 48 (August 1, 1983), p. 34910–34928, and sections 950.501 (d) and 950.403 (1)(6).

21. 5 CFR Part 950, section 501, *Federal Register*, 48 (August 1, 1983), p. 34910.

22. *NAACP Legal Defense and Educational Fund v. Devine*, 567 F. Supp. 401 (D.D.C. 1983).

23. Statement of Devine before the Subcommittee on Manpower and Housing, July 19, 1983, in U.S. Congress, House, *Executive Orders 12353 and 12404*, Part 2, 1983, p. 79.

24. See the language of President Kennedy's Executive Order 10927, March 18, 1961, particularly Section 2 (a), "The Chairman of the Civil Service Commission *shall make arrangements for such voluntary health and welfare agencies* and such other national voluntary agencies . . . *to solicit funds* from Federal employees and members of the armed forces" (emphasis added). By 1977 the CFC Manual stated that "within the basic ground rules established by the Chairman of the Civil Service Commission, the local Federal Coordinating group is authorized to make decisions on all matters on which the voluntary groups cannot agree." Elsewhere the voluntary groups are defined as a local united fund (community chest or other federated group), the NHAs, the ISAs, and the American Red Cross. *Manual on Fund Raising Within the Federal*

Service for Voluntary Health and Welfare Agencies, CFC, U.S. Civil Service Commission, April 1977, chapter 4.6.

25. See *NAACP Legal Defense and Educational Fund v. Donald Devine*, 560 F. Supp. 667 (D.D.C. 1983).

26. Statement of Boris Feldman on behalf of National Coalition to Expand Charitable Giving before the Subcommittee on Manpower and Housing of the Committee on Government Operations, in U.S. Congress, House, *Executive Orders 12353 and 12404*, Part 2, 1983, p. 115.

27. Pointed out by respondents in interviews with author. See also, for example, Dorothy Gilliam, "Fallacy," *Washington Post*, "Metro," February 1, 1982; "How Ideology Drowns Charity," Editorial, *New York Times*, December 23, 1981; Robert O. Bothwell and Timothy Saasta, "What is Charity?" *Grantsmanship News*, March/April 1982, pp. 68–69; Carlyle Murphy, "The Boss, Donald Devine: The Man Federal Workers Love To Hate," *Washington Post Magazine*, April 15, 1984; and Colman McCarthy, "Now They're Going After Charities," *Washington Post*, May 26, 1984.

28. Executive Order 12404 limited the campaign considerably, while Executive Order 12353 appeared to have opened it up more broadly; see above, chapter 5.

29. Originally, Planned Parenthood–World Population was in the CFC as part of the ISA group, which meant that it did not have to show activity in local communities across the country. In 1981 the eligibility of Planned Parenthood–World Population was challenged by Devine, who also stalled admitting the national (U.S.) organization under the new NSA group. See U.S. Office of Personnel Management, CFC Memorandum No. 81-2, Subject: 1981–1982 Fund Raising Bulletin for the Combined Federal Campaign, June 9, 1981 (Section 6, Borderline Cases), and also the Temporary Restraining Order issued in the case of *Planned Parenthood Federation of America et al., Plaintiffs, v. Donald Devine, Defendant*, September 15, 1983, Civil Action No. 83-2118.

30. Letter from Congressman Barney Frank to Donald Devine, director, Office of Personnel Management, September 20, 1983.

31. *NAACP Legal Defense and Educational Fund v. Devine*, 567 F. Supp. 401 (D.D.C. 1983) affirmed, 727 F.2d 1247 (D.C. Cir. 1984).

32. For the regulations, see 5 CFR Part 950, *Federal Register*, 49 (April 13, 1984), p. 14752. See also the extensive discussion of the 1984 regulations at 5 CFR Part 950 in *Federal Register*, 49 (August 16, 1984, pp. 32735–32753), and in U.S. Congress, House, Committee on Government Operations, Subcommittee on Manpower and Housing, *Office of Personnel Management Administration of the Combined Federal Campaign*, Hearing, 98th Cong., 2nd sess., May 15, 1984. (Cited hereafter as *OPM Administration of CFC*.)

33. United Way Board of Governors, *Resolution* Supporting Proposed Rules for Combined Federal Campaign, in U.S. Congress, House, *OPM Administration of CFC*, 1984, p. 248. Local United Ways also were requested to communicate their support of these regulations; see, for example, Memorandum on the Subject of the Combined Federal Campaign, from I. Jerome Stern, President of the United Way of Southeastern Pennsylvania, to Presidents and Executive Directors of Member and Affiliated Agencies, May 15, 1984.

34. "Minority Charities Could Lose $2 Million," *New York Voice*, May 12, 1984.

35. See, for example, Colman McCarthy, "Now They're Going After Charities," *Washington Post*, May 26, 1984.

36. *NAACP Legal Defense and Educational Fund v. Devine*, 567 F. Supp. 401 (D.D.C. 1983) affirmed, 727 F. 2d 1247 (D.C. Cir. 1984).

37. U.S. Congress, House, *OPM Administration of CFC*, May 15, 1984.

38. U.S. Congress, Senate, Committee on Appropriations, *Report to Accompany S. 2853, The Treasury, Postal Service, and General Appropriation Bill, 1985* 98th Cong., 2d sess. (Report 98-562), July 17, 1984, p. 70.

6. CHARITABLE CONTROVERSY TO CONGRESSIONAL ACTION 349

39. See, for example, Steve Farnsworth, "Charities Denounce Federal Drive Rules," *Los Angeles Times,* April 21, 1984, and numerous letters and statements submitted by representatives of the various alternative funds and organizations, including the ISAs, in U.S. Congress, House, *OPM Administration of CFC,* May 15, 1984.

40. "Prepared Statement of James A. Fitzgerald, Jr., Vice Chairman, National Health Agencies," before the Subcommittee on Manpower and Housing of the Committee on Government Operations, in U.S. Congress, House, *OPM Administration of CFC,* May 15, 1984.

41. Statement of Rep. Patricia Schroeder before the Subcommittee on Manpower and Housing of the Committee on Government Operations, in U.S. Congress, House, *OPM Administration of CFC,* May 15, 1986, pp. 6–11. Schroeder was still pushing for a totally open, market-dominated campaign, and she was not a co-signer of a congressional letter sent to the president in protest of the write-in system of designations. See letter to the president of the United States, May 30, 1984, signed by Congressman Jack Brooks, chairman of the Committee on Government Operations and Barney Frank, chairman of the Subcommittee on Manpower and Housing, U.S. House of Representatives, 98th Cong., and including more than 75 other congressional signatures.

42. See discussion, 5 CFR Part 950, *Federal Register,* 49 (August 16, 1984), p. 32736.

43. Statement of Deirne before the Subcommittee on Manpower and Housing, July 19, 1983, in U.S. Congress, House, *Executive Orders 12353 and 12406,* Part 2, 1983, p. 79.

44. See 5 CFR Part 950, *Federal Register* 49 (August 16, 1984), p. 32736.

45. United Way's support for the new rules is expressed in "Statement of Jack Moskowitz, Senior Vice President, United Way of America, before the Subcommittee on Manpower and Housing of the Committee on Government Operations," in U.S. Congress, House, *OPM Administration of CFC,* May 15, 1984, pp. 208–213.

46. Data in this paragraph were provided by OPM directly to the author. See also appendixes G. 1 and 4.

47. Telephone interviews with staff at OPM, United Way of America, and local United Way staff. There was some reluctance, however, on everyone's part to disclose the list of write-in agencies.

48. Interviews with United Way staff. For official evidence of this system for reporting see also UWA, *International Directory, 1986* (Alexandria, Va., 1985), "Amount Raised and Population Figures," covering campaign year 1984 (unpaginated).

49. See, for example, Minutes of the Executive Committee of the United Way of America, September 8, 1982, where William Aramony (president) makes this point explicitly: "Originally the IAM action (in the Boycott) was taken in the *evidently mistaken belief* that the CFC is a United Way campaign" (emphasis added).

50. *Loretta Cornelius, Acting Director, OPM Petitioner v. NAACP Legal Defense and Educational Fund, Inc. et al.* Argued February 19, 1985. Decided July 2, 1985. 53 LW 5116. Justice O'Connor delivered the opinion of the court in which Chief Justice Berger, Justice White, and Justice Rehnquist joined; Justices Blackmun and Brenner filed a joint dissenting opinion; and Justice Stevens filed a separate dissenting opinion. The two remaining justices were not part of the opinion process in this case.

51. *Loretta Cornelius v. NAACP Legal Defense and Educational Fund,* 105 S. Ct. 3439 (1985) rev'g. 727 F. 2d 1247 (1984). The opinions of the three dissenting justices suggested that excluding controversial agencies from the campaign did not appear to be reasonable and could be construed as "viewpoint discrimination."

52. See 5 CFR Part 950, *Federal Register,* 50 (August 22, 1985), p. 33962. Note that write-in designations were to be eliminated as well.

53. See *Responsive Philanthropy,* Newsletter of the National Committee for Responsive Philanthropy, Fall 1985, pp. 5–6.

6. CHARITABLE CONTROVERSY TO CONGRESSIONAL ACTION

54. Cited in "Victory! Activist Charities Will Get Federal Work Gifts for the Campaign," *Responsive Philanthropy*, Fall 1985, p. 5.
55. U.S. Congress, Senate, Committee on Government Affairs, *Nomination of Constance J. Horner, to be the Director of the Office of Personnel Management*, Hearing, 99th. Cong., 1st sess., July 30, 1985 (Washington, D.C.: U.S. Government Printing Office, 1985).
56. U.S. Congress, Senate, Committee on Appropriations, *Report to Accompany H.R. 3036, Treasury, Postal Service and General Appropriations Bill, 1986* 99th Cong., 1st sess. (Report 99-1337), p. 59. The bill was passed by the Senate, but was no longer necessary at that point because of the agreement made along with Horner's confirmation.
57. Data supplied by OPM. See appendix G1 and G4.
58. The figure of 2,330,000 comes from *Giving USA: Estimates of Philanthropic Giving in 1985 and the Trends They Show* (New York: AAFRC Trust for Philanthropy, 1986), p. 78. According to United Way figures (August 1986) the campaign that year registered a 9.0 percent increase over the previous year.
59. Data supplied by the OPM and UWA. For discussion of market share, see UWA, "Highlights, 1985–86 Analysis of the Combined Federal Campaign," UWA, Research Division, August 1986.
60. Interview with OPM staff, NCRP, and United Way staff. NCRP was instrumental in producing brochures for national social action organizations and some local organizations in 1984 and 1985, particularly in the Washington area.
61. Data and analysis of these trends comes from "Highlights, 1985–86 Analysis of the Combined Federal Campaign." I am also indebted to Robert Bothwell for suggesting the implications of the mandated listings of agencies funded in the previous year's campaign.
62. See U.S. Congress House, *Federal Personnel Should Be Better Informed*, Report prepared by The Comptroller General, June 27, 1984, and U.S. Congress, House, Committee on Government Operations, *Fiscal Management of the Combined Federal Campaign*, Report, U.S. General Accounting Office, July 29, 1985.
63. See U.S. Congress, House, *Fiscal Management of the Combined Federal Campaign*, 1985, p. 2. Interviews with OPM and United Way staff indicated problems of data collection, particularly aggravated by the difficulties of dealing with write-ins, which were often illegible. OPM indicated that amounts collected for the CFC of 1985 were still being adjusted as of January 1987.
64. *NAACP Legal Defense and Educational Fund et al. v. Constance Horner* and *Planned Parenthood Federation of America v. Constance J. Horner*, Civil Action No. 83-0928 and Civil Action No. 86-1367, *Memorandum Opinion* and *Order* for a preliminary injunction, May 30, 1986.
65. The amendment, referred to by Bothwell as the "Hoyer-Hatfield Amendment," was proposed in the Senate by Senator Dennis De Concinni (a Democrat from Arizona) and included in the Urgent Supplemental Appropriations Act for Fiscal Year 1986, P.L. 99-349 (HR 4515), Title II, section 204, signed into law by President Reagan on July 2, 1986. This law essentially made the injunction—and legal action—moot at that point.
66. Public Law 99-591, Continuing Appropriations, Fiscal Year 1987, Title VI, Sections 618 and 619, signed into law by President Reagan, October 30, 1986.
67. Personal comment to author, fall 1986.

7. Corporate Responsibility and the United Way

1. The emergence of charity in America is discussed generally in chapter 1. For other discussion of business involvement in early organized charity specifically, see Scott M. Cutlip, *Fund Raising in the United States: Its Role in America's Philanthropy* (New Brunswick, N.J.: Rutgers University Press, 1965), pp. 69–74; Morrell Heald, *The Social Responsibilities of Business* (Cleveland: Case Western Reserve University, 1970), pp. 117–145; Roy Lubove, *The Professional Altruist* (New York: Atheneum, 1969), pp. 180–182; William D. Norton, *The Cooperative Movement in Social Work* (New York: MacMillan, 1927), pp. 62–82; John R. Seeley et al., *Community Chest* (Toronto: University of Toronto, 1957), pp. 15–20; and Walter Ufford, General Secretary of the Baltimore Federated Charities, "Methods of Raising Funds for a Charitable Society," in *Proceedings of the Thirty-Third Annual Conference of Charities and Corrections* (Philadelphia, May 9–16, 1906), pp. 213–222.

2. See above, chapter 1. See also discussion of Cleveland's early history as a federation in Herbert Hewitt Stroup, *Community Welfare Organization* (New York: Harper and Brothers, 1952), pp. 368–369; and Frank Dekker Watson, *The Charity Organization Movement in the United States: A Study in American Philanthropy* (New York: Macmillan, 1922), pp. 29, 44.

3. F. Emerson Andrews, *Corporation Giving* (New York: Russell Sage Foundation, 1952), pp. 29–30.

4. Andrews, *Corporation Giving*, p. 28; P. Williams and F. E. Croxton, *Corporation Contributions to Organized Community Welfare Services* (New York: National Bureau of Economic Research, 1930); and Heald, *Social Responsibilities of Business*, pp. 117–147.

5. Marion R. Fremont-Smith, *Philanthropy and the Business Corporation* (New York: Russell Sage Foundation, 1972), pp. 7–13; Heald, *Social Responsibilities of Business*, pp. 83–116.

6. Heald, *Social Responsibilities of Business*, pp. 128–129.

7. See also Chapter 1, note 24. This case, *Corning Glass Works v. Lucas, Commissioner of Internal Revenue* (37 F.2d 798) is also discussed in Heald, *Social Responsibilities*, pp. 158–159. The later case, American Rolling Mill Co., was decided in the U.S. Circuit Court of Appeals, Sixth Circuit, June 11, 1930. There the court held that contributions to a civic improvement fund were deductible as business expenses but were not allowable as a "charitable deduction" and were "not deductible from corporation's taxable income," citing the Revenue Act of 1918, sections 214(a)(11), 234(a)(1). See *American Rolling Mill Co. v. Commissioner of Internal Revenue*, 41 F.2d 314. For evidence of the concern of the chests see their discussion of this latter case in ACCC, *News Bulletin*, January 20, 1931, pp. 3–4.

8. This was the opinion of a leading businessman connected with the chest, as indicated in ACCC, *News Bulletin*, January 20, 1931, pp. 3–4.

9. *Old Mission Portland Cement Co. v. Helvering, Commissioner of Internal Revenue*, 293 U.S. 289 (1934) affirming 69 F.2d 676 (9th Cir. 1934).

10. For discussion of the events of this period and the relationship between business leaders and chest officials in securing this law (from two somewhat different points of view), see Cutlip, *Fund Raising*, pp. 324–326, and Heald, *Social Responsibilities*, pp. 148–173.

11. Andrews, *Corporation Giving*, pp. 35–39, and Cutlip, *Fund Raising*, pp. 329–330. See also appendix A "Fund Raising Record of United Way Campaigns United States and Canada—1919–1976."

12. Andrews, *Corporation Giving*, p. 158.

13. "Yardstick for Donations," *Business Week*, September 26, 1936, p. 26. The proposed formula is also discussed in Heald, *Social Responsibilities*, pp. 177–190.

14. Under Section 157 of this act, employees have the right to self-organization and also have the right to refrain from such activities except where expressly authorized as a condition of employment. Section 157 also mentions the right "to engage in other concerted activities for the purpose of . . . mutual aid or protection," for which workers shall have "full freedom of association [and] self-organization."

15. The original provisions of the Taft-Hartley Act, while still protecting the rights of workers to organize, at the same time limited the potential for closed shops. See Taft-Hartley Act, Ch. 120, Title I, Section 101, 61 Stat. 140 and 61 Stat. 139. (Current versions at 29 USC Section 157 and 153 [a].) For discussion of later implications of NLRB decisions on charitable organization, see below, chapter 8.

16. *A. P. Smith Mfg. Co. v. Barlow* (13, N.J. 145, 160–161), 98 A.2d, quotation at 590. In holding that a corporation could give a donation to Princeton University, the New Jersey Supreme Court definitively set aside the "direct benefit" rule. See Fremont-Smith, *Philanthropy and the Business Corporation*, pp. 11–13; and Cutlip, *Fund Raising*, pp. 513–514.

17. Ralph L. Nelson, *Economic Factors in the Growth of Corporation Giving* (New York: National Bureau of Economic Research and Russell Sage Foundation, 1970), p. 75.

18. Based on extensive interviews with corporate contributions managers and personal observation at meetings with philanthropists in the years 1982–1986. See also Eleanor Brilliant and Kimberlee Rice, "Influencing Corporate Philanthropy," in Gary Gould and Michael Smith, eds., *Social Work in the Workplace*, pp. 299–313 (New York: Springer 1988). See also Council on Foundations, *Corporate Philanthropy: Philosophy, Management, Trends, Future, Background* (New York, 1982); and many publications on this issue by the Conference Board, including Kathryn Troy, *The Corporate Contributions Function*, Report No. 820 (New York: The Conference Board, 1982); Anne Klepper and Selma Mackler, *Screening Requests for Corporate Contributions*, Report No. 887 (New York: The Conference Board, 1986).

19. I am indebted to Anne Klepper of the Conference Board for pointing this out to me. See chapter 9 for further discussion.

20. By 1970, according to Conference Board figures, the category of civic (and community) was receiving 8.1 percent of corporate contributions of the reported contributions of major corporations, compared to under 4 percent in 1960. This percentage continued to increase during the 1970s, leveling off in 1979. See table 9.1 (chapter 9). Note also that some corporate groups were more directly sensitive to the situation of the 1960s because of their own investment in the cities. For example, according to one study, in September 1967, "the Life Insurance Association of America announced that its member companies had pledged to invest one billion dollars to bring housing and employment to the nation's slums." See Karen Orren, *Corporate Power and Social Change: The Politics of the Life Insurance Industry* (Baltimore, Md.: Johns Hopkins, 1984), p. 1.

21. See *Giving USA: Philanthropic Giving in 1985*, 31st annual issue (New York: AAFRC Trust for Philanthropy, 1986), pp. 39–51, for history and trends of giving in that period. For figures on federation/health and welfare giving see *Annual Survey of Corporate Contributions, 1982 Edition*, Report No. 822, The Conference Board, pp. 30–31.

22. Slightly different figures are used by Thomas Vasquez, "Corporate Giving Measures." In this contribution to the *Research Papers* (Filer Commission), 1977, vol. 3, pp. 1839–1852, he also emphasizes the overall *increase* in contributions from a few large corporations, which indicates that corporations might have taken into account the declining share of contributions by *individuals*. See below, chapter 9. Figures cited here come from Virginia Ann Hodgkinson and Murray S. Weitzman, *Dimensions of the*

7. CORPORATE RESPONSIBILITY AND UNITED WAY   353

Independent Sector: A Statistical Profile (Washington, D.C.: Independent Sector, 1986), table 3.46, p. 93. Their figures also rely extensively on compilations of the Conference Board.

23. See *Giving in America: Toward a Stronger Voluntary Sector* (Filer Commission, 1975), pp. 15–16. See also the highly influential studies done by Ralph Nelson for the Commission, including "Giving in the American Economy, 1960–1972" and "Analysis of Trends in Giving Since 1960," in *Research Papers*, (Filer Commission, 1977), vol. 1, pp. 115–134.

24. *Giving in America: Toward a Stronger Voluntary Sector* (Report of the Commission on Private Philanthropy, 1975), p. 154.

25. *Giving in America*, pp. 103–114. Numerous studies and reports utilized to reach this conclusion are cited on p. 115 following the summary discussion in that report. For analysis of the implications of tax considerations for charitable contributions, see Martin S. Feldstein and Charles Clotfelter, "Tax Incentives and Charitable Contributions in the United States: A Microeconometric Analysis," in *Research Papers* (Filer Commission), vol. 3, pp. 1393–1417.

26. See also the discussion in regard to the CFC in chapters 5 and 6 above, and earlier history of the chest-fund movement, in chapter 2. This point was also made by a number of key respondents inside the United Way system, both locally and nationally. The minutes for the years preceding the change (1968–69) suggested the degree to which United Way professionals were dominating policy discussions at the board level. See also the change in the by-laws of United Way of America, article 8 (1970) referring to the directors, "all of whom shall be volunteers."

27. Interviews in the United Way system and personal observation.

28. The author observed this situation for herself when she passed miles of automobile plants idle in the industrial stretch between Toledo and Detroit. For data on this phenomenon, see U.S. Department of Labor, Bureau of Labor Statistics, *Handbook of Labor Statistics*, Bulletin 2217 (June 1985), Table 30, "Unemployed Persons and Unemployment Rates by Industry, 1948–83," pp. 76–77. Although 1983 was regarded as a year of relative recovery, in August 1983 predominantly smokestack cities were still reporting heavy unemployment. The United Way, however, noted that despite continuing adverse conditions many United Ways in these communities had outstanding campaigns. See "Campaigning in 1983: Amounts Raised in a Climate of Economic Recovery. Final Results, Local United Ways Raising Over $2 Million" (UWA, Research Division, April 1984).

29. Thought-provoking discussions of this issue include Earl F. Cheit, "The New Place of Business: Why Managers Cultivate Social Responsibility," in Cheit, *The Business Establishment* (New York: John Wiley, 1964); Milton Friedman, "Does Business Have a Social Responsibility?" *Bank Administration*, April 1971, pp. 13–14; Ronald S. Burt, "Corporate Philanthropy as a Cooptive Relation," *Social Forces* (December 1983), 62(2):419–449; C. Lowell Harris, "Corporate Giving: Rationale, Issues and Opportunities," in *Research Papers* (Filer Commission, 1977), vol. 3, pp. 1789–1825; and Marvin Olasky, "Corporate Givers Beware," *Wall Street Journal*, June 28, 1985, p. 22. For literature arguing the pros and cons of corporate giving, and the variety of motivations involved, see, for example, David R. Farber, *Corporate Philanthropy: An Annotated Bibliography* (Chicago, Ill.: Donors Forum, 1982), and Seth M. Lahn, *Corporate Philanthropy: Issues in the Current Literature*, Working Paper no. 29 (Yale University, Program on Non-Profit Organizations, n.d.).

30. Kenneth N. Dayton, "Five Percent: An Insurance Policy for the Free Enterprise System," *Response* (January 1981), 10(1):15–16; James N. Morgan, Richard F. Dye, and Judith H. Hybels, "Results from The National Surveys of Philanthropic Activity," in *Research Papers* (Filer Commission, 1977), vol. 1, pp. 157–323; Nelson, *Economic*

Factors; Hayden W. Smith, *A Profile of Corporate Contributions* (New York: The Council for Financial Aid to Education, 1983); and Thomas Vasquez, "Corporate Giving Measures," *Research Papers.*

31. This is implied by many of the authors cited above in note 1. See, e.g., Lubove, *The Professional Altruist;* Heald, *The Social Responsibilities of Business;* and Norton, *The Cooperative Movement in Social Work.*

32. Although it is often argued that the overlapping board membership of agencies with local United Ways causes conflicts of interest, it can also be argued that it facilitates understanding of social service needs and agency roles between agency and funding source.

33. The program was featured in materials publicizing the United Way Centennial Volunteer Leaders Celebration (Washington, D.C., April 1987), and literature distributed in connection with the Second Century Initiative. See, for example, discussion of the National Corporate Development Program (NCD) and the single communitywide campaign, in *A Vision of Service* (UWA, 1987). The NCD, now renamed the National Corporate Leadership Program, was highlighted in the address of Richard J. Ferris, chairman-elect of the UWA, at the Centennial Volunteer Leaders Conference, on April 28, 1987.

34. United Way literature, and campaign manuals, all stress this kind of information as relevant to giving, and it is included as part of the data supplied by the UWA research division in their *Leaderboard* and other corporate giving information in connection with annual campaign performance analysis. The influence of these factors and others in one community were also discussed by Joseph Galaskiewicz in *Social Organization of the Urban Grants Economy: A Study of Business Philanthropy and Nonprofit Organizations* (New York: Academic, 1985). For an in-depth discussion of this process from the United Way viewpoint see Dennis J. Murphy, *Corporate Contributions: Understanding the Decision-Making Process* (UWA, 1982).

35. Stated repeatedly in personal interviews. See also Eleanor L. Brilliant and Kimberlee A. Rice, "Influencing Corporate Philanthropy," in *Social Work in the Workplace,* Gary M. Gould and Michael L. Smith, eds., pp. 299–313 (New York: Springer, 1988).

36. Respondents at several corporations, including IBM, Ciba-Geigy, and Pfizer Chemical Company, noted this.

37. Such sweepstake prizes of course vary greatly. The grand prize of the 1982 campaign at Seagrams was a 1982 Subaru automobile, and departments that had 100 percent participation of employee giving or achieved their goals also received a "bonus" of a day off for their employees. (Respondent inside Seagram; also cited in Seagram/United Way *Newsletter,* October 1982, p. 1).

38. See Deborah Kaplan Polivy, *Increasing Giving Options in Corporate Charitable Payroll Deduction Programs: Who Benefits?* PONPO Working Paper no. 83 and ISPS Working Paper no. 2083 (New Haven: Yale University, January 1985). Polivy discusses in-plant federations as one kind of option for employee giving, but does not analyze the reasons why these in-plant federations generally tend to be United Way–dominated.

39. They were apparently discussed in the early 1950s by the CCCA, which had mixed opinions. See, for example, *Experiments with More Inclusive Federation* (New York: CCCA, 1951), and *A Plan To Eliminate All Drives and Solicitations Within Your Place of Business Through a Community Services Fund* (Phoenix, Arizona: Phoenix Endorsement Council, n.d.). They are also mentioned in Seeley, *Community Chest,* p. 380.

40. That is, they have boards and committees specifically for this purpose. See also Polivy, *Increasing Giving Options* (1985), for a discussion of one in-plant federation.

7. CORPORATE RESPONSIBILITY AND UNITED WAY 355

The best available discussion of how they function may, however, still be the old one given by the CCCA, *Experiments with More Inclusive Federation* (1951).

41. Chester Burger and Company, "A Study of Employee-Donation Philanthropy and Policy Recommendations," prepared for American Telephone and Telegraph Company, July 1982. Knowledge of General Electric Federation and Boeing also derived from personal interviews.

42. In effect, while recognizing the existence of employee clubs, critics of United Way concentrate on the importance of offering alternative federations or choices to employees, and *underplay* the fact that in actuality the employee in many corporations already has the possibility of choice through the mechanism of the in-plant federation.

43. Problems with the airlines industry and Boeing sales, and the success of the BEGNF campaign in terms of percentage of employees, are noted in two articles in *Boeing News*, "Boeing Has 9-months Earnings of 201M" and " 'All Together Now' Effort—Record BEGNF Boost," *Boeing News* (October 28, 1982), 41(43):1. Boeing net earnings were reported down to $201 million in 1982 from $377 million in 1981, corresponding to a decrease in sales. At the same time the percentage of Boeing employees participating in BEGNF had grown 13.9 percent after seven weeks of the eight-week campaign. By November 4, 1982, the *Boeing News* reported participation up by 16.7 percent.

44. Census figures from United States Bureau of the Census, *County and City Data Book, 1983* (Washington, D.C.: U.S. Government Printing Office, 1983), "County Area and Population, Table B," p. 592. See also United Way of King County, "Strategic Plan, 1982" (December 17, 1981), which gives the following numbers for 1982: Spanish surname, 32,800; black, 49,000; native American, 12,000; and Asian, 54,500.

45. Observations of the author at site visit; also interviews with key respondents.

46. The United Way of King County in Seattle had developed within the United Way a mini-board and staff structure called COPA, Council of Planning Affiliates. This group apparently took over many of the functions formerly performed by the health and welfare council of the Seattle area. Interviews with local government officials made it plain that they still considered COPA an important ally in public policy matters.

47. Boeing employment figures fluctuate greatly, according to airplane orders, but one Boeing respondent reported that in 1987 Boeing had about 85,000 employees in the Puget Sound area (which covers more than King County) and that the next private employer only had close to 10,000 employees. There were 18,974 federal civilian employees in King County according to the 1980 census. See also "United Way of King County, 1982 Marketing Plan" approved by United Way of King County Board of Directors, December 17, 1981.

48. Eleanor L. Brilliant, "United Way at the Crossroads," in *The Social Welfare Forum, 1982–1983* (Washington, D.C.: National Conference on Social Welfare, 1985), pp. 250–262. See also "Project Transition," Report of the Project Transition Committee, Seattle, 1982.

49. Personal interviews; see also "Alternative Fund Statistics," National Committee for Responsive Philanthropy, February 1988, Table 5A, Payroll Deduction Revenues from Direct Access Campaigns. The Women's Funding Alliance had raised $42,000 in two public workplace campaigns in 1987, none in private sector campaigns.

50. Telephone interview with key respondent, in Boeing, December 1986.

51. See chapter 5 above. Story about IAM and Boeing is based on interviews with key respondents at the time of the site visit (August 1982) and after. See also "16.7 BEGNF Member Increase During Campaign," *Boeing News*, November 4, 1982, and "BEGNF responds to IAM Boycott of United Way," *Boeing News* (September 16, 1982), vol. 41, no. 37.

7. CORPORATE RESPONSIBILITY AND UNITED WAY

52. Figures supplied by the United Way of King County.
53. Letter from Lois E. Knutson, president, BEGNF board of trustees to President Ronald Reagan, dated September 3, 1982, quoted in "BEGNF Responds to IAM Boycott of United Way," *Boeing News*, September 16, 1982.
54. This is a well-known general representation. For specific discussion of some personnel policies in IBM, see Thomas J. Peters and Robert H. Waterman, *In Search of Excellence: Lessons from America's Best-Run Companies* (New York: Warner Books, 1982), pp. 122, 312. See also discussion of IBM personnel practices, and citation of Professor Fred K. Foulkes, called as an expert witness in the case against IBM, *Equal Employment Opportunity Commission, International Business Machine Corporation*, 583 F. Supp. 875 (1984), pp. 902–903.

8. Changing the Rules of the Game: Corporate Response to Challenge

1. Interviews with United Way personnel, and discussed above, chapter 3. See also numerous newspaper articles; for example, "United Way Accused of Monopolizing Donations," *Los Angeles Herald Examiner*, March 14, 1978, cited in Concerned Citizens for Charity (CCC), *The Charity Wars*, June 1978 (compilation of documents), p. 72. Jerrold B. Thorper, president of AID, was quoted as saying that AID had lost 182 accounts.
2. J. Robert Flour, chairman of the 1976–77 United Way drive in Los Angeles County, is quoted in CCC, *The Charity Wars*, p. 51, with remarks made at a March 5, 1977 reception for United Way volunteers.
3. Interviews with United Way personnel and with David Johnston, reporter for the *Los Angeles Times*, and narrative supplied to the author by Johnston. During the late 1970s and through the mid-1980s, the United Way of Los Angeles included in its leadership numerous high officials of major companies in the Los Angeles area. David Johnston cited these individuals in a series of articles dealing with irregularities in the use of funds in the Los Angeles–area United Way, and in personal interviews with the author he also noted the reluctance of the corporate executives to face problems of the United Way. For one discussion of corporate reaction when finally forced to recognize the situation, see David Johnston, "United Way Chief Orders Two Executives to Repay Loans," *Los Angeles Times*, Sunday, June 8, 1986. On July 2, 1986, Johnston was removed from coverage of the United Way and the Charity "beat." In the spring of 1988, he went to work at the *Philadelphia Inquirer*.
4. *California State Combined Health Agencies v. United Way of Santa Clara County*, Superior Court of the State of California, County of Santa Clara (Docket No. 382-156). The Superior Court in Santa Clara County decided in favor of the United Ways. See also Internal Memorandum to United Way Executive Directors, from Bill Aramony, on the Subject "New Information Materials," September 25, 1979, p. 8 and accompanying fact sheet on Combined Health Agencies Drive (CHADs); also, Raul Ramirez, "United Way Sued by Rival Fund Raisers," *San Francisco Examiner*, August 17, 1977, p. 4.
5. The confidential memorandum is to be found in CCC, *Charity Wars*, pp. 36–40, and is decidedly pro–United Way. It should however also be noted that in the same materials, *Charity Wars*, there are numerous documents citing opposition to United Way's "take-over of the AID campaigns," as, for example, memo to telephone industry employees, from E. A. King, President, Local 11590 (Western Electric), on the subject of the Union Boycott of United Way, October 12, 1977 (*Charity Wars*, p. 62).
6. This is discussed above in chapter 4. Sources for this information came from personal interviews with the author, and from the memo to Gerald O. Kennedy from

8. CORPORATE RESPONSE TO CHALLENGE 357

Brian P. Moore, executive of CHA, "History of the United Way with CHA of the National Capital Area; As Well As Experiences of Other CHA's with Respective United Way Organizations," March 12, 1984. The acronym "CHAD" is used throughout, although the group used different names at different times and places.

7. See Memorandum to state executives, "United Way/American Cancer Society Relationships," from Robert M. Beggan, March 1, 1984, which indicates that ACS refers to the relationship between the two organizations as an "Educational and Fund Raising Agreement." "The relationship is reported to be broader than funding. It is through cancer 'education' cooperation that added benefits accrue to the community and the United Way." In another file document, "United Way and Health: *One of Our Best Kept Secrets*," the author notes that "national market research indicates that 48% of those currently giving would give more if we [United Way] were heavier in health" (n.d., supplied to author by respondent in United Way in 1984). For discussion of the problem of definition of "educational" in relation to non-profit organizations in the "Big Mama Rag" case (1980), see below in this chapter.

8. It seems local United Ways on the whole did not benefit from contractual relationships with that organization. According to United Way data, for example, in 1983, comparison of thirty-two United Ways with AHA agreements and those without in Metros I–IV revealed that those with AHA agreements did less well in increasing amounts raised (9.1 percent increase over the 1982 campaign) in comparison with those without AHA agreements (9.4 percent over the 1982 amount raised). "Summary, United Ways with American Heart Association (AHA) Contracts" (United Way of America, Research Division, March 1984, file material).

9. See chapter 3 above.

10. According to United Way respondents, the United Airline change was largely due to the efforts of Tanya Glazebrook, the first female campaign director in a Metro I United Way (the San Francisco, Bay Area United Way), who later became the first female executive director of a Metro I United Way, the United Way of Greater Miami. For discussion of the Crocker Bank history see also Deborah K. Polivy, *Increasing Giving Options in Corporate Charitable Deduction Programs: Who Benefits?* PONPO Working Paper no. 83 and ISPS Working Paper no. 2083 (New Haven: Yale University, January 1985).

11. See United Way of the Bay Area, "A Time for Leadership," Report of the Strategic Planning Committee, May 1982, pp. 33–35.

12. *United Black Fund (UBF) v. Hampton* 352 F. Supp. 898 (1972). See also discussion above, chapter 5.

13. Major credit for the initial growth and development of the BUF movement must be given to King Davis for the philosophic underpinnings, and to Walter Bremmond for activating and implementing the organization. See chapter 4 above.

14. *Lew Moye et al. v. Chrysler Corporation*, 465 F. Supp 1189 (E.D. Mo. 1979) affirmed U.S. Court of Appeals, Eighth Circuit.

15. Letter from Roderick DeArment, attorney with Covington and Burling, to John E. Higgins, Esq., deputy general counsel, National Labor Relations Board, September 30, 1976.

16. DeArment letter to John E. Higgins (September 30, 1976), pp. 1 and 2. Letter is attached as Exhibit A to Affidavit of Leo E. Benade, in support of the Motion of United Way of America to Modify or To Set Aside the Board's Decision and Order, in Case No. 11-CA-8232, Hammary Manufacturing Corporation, A Division of U.S. Industries, Inc. and Upholsterers' International Union of North America, AFL-CIO (motion filed by John S. Koch and Douglas S. Abel, Covington and Burling, attorneys for United Way of America, January 15, 1982, before the National Labor Relations Board, Washington, D.C.).

8. CORPORATE RESPONSE TO CHALLENGE

17. See "Memorandum to Executive Directors of United Ways (Metros I–V), State Organizations, and Regional Vice Presidents, Leo E. Benade, General Counsel of the United Way of America, Re *'No-solicitation rules'* " (December 18, 1981). Benade states: "The Hammary case represents a distinct departure from prior decisions of the NLRB and the courts."

18. The arguments in relation to this issue are discussed extensively in the UWA Motion in the Hammary Manufacturing case (January 15, 1982), referred to above, footnote 16. See also Second Supplemental Motion in Response to Motion for Reconsideration, Case No. 11-CA-8232, (the Hammary case), filed by William A. Lubbers, general counsel of the NLRB, February 12, 1982.

19. Note that there may be some parallel issues in relation to raising funds for PACs and for in-plant federations, such as who controls the funds. With in-plant federations, the employee group, and *not* the corporation or the United Way, appears to control the funds initially.

20. This opinion, commonly stated by respondents (even within the companies), was not always said with disapproval, but with respect for the company's socialization process and benefits, etc. Both companies have been discussed in relation to enlightened employee policies and morale. For IBM, see, for example, Frank Koch, *The New Corporate Philanthropy* (New York: Plenum, 1981), pp. 29, 57, and David W. Ewing, *Freedom Inside the Corporation* (New York: Dutton, 1977), p. 133.

21. Benade *Affadavit*, January 12, 1982, attached to UWA Motion concerning Hammary Case (January 15, 1982), pp. 2–3.

22. The well known labor law reporting service is not named, but the quote cited by DeArment refers to the decision in C. G. Murphy Co., 213 NLRB No. 31 (1974), and is cited on page 3 of the Benade *Affadavit*.

23. Benade *Affadavit*, p. 3.

24. Benade *Affadavit*, pp. 3–4.

25. *City of Charlotte et al. v. Local 660, International Association of Firefighters, et al.*, 426 US 283, 48 L Ed 2d 636, 96 S Ct 2036 (decided June 7, 1976), at 637.

26. *City of Charlotte et al. v. Local 660*, at 641.

27. Marshall's opinion stated that "respondents have wholly failed . . . to present any reasons why the present standards are not fair and reasonable—other than the fact that the standards exclude them."

28. Among sources for this, see John Naisbitt, *Megatrends* (New York: Warner Books, 1984), pp. 201–203; and David W. Ewing, *Freedom Inside the Organization*. See also numerous cases in this chapter involving issues raised in relation to equal opportunity (IBM and AT&T), and rights for solicitation at the workplace before the NLRB.

29. Cases cited in Lubber's *Second Supplemental Motion* and in the UWA *Motion to Modify or Set Aside the Board's Decision* in the Hammary case (January, 1982).

30. Memorandum from Leo E. Benade to Local United Ways, December 18, 1981.

31. Hammary Manufacturing Corporation, a Division of U.S. Industries, Inc., 258 NLRB No. 182, 108 LRRM 1200 (1981), Footnote 2.

32. Benade Memorandum, December 1981, p. 2.

33. Order Granting Motion and Amending Decision and Order, *Hammary Manufacturing Corporation and Upholsterers' International Union of North Affadavit, AFL-CIO*, (Case 11-CA-8232), 265 NLRB No. 7, October 8, 1982.

34. The Polivy study, *Increasing Giving Options in Corporate Charitable Payroll Deduction Programs*, in fact suggested that there were several companies with units or branches in which more open campaigns were taking place.

35. NBUF was at that time developing organizational strength nationally under the leadership of Walter Bremond, although there was some confusion apparently

8. CORPORATE RESPONSE TO CHALLENGE 359

about the relationship of local units (such as those in New Jersey and New York) to the national organization.

36. There were initial discussions with Clark, Phipps, Clark, and Harris, summarized in a memorandum of June 1, 1981, and cited in the Summary Report by Kenneth B. Clark, "Summary of Observations, Findings and Recommendations: The New Jersey Bell Laboratories First Year Trial Period for Payroll Deductions to the Black United Fund," January 18, 1982.

37. Recommendations following from the original meetings and an earlier study (which more than one respondent suggested had been repressed), cited in Clark, "Summary of Observations," p. 1.

38. Clark, "Summary of Observations," p. 2.

39. "Summary of Observations," p. 2.

40. "Summary of Observations," p. 6.

41. Reported by several key respondents. See also, Polivy, *Increasing Giving Options in Corporate Charitable Payroll Deduction Programs*, p. 34. Polivy cites a letter from Kermit Eady, executive director of the BUF (NYC), August 17, 1982, to E. M. Block, a vice-president of AT&T, as a source for this information (p. 34, n. 18).

42. Chester Burger and Co., "A Study of Employee-Donation Philanthropy and Policy Recommendations," prepared for American Telephone and Telegraph Co., July 1982, p. 5.

43. "Report of the AT&T Working Committee on Donor Option," December 15, 1982, p. 2.

44. "Amended Statement of Consensus" (November 19, 1982), Attachment A to the "Report of the AT&T Working Committee on Donor Option."

45. Figures in this paragraph come from Polivy, *Increasing Giving Options in Corporate Charitable Payroll Deduction Programs*, p. 16, table 1, "Giving Through Payroll Deduction at Bell Labs, 1981–1983." United Way of Tri-State, on the other hand, suggests that employee contributions actually increased from $329,974 pledged in the 1982 campaign to $539,398 pledged in the 1983 campaign; they did not indicate other comparative figures.

46. Figures supplied by the United Way of Tri-State. See also appendix C.6 for complete outline of these donor designation figures.

47. Information supplied by United Way. Despite efforts to clarify matters, there were some differences between AT&T explanations of data concerning campaigns and those United Way of Tri-State. I wish to express my appreciation to Katharine Berry of Tri-State and Gary Doran of AT&T for their assistance with these efforts.

48. Interview with key respondents in United Way, BUF and AT&T.

49. For example, the United Way of Morris County was designated $65,422 in the 1984 campaign, and only $27,285 in 1985; the United Way of Somerset Valley, $49,572 in 1984 and $26,663 in 1985; and the United Way of Central Jersey, $29,640 in 1984 and $12,749 in 1985.

50. See *Black United Fund of New Jersey v. Kean*, 763 F 2d 156 (1985).

51. Personal interviews with NBUF and NYBUB staff. See also Larry Jaffe, "Black United Funds Battle Over Work Place Solicitation," *Fund Raising Management*, September 1984, pp. 89–90; and Kathleen Teltsch, "Changing Patterns in Donations Challenge United Way Methods," *New York Times*, March 8, 1985.

52. Respondents in BUF and IBM. See also Syd Cassese, "Black Charity Groups Strive for Equal Access," *Newsday*, December 4, 1980.

53. Sheila Rule, "IBM Agrees to Deductions for the Black United Fund," *New York Times*, July 30, 1981.

54. Interviews with IBM and BUF staff. See also Cassese, "Black Charity Groups."

360   8. CORPORATE RESPONSE TO CHALLENGE

55. Questions about slow payments, and differing amounts, were raised by Kermit Eady, executive of NYC-BUF throughout this period. Reference is apparently made to these questions in a letter to the New York City Black United Fund from M. F. Little, Program Manager, Employee Services, IBM (Armonk), January 9, 1984, which states that "the actual total received may differ from this amount [cited in letter] since we cannot account for employee transfers or pledge cancellations which could impact donations."

56. Figures for 1981 pledges come from letter to Kermit Eady, executive director of NYC-BUF from C. E. Pilger, IBM (One Citicorp Center, NYC), January 14, 1982; figures for 1982 campaign come from letter to Mr. Eady from Peter D. Kennedy, IBM (Port Chester, New York); figures from 1983 are cited in letter addressed to New York City Black United Fund (not to Mr. Eady), from M. F. Little, IBM (Armonk), January 9, 1984.

57. See Kermit Eady, "The Illegal Way of the United Way," *Black American*, November 14–20, 1985; also John Amamoo, "Black United Fund: A Notion of Self Investment," *Focus*, August/September 1984, pp. 34–35. The formation of the Associated Black Charities (ABC) was reported in the press at that time; see Sheila Rule, "Group of Black Executives Form New Charity for Their Community," *New York Times*, June 3, 1982; and photographs with captions, *New York Voice*, Saturday, June 19, 1982. The formation of the ABC was preceded by a "Black Federation Feasibility and Implementation Study" and appears to have been influenced directly and indirectly by the United Way and its supporters. See also *Report to Black Agency Executives on the Feasibility Study of a Black Federation in New York City*, Mitchell/Titus and Co., Certified Public Accountants (n.d.) (and accompanying letter, April 28, 1982), p. 19, which suggests that there would be cooperation, or affiliation with the United Way in the workplace. This point is echoed in an article by Robert McNatt, "Charity Begins with Your Paycheck," *Black Enterprise*, December 1982, pp. 51–52.

58. The seminar was held at a conference center in Westchester and was well attended by United Way staff in the Tri-State area, some of whom evidently believed IBM was giving them a message about the future. The importance of marketing to IBM is well known; for one discussion of this, see Richard I. Kirkland, Jr., "Ma Blue: IBM's Move Into Communications," *Fortune*, October 15, 1984, p. 52.

59. Personal interview with author. See also Cedric McClester, "Black Charity Battles for Share of Payroll Deductions," *Big Red News*, August 3, 1985, p. 2, and Kathleen Teltsch, "Charity Dispute Splits Two Funds," *New York Times*, Wednesday, June 13, 1984.

60. Personal observation, interviews, and material supplied by the NYC-BUF all suggest this. By 1984 NYC-BUF had become a statewide organization, had changed its name to Black United Fund of New York (BUFNY), and was announcing "historic results" in the 1983 campaign within the Bell system; see "BUF Makes Historic Breakthrough in Payroll Giving at Bell Systems," *Big Red News*, April 28, 1984.

61. See, for example, Kermit Eady, "Beyond the Grant," statement presented to the Black United Fund of New York, Board and Staff (n.d., but given to the author in 1985); "National Black United Fund and Land Development: A Proposal," submitted by Kermit Eady to National Black United Fund Board of Directors. This point was also made in discussion with Dana Alston, executive director of NBUF in those years, and was apparently related to CFC regulations at that time.

62. *Equal Employment Opportunity Commission v. International Business Machines Corporation*, 583 F. Supp. 875 (1984).

63. See *Big Mama Rag v. United States*, 631 F. 2d 1030 (D.C. Cir. 1980).

64. In June 1981 the federal government had agreed to allow twenty additional national charities into the CFC, and chief among these new charities was the National

8. CORPORATE RESPONSE TO CHALLENGE 361

Black United Fund. (The NAACP Legal Defense and Education Funds had already received funds under an earlier court ruling.) See above, chapter 6.

65. *United States of America v. International Business Machines Corporation*, 69 Civ. 200 (DNE). Stipulation of Dismissal, United States District Court, Southern District of New York (January 8, 1982), case withdrawn by the government. This stipulation of dismissal was entered into almost thirteen years after the federal government had commenced its action against IBM (in 1969), and it should be noted took place under a conservative administration.

66. As an example of utility regulation, note that action against the utilities (under an old PSC ruling) for including costs of their contribution in the rates was being considered by the attorney general of New York State in 1985; see Christopher Atwell, "PSC Ruling May Affect Funding for Black Charities," *Brooklyn, New York City Sun,* September 25, 1985. See also Arnold H. Lubasch, "Suit Demands Utilities Cease Use of Payments for Charities," *New York Times,* August 6, 1984; the argument for this suit is given in *Joseph Cahill v. the Public Service Commission,* Memorandum in Support of Article 78, C.P.L.R. Petition, by Richard Emery, New York Civil Liberties Union, October 18, 1984. The state's highest court ruled against the PSC and the utilities; see Bruce Lambert, "Albany Court Bars Utilities' Gifts to Charities from Rate Revenue," *New York Times,* December 20, 1986. The Cahill action was brought under First Amendment rights and raised a series of issues which were unresolved at the time.

67. U.S. Department of Commerce, Bureau of the Census, *County and City Data Book,* 10th ed. (Washington, D.C.: U.S. Government Printing Office, 1983), Table C, "Cities—Area and Population," p. 730.

68. "Demographic Characteristics of Users of United Way Agencies' Services: A Survey," conducted for General Mills, Inc., by Mid-Continent Surveys, Inc. (Minneapolis, Minnesota, January 21, 1983). See Joe Rigert and Lori Sturdevant, "United Way: Behind the Image," a series of articles in the *Minneapolis Tribune,* December 11–18, 1977. This series of articles was written with the cooperation of the United Way and was considered to have presented the United Way fairly. In a follow-up article, "Area United Way Moves on Problems," the reporter, Joe Rigert, also discussed United Way's efforts to correct problems uncovered. See CCC, *The Charity Wars,* June 1978, pp. 128–149.

69. Discussions with local United Way staff. Although there may be some justification for questioning the methodology, the findings are not surprising given the "package of United Way" services, which include a preponderance of the "traditional" Scouts, YMCAs and YWCAs, and Red Cross services, along with other neighborhood centers. In any case, by 1983 United Way had already completed a priorities study, and used it in allocations that year. United Way also surpassed its goal in the 1983 campaign.

70. Steve Paprocki was one of the co-founders (and first executive director of the Cooperating Fund Drive), and later a consultant to NCRP. Under the leadership of Jean Anderson, executive director, and Katie Lowery, campaign director, the drive really took off, and by 1984, in its fourth year of workplace campaigning the Cooperating Fund Drive raised a total of $348,000 ($231,000 or 67 percent of which came from 11 local government units and 44 businesses and non-profit organizations. CFD was instrumental in obtaining passage of state legislation which allowed a more open State Employees Campaign in Minnesota. Figures on the campaign come from National Committee for Responsive Philanthropy, "Alternatives to United Ways Expand Rapidly in 1984," April 2, 1985.

71. Personal observation at NCRP-BUF sponsored alternative fund conference in Philadelphia, July 1984, suggesting that maybe a campaigner has, in fact, to be a campaigner.

362   8. CORPORATE RESPONSE TO CHALLENGE

72. Interviews with respondents in the Cooperating Fund Drive and the St. Paul Companies verified this. Note, however, that the Cooperating Fund Drive continued to have a successful campaign, based largely on its successes in the public sector, and in 1985 it expanded amounts raised by 40 percent over the 1984 campaign, to a total raised of $422,000. Figures from NCRP, *The Workplace Giving Resolution: A Special Report*, Spring 1987.
73. Interviews with Director of Communications and Community Relations, Economics Laboratory, Inc., St. Paul, Minnesota.
74. Letter from Kristie L. Greve to Eleanor Brilliant, April 15, 1987.
75. Although precise figures are hard to obtain, Tom Nunan, director of Community Problem Solving for UWA, is quoted as saying: "Most [of United Way money] goes to what we call system support," which is defined as the ongoing programs of member agencies, such as the Boy Scouts and the YWCA. Noonan is cited in "Aramony's Risky Plan: What is UWA Really Up To?" *Corporate Philanthropy Report* (April 1986), 1(10):3. The article also states that "according to UWA figures, over 50% of the funding goes to just 20 'traditional' charities which, Mr. Aramony insists, all have updated their programming in keeping with the times." See also discussion above, in chapter 4.

9. *Company Choices and United Way Agencies: The Bottom Line*

1. "Non-United Way Charities Top $100 Million in Workplace Gifts," *The Workplace Giving Revolution: A Special Report* (NCRP, Spring 1987), p. 1.
2. Hayden W. Smith, *A Profile of Corporate Contributions* (New York: Council for Financial Aid to Education, 1983).
3. See Smith, *A Profile of Corporate Contributions*.
4. Questionnaires were sent to a stratified random sample of 245 local United Ways in Metros I–VII, with 131 responses. For Corporate Giving Table, see appendix C.5.
5. *Giving USA: Estimates of Philanthropic Giving in 1985 and the Trends They Show* (New York: AAFRC Trust for Philanthropy, 1986), p. 33.
6. Figures from *Giving USA, 1985*, p. 33. These appear to be an update of similar figures given by Kathryn Troy, *Annual Survey of Corporate Contributions, 1984 Edition* (New York: The Conference Board, Report No. 822), pp. 1–2 and p. 5.
7. In a tight economy Company Foundations began in 1980 to pay out more money than they received from their parent companies. See Kathryn Troy, *Annual Survey of Corporate Contributions, 1984 Edition* (New York: The Conference Board, Report No. 822, p. 5.
8. Troy, *Annual Survey, 1984 Edition*, p. 2. See also Linda Cardillo Platzer, *Annual Survey, 1986 Edition*.
9. Non-cash contributions rose to 22 percent of all corporate gifts in 1984, compared with 11 percent in 1983 and 1982. See Platzer, *Annual Survey, 1986 Edition*, p. 2. See also Alex J. Plinsio and Joanne B. Scanlon, *Resource Raising: The Role of Non-Cash Assistance in Corporate Philanthropy* (Washington, D.C.: The Independent Sector, n.d.).
10. *Giving USA, 1986.*
11. Lester M. Salamon, "Federal Budget Cuts: Documenting the Damage," *Foundation News*, July–August 1984, pp. 16–23. See also the complete report, Alan J. Abrahamson and Lester M. Salamon, *The Nonprofit Sector and the New Federal Budget* (Washington, D.C.: The Urban Institute Press, 1986).
12. See Eleanor L. Brilliant, "United Way at the Crossroads," in *Social Welfare Form, 1982–1983*, pp. 251–262 (Washington, D.C.: National Conference on Social Wel-

9. THE BOTTOM LINE 363

fare, 1984). See also Kathryn Troy, *Meeting Human Needs: Corporate Programs and Partnerships*, Report No. 881 (New York: The Conference Board, 1986).

13. Lester M. Salamon and Alan J. Abramson, "Nonprofits and the Federal Budget: Deeper Cuts Ahead," *Foundation News*, April 1985.

14. Figures from the United Way of America. See appendix C.3.

15. In recent years the number of companies reporting their contributions to the Conference Board has dropped fairly sharply. In the 1982 analysis 534 companies were included; in 1983, 471 companies; in 1984, only 422 companies. It should also be noted that the survey results are published at least a year later than the figures reflect; thus, for example, giving for 1984 was reported in the 1986 edition of the Conference Board *Annual Survey*. For figures, see Platzer, *Annual Survey, 1986*, pp. 20–21.

16. Platzer, *Annual Survey, 1986*, p. 21.

17. Platzer, *Annual Survey, 1986*, p. 19.

18. Ibid., p. 20.

19. Ibid., p. 21.

20. Ibid., pp. 18–24.

21. In our survey we asked local United Ways to name their five biggest contributors. The Conference Board survey on the other hand addresses the corporations, and their analysis is in terms of the biggest contributions of responding corporations.

22. This conclusion is partially based on the author's personal observations over a period of five years as a United Way professional. See also discussion in chapter 8 above. For general background on the reasons why corporations give locally, see also Joseph Galskiewicz, *Social Organization of an Urban Grants Economy: A Study of Business Philanthropy and Nonprofit Organizations* (Orlando, Florida: Academic, 1985), and Arthur White and John Bartholomeo, "The Attitudes and Motivations of Chief Executive Officers," in *Corporate Philanthropy*, pp. 102–110 (Washington, D.C.: Council on Foundations, 1982). Banks (and utilities) are discussed in this context specifically in Michael Useem, "The Decision Making and Allocation Process in Corporate Philanthropy," in *Working Papers of the 1987 Spring Research Forum* (Independent Sector and the United Way Institute), pp. 53–69.

23. For a discussion of some of the issues involved in discussions by utilities, see above, chapter 8. See also *Brief on Behalf of Petitioner-Respondent, Joseph Cahill*, in *Joseph Cahill v. The Public Service Commission et al.*, Richard Emery, Attorney for Petitioner, Supreme Court of the State of New York, Appellate Division, Third Department (Index No. 12464-84).

24. Thomas A. Reiner and Julian Wolpert, "The Non-Profit Sector in the Metropolitan Economy," *Economic Geography*, (September 1981), 57:23–33.

25. Although our findings may have been affected somewhat by the failure of three Metro I United Ways to respond to our survey (Hartford, Los Angeles, and Rochester), our study is statistically valid. In any case, at least two of these United Ways, Hartford and Los Angeles, would probably have shown large insurance company involvement; while two of them, Hartford and Rochester, would have also reflected dominance by some major large manufacturing companies, United Technologies in the former area, and Xerox and Eastman Kodak in the latter.

26. Platzer, *Annual Survey, 1986*, p. 21.

27. Interviews with AT&T Foundation staff. See also *AT&T Public Service Activity, 1984–1985: A Biennial Report* (AT&T, July 15, 1986).

28. Interviews by the author with corporate contributions staff across the country provide further evidence that corporate contributions staff wish to use their own expertise in directing the allocation of corporate philanthropy. In a time of generally shrinking resources, this inevitably means taking some money out of the United Way pocket. The existence of corporate foundations makes this even more feasible.

29. Based in information from Pfizer.
30. See above, chapters 6 and 7. Note also that there was continued pressure about revisions in the IRS code and its interpretation in relation to advocacy for 501(c)3 organizations under the Reagan administration (1980–88).
31. "Employee Contributions to Alternative Charities," table 4 in *The Workplace Giving Revolution: A Special Report* (NCRP, Spring 1987), p. 5.
32. From talk by executive director of BUF at the NCRP-BUF alternative funds conference, Philadelphia, July 1982; discussions with BUF leaders at the alternative funds conference, New Orleans, 1984; and discussions with BUF staff.
33. Material supplied from UW files, "United Way and Health: One of Our Best Kept Secrets," n.d., and "Partial Listing, Local United Way Allocations to Selected National Health Agencies" for figures, also no date, but given to the author in 1984.
34. Internal United Way file documents, "United Ways with American Heart Association Contracts," and memorandum to state executive from Robert M. Beggan, "United Way/American Cancer Society Relationships, March, 1984."
35. I wish to acknowledge the assistance of Elizabeth A. Essex in collecting this data.
36. Deborah Kaplan Polivy, *A Study of the Admissions Policies and Practices of Eight Local United Way Organizations* (New Haven: Program on Non-Profit Organizations, Working Paper #49, May 1982.)
37. *1985 Local United Way Allocations to Agencies and Program Services: Metros I–VIII*, (UWA, Fall 1985), pp. 30–81.
38. *1985 Local United Way Allocations*, pp. 80–81.

10. Structure and Function

1. The term "affiliated agencies" has gradually replaced the term "member agencies" in United Way literature, but other terminology is also used, such as "funded agencies" and "participating agencies." The latter is the term used in the *1985 Local United Way Allocations to Agencies and Program Services: Metro I–VIII*, (UWA, Fall 1985), Table 10, pp. 80–81.
2. See Lester M. Salamon, "Nonprofits: The Results Are Coming In," *Foundation News*, July–August 1984.
3. See table in appendix E.2. Note also that of the approximately ninety donor option programs, only about 40 percent were actually communitywide campaigns in the fullest sense. "Highlights, 1986–87 Donor Option Programs" (UWA, unpublished report, October 1987).
4. Jacqueline Trescott, "United Way: Recollections of a Century," *The Washington Post*, Saturday, April 25, 1987.
5. Although this may have been the practice of some local United Ways even before this, it became official practice of all United Ways to report all funds raised through United Way donor option campaigns as part of their total raised. See, for example, the statement in the *1984–85 UWA International Directory*, in the section "Member United Way Organizations in United States," relating to "Amounts Raised and Population Figures," quoted at the beginning of this chapter.
6. The figures raised are from The United Way Public Relations Office. See also United Way Fact Sheets, "Basic Facts About United Way" (July 1987); and "Challenges to the Single United Way Campaign: Issues, Tactics, and Competing Organizations" (July 1987). For alternative fund figures and discussion, see *The Workplace Giving Revolution: A Special Report* (NCRP, Spring 1987).
7. AT&T had, with the United Way of Tri-State, developed what might have become a model for a United Way–administered, companywide, donor option cam-

10. STRUCTURE AND FUNCTION 365

paign. From discussions with officials of AT&T it appears that they thought this might become a model for other companies nationwide, but this did not occur.

8. See chapter 4 above.

9. Information supplied by United Way. Also based on discussions with AT&T and the Black United Fund of New Jersey. The reason given by AT&T for doing this was that there had been disagreements and confusion over the amounts designated to BUF and the timeliness of payments as well, and that they (AT&T) "get along well with the New Jersey BUF."

10. This was commonly said by United Way professionals, openly and in private conversations.

11. For analysis of donor option, see above, chapters 4 and 5. The issue is also discussed in relation to the CFC in chapter 6.

12. This was clearly a problem both in the CFC and in the open plan of the New York City municipal workers. For discussion of the problem in the CFC specifically, see above, chapter 6.

13. This issue was brought up in the author's site visit to Denver, in discussions with executive staff of the Mile High United Way, June 1982, and it was also indicated that the United Way of America's president, Bill Aramony, was discussing this issue with local United Way leadership. The issue was raised in regard to the CFC subsequent to the court decision in regard to the NAACP (in *NAACP Legal Defense and Education Fund v. Campbell*, 504 F. Supp. 1365 (D.D.C. 1981), related to *Schaumburg v. Citizens for a Better Environment*. For further discussion, see also *Executive Orders 12353 and 12404 as They Regulate the Combined Federal Campaign*, Part 2, Hearings, June 23 and July 19, 1983, particularly pp. 96–100.

14. Although they realized that corporations could not make up for declining support from the government, numerous corporate philanthropic officers suggested that they were making an effort to show increases in some areas of federal cutbacks. See discussion of corporate foundations above, chapter 9, and also refer to publications of the Conference Board during these years; in particular, see *Annual Survey of Corporate Contributions* (Conference Board, Report No. 869), p. 10. See also the discussion of the growing use of non-cash contributions, in Alex J. Plinio and Joanne B. Scanlon, *Resource Raising: The Role of Non-Cash Assistance in Corporate Philanthropy* (Washington, D.C.: Independent Sector, n.d.).

15. The gap between funds raised and allocations was particularly acute in the Tri-State communities, where a large percentage was apparently absorbed by the administration of Tri-State. The United Way of Westchester did not issue an Annual Report for 1986, and other communities, including Westchester, were in various stages of threatening to withdraw from the Tri-State partnership.

16. For example, United Way in its *1985 Local United Way Allocations to Agencies and Program Services*, referring to Allocations to Program Goal Areas, Metros I–IV (figure 5, p. 29), was the following categories: Family Service, Health, Safety and Justice, Social Organization, Employment, Food and Shelter, and Education. In an earlier Fact Sheet (Basic Fact Sheets about United Way, February 1984), the categories listed for allocations were the following, "by service area": Family Service, Social Development, Health, Recreation, Neighborhood and Community Development, Protection and Safety, Daycare, Jobs and Income, Education, and Other. In another pie chart supplied by the United Way public information officer, "Where the Money Goes" (1986), the categories used are: Family Services, Health, Disaster Relief and Crime Prevention, Volunteer and Social Service Coordination, Job Training and Placement, Food and Shelter, and Special and Supplementary Education.

17. Local United Ways are surveyed for data about their campaign revenues and allocations every year. In return for their participation in the survey (i.e., returning

the forms with the requested data), they gain access to the various data bases, and receive copies of the overall printed summaries (for example, the Allocations Profiles, and other selected reports) as requested. Response rates are essentially proportionate to size: thus, 49 out of 50 (98 percent) of the Metro I United Ways responded to the 1985 survey, while only 50 out of 186 of the Metro VIII United Ways responded that year. Over 90 percent of the Metro I–IV United Ways responded in contrast with 59.6 percent of the total of Metros I–VIII.

18. For example, as cited earlier, in April 1987 the percentage of United Way money to such agencies was reported as follows: "Forty percent of United Way money goes to 12 national charities"; in Trescott, "United Way: Recollections of a Century." See also discussion in chapters 4 and 5 above.

19. The so-called "immunity clause" dates back to the earliest days of the community chest and was already cited in William J. Norton, *The Cooperative Movement in Social Work* (New York: Macmillan, 1927), pp. 226–230. United Ways still have formal policies which limit participating agencies in direct solicitations of businesses for major donations. See above, chapter 9, for further discussion.

20. For a discussion of this issue, see above, chapter 4. See also Norton, *The Cooperative Movement*, pp. 173–191 and 256–278.

21. Personal observation of the author. Also reports and discussions at conferences and NAV courses in which the author participated. See also Timothy Saasta, "Accusing the Biggest Charity of Greed," *Newsday* (Viewpoints), November 30, 1979.

22. The Salvation Army in this country has generally set aside a large amount of its funds as "reserves" which ultimately are used for mission work, and apparently primarily overseas, and this adds to the difficulty in accountability.

23. See "Serving Community Need: the Nonprofit Sector in an Era of Government Retrenchment," The Nonprofit Sector Project, Progress Report No. 3 (Washington, D.C.: The Urban Institute, September 1983), Table 3, p. 3.

24. Sensitivity to issues of minority involvement and needs of special populations, such as children, single parent families, and the homeless is indicated in "What Lies Ahead—A Mid-Decade View," Strategic Planning Report (UWA, 1985), released around the same time as the U.S. Supreme Court was considering the case of the CFC (see chapter 6, above). Although there is a continual change in the number of agencies included, these percentages can be considered indicative of general trends.

25. *1985 Local United Way Allocations*, pp. 4, 11.

26. Information and referral services, and volunteer services, are often provided by United Ways, and several United Ways in our site visits—for example, Toledo—were moving in this direction as planning councils were closed down.

27. According to figures supplied to the author by Family Service America, there has been a dramatic drop in the United Way share of total income raised by family service agencies nationwide, from over 65 percent (1965) to 53 percent (1975) and down to 38 percent (1985).

28. This point was made explicitly to the author by a staff person at the Planned Parenthood organization in Corpus Christi, which had been forced out of the United Way by a controversy with the Catholic bishop in that city. It is evident also in the funds raised by Women's Way, as described above in chapter 5. See also, for reference to Planned Parenthoods in general, and to the Boise situation specifically, Trescott, "United Way: Recollections of a Century."

29. John R. Seeley et al., *Community Chest: A Case Study in Philanthropy* (Toronto, Canada: University of Toronto Press, 1957).

30. This sentiment is evident in the Tri-State designation figures from the AT&T campaign, and has been a factor of United Way life since commuting separated workers in the workplace from their community of residence increasingly after World

War II. Note that AT&T and IBM, as well as many other corporations, have listed numbers of local United Ways on donor cards for designation, for many years.

31. Tri-State has a fairly standard percentage (6 percent) for shrinkage of unfilled pledges, but a growing administrative/operational budget. The money taken "off the top" generally by Tri-State, however, has been a continual source of controversy within the Tri-State system, according to key informants, so that there is considerable question about differences between amounts raised and those allocated back to local United Ways.

32. Figures from "Introducing—United Way of Tri-State," *Together*, September 1977 (first issue of the magazine of the United Way of Tri-State) pp. 1–3.

33. "Introducing—United Way of Tri-State," p. 3.

34. Personal observation of author at the time of the process, 1977–78. Also expressed by various key respondents in interviews with the author.

35. "Introducing—United Way of Tri-State," p. 2. A similar sentiment is expressed in the UWA journal by the northeast regional director of UWA; see Robert V. Donahoe, "The Tri-State United Way: A New Thrust to Areawide Fund Raising," *Community Focus*, September 1977, p. 6.

36. "Introducing—United Way of Tri-State," p. 2. This basic proposal for fund distribution is in the original document of the study committee recommending the formation of the United Way, and written by Dennis Murphy, executive director of the United Way of Westchester, *Tri-State Area United Ways* (January 1976), p. 4.

37. Transition status meant that the local United Way essentially had a special deal with Tri-State, whereby it could keep all the increments in revenues it raised, for a defined period of time, and thereby raise its base for the future.

38. *United Way of Tri-State Annual Report 1985–1986*, pp. 4–6, gives total amount raised and number of partners. The new per capita is derived by dividing the amount raised by the population reported for the region, which remains at approximately eighteen million. Numbers of partners fluctuated in these years, however.

39. Cited in "A Personal Statement Regarding the United Way of Tri-State," John N. Pike, Ph.D., member of the board of directors of the United Way of Westchester, and former member (for three years) of the Partner Relations Committee of Tri-State, where he was an active proponent of the need for a change in the partner distribution formula. Statement is dated December 5, 1986.

40. Conclusions nos. 2 and 4 from "A Personal Statement," John N. Pike, December 5, 1986. Shared with the author by Dr. Pike.

11. *United Way as a National Organization: The Aramony Era*

1. Typically, a United Way press release in connection with the Centennial Volunteer Leaders Conference (April 27, 1988) stated in regard to this award, "The winners of the prestigious award were chosen for their lifelong commitment to voluntarism and *community* service, and for improving the lives of the people and *communities* around them" (emphasis added). See also chapter 10.

2. "Federation" is a much more common term than "confederation," but the two should be distinguished. American history provides evidence of their distinctness: the southern states during the Civil War formed a *confederacy* to maintain a high degree of autonomy for the separate states; the United States has been defined as a *federation* of states, which cedes more functional control to the central unit. Stanley Wenocur used the term "confederation," and discussed it in Stanley Wenocur, "Confederation Adaptability to External Change Pressures" (dissertation for the D.S.W., University of California, Berkeley, 1974), particularly pp. 22–32.

3. From "Basic Facts," file document of UWA, 1979.

4. Interview with Public Relations Department of United Way. Figures for NAV training also found in "Fact Sheet: United Way National Service and Training Center," July 1987.

5. The business emphasis during the decade 1975–1985 in the courses for United Way personnel is noted in *1979 Report of Evaluation Committee: Program for the Future* (UWA), p. 21.

6. Although the pageantry at both places was impressive, it may have been overdone, judging from comments overheard, and discussions with participants later, who suggested that there was too much blatant "propaganda" and oversell of the theme of Americanism.

7. "The Philadelphia Donor Option Story," presentation by Robert W. Reifsnyder, executive director, United Way of Southeastern Pennsylvania, 1981 United Way Northeast Regional Staff Conference.

8. For discussion of this issue, see Eleanor L. Brilliant, "United Way at the Crossroads," in *The Social Welfare Forum*, pp. 251–262 (Washington, D.C.: National Conference on Social Welfare, 1984); Richard Bartlet, "United Charities and the Sherman Act," *Yale Law Journal* (July 1982), 91(8):93–1613; and David Horton Smith, "The Philanthropy Business," *Society*, January–February 1978, pp. 8–15.

9. The United Way charges for many of these services, and has set up an extensive communications department with "business-like" sales promotions.

10. In effect, the UWA thus acts like the national office of McDonalds or Howard Johnson. While the UWA does not actually impose site visits on its local organizations, there is of course frequent contact between the national office and the local units. While reporting is not entirely mandated, there are rewards for providing data, including receiving reports of all information obtained. Note also that the United Way promulgated its own *Standards of Excellence for Local United Ways* in 1973, updated in 1977, which are widely referred to within the United Way system.

11. Numbers of United Ways and totals raised by all of them are generally presented as if they are precisely determined and based on complete data. In fact, they are estimates based on mathematical projections and calculations from a far smaller number of reporting United Ways regularly supplying information over the years.

12. Personal observation, and interviews with key respondents inside and outside the United Way.

13. See, for example, the letter from the president, signed "Ronald Reagan," to James Robinson III, addressed as "Jim," January 17, 1986, accepting the position of honorary chairman of the United Way's centennial in 1987, and the president's proclamation, p. xv above. Mrs. Reagan was honorary chairwoman, and also had a special role at the United Way's Young Leaders Conference held in conjunction with the centennial celebration.

14. This bill, passed in March 1983, included a $50 million grant to be administered by a group of national voluntary agencies, through a board connected to the Federal Emergency Management Agency (FEMA), and local boards to allocate funds to private voluntary organizations. United Way was a logical choice in addition because it was well established in local communities nationwide and also because UWA had working relationships with agencies on the national FEMA board, including the Salvation Army, the Conference of Catholic Charities, the Council of Jewish Federations, and the American Red Cross. According to the United Way, local "United Ways in hundreds of communities across the country helped to administer the grants," which provided millions of meals and nights' lodgings for people in need.

15. "Final Report of the Study Committee of United Way of Tri-State," United Way of America, June 1981, p. 17.

11. THE ARAMONY ERA

16. Discussed above in chapter 5, and based on extensive interviews with local United Way professionals. In fact, despite the influence of the UWA, the majority of the United Ways in Metros I–IV did not adopt a donor option plan.

17. United Way's total expenditures as reported to the IRS in 1983 were $16,762,001, of which membership support was reported as $4,021,836, so that it appears that most United Ways did not meet their fair-share expectations. Figures are from United Way of America's 990 Form, the Income tax form for Organizations Exempt from Income Tax, filed with the Department of the Treasury, Internal Revenue Service, by the United Way of America in May 1984, for 1983.

18. This information is based on interviews with key respondents and personal observation. By the past decade, United Way developed an extensive Professional Advisory Council (NPAC)—with subcommittees—to help improve communication with local United Way professionals.

19. See "1979 Report of Evaluation Committee," p. 17. Also based on discussion with numerous executives involved in the program.

20. This is a well known "fact" of United Way life. Staff who have had trouble in their local communities, but have paid their "dues" to the national organization (and are not considered to blame for the problems) are even transferred for a period of time to the UWA, or actively helped to find positions in other communities. Thus, for example, after one community ran into difficulties in its campaign, and lost over $1 million as a result of backlash from a civil rights–busing issue, the executive was brought to the UWA, where he worked for several years.

21. Figures provided by the UWA public relations office. Also numbers of minority and women staff are found in "Staffing Report on Minority and Women Professionals," UWA, 1985, which indicates that there were only 4,142 professional positions in total. The report also does not separate out staff by Metro size, thus leaving out a valuable piece of information. The data about the three Metro I positions was supplied by respondents inside the United Way.

22. Based on interviews and personal observation of the author. By 1980 United Way professional women were attempting to organize, eventually, it seems, without success. However, a northeast regional chapter was initiated on June 9, 1980, with the hope that "other United Way of America regions would organize like chapters" (Articles of Organization, United Way Professional Women [internal document]).

23. Nashville moved into that category in the 1986 United Way Directory when it raised over $9,000,000.

24. See, for example, the "message strategies" outlined in "The Report on Centennial Celebration Committee" by Charles D. Peebler, Jr., to the UWA, September 11, 1985, which includes a rededication to the "voluntary spirit" and attention to involvement of young people, with renewed emphasis on the United Way concept as "rooted in fundamental American values." Note also UWA environmental scan reports, and futurist projections of such authors as Naisbitt, used to emphasize individualizing the United Way message and personalization in the workplace.

Index

Abortion, controversy of, 96, 97, 347*n*14
Accountability: in agency budgeting, 24; and national health agencies, 36; in United Way system 49, 88-89, 235, 246, 251
Addams, Jane, 20
Aetna Life and Casualty, 75, 133, 178, 254
AFL-CIO: and community fund raising, 26; formation of, 55
Aft, Richard N., 258
Aid to Dependent Children (ADC), 25, 41
AID-United Givers, *see* Associated-in-Group Donors
Akana, Paul, 61-65
Alston, Dana, 181
Alternative fund movement, 8, 9, 111, 186, 208, 222, 263; amounts raised, 231, 232, 262, 318*n*15; and CFC, 137, 141; and Cooperating Fund Drive, 205; in Seattle, 173; *see also* Black United Fund; Combined Health Agencies Drives; Women's funds
American Association for Community Organization, 21, 22, 24, 245, 320*n*14
American Association for Organizing Charity, 22, 245
American Cancer Society (ACS), 32-33, 38, 86, 89, 139, 140, 144-45, 157, 170, 178-79, 208, 221-22; agreements with local United Ways, 71, 72, 83, 178-80, 223, 357*n*7; and CFC, 140, 144, 194, 195; and IBM campaign, 196, 198; non-participation in United Funds, 38, 325*n*34

American Civil Liberties Union (ACLU), 176
American culture: changes in, 8, 74, 240-41, 264; subgroups, 43, 88, 261-262
American Heart Association (AHA), 33, 38, 89, 170, 178-79, 208, 221, 222, 252, 325; agreements with local United Ways, 179-80, 357*n*8; and United Funds, 32
American Lung Association, Denver, 347*n*14
American Red Cross, 26, 33, 39, 77, 78, 104, 110, 112-13, 119, 162, 325*nn*28-31; budget share from United Ways, 236-38; relationship with federated (community) funds, 10, 32, 36, 37, 230, 334*n*53, 337*n*24; in Toledo, 67, 71, 238, 334*n*53; in world wars, 22, 36, 37, 154
Andrews, John, 174
Aramony, William, 50, 52, 60, 61, 159-60, 222, 246, 255; and the Combined Federal Campaign, 142; and corporations, 188, 252; influence on local United Ways, 242, 259, 365*n*13; and United Way organizational culture, 257; and United Way professionals, 254, 255, 259
Arthritis Foundation, Toledo, 71
Arts funds, *see* United Arts Funds
Associated Black Charities (ABC), 198, 360*n*57
Associated Charities of Denver, 19; *see also* Charity Organization Societies; Councils of Social Agencies
Associated in-Group Donors (AID), 89, 92-94, 177, 180; court order, 93, 182, 356*n*5

371

Association of Black Laboratories Employees (ABLE), see AT&T
Association of Federal, State, County and Municipal Employees, (AFSCME), District Council, 37, 201
AT&T, 104, 153, 183, 188, 196, 255; Affirmative action, 201; Association of Black Laboratories Employees, 186, 201; Bell Laboratories, 186-87, 190, 193; Black United Funds, 186-87, 191, 195; Burger study, "Employee-Donation Philanthropy," 188; compared with IBM, 198-203; divestiture, 191, 202; donor option, 189–91, 220-21; 364n7; employee campaign, 190-93; employee, top designations of, 194-95, 223; Foundation, 193, 209; monopoly charges, 202

Baker, Newton D., 22
Baker, Tom F., 174
Baltimore, The United Way of Central Maryland, 90, 109, 178, 233; see also Combined Health Agencies Drives
Benade, Leo, 183
Bergen County, New Jersey, 241
Big Brothers, Pittsburgh, 239
Black Workers Alliance (BWA), see IBM
Blacks: in California cities, 73, 179; and employee rights, 181-82, 184; leadership in War on Poverty, 43; separate service system in United States, 17
Black United Fund (BUF), 9, 91, 122, 146, 173, 196, 198, 222, 263; AT&T, 186-95; Black United Funds distinguished from other black groups, 180-81, 343n42; CFC and government workplaces, 117-22, 125, 146, 181; as growing movement, 180, 263; and IBM, 196-99, 201, 203, 224; origins, 91, 180; payroll deduction in corporations, 181-82, 199, 200; pressure on corporations, 196; see also National Black United Fund
Black United Fund, local organizations, see also under Los Angeles,

New Jersey, New York, St. Louis, Washington, D.C.
Blakewell, Daniel, 181
Blechman, Frank, 74
Boeing, 169, 172, 353n47
Boeing Good Neighbor Fund (BEGNF), 165, 170-73, 197, 232, 355n43; and the IAM boycott, 173, 174
Boston, 22; early Jewish federation, 19; United Way of Massachusetts Bay, 82, 241-42, 254
Bothwell, Robert O., 132, 139
Boys Clubs, 21, 77, 234-35, 237
Boy Scouts, 21, 77, 78, 162, 234, 236-38
Bremond, Walter, 92, 181, 200, 257n13
Brilliant, Eleanor L., 89, 168-69, 216, 224, 363n25
Brown, Tom B., 126
Burger, Chester, 188, 189

California, Charity Wars, 90, 177
Campbell, Alan, 122, 123
Canada, 5, 20, 23, 321n22
Carnegie, Andrew, 17
Carter, Lisle, 188
CCC, see Community Chests and Councils
Center for Community Change, 75
Center for Responsible Funding, Philadelphia, 98, 195, 108
CFC, see Combined Federal Campaign
CHAD, see Combined Health Agencies Drives
Chamber(s) of Commerce, 19, 54, 154, 178, 224
Champion Spark Plug, 66, 67
Charity Organization Societies (COS), 18-21, 54; and early federated funds, 19-21, 317n7
Check-off: for BUFs, 184; for charity, 30, 40, 185; and Fourteenth Amendment, 184; origins, 323n4; related to withholding of federal taxes, 26, 27; for union dues, 27; see also Payroll deduction
Chicago, United Way/Crusade of Mercy, 241-42, 254
Ciba-Geigy, 200, 219
Cincinnati, Ohio, 260; early Jewish federation, 19; United Appeal and

INDEX   373

Community Chest of the Greater
  Cincinnati Area, 253, 254
CIO, 31, 38, 55, 156
Civil Rights Act: of 1957, 44; of 1964,
  43
Civil Rights movement, 41, 43, 332n17
Civil Service Reform Act of 1978, 115
Civil War, 17
Clark, Phipps, Clark and Harris, 187
Cleveland: Federation for Charity and
  Philanthropy, 19, 20, 154, 162; as
  first modern federated fund, 19;
  Planning Council, 54, 333n46;
  United Way Services, 241-42, 253-
  54
Combined Federal Campaign (CFC):
  advocacy and social action issues
  in, 122, 133-38, 142-46, 344n50,
  346n2, 350n60; American Red
  Cross, 110; and business, 129, 160,
  175, 201, 204, 263; campaign of
  1982, 123-28, 130-32; campaign of
  1983, 138; campaign of 1984, 141,
  146; campaign of 1985, 143, 146;
  Congressional hearings, 115, 117,
  134-38, 140, 143, 145; coercion in,
  117, 160; court definition, public
  or private, 120-21, 136, 138, 142,
  263; direct service requirement,
  123, 133, 135-36, 140, 142; and donor choices, 139-41, 265-66; early
  history, 109, 110, 112-13, 341n11,
  342n19; eligibility rules, 115, 116,
  121-26, 133-43, 145-46, 344n55,
  346nn9, 10, 347n24; federated
  groups defined, 124, 125; First
  Amendment issues, 118, 121-22,
  135-39, 142; and government role,
  132, 135-38, 140, 143, 151; International Service Agencies (ISA)
  group, 110, 114-15, 124, 131-32,
  140-41, 144; legal challenges, 117-
  22, 135-43, 263; local non-affiliated
  agencies, 141, 145; Manual, 121-23;
  national agencies defined, 124-25;
  National Health Agencies (NHA)
  group, 110, 114-15, 124, 131-42,
  137, 140-41, 345n64; Principal
  Combined Fund Organization(s),
  124-25, 128, 133, 137-141, 144, 198,
  229, 231, 252, 341n13, 344n56; San

Diego Naval Base, 132; and United
  Black Fund (Washington, D.C.),
  180; and United Way of America
  Board, 126; write-in agencies, 139,
  141
Combined Health Agencies Drives
  (CHADs), 89, 90, 98, 177-79, 223-
  24, 232-33; agreement with local
  United Ways, 178, 233; Commerce
  and Industry Combined Health
  Appeal (CICHA), Baltimore, 89,
  90, 178, 233; litigation in Califor-
  nia, 177-78, 181
Commission on Private Philanthropy,
  see Filer Commission
Communications Workers of America
  (CWA), 127
Community Chest campaigns: in Great
  Depression, 125-26, 155, 156, 321;
  1918–29, 23; 1944, 26, 33
Community Chests, in relation to
  United Funds, 33, 39, 40, 324n22;
  see also United Funds
Community Chests and Councils
  (CCC), 29, 32, 34, 54, 245; influ-
  ence on income tax laws, 26; see
  also United Funds and Councils of
  America
Community Health ad Welfare Coun-
  cils, see Planning councils
Community organization, see Social
  Work profession
Community planning, defined, 59-61;
  and UCFCA, 45, 46
Community problem solving, and
  United Way, 52, 53, 60, 73, 261,
  265
Concerned Citizens for Charity, San
  Francisco, 338n31
Conference Board, 210, 211, 213-14,
  216-18, 365n15
Consensus: in American society, 8, 10,
  43, 87, 261; and federated fund
  raising organizations, 8, 128, 131,
  183, 260-61; and planning coun-
  cils, 8, 55
Cooper, Alan, 249, 259
Cooperating Fund Drive (CFC), 204-7,
  221-22, 233, 361n70, 362n72
Corporate contributions officers, 205-
  07, 218-19, 264, 365n14

Corporate giving: and community base, 216-17; company foundations, 161; difficulty with data, 21; direct benefit doctrine, 154, 155; diversification, 213, 219; and federated fund drive, 213-15; in Great Depression, 155-56; health and welfare share, 158, 213; industry comparisons, 164, 216-18; legal questions, 23; non-cash contributions, 216-17; and Reagan cutbacks, 212-13; and taxes, 154, 161, 211-12, 323n9; trends, 1975–84, 211-15; in world wars, 154, 156
Corporations: as good citizens, 162; linkage to federated funds, 161-62, 265, 341n15; response to minorities and advocacy groups, 158, 196, 199-201, 210, 212; and social welfare, 151
Council on Financial Aid to Education, 211
Councils of Social Agencies, 4, 20, 24, 50; see also Planning councils
Corpus Christi, 80, 96
Corpus Christi, United Way of the Coastal Bend: allocations program, 80–85; campaign, 80, 336n16, 337n21
Covenant House, New York, 191, 194-95
Croxton Study of Corporate Contributions, 155, 323n24
Cystic Fibrosis, 38

Davis, King, 91, 181, 357n13
Davison, Owen, 52
De Arment, Roderick, 182-85
Delaware, 92
Delfin, Steve, 127
Denver: Charity Organization Society, 19, 82, 320n7; Federation for Charity and Philanthropy, 19; Mile High United Way, 82
Des Moines, United Way of Central Iowa, 235
de Toquevillle, Alexis, 1
Detroit, 6, 8, 56, 168, 200; riots of 1967, 43, 50; United Foundation, 30, 32, 34, 36-37, 241, 253-54

Devine, Charles, 171-72, 174
Devine, Donald J., 123, 138, 133, 137, 140, 146
Devine, Edward T., 15
Donee Group, see Filer Commission
Donor Option, 94, 95, 103-5, 108-9; and AT&T 104, 188-92; comparison, by industry, 220-21; comparison among local United Ways, 105-7, 341n6, 364n3; in Cooperating Fund Drive, 206-7; Philadelphia, 97-99, 105, 108, 199; San Francisco, 105, 180, 199; United Way of America Resolution, 94, 95, 103, 199; see also CFC
Drucker, Peter, 249

Eady, Kermit, 181, 360n55, 56
Eastman Kodak, 154, 254
Ecolab, 203, 206, 220, 233
Economic Opportunity Act of 1964, 41-42
Edelston, Harold, 63, 65, 333n56
Eisenberg, Pablo, 75-76
Eisenhower, Dwight D., 112, 157
Elizabeth Blackwell Center, Philadelphia, 97
Employee clubs, see In-plant federations
Employee giving, 31, 240, 264; to alternative funds, 231, 232, 262; blue collar workers, 201; Boeing Corporation, 172; and donor option, 205, 220, 262; in relation to corporate giving, 33n10, 157, 167, 177
Employee rights, 181-82, 184, 202, 261-64, 352n14; in CFC, 117-18, 137, 140
Executive Orders: 10728 (Eisenhower), 113; 10927 (Kennedy), 114; 12353 (Reagan), 123, 126, 137; 12404 (Reagan), 133-38
Exxon, 200, 254

Family Service Agencies, 77; budget share from United Way, 236-37, 366n27; in the Great Depression, 25; national organization, 21, 258; origins, 4, 21; in Pittsburgh, 239

INDEX 375

Federal Emergency Management Agency (FEMA), 252, 368n14
Federal employee campaign, see Combined Federal Campaign
Federal Register, The, 122-24, 135, 140
Federal Service Fund Raising Policy (Eisenhower), 112-13
Federation for Community Planning, Cleveland see Cleveland, Planning Council
Ferris, Richard J., 260
Filer, John H., 3, 75
Filer Commission, the, 1, 2, 3, 58, 75-77, 79, 86, 88, 159-60, 176, 211, 230, 337n29; Donee group, 76, 88, 336nn6, 7, 9
Flour, Robert K., 177
Ford, Henry, 30
Ford, Henry II, 29-30
Ford, Lyman, 45, 52
Ford Foundation, 41
Ford Motor Company, 27, 30, 254
Foundations, 157
Frank, Barney, 134-35, 138
Freedman's Bureau, 17
Fund raising and controversy, 37, 127-29, 131, 266, 277

GAO (U.S. General Accounting Office), 344-45n56
Garber, John, 255
Gay and lesbian groups, 206, 263
G. C. Murphy, 183
General Electric, 169, 232
General Food, 254
General Mills, study of United Way services, 204, 224, 361n69
General Motors, 32, 254
Gentle Legions, The (Carter), 33
Gesell, Gerhard, 135
Girl Scouts, 77-78
Goodwill Industries, 21
Green, Joyce Hens, 136-39, 145
Glazebrook, Tanya, 357n10
Great Society, 41, 88; see also Johnson, Lyndon B.; Kennedy administration; War on Poverty
Gurteen, S. H., 18

Haggerty, Joseph, 80, 205
Hampton, Robert E., 114-15, 119

Harrington, Michael, 41, 326n41
Hartford, 178; Chamber of Commerce, 224; United Way of the Capital Area, 233, 234, 254
Hatfield, Mark, 143, 145
Hayes, John S., 113
Health and Welfare Councils, see Planning councils
Health and wealth needs, 55, 59; see also Social welfare
Health Systems Agencies, 57
Hoover, Herbert, 24
Horner, Constance, 143
Houston, United Way of Texas Gulf Coast, 254
Hoyer, Steny H., 145-46

IAM, see International Association of Machinists
IBM, 169, 175, 180, 254; anti-trust case, 202; Black United Fund, 180-81, 196-98, 200-1, 360nn55, 60; Black Workers Alliance (BWA), 196; compared with AT&T, 198-203; employee designations, 196-98; and Equal Employment Opportunity Commission, 201; marketing training, 198, 360n58; United Way campaign of, 164-65, 175, 196-98; and United Way National Corporate Development Program, 199
Immunity clause in federated funds/United Way, 22, 162, 366n19
Inclusiveness: in earlier federated funds, 33, 40, 79; in United Ways, 58, 86, 94, 221-23, 229, 230, 239, 251
Indianapolis Community Chest, study of (Seeley), 78
Industrial Chest, see In-plant federations
Information and Referral Services: in Corpus Christi, 83; as United Way function, 238
In-plant federations, 33-35, 89-90, 157, 163, 168-69, 175, 193, 232, 354n38, 355n42; compared with Political Action Committees, 358n19; in San Francisco, 179
International Association of Machinists (IAM), 125-26, 173-74

International Labor Union, 17
Internal Revenue Code, Section 501(c)(3) organizations, 2, 15-16, 129, 139, 317*n*2
Internal Revenue Service: and challenge to advocacy organizations, 133-34, 140-41, 211; list of 501(c)(3) organizations, 6; *see also* United States Office of Management and Budget, Circular A-122

Jacobs, Frances, 19, 320*n*7
Japan, 5, 28
J. C. Penny, 126
Jewish Community Council, Corpus Christi, 85
Johnson, Geneva, 258
Johnson, Lyndon B., 41, 55
Johnson and Johnson, 219, 254
Johnston, David, 356*n*3

Kennedy, John F., 55, 113-14, 134-35
Korean War, 31; United Defense Funds, 39
Koch, Edward I., 201
Ku Klux Klan, 44

Labor unions: boycott of, CFC, 125-26, 131, 345*n*38; and community health and welfare, 28, 30-31, 38-39, 55, 322*n*1, and 331*n*15; criticism of American Red Cross, 325*n*28; gains under New Deal, 31; leadership in United Fund, 30-31; and payroll deduction, 164, 181; relationship with business, 23-24, 28, 32; and World War II fund raising, 26
Laidlaw, Walter, 30
La Raza, San Francisco, 89
Legal Defense Funds (LDFs), 122, 135-39, 142
Lewis, Gerald F., 258
Libbey-Owens-Ford, 66
Lipton tea, 254
Litigation: *AID v. United Way*, 339*n*47; *American Rolling Mill Co. v. Commissioner of Internal Revenue*, 351*n*7; *A.P. Smith Mfg. Co. v. Barlow*, 157,
352*n*16; *Big Mama Rag v. United States*, 121, 201; *Black United Fund of New Jersey v. Kean*, 359*n*50; *Brown v. Board of Education in Topeka*, 40, 331*n*17; *Cahill v. Public Service Commission*, 361*n*66; *California State Combined Health Agencies v. United Way of Santa Clara et al.*, 181-82, 356*n*4; *City of Charlotte et al. v. Local 660 International Association of Firefighters et al.*, 184-85; *Cornelius v. NAACP Legal Defense and Educational Fund*, 142, 263, 349*nn*50, 51; *Corning Glass Works v. Lucas*, 23, 155, 321*n*24, 351*n*7; Hammary Corporation Case (NLRB), 183, 185-86, 189, 204; *Lew Moye v. Chrysler*, 181; *NAACP Legal Defense and Educational Fund et al. v. Campbell*, 122; *NAACP Legal Defense and Educational Fund v. Devine*, 136-37; *NAACP Legal Defense and Educational Fund v. Devine* (1983), affirmed (1984), 138, 348*nn*31, 36; *NAACP Legal Defense and Educational Fund v. Horner, and Planned Parenthood Federation of America v. Horner*, 145; *National Black United Fund v. Campbell*, 121, 343*n*45; *National Black United Fund v. Devine*, 121, 343*n*43; *National Health Agencies Committee for the Combined Federal Campaign v. Campbell*, 137-38; *Old Mission Portland Cement Co. v. Helvering*, 351*n*9; *Riddles et al v. the Department of the Army*, 117-18, 128; *United Black Fund v. Hampton et al.*, 119; *United States of America v. International Business Machines Co.*, 201, 361*n*65; *Village of Schaumburg v. Citizens for a Better Environment*, 121, 343*n*48
Los Angeles, 90-91, 93; Brotherhood Crusade (BUF), 91-92, 180; United Fund Study (Dinerman), 78; United Way, Inc., 91-94, 253-54
Los Angeles Times, The, 177
Losh, Stephen R., 126-27
Lowery, Kate, 361*n*70
Lubove, Roy, 15

INDEX 377

Mable, Robert, 52, 255
McNaughton, Donald S., 60-61
MACSI, see United Way of America, Management and Community Studies Institute
Manpower Development Training Act off 1962, 41
Marshall, George, 36
Marshall, Thurgood, 184
Medicaid, 41
Medicare, 41
Memorial-Sloan Kettering Cancer Center, 225
Memphis, Tennessee, United Way of Greater Memphis, 258
Merck and Company, 219
Mexican-American community in Corpus Christi, 82-83, 85
Michigan Cancer Foundation, 32
Michigan Health and Welfare Fund, 29-32
Michigan Tuberculosis Association, 32, 37
Mills, Wilbur, 75
Milwaukee, 54
Minneapolis-St. Paul, 203-4
Minneapolis, United Way of Minneapolis Area, 204
Minneapolis Tribune, The, 361*n*68
Model Cities Program, 41, 92, 327*n*43, 338*n*42
Monsanto Fund, 209
Moore, Ted L., 249, 254
Morgan, J. P., 17
Morris County, United Way of Morris County, see Tri-State United Way
Multiple Sclerosis Association, 38
Mobil Oil, 200
Myth: of American consensus, 43; and corporate commitment, 209; of one campaign for all, 86; and the United Way, 10, 29, 74, 109, 209, 234, 236, 240, 246-47, 266, 322*n*3

NAACP (National Association for the Advancement of Colored People), 9; in Corpus Christi, 85
NAACP Legal Defense and Educational Fund, 16, 135-38, 142, 145-46

NAACP Special Contribution Fund, 344*n*50
Nashville, Tennessee, United Way of Nashville and Middle Tennessee, 258
National Association of Letter Carriers, 125
National Black United Fund (NBUF), 92, 117, 120-21, 125, 180-81, 200-1, 360*n*64; and AT&T, 186-88, 196; in the CFC, 117, 120-21, 125, 201; and individual BUFs, 358*n*35; origins, 336*n*43; pressure on companies, 199, 200
National CIO War Relief Committee, 38
National Committee for Responsive Philanthropy (NCRP), 76, 111, 132, 181, 197-98, 205, 210, 350*n*60; amounts raised by alternative funds, 233; and minority charities in CFC, 139
National Conference of Charities and Corrections, 17
National Conference of Social Work, 55
National Football League (NFL), public service announcements, 3, 4
National Foundation for Infantile Paralysis, 32, 37
National Health Agencies, 22, 29, 32-36, 39, 110, 114, 222, 253; Gunn and Platt Report, 34-35, 322*n*1; Hamlin study, 36, 325*n*23, 24; Rockefeller Foundation, 325*n*23
National Labor Relations Board (NLRB), "no solicitation rule" and United Way sole exception, 156, 182, 185-86, 201, 204, 263
National Planning and Resources Development Act of 1974, 57
National Right to Life Educational Trust Fund, 125, 131, 175
National Right to Work Legal Defense Foundation, 125-26, 131, 175
National Treasury Employees Union, 125
Native American Rights Fund (NARF), 122, 127, 345*n*64
New Deal and federal aid, 25, 42
New Haven, 54

New Jersey, Black United Fund of New Jersey (BUF/NJ): and AT&T, 187, 189, 191-94, 200, 203; and IBM, 196-97; and State employee campaign, 193
New York, Black United Fund of New York (BUF/NY), 233; and AT&T, 187-89, 191-95, 203; and IBM, 196-97; and NYC municipal campaign, 201
New York City (NYC), 181, 254, 255; municipal campaign, 201, 221; United Way of New York City, 90, 242, 244, 254
New York School of Philanthropy, 20
New York Telephone, 191
Non-profit sector: and business, 9, 16, 153; environmental pressures on, 87; exempted from income tax, 21; and government, 44, 159; and individual philanthropists, 18; influenced by public policy, 9; in the 1920s, 24; place in American society, 1, 2, 15, 16, 87; and social work, 26; state of the GNP, 87
NOW Legal Defense and Education Fund, 76, 122
Norton, William J., 15
Nunan, Thomas, 362*n*75

O'Brien, Richard, 255, 333*n*47
O'Connell, Mark L., 259
O'Connor, Basil, 34, 36, 324*n*18
Organizations: and change, 8, 15; secrets of, 78, 336*n*12
Older Americans Act, 41
Omaha, Nebraska, 20
OMB, *see* U.S. Office of Management and Budget
Orange County, United Way of Orange County, 94
Owens-Illinois, 66

Painful Necessity of Choice, The (UWA), 86
Paprocki, Steve, 361*n*70
Payroll deduction, 33, 40, 113, 164, 181
Peat, Marwick, and Mitchell, 45, 46, 49, 51, 57
Perlis, Leo, 44, 55, 328*n*53
Pfizer, 200, 219, 255

Philadelphia, 96; alternative funds in, 98; Archdiocese of, 96-97
Philadelphia, United Way of Southeastern Pennsylvania, 91, 96-97, 247, 250, 254, 341*n*7; influence on other United Ways, 247, 254
Philanthropy: funding for women's causes, 76; funding for minorities, 76; individual fortunes and uses of wealth, 17-18; questions addressed by Filer Commission, 74-75; *see also* Corporate giving; Non-profit sector; and Employee giving
Phoenix, Valley of the Sun United Way, 259
Pike, John N., 244, 367*n*40
Pittsburgh, 34, 54; United Way of Allegheny County, 253
Planned Parenthood, 37, 221-22, 239, 326*n*32, 337*n*21; and the CFC, 125, 135, 137
Planned Parenthood–World Population and the CFC, 123
Planning, *see* Community planning; United Way planning
Planning councils: early history, 4, 20, 54; executive's group, 64; and funding sources, 56, 58, 60, 332*nn*24, 26, 30; name changes, 330*n*7; numbers of, 5, 54, 58-59, 65, 330*n*9; priority setting, 57, 59, 60, 69, 79, 80, 332*n*29; priority setting in Cleveland, 54, 333*n*46, in Seattle, 171-72, in Toledo, 67-73; and the war on poverty, 45, 56, 331*n*19; *see also* Councils of Social Agencies
Political conservatism, 31, 40, 129, 134, 151
Pratt, Edward T., Jr., 219
Pratt and Whitney, 178
Progressive era, 20-21
Prudential Insurance Company of America, 60, 133, 153
Puerto Rican Legal Defense and Education Fund, 344*n*50

Ranier Bancorporation, 172
Reagan, Nancy, 252, 368*n*13
Reagan, Ronald, 123, 132, 138, 140,

142, 211, 264; and United Way
centennial, 245, 252, 368n13
Red Feather, 33
Residential fund raising campaigns, 7,
29, 35, 240, 324n22
Reuther, Walter, 31
Richmond, Mary, 24
Richter, Glenn, 73
Riddles, Benjamin, T., 117-18
Rivera, Edward J., 85
Robinson, James D., III, 260
Rochester: Community Chest, 23, 154;
United Way of Greater Rochester,
254
Rockefeller, John D., 17
Rockefeller, John D., III, 3, 75
Rolark, Calvin, 118-19, 180
Roosevelt, Franklin D., 25
Rosa Morgan Enrichment Center, Toledo, 71
Rudney, Gabriel, 335n2

Sacramento, United Way Sacramento
Area, 94
St. Louis: United Black Community
Fund (UBCF), 181; United Way of
Greater St. Louis, 254
St. Paul, United Way of the St. Paul
Area, 205
St. Paul Companies, 203–6
Salvation Army, 40, 77-78, 162, 236,
250
Sampson, Charles, 52
San Antonio, United Way of San Antonio and Bexar County, 96
San Diego, United Way of San Diego
County, 82, 86, 109, 178, 233,
337n24
San Francisco, 69, 91, 177-78, 197;
adoption of donor option plan,
105, 182; Black United Fund, 180,
222, 233; partnership agreements,
180; United Way of the Bay Area,
88, 94, 180, 241-42, 247, 250, 254,
338nn32, 38
Santa Clara, United Way of Santa
Clara County, 94
Schoderbeck, Peter, 249
Schools of Social Work, 52, 55, 330n2;
Boston College, 52, 255; Bryn
Mawr College, 52; Columbia University, 20; Ohio State, 52; University of California, 52, 255; University of Pittsburgh, 52, 255
Schroeder, Patricia, 116-17, 123-24,
131-34, 140, 349n41
Scolar, Milton J., 130
Seagram campaign, 166-67, 354n37
Seattle, 126, 171, 355n44; alternative
funds in, 173; Council of Planning
Agencies (COPA), 171-72, 355n46;
public-private coalition for displaced workers, 173; United Way
of King County, 82, 86, 171-73,
174
SEFA, see State Employees Federated
Appeal
Seibert, Donald K., 126, 132, 134
Settlement movement, 20, 21
Seymour, Harold, 28
Shaffer, Charlotte, 68, 73
Shiffman, Bernard, 333n44
Shriver, Sargent, 45
Shroder, Jerry A., 333n44
Sierra Club, 127
Silverstein, Leonard L., 335n2
Simon, William E., 75
Sister Kenny Foundation, Michigan, 32
Smith, David Horton, 3, 76
Social Darwinism, 18
Social Security Act, Amendments: of
1962, 41; of 1967, 42, 57; of 1974,
57, 332n27
Social welfare: after civil war, 17; and
charity, 15, 16; disengagement
from poor, 24; federal government
initiatives in, 17, 42-43
Social welfare planning and federal
government, 56-57
Social work profession: and business
community, 154; definitions of
community organization, 43, 54-
55, 328n52; development of social
casework, 24; see also Schools of
Social Work
South Africa, 5
Spencer, Herbert, 18
Spillane, James B., 167
Springfield, Missouri, United Way of
the Ozarks, 126-27
Stamford, Connecticut, 241; United
Way of Stamford, 254

State Employees Federated Appeal (SEFA), 151, 231; and national health agencies, 34; New Jersey, 193
Steketee, Nancy L., 98, 108, 340n65
Stevens, Theodore, 143
Stranahan, Duane ("Pat"), Jr., 67, 335n62
Street, Elwood, 15
Sumariwalla, Russy D., 63-65, 333n47
Sumner, William Graham, 18
Symes, William F., 209

Taft-Hartley Act 31, 156, 352n15
Taxes, federal: on corporate giving, 26; excess profit taxes, 21, 35; exemption for non-profit organizations, 21; mandated witholding by employer, 26-27, 156; personal income taxes in depression, 25
Tax Reform Act(s): 1969, 158; 1981, 161, 211; 1986, 264
Texaco, 200, 254
Three Critical Issue Reports (UWA), 261
Toledo, 53-54, 65-66, 334n51; Community Planning Council, 67-73; United Way of Greater Toledo, campaign, 66-67, 72, 334n52, 53
Tri-State area, 242; major companies in, 254-55; per capita giving, 242-43
Tri-State, United Way of Tri-State, 5, 189, 194-99, 203; and corporate leadership, 242; designations, 221, 359n47; local partners, 242-44, 365n15, 367nn37, 38; Woodcliff Lake, agreement on donor option, 189
Tuberculosis Association, Michigan, 32, 37
Tully, Mary Jean, 75-76

UCFCA, *see* United Community Funds and Councils of America
United Airlines, 180, 199, 260
United Arts Funds, 234; in St. Paul, 205-6
United Auto Workers (UAW), 27, 31
United Charities of Denver, *see* Denver, Charity Organization Society

United Community Funds and Councils of America (UCFCA), 40, 43, 57, 245, 330n2; Board, 49, 52, 247, 353n26; and civil rights, 44, 329n54; and Combined Federal Campaign, 113-15; and health wars, 40, 43; Organization and Management Committee Report, 49-50, 79; search for identity, 46, 51-52, 74-75; and war on poverty, 44-45, 329n56; *see also* United Way of America
United Community Services, Toledo, 69, 71
United Fund(s): and business, 34-35, 38, 157; campaign of 1969–70, 50; characteristics of, 29, 30, 33-35, 39-40, 74, 324n22, 326n38 and Combined Federal Campaign, 110, 112–15, 118; Detroit model, 156; and grass roots ideal, 28-32; and national agencies, 157, 325n31; *see also* United Way
United Negro College Fund, 146, 191-92, 194, 221
United Service Organizations (USO), 26, 238
United States Civil Service Commission, 114, 120
United States Congress: Appropriations Bill, 1987 (Hoyer 2), 146; House, Committee on Appropriations, Subcommittee on the Civil Service, hearings, 134-35; House, Committee on Appropriations, Treasury, Postal Service and Government Appropriations Subcommittee, 145; House, Committee on Government Operations, 130, 145, Subcommittee on Manpower and Housing, hearings, 134, 140; Senate, Committee on Appropriations, 140, 143, 145; Supplemental Appropriations Bill, fiscal year 1986, 145-46, 350n65; Treasury, Postal Service, and General Appropriations Bill, 1985, 143
United States Department of Defense, 117-18
United States Department of Health, Education, and Welfare, 44

INDEX   381

United States Department of the Treasury, 3
United States Office of Management and Budget (OMB), Circular A-122, 133, 220, 345n7
United States Olympic Committee, 127, 133
United States Supreme Court and issue of viewpoint neutrality, 263
United Way allocations: by category, 238, 365n16; funding of advocacy groups, 225; funding of minorities, 238; profile of, 224, 235, 365n17; to traditional core agencies, 77, 79, 89, 225, 230, 235-40; women and children's services, 238
United Way allocations process, 59, 60, 78-86; and multi-year funding, 82
United Way area-wide organizations, 241-42; *see also* Tri-State, United Way
United Way as business, 6, 250-51
United Way campaign: and the CFC, 132, 141-42; competition for employee dollars, 8, 208, 262-64; corporate call and case for the CEO, 163-65; dollars raised by Metro groups, 5, 6, 50; dollars raised by top 12 United Ways, 254; dollars raised in 1970s, 58; dollars raised in 1986 campaign, 350n58; inclusion of designations in totals raised, 229-33
United Way centennial celebration, 230, 250, 252, 261-62, 264-65, 369n24
United Way citizen review process, 11, 39, 79, 82, 96, 194, 108-10, 130, 239, 246, 337n18
United Way early history, 3, 4, 19, 21
United Way *International Directory*, 5, 58, 67, 229
United Way local organizations: as full service organizations, 72, 264; community role, 8, 10, 52-53, 55, 128, 245-47, 261, 264-65; new agencies and programs, 78, 88, 224-25, 338n32; and planning role, 53, 60-61; relationship to core member agencies, 88-89, 90, 94, 230, 239, 338n33, 364n1; structure and function, 4, 53, 60-65, 72, 247, 257, 259, 264, 318; *see also under individual cities*, e.g., Boston; Chicago; etc.
United Way marketing, 4, 265
United Way of America (UWA): corporate leadership and federal government, 132-34, 159-60; data collection, 368n10; donor option resolution of Board, 94-95, 103; internship program, 257; Management and Community Studies Institute, 253, 333n47; and member United Way organizations, 5, 53, 245, 254, 258-59, 317n8, 329n5; move to Alexandria, 50; name changes, 50, 245; National Academy for Voluntarism (NAV), 53, 248-49, 251, 256, 330n3 National Corporate Development Program (NCD), 160, 163, 199, 210, 219, 252, 264, 354n33; and the NLRB, 182-84; National Professional Advisory Council (NPAC), 254-55, 369n18; Personnel Development Program (PDP), 258; Program for the Future, 264; Second Century Initiative, 260-61; Service Identification System (UWASIS), 64; *Standards of Excellence for Local United Ways*, 251, 368n10
United Way planning: long range and strategic planning, 94, 253, 261; Model Planning Organizations (MPO), 64; planning models, 59-65; Plans Y and Z, 61-62; priority planning, 69, 80, 86
United Way professionals, 6, 53, 247-49; and allocations process, 79-80, 96; Big Ten group, 254-55; and donor option, 103-4, 253-54; executives, business programs for, at Harvard and University of Miami, 258; Minorities and women, 254, 256-57, 351n22, 369nn21, 22; Select Cities, 255; and social work, 6, 52, 171, 255-56, 259
United Way share of agency budgets, 6-7, 59, 236, 318n13

United Way *Standards of Excellence for Local United Way Organizations*, 59-60, 253
United Way State Organizations, 5, 29, 32, 323*n*7; *see also* Michigan United Health and Welfare Fund
United Way system: characteristics of larger Metro cities, 53, 58-59, 79, 169, 180, 224-45, 248, 256; corporate giving guidelines, 253; description and scope, 4, 5, 6, 248, 368*n*11; as a federation, 7, 11, 246-47, 367*n*2; inclusiveness, 33, 40, 58, 79, 86, 94, 221-23, 229-30, 239, 250; International United Ways, 5; minorities in, 254, 256-57, 361*n*22; sectarian groups and federations, 19, 89-90, 96-97, 237, 337*n*21, 339*n*56; slogans and symbols, 3, 4, 113, 234; social workers in, 255-56, 258; sources of funds raised, 7; strains in, 8, 220-21, 229-30, 239, 252, 253, 254, 265; women in, 68, 254, 256, 369*nn*21, 22; *see also* Myth, and the United Way
United Way Volunteer Leaders Conferences (VLC), 60, 74, 249-50, 260

Valentine, Joseph, 180
Ventura, United Way of Ventura County, 92, 94
Vietnam War, 43

War on Poverty, 42-43, 55-56; maximum feasible participation, 55-56, 327*n*57; Office of Economic Opportunity and community action agencies, 44-45, 56, 329*n*57; *see also* Planning councils; United Community Funds and Councils of America
Washington, D.C.: United Black Fund, 118-19, 180-81; United Way of the National Capital area, 119-120
Werbaneth, Louis A., 74

Westchester County, 69, 241; United Way of Westchester, 254
Weyerhauser Corporation, 172
Wilkinson, George, 253
Wilson, Charles, 32
Winpisinger, William W., 174-75, 202
Women: increase in employment, 240; and voluntary organizations, 17, 206, 222, 263, 326*n*32; *see also* United Way allocations; United Way system, Women in
Women's funds: Women's Funding Alliance, Seattle, 173, 359*n*49; Womens Way, Philadelphia, 96-99, 105, 221, 231, 233, 262
Women's Shelter, Corpus Christi, 83, 86
Woodrow, Wilson, 22
Workplace: access to, 29, 38, 63, 110-11, 156-57, 162, 182, 210; access to, and United Way control, 8, 9, 169, 229, 265; cafeteria choices, 203, 232, 233; changing environment, 240, 262-65; fund raising, 7-9, 23, 35, 88, 111, 156, 183; fund raising and fair share giving, 113; pressure on employees, 117, 160, 166-67, 181, 264; single campaign in, 31, 95, 168, 182-85, 234, 265; *see also* CFC; Employee giving; Labor unions
World War I, 22, 36, 156; war chests in, 26, 154, 321*n*21
World War II, 28, 36; corporate giving in, 156; fund raising in government workplace, 112; state war chests and National War Fund, 26

Yeakel, Lynn, 198
YMCA, 22, 77-78, 89, 153-54, 238; intensive fund raising model, 20; as residence for workers, 153
Yonkers, New York, Community Planning Council, 33*n*46
YWCA, 77-78